# A Musician Talks

## 1. THE INTEGRITY OF MUSIC

By

Donald Francis Tovey

Oxford University Press

LONDON  NEW YORK  TORONTO

1941

OXFORD UNIVERSITY PRESS
AMEN HOUSE, E.C. 4
London Edinburgh Glasgow New York
Toronto Melbourne Capetown Bombay
Calcutta Madras
HUMPHREY MILFORD
PUBLISHER TO THE UNIVERSITY

PRINTED IN GREAT BRITAIN

# A Musician Talks

---

## 1. THE INTEGRITY OF MUSIC

# EDITOR'S NOTE

DONALD FRANCIS TOVEY was invited in
1936 by the University of Glasgow to deliver
the Cramb Lectures, and in 1938 by the University of
Liverpool to deliver the Alsop Lectures. University
Lectures, daily or occasional, provided a medium
in which Tovey felt comfortable, and these courses
gave him an equal pleasure and incentive to express
his ideas.

In prose-writing Tovey worked at his best with
the printer's devil at his elbow. Not one of his now
famous programme analyses had its origin save in a
performance, not even from the days of the Meinin-
gen Orchestra. He projected a number of books and
editions. Yet of his published works only one, as
far as I know, was the result of ignition without the
tinder of performance—and that one was not entirely
the result of spontaneous combustion. I refer to the
*Companion to the Art of Fugue*. Even the cadenzas
to classical concertos and the redistribution of the
Haydn trios could trace a lineage from actual concerts, and the *Companion* would never have been
written had not Tovey delighted in playing the
last Fugue of *Die Kunst der Fuge* with his own
superlative ending.

For the appearance of these two volumes, issued
under the name of *A Musician Talks*, I am partly
responsible. To an extent Tovey needed his books
to be made for him. One of the projects mentioned
above was planned to fill a big frame. It was a series

of text-books on music, to comprehend his own system of musical education. Their subjects were to be Counterpoint, Thorough-Bass, Form, and Orchestration. Not a word of them was ever written down. The scheme, however, simmered in his brain, and was after some years reduced to two composite books by his own wish. Still pen was not put to paper. Then came the call of the lectures, and at last Tovey, having accepted the invitations, was obliged to produce the matter in prose.

He dictated the lectures to his secretary and allowed the duplicate of the typescript to go to the printer and to be set up in type. But only those who were present at the delivery of the lectures can by comparison with this text have a real sense of how Tovey illuminated his words with the magic of his pianoforte playing. That a large part of the lectures was occupied by music is obvious: not only were there many long passages from the classical composers, but there were long improvisations in one style or another (cf. p. 27 of 'Musical Textures', where the lecturer showed how Klengel might have treated a given fugue subject).

On receiving his proofs Tovey was a little doubtful what to do about musical examples, as he was about the obvious overlapping of the two books in certain arguments and illustrations. To quote at anything like the length required would have turned a book into an album of music with annotations. But it was soon agreed that minor adjustments would avoid long citation. The overlapping I made light of, and Tovey also agreed to the issue of the books under the informal title they now bear. All was ready, but he was no diligent proof-reader, and he never corrected the proofs himself.

On his death, Lady Tovey kindly gave her consent to the publication of the books as they now stand. Also with her consent I invited Dr. Ernest Walker to contribute a Preface and give the proofs a final approval. The text exactly follows Tovey's words except for the main title, and except that certain small circumlocutions have been necessary, as I have explained above, to avoid musical examples, and certain corrections where the prose style betrayed dictation and lack of later revision. But I can testify that they are less in number than Tovey himself would probably have made.

For one admirer, at least, repetitions are but a slight disadvantage against the enormous advantage of the possession of two more of Tovey's writings.

HUBERT J. FOSS

*November 1940.*

# PREFACE

DONALD FRANCIS TOVEY was born at Eton on 17 July 1875 and died at Edinburgh on 10 July 1940. My own acquaintance dates from October 1894, when he came up to Balliol as the first holder of the Lewis Nettleship Musical Scholarship: an undergraduate whose age was the only ordinary thing about him. With a winning personality keenly appreciative of the humorous, and abundant non-musical interests, he dropped easily into normal college life; but he had never been to a school of any kind, and had from early childhood been privately trained for the musical profession. There were other musically minded undergraduates in Oxford, but Tovey was very obviously in a class altogether by himself; not only was he an outstanding pianist, but the Bach-Gesellschaft scores were his regular bedside literature, and he had written full-dress symphonies—I still recall the opening page of one in E minor, and its author's innocent pleasure in the subtly artistic snag of the reiterated wind chords which, until the entry of the violins, suggested that the key was F major. A finely equipped musician in practice and in theory, the youth was father to the man. Tovey was a three-fold artist: in performance, in creation, in knowledge.

It was as a notably artistic pianist, in chamber music as well as in solo work, that Tovey was first generally known to the public: and throughout his life pianism, including problems of technique as well as of interpretation, remained a prominent though gradually a less absorbing interest. Among my own memories perhaps the most vivid are those of performances of the late Beethoven Sonatas, particularly op. 101 and op. 111: these were, very masterfully, the real thing. He was very versatile: Scriabin and Brucken-Fock and Hindemith had their turns as well as the classics. Line-drawing was nearer to his heart than niceties of colour; but anyhow it was always playing in the big manner, absolutely faithful and with finely modelled phrasing and a rhythm that could bend but never break. In his conducting, also, I always felt the same sure judgement of tempo; though he seemed less at home with London orchestras than with his more personally familiar Edinburgh folk.

Notwithstanding that he could complete Bach's *Kunst der Fuge* with dazzling certainty of style and technique, and write concerto-cadenzas that Beethoven and Brahms would have been glad to father, Tovey had as a composer a definite style of his own; and it changed little in essentials throughout his published work, from the op. 1 B minor Pianoforte Trio (dedicated to Parry as 'the first work of a grateful pupil') down to the end. In his earlier and more leisured life he was prolific; but after, in 1914, he had accepted the Reid Professorship of Music in the University of Edinburgh, and added to his other activities those of the busy and inspiring teacher and orchestral trainer, his output slackened a great deal. From time to time he showed me things that have, so far as I know, remained fragments; in these twenty-five years he produced for publication only two works, the choral setting of the Northumbrian 'Lyke-Wake Dirge', a miniature but none the less outstanding masterpiece full of a strange sombre beauty, and the spacious Violoncello Concerto, the finely massive first movement of which best, perhaps, represents his instrumental achievements. Otherwise I would direct special attention to the great closing scene of the opera *The Bride of Dionysus* (pre-1914, though not performed until later), the Variations for string quartet often played by the Busch Ensemble, the E minor Quartet for pianoforte and strings, the D major Pianoforte Trio (which I have heard its composer mention as if it were a rather favourite child), or, in lighter vein, the 'Balliol Dances' for pianoforte duet—the first five dating from undergraduate days, the remainder from considerably later. To the neophyte, these duets are the best of initiations into Tovey's compositions: we may feel the hand of Brahms in No. 5, but it is only a passing touch, and the transition from the penultimate to the last of the Dances is one of the most personal, and one of the most beautiful, things Tovey ever wrote. Though as a rule very quick in his literary work, he was a slow composer; and he suffered, possibly to his detriment, from a certain inability to leave a work alone when completed and performed, or even, in the case of the opera, when published. He could not, so to speak, refrain from fingering his creativeness. None the less, the creativeness is there.

It is, however, as a writer about rather than of music that Tovey has, at any rate up to the present, enjoyed the widest fame. He had read and remembered in detail and, what is more, methodically assimilated into his personal scheme of aesthetics, every page of live music from Byrd and Lassus and Palestrina to the end of the nineteenth century, with a great and varied mass of twentieth-century music in addition. The live music, I say; he was not the kind of scholar who is interested in a fact simply as a fact, and about dead music he did not worry. But he was not pedantically exclusive; some second-rank composers such as Méhul he had studied with minuteness, and he knew all that need be known about even third-rate folk. Unlike his Edinburgh predecessor and intimate friend, Frederick Niecks, he was not interested in composers' biographies: he knew Beethoven's works backwards, but cared nothing for his life—and less than nothing for attempts to correlate his music with the French Revolution. Definite artistic achievement of some kind was what mainly attracted him. He did not pay any very special attention to even creditable composers who, in his judgement, were merely pioneers or gap-bridgers: though his active dislikes were few—Saint-Saëns ('slick classicism' and 'thin, mundane lucidity') and, to a less extent, Liszt. Even then, he was catholic-minded enough to perform the Symphonic Poems of the former ('they are so damned clever'): and he was fond of Liszt's 'Orpheus', while often playing his transcriptions of Beethoven's Symphonies with enthusiastically admiring running comments.

Tovey was a brilliant talker: unfortunately he lacked a Boswell. But he often wrote in the same way that he talked; and we have from his pen six volumes of analytical essays, many elaborate articles in the *Encyclopedia Britannica*, the long essays on Brahms and Haydn in Cobbett's *Cyclopedic Survey of Chamber Music*, annotated editions of Bach and Beethoven, pamphlets, and many sporadic articles in journals and composite books, with various lectures —the Edinburgh inaugural, the Deneke and Romanes lectures at Oxford, the Hertz British Academy Lecture, and the Alsop and Cramb lectures first printed in these volumes. It is by these many hundreds of pages that he has achieved a world reputation; and, indeed, there is nothing like it all in English nor, so far as I know, in any other language. Perhaps we see the quintessence of his thought most completely in the Philip Maurice Deneke lecture on 'Musical Form and Matter', delivered at Lady Margaret Hall, Oxford, in June 1934: the germ from which the Cramb lectures in the present volumes have developed.

A great man must have his diversions; and, as all his acquaintances remember, Tovey had, all through his life, the keenest of appetites for wit, humour, and frank nonsense. The poetry of Edward Lear, Lewis Carroll, Hilaire Belloc, he knew by heart, set to brilliantly suitable music (unfortunately never written down), and sang *con amore*, along with advertisements, extracts from *Punch*, and so on *ad infinitum*; and in later life he added the *Galgenlieder* of Christian Morgenstern to his repertoire, though, I think, only for non-musical recitation. And, in one way or another, the same trait peeps out—or perhaps jumps out—in many a page of his critical writings: the index to his volumes of analytical essays, the last thing that he personally passed for press, contains entries that are nothing less than impish. A great man's diversions may often, to merely casual eyes, loom larger than they really are. With Tovey, anyhow, no one would have wished them otherwise. But as diversions they are a remembrance that will pass: it is the greatness that remains.

ERNEST WALKER

These Lectures were delivered in the University of Glasgow in November and December 1936, with the kind assistance of Professor W. Gillies Whittaker, M.A., D.Mus., F.R.C.O., who made the arrangements in connection therewith.

Much of the Preface has already appeared in the pages of *The Monthly Musical Record*, and thanks are due to the Editor for kindly allowing this reprint.

# CONTENTS

# LECTURE I

THE musical doctrine which I wish to illustrate in the present course of lectures was adumbrated by me in the summer of 1934 in one of the Philip Maurice Deneke lectures at Oxford. In spite of its discursive form, and even in spite of its apparent digressions, that lecture suffers from over-compression, and I always intended to make it the basis of a more systematic illustration of its subject. Hence I am specially grateful to the Cramb Trustees for honouring me by an invitation which enables me to execute this plan.

My general title, 'The Integrity of Music', may be presumed to explain itself. It indicates that music is a special illustration of the integrity of art in general. This is no vague proposition. It implies an essential difference between art and science. The task of my first lecture will be to illustrate this difference and to show that herein music has no special privileges against other arts. For this reason I have much to say before I come to definitely musical topics. The question is not merely academic. It is vitally practical and contemporary. In every period of art only a small fraction of what is produced is destined to survive to later ages, and that fraction could not have been produced without the environment which produced all the rest. Criticism might conceivably be organized on lines scientific enough to allow it to predict in terms of an actuary's tables what percentage of contemporary art would survive, but contemporary criticism has always been as helpless as an actuary when it has tried to select individual works for immortality.

To-day no sane person doubts that John Sebastian Bach is one of the greatest masters of any art that has ever lived. But no competent musical historian who honestly examines the strength of his own musical faith can suppose that if he had been a pupil of John Sebastian Bach he would have predicted the immortality of his master's works. We may hope that in such a position we should have had an irresistible conviction that for us this was the greatest music in the world; but the master himself was quite cheerful in his acceptance of the fact that such music no longer appealed to modern ears; and instead of deploring the degeneracy of the times, he said that the art had advanced to great heights, implying without bitterness that this was why his own music appealed to nobody. If any actual pupil of Bach understood him as we can, his only possible conclusion would be that for him this was the greatest music in the world, but that such was his private opinion, and *de gustibus non est disputandum*.

Such practical wisdom may seem cold, but it is at all events sane. Sanity adapts itself to its environment and minds its own business. Insanity both shuts itself up in a box and tries to convert the world to its private views. And herein lies the most serious practical importance of the distinction between science and art. Most of the perishable and decadent elements in art have been in existence at all periods, and our illusion that they are especially modern arises from our total lack of interest in the forms they have taken in works we have willingly let die. But it seems probable that modern art has suffered especially from tendencies to confuse its modes of thought with those of science. Only one thing can save the results of such a tendency from being foredoomed: and that is the very fact that, whatever the official propaganda of an artist may be, neither art nor science can make a work of art into a scientific product. The artist's scientific theories are for the most part too half-baked to detain a man of science for five minutes, and the man of science who will allow himself to be so detained by an artist will have very little conception of the meaning of art. If a theory of art helps the artist to compose, it does not matter whether it is correct, pseudo-scientific, or naïvely representational and everything else that modern criticism abhors.

A correct theory of art is seldom, if ever, a guarantee or even a help to the artist in the creating and perfecting of his work. It is not unscientific for a doctor to ask his patient to 'say 99'. It is not even unscientific to base a successful slum practice on faith and bottles of coloured tisanes. The doctor's scientific and medical object is to provoke the right reactions in the patient. Modern pseudo-scientific theories, and the classical art-forms themselves, have been serviceable in stimulating the right activity in the artist. Pedantry and quackery begin when our ninety-nines and tinctures are erected into magical devices that annoy the public and become sacred causes of martyrdom to the artist.

The first step towards understanding the integrity of art is to recognize that it consists in the integrity of each individual work of art; that, as I have expressed it elsewhere, there is no such thing as Art with a capital A. Bach was too modest if he thought that his own music could be superseded by a new art that 'had risen to great heights'. You note that even in this connexion he did not use the word 'progress'. That is a word certainly applicable to science, but almost invariably misleading when applied to art. Science with a capital S does exist as a body of organized knowledge with a definite aim. That definite aim is knowledge of the universe and is not to be frustrated by the certainty that it will never be attained, nor even by the tendency of some philosophers to cast doubts upon whether a universe in the strict sense of the term exists. The man of science must not only work in the belief that the universe does cohere as a whole, but he must be content with no lesser wholeness and must regard with grave suspicion any scientific theory which has the kind of completeness that pleases the artist. Helmholtz has some illuminating remarks on Goethe's scientific work. His criticism comes to this: that Goethe could make important discoveries in morphology because he had the artist's view of phenomena that concern concrete and relatively detachable objects; but that he was helpless and recalcitrant in scientific work on the phenomena of light, which are diffused over the whole universe and become more and more abstractly mathematical and metaphysical the more deeply they are studied. Goethe was prouder of his theory of colour than of any other work, artistic, diplomatic, or scientific, that he had achieved. Helmholtz points out that that theory is an admirable description of appearances and has precisely the qualities of observation that made Goethe a pioneer of evolution in botany and anatomy. But as a scientific theory it is as unintelligible to men of science as Newton's methods were unintelligible to Goethe, whose attacks upon Newton show that he is really bewildered to the verge of a nervous crisis by a man of science whose optical theories are so outrageously unsuggestive of what colour looks like.

The duty of the man of science is, then, to contribute to the body of knowledge called Science. In order to make his task practicable, he must isolate and confine his problem within narrow categories. He must work under laboratory conditions and must not confuse one science with another. Aesthetic prejudices must not interfere with his optics, and if his political economy is to be a science at all he must not let ethical ideas intrude nor deviate from political economy into politics and housekeeping. On the other hand, he must be prepared for the time when the subjects of his observations and experiments are to be released from their immediate laboratory conditions. Roughly speaking, the more the subjects of his science are removed from the world that satisfies the artist, the easier and safer is the scientific abstraction. Physical science is becoming more and more mathematical, not without causing symptoms of disquiet lest its applications of mathematics should outrun its discretion. But pure mathematics is not obliged to wait for physical science to keep step with it. The mathematicians proceed at their own discretion within their own category.

It would be crude to say that the artist's method is the exact opposite of that of science; but the comparing of opposite characters is the clearest way to show the difference. Moreover, it brings out the resemblances between science and art, without which there would have been neither danger of confusion nor the possibility of an intellectual pleasure in qualities common to both. Some philosophic tendencies may, with or without the intention of their promoters, shake what faith we have in the unity of the universe. There is no difficulty in believing in the unity of a convincing work of art. I cannot say whether there is any widespread belief that the individual work of art is a microcosm; but such is my own belief, and music, which has no motive for being anything but an art, is remarkably rich in examples. A work of art, in as far as its purpose is unmixed, is a single coherent whole, and as such expresses our faith in the possibility of wholeness and coherence. This conception is a first step towards the view that artistic wholeness or perfection is a type of infinity.

Before any premature objection can be raised, let us note that there is nothing in the nature of art and of its materials to make artistic perfection impossible. The elements of art are selected by human beings, and its problems are completely under human control. Many further difficulties also may be swept away by postulating that artistic wholeness may be recognized in less than the whole. Art is in this respect no worse off than science, which is committed to assume both that the universe will always make sense and that we shall never make sense of it. There is nothing to prevent scientific truths from entering into a work of art if the work is large enough for them.

There are very few straight lines or perfect circles in nature, but there is one, the horizon, which will be visible in every wide prospect and which is implied in every correct perspective. Accordingly, if pictorial art chooses to include the common but interesting human experience of perspective, it must include so much optical geometry as is inherent in the way in which we all use our eyes. But the pictorial artist must command a wide prospect before the horizon will present itself directly to him as a straight line to be expressed as such in his picture. In fact, to see the horizon amounts to seeing, at least by inference, the dome of the sky, and hence to seeing our first view of the universe. This illustration is a useful symbol of the way in which some features of a work of art may be recognizable as scientific elements without destroying the art, and I am sometimes tempted to use the word 'straight' as a symbol of such cases. The most important of these are grouped round the science or art of logic. Art can no more exist without it than science: but though it is the master of science, it must be kept in its place as the butler of art. One hears a great deal about logical development in music, and both in the analysis of the classics and in the teaching of composition this term covers some of the most dangerous fallacies in popular and academic aesthetics. You cannot get rid of logic any more than you can get rid of the horizon, but the occasions in which logic appears on the surface are as rare in music as in any art which selects an artistic sufficiency of human experience for its purposes. Here, again, if your work of art is large enough, its logical coherence will appear on the

7

surface to about the same extent as it will appear in any actual human experience of equal calibre. The most familiar and extensive appearance of crude logic in modern literature is shown in the detective story, where the logical sequence is usually inverted, its conclusion being first presented as a mystery of which the explanation is disclosed in reverse order of events. This logical dictatorship restricts the detective story from the range and depth of less mathematical forms of literature.

Artistic range and depth must be human, and they need not become less human as they become more abstract. If this were not so, pure instrumental music would be the coldest of arts: whereas those who understand it find it more intense than any other. Neither abstruse thought nor rarefied atmosphere is to be mistaken for the intrusion of science into art. They may represent human experiences as artistically as a lifelike character study of a man of science. Those who can appreciate the works of Henry James find no loss, but a gain in human interest in his progress from the early novels which could be ended by a tragic fall from a cliff to novels which tell how A's partial misconception of B's undecided impression of A's attitude towards C impelled A to offer B a cigar. Think as you will of the taste which enjoys such subtleties, neither the selection nor the treatment of the subject points to anything but purely artistic principles. Science has not intruded, and the reactions are not produced under laboratory conditions.

It is the duty of the man of science to let no sentimental or aesthetic interests interfere with his work. His first duty towards his own theories is to try to disprove them. I heard the discoverer of argon and other inert gases explain that he was led to his discoveries by one of the first principles of scientific measurement: viz. Never remove a discrepancy. Another aspect of this precept would be: Never add a pinch of salt to taste. It is obvious that the artist habitually perfects his work by removing discrepancies and adding what is needed for no other purposes than those of taste. Moreover, his selection of materials always makes a world complete in itself and not analysed into categories. The most rarefied of Henry James's later works not only presupposes a highly complex and refined civilization, but gives abundant evidence that such a civilization coheres in his mind, more perfectly than anything like it in the outer world. Such evidence is a vital necessity to works of art. To take an example of Henry James's middle period, it is not merely what Maisie knew, but what everyone knows that holds that novel together. In the last resort, no matter how works of art may have depended on their environment before they could be produced at all, once a genuine work of art has been created it carries enough of its environment with it to explain itself to future and foreign civilizations.

My favourite illustrations of this were forced upon me in my undergraduate days when I was trying to cram up enough classics to satisfy examiners who did not profess to be interested in music. Homer's civilization evidently differs considerably from that of Oxford; but this makes no difference to the vividness or even to the actuality of what he describes. Alcinous greets Odysseus with delight on finding

9

that he is the famous pirate and sacker of cities, instead of being, as he had suspected, one of those confounded merchantmen. There may have been a Homeric age in which this had the charm of a realistic trait. It now has a romantic charm just because its point of view would be disavowed by our own Royal Family. The proposition that nothing is true which a change of date can make false is perhaps the most fundamental of all aesthetic rules. The *Odyssey* remains irrefutable not because we must accept its estimate of the social status of pirates, but because it makes that estimate perfectly clear instead of taking it for granted. In those remote days of my attempts to penetrate through thick blankets of 'crib' to the original Greek, I encountered in Sophocles another point of view which, according to Mr. Bernard Shaw and many of my Oxford contemporaries, was too obsolete to have for us the tragic value that it had for Sophocles. I was told that we do not think of funerals as Antigone did. Hence it was held that the cause of Antigone's martyrdom had to modern taste an unfortunate resemblance to the taste of the little seaport which, according to Tennyson, gave the strong soul of Enoch Arden the costliest funeral within its records. I have never been able to accept this criticism. To me Tennyson has not unmistakably risen beyond a tenderly humorous patronage of the villagers' simple faith. Such patronage, even if humorous, is apt to jar without achieving irony; and in any case, like all patronage, it puts the artist hopelessly outside his work. In the case of Antigone, it always seemed to me evident that her belief in the duty of burying her brother was a tragic necessity of central importance in her universe, and that it was as impertinent to accuse Sophocles for talking Greek instead of rising to the language of my cribs as to compare the cause of Antigone's martyrdom with even the real pathos of the comfort which our poorer classes derive from a sumptuous funeral. Antigone's belief and its origins are, in fact, neither taken for granted nor presented as novelties. They are presented with the same enthusiasm for actuality as that with which Pepys writes in his *Diary* that the watchman called out the time 'as I was penning this very line'.

My luck ordained that I had to read the *Ajax* at the same time as I read the *Antigone*, and here I found an obvious instance of the way in which a contemporary feature in a work of art may be so presented as not to stand a change of climate. After the tragedy of Ajax himself is over, there is a long wrangle between Odysseus and other heroes as to whether Ajax's conduct has entitled him to an honourable funeral. The mere position of this topic makes it for us an anticlimax to be explained only by the force of beliefs that have lost their force for us; and it is evident that their force for the characters of the drama is that of a jealousy essentially unheroic and mean, or, at best, the jealousy of a technical orthodoxy. I have never since found a clearer illustration of the difference between the art that can keep its subjects alive throughout future ages and an art which has left some part of its material in a perishable state.

A work of art can never be superseded. With architecture, sculpture, and painting, time brings physical decay for which the artist is not to blame, unless for the sake of immediate effect he knowingly uses short-lived materials. Replicas and copies may be good enough to make the record of the artist's creations immune from the ravages of time, and the aesthetic value of a copy that can deceive the un-aided eye of the expert is at least equal to that of great music perfectly played. The truth must be faced that music exists only in performance. No musician will agree to this in any sense that would impel him to confine his experience to what he has leisure and opportunity for hearing; a competent musical scholar must have read and enjoyed with all the pleasures of imagination incalculably more music than he will hear in a lifetime, and his knowledge of works that he has actually heard would need many more hearings before it could attain the depth and clearness of what he can gain by reading them. But his imagination depends upon memory, and it is per-formance, not technical abstractions, that he imagines when he reads. It is an immense advantage to music that the value of the autograph is mainly sentimental. This removes from the category of musical aesthetics a large number of issues that complicate—we might even say, confuse—the judgements of connoisseurs of painting and sculpture. Far be it from me to deny the unique value of the original painting; but, to take one notorious case, my sympathies are entirely with Professor Bode in the tragedy of his insistence that a translation of *La Gioconda* into the terms of a wax bust was the authentic work of Leonardo. Bode was not alone among museum directors in thinking that this wax bust was a very beautiful thing. His only mistake was in assuming that a skilled craftsman cannot execute a masterly translation of a work that he could not have created. If the training of Sir Walter Parratt has conferred upon an organist the habit of playing a toccata of Bach perfectly in a noble style, his performance will not give me any certainty that his own compositions, or even his own general musicianship, may not be as commonplace as the roll of Victorian quilt that was found to be the core of Ralph Cockle Lucas's *Gioconda*.

The perfection of works of art is not only a question separable from external accidents. It is a quality inherent in the very conception of art, as I have already implied in suggesting that the individual work of art is a microcosm. The conditions of music are specially favourable to the actual attaining of perfection: indeed, Schweitzer goes so far as to say that there is no other art in which perfection is so necessary to the permanent value of the work. The circumstances are indeed rare in which music has any but purely artistic motives for existing; and, whereas some of the greatest monuments of literature, such as the *Aeneid*, have openly professed a patriotic or instructive purpose, most of the music that has professed anything of the kind is so poor that no composer can have any ambition to write music that will play a part in general history.

Such is the normal purity of music that it tempts the critic into many fallacies of narrowness and over-simplification. With these I must deal more fully in my next lecture. For the present, let us understand that the integrity of music—or, if you prefer it, the purity of music—in no way depends on the

13

absence of non-musical elements in the art. The most perfect, as well as the most ancient, of musical instruments is the human voice; and the human voice is normally used for human speech. Music loses none of its integrity by allowing the singing voice to utter words. The art of reconciling the claims of words with those of musical form is not simple, but neither is it impure. Apart from dance music, the main stream of musical thought originated in voices, and always advanced as an art of treating words, allowing only small scope for inarticulate vocalizing.

Not only is it impossible to think away the original rhetorical associations of music, but it is necessary to use them as criteria for even the most absolute instrumental music. If I had entitled the present course of lectures 'The Purity of Music', I might have eventually proved by logic that musical purity does not depend upon the absence of extra-musical elements and conditions; but the proof would have been laboured, and would not have outweighed the prejudices and doctrines that have cramped the musical ideas of many critics and of some composers. It is more practical to regard purity as a question-begging epithet. The word 'integrity' serves all the purposes that can be served by the word 'purity', and it allows us to consider profitable and thoroughly artistic questions about the way in which the arts can integrate a combination of their resources and of all that their material naturally suggests. Unless such an integration is allowed as a normal condition of art, our notion of purity will suffer from what is essentially a confusion between art and science. Only a scientific habit of abstraction could tolerate the view that the musical use of the voice should be dissociated from words; or that words, once admitted in music, should not be treated illustratively. The integrity of music is not preserved, but injured, by a less-than-human use of the voice; and some of you may be horrified to find that I regard Wagner as an artist who preserved the integrity of music as meticulously as Mozart. Programme music—that is to say, instrumental music unassociated with the stage, but gratuitously illustrating non-musical matters—is obviously the field in which musical integrity is most exposed to doubt; for there is no inherent necessity for it. Beethoven once said that he always composed according to some *Bild* that he had in his mind, and this remark reverberates through the ages as a summons to that kind of inattention which enables people who are not very fond of music to while away the time while a symphony is in progress. When the German word *Bild* is translated as 'picture', Beethoven's meaning is absurdly narrow. The word means little more than 'idea'; in fact, it does mean precisely 'idea' as Plato would have conceived it and is a happy instance of the genius of the German language for translating Greek terms accurately.

A still more significant point in Beethoven's confession is that he not only seldom told us what the *Bild* was, but was as rude to people who inquired about it as any of us are inclined to be to intrusions upon our private affairs. Beethoven's rudeness is justified by the cataracts of hasty criticism that have fallen upon the few important works in which he has given a name to his *Bilder*. Any popularity that his 'Pastoral'

Symphony may at one time have owed to its title has been forgotten or adduced as evidence against it by criticisms which show a brutal inability to understand it on its musical merits. The real and avowed inspiring occasion of the sonata *Les Adieux*, *l'Absence*, *et le Retour* is not romantic enough for the sentimental people to whom titles are necessary for the enjoyment of music; and so it has not even had the benefit of the cheap popularity that is brought in evidence against the 'Pastoral' Symphony, as an offset against the difficulties of its being one of Beethoven's most subtle and unusual works. In my next lecture I shall deal in more detail with the conditions of absolute music and absolute arts. Let us at present sum up the general position.

From the romanticism that pervaded most of the nineteenth century down to very recent times, programme music has tended more and more to crowd absolute music out of the field. The only objection to it is that there is no inherent necessity for instrumental music to have a programme. On the other hand, the pictorial plastic arts, and latterly even poetry itself, have developed almost a conscientious objection to anything but the most abstract treatment of their materials. It is even begging the question to speak of their materials. Outside the realms of abstract art, the material of human speech is human meaning; and you cannot proceed far or long in the handling of colours and forms without resembling natural objects in a way which, however accidental, must be distracting to the attention. No doubt it was long ago high time that not only critics, but the general public, should be drastically cured of the habit which sees and enjoys the subject, and nothing but the subject, of a picture, and it is certain that no conceivable predominance of programme music will ever reduce the general public to quite such an abject condition of seeing nothing in music except the subjects it pretends to illustrate. Music can afford a reckless extravagance in gratuitous illustration, and the other arts have doubtless needed a drastic remedy for the irrelevancies to which mere illustration betrayed them. Still, the fact remains that doctrines which insist on abstractness in painting and the use of words for their sounds rather than their sense are in essentials a confusion between science and art. They would be fallacious even if they were scientific; but the real man of science knows better. When he believes that a line is length without breadth he is under no delusion that there is any such thing in nature or art; but it is by no means clear that the artists who act upon an *a priori* abstract theory of art have any correct notion of even what an abstraction really means. It is one thing to see the fallacy of a criticism which ignores every aspect of a picture except those by which it illustrates its subject, but it is not legitimate to proceed from this to demand that the artist should shut himself into a world in which colours and forms abstain from behaving on his canvas as they behave in real life. That way madness lies; or something too much like it to be worth the trouble of distinguishing from it.

My first propositions, then, are as follows:

Science is not art, and, if a work of art can legitimately convey scientific information, that is because its material includes matters of universal scope.

Thus, for example, a whole landscape may be divided horizontally by a straight line if that straight line represents the horizon.

Secondly, a correct theory of art is not necessarily a practical method of producing works of art, any more than it is an element likely to appear explicitly in the result. It concerns criticism, not creation.

Thirdly, art consists of individual works of art, not a general growing body of knowledge like science. The integrity of science implies that science is pursued for its own sake and not for practical purposes. The integrity of art is the integrity of works of art.

Fourthly, there is nothing to prevent a work of art from being perfect. Its perfection is only its highest standard of integrity, and its integrity can be secured by the artist's choice of his materials.

Fifthly, if the artist has omitted no essential elements, his work will remain unaffected by changes in public opinion. Perhaps there was a time when Homer seemed realistic, there doubtless was a time when he seemed barbarous, and there will always be a time when he seems romantic. The difference between the three points of view is negligible. The thrill given by complete artistic integrity is always the same. The only things that change are the directions and difficulties through which we approach the work.

Sixthly, a work of art exists, as Andrew Bradley said of poetry, in countless degrees. For the most part its enjoyment cannot be a single experience, but must come from the accumulation in the memory of many and varied impressions. Music cannot properly be said to exist except in performance; and in this sense the authenticity of a piece of music can be preserved only when the performance respects the intentions of the composer and is otherwise adequate. The authenticity of the autograph is not an aesthetic factor at all; all that matters is proof of the faithfulness of copies. This is a general truth which ought to be faced by all connoisseurs of painting and sculpture to whom it may be unpalatable.

Seventhly, the integrity of an art is not preserved, but injured, by the exclusion of elements which cannot naturally be separated from its mean of existence. Pure instrumental music has so little reason to be otherwise than absolute that there is a strong presumption against the integrity of music that illustrates other subjects without the necessity forced upon it by the human voice or the stage. This presumption, however, is a difficulty that must be faced, not a prejudice that must be accepted. Absolute instrumental music is, as most musicians will agree, the highest form of the art; but it represents not more than the condition in which perfection is most easily attained and appreciated. Dean Church asserted that in literary criticism the terms 'higher' and 'lower' are unscientific; and, whatever may be the difficulties of attaining perfection in so highly compound an art as opera, we shall be well advised to avoid all criticism that implies that the art of opera is lower than that of the symphony or string quartet.

# LECTURE II

WE need not wait until the question has been settled between those who wish art to be absolute and those who deny that such a consummation is possible or desirable. The beliefs which I wish to inculcate in these lectures are beliefs which I think practical as a basis for criticism and as a guide to creative and reproductive art.

In my first lecture I have pleaded for a large view of the integrity of music, and have explained that such integrity implies the integration of whatever elements are essential to the existence of the music. Such integrity is not preserved, but violated, by inhibiting the use of words in vocal music. The foundation of my entirely unoriginal and, I hope, common-sense doctrine was laid down for me in Andrew Bradley's inaugural lecture as Professor of Poetry at Oxford, in which, dealing with poetry for poetry's sake, he demonstrated with all the skill and soundness of an experienced philosopher that it is a fallacy that would separate the sound of words from their meaning. The fallacy is only apparently less crude than that which treats words as if their sound could be replaced without damage by that of any other words that literally and grammatically purport to describe the same objects. Let me borrow Bradley's shortest illustration, the difference between the words 'steed' and 'horse'. The dictionary can distinguish them only by distinguishing between a prose and a poetic vocabulary, and in bad poetry a 'steed' and a 'horse' are the same. But Byron could not interchange them when he wrote: ' "Bring me the horse." The horse was brought. In truth he was a noble steed'; though doubtless neither grammarian nor horse-coper can be very clear why he should not have said: ' "Bring me the steed." The steed was brought. In truth he was a noble horse.'

For purposes of analysis it may be convenient to abstract form from matter; and the matter of music, even where words are involved, is so remote from any other human experience that we are overwhelmingly tempted to regard most musical problems as problems of form, so long as we have any fear lest our analysis should degenerate into a mere popular account of external things alleged, rightly or wrongly, to be described by the music. Let us by all means beware of being distracted from music by the accidents of its resemblance to other things; but, in music as in poetry and the other arts, the opposite mistake is not much less crude: the mistake by which musical forms are conceived as mere jelly-moulds which determine the shape of music from outside. Not so has absolute music attained either its absoluteness or its supremacy in art. It has become untranslatable into other terms, but it has not become meaningless. On the contrary, it has become more exact than any language, as Mendelssohn pointed out in a remarkably profound letter which he courteously took the trouble to write to a tiresome person who asked him the meaning of some of his *Songs Without Words*. The inquiry was, perhaps, not so foolish as the people who have thought fit to supply those compositions with words, an absurdity that has been committed more than once. We need not be surprised that a person insensitive enough to commit it at all should show himself uniformly perverse in attaching the sentiments of merry Hussars on horseback to some of Mendelssohn's most melancholy pieces, and should represent Mendelssohn's perkiest cheerfulness by sweet maidenly meditations.

Perhaps it is not necessary to deal further with the intrusions of external matter upon musical substance. Such questions settle themselves without the need of special or technical knowledge; but it is important and by no means easy to determine how far the forms of music are inherent in musical matter. Let us be clear from the outset that, whatever objections we may raise to programme music, no pressure from external matter can violate the integrity of music more seriously than the pressure of an external form, though it profess itself to be purely musical. Now this is a matter in which not only appearances, but actual historical and practical processes, may be very deceptive. In fact, I do not believe that any *a priori* evidence can discriminate between a musical form that has been imposed from outside and one that has grown vitally and artistically from within. Of all the arts music is perhaps that in which art-forms are most easy to analyse and classify. Consequently, an immense amount of generalized knowledge about musical form has been accumulated, and has led inevitably to the view that the form exists before the music is composed. Rockstro's pious phrase, 'the rules to which the Great Masters gave their loving obedience', is one of the most dangerous heresies that has ever been accepted as an orthodoxy.

Quite apart from the fact that, as Dr. R. O. Morris has pointed out, Rockstro himself had to confess that he could often find no suitable illustration of these rules from the works of the great masters, the truth lies in precisely the opposite direction—viz. that where the rules have been intelligently drawn up they are the record of observers who devoted their loving and faithful observation to the practice of the great masters.

The rules which Rockstro had in mind were the grammatical rules of a musical dialect that attained its Attic, or Augustan, purity at the end of the sixteenth century. At that time the contemporary theorists were good observers, and students were ready to give the rules their loving obedience, because the whole tendency of music was towards a more and more fastidious purity and sense of euphony in the treatment of the unaccompanied chorus. Against my own principles I am shortening the argument by indulging in a special licence so as to speak of general tendencies instead of making the full statement that Palestrina and his greatest contemporaries found that fastidious attention to euphony was their greatest stimulus towards producing perfect individual works of art. The rules of strict counterpoint began to degenerate into an arbitrary and morbid casuistry when teachers refused to face the issue that in instrumental music these rules were true only in as far as instruments imitated the qualities of voices. A further step in the degeneration took place when teachers realized that the tonality of the Church modes was definitely obsolete, and that students must be trained in the more solid system of tonality founded by Alessandro Scarlatti and pervading the whole musical art of the eighteenth and nineteenth centuries. The teachers of strict counterpoint then merely added the stiffness of modern tonality to the restrictions of pure sixteenth-century polyphony, entirely failing to see that those restrictions and the freedom and variety of the Church modes were intimately related. I believe it is still held by some teachers that students who are allowed to write strict counterpoint in the Church modes are thereby undermining their grasp of classical tonality. If a sense of classical tonality is to be represented by the harmonic style of our unrevised Victorian *Hymns Ancient and Modern*, it is difficult to see how any of the laxity of Palestrina's tonality could make a student's style worse. There is within the records of living memory the utterance of a venerable university don who would neither read Homer himself nor allow his pupils to read it, because such a study would be subversive of the standards of Attic Greek. This argues a very imperfect faith in the don's own capacity to retain his grasp of that noble dialect; and in any case it shows that his own education must be regarded as a total loss.

It is worth while dwelling upon the case of strict counterpoint, not merely because this is the narrowest and most unpopular of all items in musical education, but because, rightly understood, it shows the impossibility of separating technique from aesthetics. Just as it is convenient at times to disregard the integrity of the individual work of art and allow oneself to speak of general tendencies in music, so it may be convenient sometimes to say that such and such a problem is merely technical. In the same way, the astronomer talks of rising and setting and crossing the meridian, and of a planet as being stationary or retrograde in its orbit, just as if the Ptolemaic system were still accepted and nobody realized that these phenomena are merely the results of the earth's motion. But we must be not less careful than the astronomer to know when we are talking merely of phenomena and when we are dealing with what lies behind them. And it is significant that the greatest composers themselves have not only taken no trouble to separate technique from aesthetics, but have actually put forward some of their greatest works under the title of 'Exercises'. *Das Wohltemperirte Klavier* professes by its title to inculcate the tuning system of equal temperament for keyed instruments. The main bulk of the remainder of Bach's ripest keyboard works was published by him in five volumes under the title of *Klavierübung*. On the other hand, Domenico Scarlatti's sonatas show the same exalted view of technique in a negative way, for he published them with a preface warning the reader not to expect anything learned, but to regard them as written simply for his entertainment. Which is all the more remarkable since of all early keyboard music Scarlatti's sonatas notoriously make the most extravagant demands on the player's mechanical technique. But it is not even mechanical technique that is inseparable from aesthetics. Far more is it the case that nothing that concerns the composer as means to an end can be separated from that end.

Modern usage applies the term 'Studies', 'Übungen', or 'Études' to studies that inculcate technical mastery of an instrument—surely as low an aim as can be confessed by respectable artists. Even here English usage draws the line at calling such works 'exercises', though Bach himself and his early editors were less snobbish, and published the *Klavierübung* with the French title *Exercices pour le Clavecin*. It so happens that studies technically profitable to a player fall naturally into an art-form typified by some of Bach's most beautiful and characteristic preludes; a kind of musical network or lace, severely uniform in texture and rhythm, intolerant of anything obvious in the way of melody, but as capable of majestic growth and climax as a painter's finest studies in cloud perspective. Hence, there is no reason why *études* should not be great music. A goodly proportion of Chopin's twenty-seven *Études* are among his nobler works, and only three seem to me to be comparatively commonplace. The musical world was much disappointed when Debussy's collection of *études* turned out to be almost entirely preoccupied with dry, though eccentric, propositions.

It is not difficult to draw a line between pure aesthetics and these mechanical aspects of technique, and the only case in which confusion has arisen is that of the concerto. The orthodox view of concerto form has been fatally vulgarized by the assumption that the purpose of a concerto is to display the technique of the solo player. On this assumption concertos are, of course, ridiculously easy to write, and we need not wonder that the majority of them are hopelessly vulgar and trivial; but the true concerto forms and styles are represented by the highest and subtlest things in musical art, and their technical difficulty is the natural result of the condition that puts an individual player into the position of dominating an orchestra. But the real dangers of separating technique from aesthetics do not concern the skill of the player. I am not sure that Bach used the word *Übung* in any sense but that of 'exercise', but, like all his collected works, it happens also to be a series of studies in composition. However, the only work in which he avowed this has been more grossly misunderstood than anything else that he wrote. I refer to *Die Kunst der Fuge*, which is a series of fugues all on the same subject, classifying the main types of fugue and setting them forth in order of complexity; and here, by a specially annoying perversity, the fact that Bach wrote out this work in open score instead of on keyboard staves has led persons who have evidently never tried to play from score in their lives to assert that it is merely abstract music and so never meant to be played at all. I have not space to go into recent controversies about *Die Kunst der Fuge*, nor do I feel inclined to grumble because the belated recognition that that work has received has been displayed in forms which betray a scandalous prevalence of humbug in many accepted methods and schools of musical education.

*Die Kunst der Fuge* is, as its very title shows, an important *locus classicus* for the distinction between technique and aesthetics in so far as that distinction can represent facts. The whole work is founded on one subject. The task of showing all standard types of the treatment of that subject is in some cases a natural art-problem, and in some cases a discipline enforced. The subject must be capable of the most complex treatment, and it is therefore not free to have the qualities shown elsewhere by the subjects of Bach's simplest fugues. In *Die Kunst der Fuge* the fugues in which Bach is free to produce his finest music are those in which his severe main subject is combined with others. Even in the course of these Bach found himself faced by a contingency that had not occurred elsewhere in his experience. It was a mere accident that it had not occurred before; and Bach devoted the two most eccentric *tours de force* in *Die Kunst der Fuge* to working out a technique that would provide for this contingency. It seems an abstruse and useless *tour de force* to write an extended piece of music which sounds equally well right way up or upside down. In the fifteenth and sixteenth centuries composers, more especially of Flemish schools, notoriously spent immense energy on even more abstruse problems of the kind, and undoubtedly often indulged in their ingenuity for its own sake; but the ingenuity of Bach's invertible fugues is not indulged in for its own sake. It is indulged in because he discovered that totally invertible counterpoint in three or four parts was a thing that might be needed in any triple fugue, and that it could not be produced by accident.

Bach did not, as some people suppose, develop his contrapuntal skill early in life. In spite of his growing tendency to a crystalline clearness in every aspect of his art-forms, he learned neither by *a priori* theory nor by classical precedent, but by trial and error. Although his copies of the works of other composers, ancient and contemporary, fill a considerable bulk in the mass of his autographs, he did not learn anything like as much by classical precedent as he added almost automatically even in the act of copying. His precedents are, in fact, not classical, but archaic; and it was he who developed what could be learned from them into forms that we accept as classical.

Counterpoint is of all musical subjects that in which the confusion between technique and aesthetics shows itself in the most childish forms, both in criticism and in composition. We shall do well to beware of the assertion that any contrapuntal combination is ingenious. Nobody can judge of its ingenuity except people who could have produced it. In the fourteenth century polyphony was being hammered into shape by a process beginning with the more or less reckless use of ornaments in several voices simultaneously proceeding on a foundation of bare fifths, fourths, and octaves. The original conception of harmony was that of doubling a melody in perfect concords. The addition of ornaments produced imperfect chords and discords, which were acceptable in as far as the ornaments glided smoothly and the discords did not dwell on accented moments. Experiments became bolder; and sometimes a drastic leap forwards was made by *quodlibets*, compositions in which several pre-existing tunes were sung together under the order *Marche ou je t'assomme*, and the more intolerable corners were roughly knocked off. This venerable conception survives at the present day, except that we find no corners so intolerable as to be worth knocking off. I would have said, not that it survives, but that it had been recently revived; only the apostolic succession of steam-roller contrapuntists happens to have been preserved by Wagner in the famous combination of three themes in his *Meistersinger* Prelude. Moreover, it has been preserved, at

29

all events in England, by a plausible definition of counterpoint propounded by an Oxford professor, Sir Frederick Gore Ouseley, who stated that counterpoint is the art of combining melodies. Here the word 'art' begs the question. There is obviously no art in allowing Sir Toby Belch, Sir Andrew Aguecheek, and the Clown to sing anything they like in complete independence of each other. The true definition of classical counterpoint is that it is the art of conveying a mass of harmony in a combination of good melodies—that is to say, in a combination of melodies that need no extra notes to make the harmonic sense complete. The discipline by which this art is attained will naturally consist of exercise in problems both more restricted and more extended than any that need appear in free works of art. It has been said of Palestrina, and of other composers earlier and later, as it has been said of great billiard-players, that he makes the notes or the balls go where he wants instead of having to follow their track like ordinary mortals. Rockstro compared Palestrina with earlier great masters such as Josquin des Prés, in that, while Josquin could place a beautiful chord at every turn, Palestrina's proved to have placed themselves in the course of some beautiful contrapuntal imitation. Not only does this ascribe to Palestrina what should be a normal quality of good counterpoint and beautiful harmony, but it actually runs counter to the fact that, while Josquin's contrapuntal devices are present in crystalline clearness, like Bach's two centuries later, Palestrina in his ripest style has removed most of the direct evidence that a definite contrapuntal structure ever existed in his mind.

We are not to infer from this that the highest art is to conceal art. With all respect to Horace, and to the not less venerable authorities who quote him, that represents a childish view both of aesthetics and of technique; and in Great Britain, which, of all countries, is that in which amateurishness is a most dangerous affectation, it amounts in practice to a belief that the highest art is to avoid art. The art by which a composer learns to make the notes go where he wants them is one that is most easily and quickly learned by practice in canonic forms, for these forms compel us to find a possible harmonic meaning for combinations that we would not have invented for ourselves. They are like complicated rhyme-formulas, which often have a deep motive in the structure of the language far more cogent than any desire of ingenuity for its own sake. Thus, for instance, *terza rima* is a *tour de force* in English poetry, where an immense variety of rhymes is available and many rhyming syllables have individual meanings; but *terza rima* is almost forced upon Dante by a language in which rhyme is not only unavoidable, but consists almost wholly in grammatical terminations common to all verbs, nouns, and adjectives, so that the rhyme has no meaning in itself but needs an inherently interesting pattern to make it endurable throughout a long poem. There is no rule whatever by which we can say *a priori* that a contrapuntal device is justified by its ingenuity. The student who excuses a harsh harmony or a grammatical licence by the necessity of a canon must be told that neither the licence nor the canon is necessary. In no case does a contrapuntal device deserve to be called ingenious if the result is ugly, but in the case of a beautiful piece of counterpoint it is equally untrue to say that it is beautiful in spite of its ingenuity. Unquestionably it is ingenious if the beauty could have been obtained by no other means; and this is the case with most of the beautiful contrapuntal devices. Their harmony will prove to be unproducible by other means. How the composer arrived at such a result is no business of ours. By the time he has the enormous experience by which Mozart, Bach, and Brahms produced their mature works, much of it may seem to him to be a matter of luck—that is to say, he will not have thought of every contrapuntal possibility before he actually produced it, and will certainly not go through a process of first putting independent melodies together and then knocking off the intolerable roughnesses; but the luck which serves his purpose does not occur to inexperienced and unpractised artists.

It may be as well now to give some actual illustrations of this matter of counterpoint. First let us begin with the famous case of the *Meistersinger* combination. At the time when Wagner was a subject of controversy—we can afford to ignore recent attempts to belittle him—the anti-Wagnerians found in that combination plenty of occasion to blaspheme. Wagnerians in Grove's *Dictionary* and elsewhere said: 'Who can deny the title of contrapuntist to the composer who achieved this combination of melodies?' People who knew what counterpoint ought to be could deny it loudly and emphatically. The harmony made by this combination of melodies is miserable. All is well so long as the themes are all on one chord, although that chord is poorly and harshly repre-

The Song.

The Guild Banner.

The Master-Singers.

sented, with uncomfortable emphasis on a bare fourth; but in the third bar two of the melodies go crassly into unison or octaves, and in the fourth bar the one accented note of the *Preislied* that should be a sensitive appoggiatura, if it means anything, is doubled, and one can only say fouled, by a flourish in the Apprentices' theme. It has been pointed out to me that, if this combination of melodies is all that matters, it is almost a pity that Wagner did not add a very fine fourth melody, the Toreador's song in *Carmen*, which by no connivance of his own can be added for no less than six bars at the top without making matters any worse. This closes the anti-Wagnerian case. For most of us a sufficient reply is the triumphant fact that the passage as a whole, properly played, sounds magnificent and perfectly smooth. But as the mere combination of melodies sounds nothing of the kind, it is evident that, if Wagner is a great contrapuntist, his genuine counterpoint must lie elsewhere; and as a matter of fact, the combination is held together by some classically perfect counterpoint to which nobody pays any attention.

Let me illustrate in detail how the points which I have censured are absorbed into chromatic harmony of classical beauty and naturalness, how the hideous fourth that aggravates the pair of octaves in the third bar turns out to be part of a progression of interesting chords with the top part moving in smooth contrary motion with the bass, and how the sensitive appoggiatura of the *Preislied* turns out to be an essential part of quite a different chord, well able to bear doubling at the moment of its occurrence, and becomes something equally important but quite different by means of the very flourish in the Apprentices' theme which seemed merely to foul it when we had only the bare combination before us.

Wagner evidently never supposed that his combination of melodies could make counterpoint by itself. The melodies had, in fact, been conceived independently; and the art which combines them lies in the unobtrusive accompaniment. Wagner promptly proceeds to demonstrate this; because after the first four bars he is obliged to keep his counterpoint in play, but has no longer to force a rigid pre-existing material into combination, and there is far less crudity in the whole tangle that develops in complex liveliness for the next twenty bars. Every suspicion of awkwardness is explained away by unobtrusive harmonies, but the occasions for such explanation are few and momentary, and the explanatory harmonies are produced mainly by sustaining notes already present in the themes; which almost proves that the combination tends to explain itself.

The motive for the ostentatious roughness that is the fashion in the most modern counterpoint comes from the fact that classical counterpoint actually attracts no attention. The *Meistersinger* combination itself is already a case that, apart from its accompanying harmonic explanation, may be described as 'stage' counterpoint. It might be argued that there ought to be a certain awkwardness in the fitting of the melodies if they are to be heard as independent things, and the modern composer scornfully rejects the scrupulous art by which Wagner's classical harmony smooths out the primitive roughness of the ostensible counterpoint. Many errors of criticism consist in confusing methods with results. When a critic suspects a composer of pedantic ingenuity, he is apt to tell us that counterpoint is only a means to an end. This is not true. Counterpoint is the art by which a combination of good melodic lines produces complete harmony without the need of any inferior accessory matter. It is ridiculous to say that such art is only a means and not an end in itself. If the counterpoint, with or without accessory matter, is not beautiful, why complain that it is too ingenious? It is not ingenious at all.

Another *a priori* objection must be mentioned, in order to be dismissed as thoroughly unsound in form. We are told that it is psychologically impossible to attend to many things at once. In fact, the psychologists tell us as a scientific fact that nobody can attend to more than two. This is quite true, but it has no effect whatever in limiting the complexities admissible in polyphonic music. No psychologist denies that you cannot hear any number of things at once. He denies only that you attend to more than two; but for my own part I seriously doubt whether in listening to polyphonic music I attend to more than one thing, and that is the total impression. From moment to moment I may notice an effect produced by this or that inner or outer part, but my enjoyment would be a sadly strenuous and uncomfortable affair if I made any conscientious effort to identify in a single hearing all the details which prove that the harmony and form are alive.

If a painter or sculptor shows a consummate knowledge of anatomy, this does not mean that a staff of X-ray experts can reveal actual bones and muscles in the interior of works of art. Nor does it mean that the artist could be entrusted with a surgical operation. It means that his figures present to the eye of the man of science as well as to the eye of the layman the appearance of living figures and not of sacks stuffed with straw or flock. The total impression of good counterpoint is good harmony.

I will conclude with a few classical examples. Triple counterpoint is harmony made by a combination of melodies so contrived that any of them can be a bass to the others. The necessity for its existence is evident in an art-form like that of fugue; for, if any of the melodies is not capable of making a good bass to the others, the bass will be deprived of its fair share of the themes. The question whether the listener can attend to all three at once does not arise. He can recognize the whole combination, and he can enjoy the unity in variety which results from presenting the same harmonic and melodic elements in six different positions. As a matter of fact, in Bach's standard type of triple counterpoint the three themes are remarkably transparent to each other. Psychologists may say that you cannot attend to all three: but you certainly cannot only attend to the combination as a single impression, while you can detect at any moment the elements of contrast between the three members. There is usually one theme that skips energetically, another that trickles smoothly, and a third which completes and enriches the whole harmony with a slow chain of suspensions. Bach attained maturity in the art of combining different melodies much sooner than he attained it in stretti or combinations of a theme with itself. I cannot think of any crude examples of double, triple, and quadruple counterpoint in Bach's works; but there are early works in which he treated a single theme awkwardly. Opinions will differ where the line should be drawn. In my opinion Busoni draws it for Bach with a fastidiousness which he certainly does not apply to his own compositions: rejecting, for example, the D major fugue in the second book of *Das Wohltemperirte Klavier*, a stretto fugue which I shall always maintain to be magnificent. For my own part, I put decidedly outside the pale the famous fugues in D sharp minor and A minor in the first book. When I am told that these are learned and ingenious I dispute the learning and ingenuity of their admirers.

37

A common prejudice, unworthy of grown-up persons, assumes that of two kinds of technical problem whichever is studied later is the more difficult. This mistake is quite common in the schedules of examinations in playing. On the pianoforte scales in thirds are naturally studied later than plain scales; and a piece that contains a scale in thirds is without further inquiry graded as more difficult than a piece which does not. I once encountered an exalted person who played the violin—it were indiscreet to ask how—and he was convinced that Beethoven's Violin Concerto was easy, because at no moment does it contain a scheduled *tour de force*. Belief in this naïve criterion is very harmful in the education of players. In the technique of composition it is too ridiculous to do much harm, and the nonsense that it produces in analysis and criticism is too perishable to matter.

When we are told in the preface to an excellent miniature score of Mendelssohn's *Elijah* that the Overture deals with some of the more difficult contrapuntal problems, such as treatment by inversion, the *naïveté* calls for comment, because, incredible as it may seem, it represents a belief seriously held by some teachers. Any theme will invert. All that you need do is to write it upside down. You need not even write it. If you hold the theme upside down, it will be inverted and turned backwards as well; and if you do not wish it to be thus also what the learned in such matters call *cancrizans*, you must hold it before a looking-glass to get it reflected in the right direction.

If the inversion is ugly, why does the composer use it? The only art in the use of an inversion is the

38

choice of themes and positions of which the inversion happens to be good. A composer who works habitually at contrapuntal forms is likely to conceive a large number of themes that will invert well. This sets up a habit of mind that is favourable to the invention of such themes. It does not set up a skill in tinkering preconceived ideas until they will invert. If a theme needs tinkering before it will invert, the composer will simply not invert it. Purcell's themes will invert more often than not; Brahms's almost as often as Purcell's; Beethoven's seldom, and then in compositions avowedly fugal.

Now the D sharp minor and A minor fugues in the first book of the Forty-Eight have themes which Bach treats by inversion, though the inversions are definitely ugly. The inversion of the D sharp minor theme produces a feeble tautology not evident in the original. The inversion of the A minor theme begins well, but risks lockjaw when the downward plunge which was originally its best feature becomes like the upwards force of a dentist's gag.

Both fugues exhaust, I hope, the possibilities of stretto; but the stretti do not make beautiful harmony. They narrowly achieve grammatic sense. The composer's material is not naturally giving rise to these forms. The forms are forced upon it from outside, and noble musical rhetoric asserts itself with evident relief when the devices are abandoned.

There is something almost uncanny in the difference between such exercises and the masterpieces where the matter produces the form. I wish I had time to vindicate the D major fugue in the second book, which Busoni rejects, and also to discriminate between the elements of pure art and of technical exercise in *Die Kunst der Fuge*, which at its worst contains nothing like the crudeness of the D sharp minor and A minor fugues; but I end this lecture by directing special attention to the great B flat minor from the second book of the Forty-Eight. I choose this in preference to the more famous and equally noble B flat minor from the first book, just because it is a schematic composition of which a superficial description might lead one to suspect it of being an exercise.

The points which illustrate my arguments are: first, that the inversions of the theme and of its counter-subject, singly and in combination, are not less beautiful than the originals; secondly, that the stretti all make beautiful harmony without the slightest effort; thirdly, that, instead of abandoning the ingenuities in order to make a purely musical climax, Bach achieves his highest rhetoric by the closest combination of all. (This, by the way, is also the case in the D major fugue which Busoni dislikes.) But there is another point, which lies outside the composition, and which shows what happens when material and form are true functions of each other. I have expressed the hope that in the A minor and D sharp minor fugues Bach had exhausted the possible combinations. He had, in fact, done more, since he included several that he would later have thought impossible; but he could have designed at least eight other fugues with the subject and scheme of this B flat minor fugue. And probably these would not have exhausted the combinations. He has taken the closest stretti, those in which the answer follows the subject at the second note and at the interval of a seventh; but there is another set of stretti at two beats and an octave, and a third set at a whole bar and a ninth. And in the present set of stretti Bach has used only a quarter of the combinations where the direct theme and its inversion answer each other.

# LECTURE III

PERFECT integrity in a work of art implies that all it needs for its explanation is to be found within it. We have already seen a few of the more obvious illustrations of this in showing that technical problems are essentially aesthetic problems, which concern every lover of the art, and not professional or trade secrets.

To the non-musician it may seem hopeless to maintain the paradox that there is nothing in purely instrumental music that does not explain itself, and most musicians are apt to be equally sceptical in this matter. Nevertheless, I hope to show that the experience which makes a piece of music enjoyable is an experience accessible to all, and that no technical knowledge is relevant to it except that which enables us to become more quickly familiar with the music. Although art exists and must be judged only in individual works, the experience necessary for enjoying each work cannot be confined to that work. And we must not forbid, though we must severely control, the influence of many human experiences, general and artistic, on our enjoyment of the single work. Poetry uses human speech. You cannot learn a language from a single poem, and the most rigorously abstract of modern poets cannot even enjoy their meaningless word-patterns unless in daily life they still understand language normally enough to recognize nonsense when they see or hear it.

If any work of art could explain itself to an experience confined to its own materials, a musical composition might be able to do so; and music and architecture certainly make themselves understood more universally and with less appeal to outside experience than any other arts. We have lost our simple Victorian faith in the universal intelligibility of classical music. In the seventies Macfarren, though he suffered from the most naïve readiness to interpret medieval music by nineteenth-century habits, had the wisdom to point out that the cultivated Chinaman finds European music as unintelligible as we find Chinese music. Neither Macfarren nor all but few, if any, of modern European orientalists and musical folk-lorists can be trusted to keep their interpretations of oriental and ancient music free from unconscious confusion with ideas of their own civilization. Hannibal crossed the Alps with the utmost expedition, but the schoolboy who translated *summa diligentia* by 'on the top of a diligence' was less confused in his notions than the learned writer who tells us in one of our chief works of reference that we need not expect to find written records of so simple a procedure as singing in thirds.

I shall not attempt to deal, here or at any other time, with any music but the classics of our own Western civilization. Two cardinal errors are to be avoided, both in dealing with these classics and their merits and in comparing them with alien systems. The first error I have just mentioned. Macfarren avoided it in as far as he recognized that music cannot be said to be universally intelligible, but he constantly fell into it whenever he tried to describe any music that he could not conceive as written by himself.

This is a natural, and not always unamiable, error. Dame Ethel Smyth has quoted as a perfect example of psychological blindness the case of a friend who said: 'I consider that I understand a person when, if I were to be in the same position as that person, I should act in the same way'. It is impossible to frame a more accurate illustration of a person whose point of view is exclusively self-centred. But Macfarren's very efforts to attain a detached point of view betrayed him constantly into the opposite error, which is perhaps more serious. The self-centred person may not know himself as thoroughly as the oracle required, but at all events he does not disbelieve in his own existence, and a broad-minded view on ancient and oriental music is easily affected by persons who are really only substituting a profound scepticism about music of all kinds. In a famous passage more valuable as prose than as a contribution to musical thought, Cardinal Newman has expressed a not uncommon doubt whether our music is not after all a game rather than an art with foundations in truth. Now, those of us who have no time to study oriental and ancient music may be pardoned for suspecting that arts so remote from their comprehension may be arbitrary games; but for European musicians who devote their lives to the study of our musical classics of the last five hundred years there is no excuse for such an attitude. If they are wrong they have failed to understand the essentials of music; if they are right they expose themselves to the condemnation of Herbert Spencer, who on playing a friendly game of billiards with a stranger put away his cue when the stranger made a break of sixty and said that the attainment of such preposterous skill in a mere game was proof of a mis-spent life.

There is a difference between a work of art and a chess problem. Problems have been called the 'poetry of chess', a proposition often hotly disputed by chess-players. They certainly are selections of the elements of chess arranged on highly artificial principles with the utmost regard for economy and several other qualities of high aesthetic value. Still, it cannot be claimed that the materials of chess, whether in play or problem, have any power to explain themselves without instruction in the rules of the game. Capablanca tells us that at a very early age, without any lessons in chess, he had by merely watching his father and his uncle at play discovered that his uncle moved a knight incorrectly; but the observant eye of the *enfant terrible* is not restricted to so narrow a field of observation, and we might study the shapes of chessmen till Doomsday before we could discover any necessary connexion between them and their correct moves.

Musical theory has been wrecked again and again by efforts to base it upon natural acoustic principles. The attempt is vain, as are all attempts to reduce art to science. In as far as theories of harmony go beyond empiric observation of the practice of great masters, they tend towards uncontrollable pseudo-scientific speculations. And I frankly have more faith in your patience to listen to the discussion of such things than I have in my own patience to discuss them; but I have no doubt that the coherence of musical works of art rests on principles more universal and more self-explanatory than the laws of chess. Nor am I deterred from asserting this belief by the fact that some of the most essential elements of music cannot possibly be described except in technical terms. This does not mean that they are professional matters. Why should it mean anything of the kind?

Let me devote the rest of this lecture to an illustration of the most technical subject in all music: the subject on which text-books are inadequate and on which many questions which still survive in examinations show not the slightest sign of intelligence. Before I terrify any of you by naming the subject, I will ask you : first, whether the taste of a peach can be appreciated by any but a connoisseur? and secondly, whether connoisseurship in peaches carries with it any capacity to describe the taste of a peach in terms that will convey an idea of it to a person who has never had the experience? If your reply to these questions is that this is a profound professional matter and a field for connoisseurship not less exalted than that of wine, I shall then be prepared to believe that tonality is a profound professional matter of which the sense is inaccessible to any but professional musicians. The taste of venison is not an everyday experience for all people, and those to whom it is new, even when they are so highly professional as cooks, have been known, when not forewarned, to assume that the haunch of venison is some more familiar joint that has been kept too long. Doubts aesthetically analogous were cast upon Wagner's tonality by anti-Wagnerians. The extension of the word 'taste' over all the five senses has been very useful to critics and connoisseurs, especially in the light of the Latin proverb, which firmly removes it from the sphere of a dispute. Tonality is a thing which you can no more describe except by metaphors and comparisons than you can describe the taste of a peach, or the precise difference between venison and mutton or beef that has been kept too long.

The nearest parallel to tonality that I can find in other arts or senses is perspective. I have, both in lectures and in writings, carefully worked out the objections and limits to this analogy. The shortest working-out would take at least twenty minutes to deliver, and I am tired of the comments of critics who skip my explanations and assail me with the very objections which these explanations have discussed; so please believe that I know and have considered all that can be said against the parallel between tonality and perspective. The objections are not more serious than those which can be raised to the statement that 'scarlet is like the sound of a trumpet', the famous remark made by a man who, having been blind from birth, received sight by means of an operation.

A picture that is in correct perspective represents three dimensions on a flat surface by faithfully obeying the laws of optics within the limits of single-eye vision. If in a picture gallery you shut one eye, the perspective of most of the pictures will seem far more realistic. What has really happened is that by shutting one eye you make the walls and frames appear flat, only you ignore that appearance, and therefore the flat picture is at no disadvantage. The correctness of the perspective depends upon the painter's having referred all the objects in his picture to one horizon; or, conversely, to his having painted the picture from one point of view, the point of view being that of the spectator and the vanishing-point of all lines being within the picture in the middle of its horizon.

A musical composition in classical tonality has a tonic chord, which will normally be the final chord of the whole, and round which all other chords will be grouped in definite relation. Before the art of harmony was developed this tonic sense asserted itself in melody, though not always in ways that lend themselves to our harmonic interpretations. The non-musician who is accustomed to as much music as assaults his ears from the common barrel-organ is by no means without a sense of classical tonality. It may be a very bad sense, but it is no more primitive than a diet of tripe and onions. Few people can be so stone-deaf as not to realize when they hear it that a chord of the subdominant will not fit the sixth bar of our National Anthem; and if there is anyone who does not recognize something wrong there I will not inquire further into his capacity to enjoy music.

In what has been called the Golden Age of music, the age of pure vocal polyphony that became a great art in the fifteenth century and reached its perfect maturity at the end of the sixteenth, there was no need for tonality to be constantly asserting the kind of harmonic perspective analogous to that of a picture with no vestiges of primitive technique. There are plenty of beautiful pictures that imply a different horizon for each item that can be viewed separately; and, while we label the masters of such art primitive, we have outgrown the philistinism that prefers consistent perspective to all decorative merits, and we have learned humility in our criticisms of Chinese and Japanese art which, as Macaulay would have put it, violates every rule of perspective.

In the eighteen-forties an editor of the Musical Antiquarian Society acquired merit by publishing a volume of motets by William Byrd. Perhaps he acquired the more merit since he disapproved of them strongly, and expressed his opinions honestly in a preface in which, while deprecating the judgement of Byrd's contemporaries that they were 'angellical and divine', he grudgingly conceded that, in spite of certain monstrous false relations, they were as good as could be expected of a composer who was shackled by the Church modes, in illustration of which he quoted one of the most wonderful passages in all sixteenth-century music, the opening of Palestrina's *Stabat Mater*, as a curious instance of the uncertainty regarding the scale prevalent in the time of the author.

A favourite examination question of mine is this: 'Quote from memory, or invent, some progression characteristic of the Elizabethan period.' One of the answers I got was the opening of 'O who will o'er the downs so free?' If the Palestrina example has the perspective of a Chinese painting, my candidate's example has the painted relief of letters in a trade sign. I am afraid that the Victorian editor of the Musical Antiquarian Society would have thought this an advance upon Palestrina's tonality. As a matter of fact, in all the large-scale uses of tonality the exponents of the unrevised *Hymns Ancient and Modern* style were crassly ignorant; and the statements

E 49

and rules about tonality that survive to this day in text-books are as misleading as the phlogiston theory of chemistry. Unfortunately, the large-scale facts of tonality would need the whole of the present course of lectures to present even in outline. I once rashly undertook to demonstrate for my Edinburgh classes the balance of keys in a single Mozart rondo; and I found that the demonstration of that one piece occupied three lectures. Perhaps I may risk merely mentioning what I undertook to demonstrate.

The subject was the finale of Mozart's Trio for Piano, Clarinet, and Viola. The demonstration took for granted how the home tonic was defined, and ignored all possibility of any more primitive and less rigid earlier and later systems of tonality. It undertook to show that as soon as the key-centre was changed the original tonic chord no longer suggested the tonic, but quite unequivocally took its proper place in the new key. It showed that, nevertheless, if the new key was not too remote, a return could be made to the home tonic without any feeling that the bounds of a single flow of melody had been exceeded.

The first change of key in an actively disposed composition in the major mode will normally be to the dominant. Within the original key the chord on the dominant is penultimate in every normal cadence. When this chord has become a key-centre in its own right, the home-tonic chord becomes its subdominant, and retains no vestige of its original tonic sense. This and all other facts I demonstrated by showing the effect of a return to the main theme in the tonic at each point where the local sequence of chords would permit if we knew nothing of the larger context. It soon became evident that quite a long stay in the key of the dominant was powerless to convey a sense that the music had travelled beyond the bounds of an extended lyric melody, and that the home tonic would not sink below the horizon until some stress had been laid upon the dominant of the dominant. For this I have found it necessary to coin the term 'enhanced dominant'. And it is a shocking evidence of the incompetence of much widely accepted teaching that there are few, if any, commentaries that can be trusted not to treat an enhanced dominant as a key in its own right.

The rondo of Mozart's Clarinet Trio is almost an encyclopedia of the facts of simple key-relations, which it demonstrates all the more impressively because the whole composition is ostentatiously unintellectual and devoted to pleasure in the alternation of simple melodies. If we appreciate the Greek accuracy and subtlety of its key-relations, and their connexion with its thematic structure, we shall find grim satisfaction, such as Tertullian ascribes to the angels who rejoice to contemplate the torments of the damned, in our superiority to the childish critics who tell us that this movement is an unimportant and lazy piece of work. I regret that I cannot illustrate it further, or give you the very convincing demonstrations of what will happen if we substitute one thing for another, or return to our tonic at the wrong moment, or shorten any of the passages which delay Mozart's return until the right moment. I can only tell you that his final stroke is to repeat as the triumphant end of the whole composition a passage which had earlier been heard at the very same pitch as being on the dominant of the key of the subdominant. Some of our bright young men, or dull old men, sneer at the two pages of leisurely epilogue that precedes this close, and that has thematically no more connexion with the rest of the movement than the other passages have with each other; but if you leave it out or shorten it the close of the movement will be disastrously suggestive of a return to the subdominant, and if the two pages of epilogue had more connexion with the other themes the style of the whole movement would have been stultified.

I shall have more to say about tonality in later lectures. The harmony of classical music from Haydn to Beethoven is far less elaborate in detail than that of Bach. And commentators have been known to remark that no great composer has contributed less to the progress of harmony than Beethoven. Such a remark can be made only by a critic who has never regarded the facts of harmony on a large scale at all; and to this day harmony books, even of a most advanced kind, never seem to take a longer view than some half-dozen chords at a time. The harmony of the dramatic sonata-style of Haydn, Mozart, and Beethoven is in detail simpler than that of Bach, because you cannot build large-scale relations of key on a basis of elaborate harmonic detail, any more than you can construct a dramatically exciting play out of epigrams. Beethoven's harmony may become as abstruse as the profoundest of Bach's figured chorales if his task allows him to devote a short section of a work to matters of local harmonic interest, as in the *Variations on a Waltz of Diabelli*.

Large-scale harmony once more became abstruse when Wagner, anticipated in detail by Chopin and Liszt, developed the art of so accentuating an ornamental note in one key that it conveyed a sense of some vastly remote key. If the extended use of such an art is not to degenerate into nonsense, the composer's sense of large-scale tonality must be very powerful, and he must be able to convey it to the listener. The permanently astounding paradoxes of the *Tristan* Prelude are not more characteristic of Wagner than the opening of *Das Rheingold* with its several minutes of one single chord, or the opening of *Die Walküre* in sequences which take sixteen bars to move one step up the scale of D minor.

I have not time to deal with more modern developments of harmony, and any attempt to do so will involve me in controversies more interesting humanly for the acrimony which they may develop than musically for the enlightenment they may give. I will only say that one thing is unquestionably missing in most of our new harmonic experiments : and that is, evidence that they are helpful to the development of music on a large scale. When a tendency in recent harmony is definite enough to be the subject of propaganda, the propagandists still seem to concern themselves with six bars at a time at the utmost. Atonality and polytonality are severe discipline. I feel sceptical about their independence and novelty, especially when I find that a violinist who has great difficulty in finding the correct intonation of a thread in a polytonal composition can play it with ease if I support it on the commonplace and slightly oily Spohr-like harmonies which I suspect to have been lurking at the back of the composer's mind. Not so can the harmonic profundities of Wagner be made to vanish.

# LECTURE IV

WE have now to consider some paradoxes that are far more deeply involved in the integrity of works of art than any questions of the influence of one kind of art upon another. The vexed questions of programme music, and of conflict between the claims of musical form and the treatment of words in vocal music, and the endless possibilities of confusion and imperfection in the art of opera, are all easy and trivial matters compared with the dangers that arise from confusing processes with results. This confusion is not the same as that which confuses means with ends. The ingenious work of art is often criticized for sacrificing means to ends by critics whose views are not sound as to how far things that happen to be means are worthy to be regarded as ends in themselves; and in any case we are inclined greatly to overrate the practical danger of such a confusion. The golfer's end is the hole, and he must know its direction and be able, like any other marksman, to allow for the force of the wind; but his duty is to keep his eye on the ball. It is a brutal truth that in music, as in all the arts, most composers produce their worst work in the avowed pursuit of lofty ideals, and there are abundant classical examples of great works produced, not only with an avowedly technical aim, but even with an appeal for immediate popularity.

The question now before us is this: every work of art being produced under stress of practical necessities without which it could not have existed, how far do these necessities remain in the finished result in such a form that we must know them in order to enjoy the work? If there is any such thing as perfection and integrity in art, the only possible answer to this question is that, to use an inelegant metaphor, what the finished result cannot digest must be ignored or regarded as outside it. The historian must not confuse between his estimate of the historical influence of a work and the permanent value of the work in itself. The student of technique must neither be too ready to dismiss means from the category of ends, nor to confuse the way in which a thing is done with what is done. Smooth harmony can be achieved by avoiding consecutive fifths and octaves, by resolving all discords immediately downwards by step and all leading notes upwards by step, and by avoiding progressions that are ambiguous in tonality, especially those that follow the dominant by the subdominant in such a way as to draw attention to the tritone fourth. But this is not even a technical definition of smooth harmony. The observance of these rules does not even amount to 'safety first', though there are exercises in which these rules will enable a beginner to express the musical equivalent of 'a cat sat on a mat'.

Unfortunately, a great deal of quite advanced training is often devoted to inculcating the notion that the more closely a style obeys such rules the purer it will be. For instance, the rule against consecutive fifths is very stringent in pure polyphony, and there are conditions in which Beethoven and Wagner, sometimes even Strauss, will show themselves extremely scrupulous to observe it. As a teacher I find myself all in favour of enforcing it upon students with a strictness which most examiners will to-day consider old-fashioned and pedantic; but such broad-minded people are in revolt against a doctrine current in my youth, which inculcated that the more nearly you approach to a pair of consecutive fifths the less smooth is your style. Now there is no period of history or phase of musical education in which such a view ought ever to have been orthodox.

Time fails to work out the very difficult arguments that arise from this rule, but it is possible to show the conclusion of the whole matter in two illustrations. The object of training students in exercises where the rule is enforced under difficulties is to develop in them an ear sensitive enough to such matters to appreciate genuine refinements of musical style when they hear them, and eventually to be able to achieve such a style themselves.

In a composition called a *moresca* or *frottola*, Orlando di Lasso has written a certain progression of chords to the text *miaow, miaow*. The progression breaks the most elementary rule of counterpoint or harmony and is utterly inadmissible in pure polyphony. If you find any trace of it in Palestrina you have to deal with a misprint or a slip of the pen. Orlando di Lasso is quite as great a master of polyphony as Palestrina, and has a very much wider range of style, being not only a writer of great motets and not much less great masses, but perhaps the most prolific sixteenth-century musical illustrator of every kind of secular poetry, French, German, Italian, and Latin. Traces of such a progression are as non-existent in a motet or madrigal by Lasso as in the works of Palestrina; but Lasso did write this progression as part of a coherent, if naughty, scheme. In the aesthetic system of Debussy they would be perfectly proper, because his system is in many respects the reverse of that of classical polyphony, or of any kind of polyphony; and as such it has a purity of its own which he maintains with the scrupulousness of antiseptic surgery. There is room in musical aesthetics for the most opposite doctrines, but there is no room whatever for the doctrine that you must keep away from the risk of a direct collision of consecutive fifths.

The mature, broad-minded view is that such things may be done if one of the peccant notes is *only* a passing note. Captain Marryat with his bluff humanity persuaded even the mid-Victorian circulating libraries and British parents to accept a view at once severe and humane of the inadmissibility of the word 'only'. I refer to the case of the poor little nurse who had been in trouble, but who for that very reason was a suitable nurse if the guardians of the baby who was in need of her could only be persuaded to overlook the fact that she had had no right to have a baby of her own. They were not satisfied with her excuse that it was 'only a little one'. You may take it that when a licence is found in a great style, the excuse for it will never prove to be that the peccant element is *only* this or that. The explanation will always turn out to involve a wide context, and to be something by no means to be ignored, but, on the contrary, to be regarded as highly important.

There is a wonderful Amen of Palestrina, so wonderful that you may listen to it for years without adding to your quiet satisfaction in it the discovery that it is unusual. Its harmony is perfectly pure, but seven pairs of consecutive fifths and octaves are avoided only by a crotchet which is not even a passing note, but is part of the prevalent concords. Of course, it is evident that this crotchet is part of a theme, a fact which makes it easy to recognize; but few vaulted buildings, such as are generally favourable for the sound of Palestrina's choral writing, are so free from confusion in their re-verberations that any listener can count upon always distinguishing this very essential note. Now the broad-minded examiner will think me pedantic for blue-pencilling such a progression as this in an answer to an examination question. But I cannot accept the excuse that the fifths are produced by something which is only a passing note. That presupposes that we do not notice that the passing note is a fifth. The most old-fashioned examiner would object if we magnified the passage until this fifth evidently made a chord. Tempo is one of the vital elements in all harmony, and I am far from main-taining that the passage thus magnified is the same as the passage at a quick flow; but I do stoutly maintain that even naïve listeners—I mean listeners un-corrupted by professional information—should be credited with the ability to develop ears highly sensitive to the most delicate meanings of melody and harmony, and that to this end all musical students should be trained to recognize harmonic meanings in rapid details—in other words, that their exercises should be in a harmony that bears magnifying. And it is quite certain that you cannot have it both ways. This progression does not bear magnifying and if you are content habitually to dismiss the passing note as only a passing note, how is it that you can claim to appreciate the beauty of Palestrina's *Amen*?

Most of the confusion that is set up in the minds both of students and of teachers on this subject comes from the natural tendency when correcting an exercise to recognize each mistake with an agonized intake of the breath and with other symptoms of imminent lockjaw. It is true, as I have pointed out before, that Professor Higgins and Eliza Doolittle needed to devote unremitting attention to the utmost refinements that phonograph records could show in distinguishing between innumerable sounds of human speech before she could control her utterance well enough to pass as a person fit to present at a Royal garden party. It is equally true that she passed through an intermediate stage in which every syllable was enunciated in a voice of beautiful quality and accurate intonation, while the substance of what she said produced the greatest shock that the modern stage has received since the box on the ear which devastated the French theatre in the time of Molière. The moral of which is that the musical student needs more protection from debilitating and unsound technical precautions than from any risks of making his own mistakes.

The doctrine that not only fifths, but the remote risk of fifths, must be avoided has not, I think, been officially avowed, but a statement arising from the same assumption has often been current from classical times onwards, with results not less disastrous because it asserts a fact, though it gives the wrong reason for it. We are told that the severity of rules for two-part and three-part harmony becomes relaxed as the difficulty of observing them increases with the number of parts. A student who has been taught this has practically been told that he need never trouble to acquire a good technique. I was told by a pupil of Liszt that one of his proverbs was : 'There is no mercy in art'.

The student of two-part and three-part harmony is confronted with a large number of vexatious rules. Most of these are necessary because with two or three parts it is difficult to produce rich and full harmony. Such rules automatically cease to have any meaning in harmony of more parts, where the difficulty is rather to be clear and to prevent any of the parts from sounding superfluous. Of course, the student really should study two-part and three-part harmony in two widely separated stages. So long as he is handling two and three parts merely because he has not the skill to spell out four or more, his exercises should be elementary; and he should not be kept at them too long, but should proceed betimes to what is a more normal kind of music. The advanced student should then return to the noble economy and the lean athletic styles by which two parts or three parts can be made to sound as rich as eight.

Meantime, all teaching and criticism of musical texture should be designed so as never to confuse between methods and results. The student need not expect to see a direct connexion between such exercises as those of scholastic counterpoint and actual music. For musical criticism and analysis the danger of such a confusion might have existed with sixteenth-century music, but for the fact that the teaching of counterpoint was during the nineteenth century so distorted by feeble attempts to bring it up to date that no accurate observer can possibly suppose that from Cherubini onwards its academically accepted rules refer to any known artistic language.

The general type of confusion between means and ends persists to-day with subjects much more advanced and of popular interest. Few musicians can be trusted to keep their power of appreciating classical orchestration free from contamination with their experience of what is good practical advice for students. If we can see no more in Beethoven's orchestration than was seen by Rimsky-Korsakov, to whom it was nearly as obsolete as a tricycle with solid tyres is to the owner of a Rolls-Royce, then we shall certainly not appreciate, much less achieve, the splendours of Rimsky-Korsakov's brilliant and meticulously pure orchestration; and though we may easily emulate the perky provinciality and pedantry of his mind, we shall suffer in our own estimation from the hopeless disadvantages of being British, whether Northern or Southern, instead of having the privilege of being Russian, and therefore romantic and exotic.

The conclusion of this matter is that, whether in counterpoint or in orchestration, the student must be trained in a meticulous, but genuine, purity of style. At present, much of our academic training is lax where it ought to be severe, and timid where it ought to stimulate the student to be bold; but even the soundest practical training will not protect the critic and lover of music from confusing between methods and results. I have often had occasion to point out by way of illustration that the doctor who asks his patient to say 'ninety-nine' is not pronouncing a magic formula. I do not know how French doctors obtain the requisite resonances from their patients' interiors, but I know that they do not ask them to say 'Quatrevingt-dix-neuf'. Many of the rules and practices which the best training will enforce upon students have the purpose of producing habits and skills quite as remote from the superficial appearance of the exercise. I need not illustrate this subject further, but pass at once to the conclusion that one of the most cramping and inadequate of criteria is that which estimates the value of a work of art according to whether it is a good model for students. Students themselves, if they are allowed to believe this, may perhaps not degenerate on the lines of the don who refused to read Homer for fear of spoiling his grasp of Attic Greek, but they will assuredly develop the perkiness of Rimsky-Korsakov without his genius; and, given opportunity, will do far worse by way of bowdlerizing works of genius than Rimsky-Korsakov did with his friend Moussorgsky's *Boris Godounov*. The confusion between history and aesthetics can be even more disastrous to our capacity to understand music than the confusion arising from methods of training. The historic importance of a work of art is obviously separable from its aesthetic value. *Lilliburlero* jingled a king off his throne, but effected nothing that directly concerns musical history; though it is not merely external politics that are irrelevant to musical values, but many of the most important factors and tendencies in music itself.

My beloved master Parry presents in his numerous and stimulating writings on music abundant instances of the fallacies which arise from confusing history with aesthetics. Between him and the art of Mozart there was an obvious incompatibility of temper, aggravated, no doubt, by the revolt from the curiously ignorant idolatry of Mozart prevalent in his youth: an idolatry which not only consistently selected the more trivial of Mozart's numerous works for its worship, but displayed the utmost reverence for spurious works, like the so-called Twelfth Mass, which ought never to have deceived a competent musician for a moment. We have not yet freed ourselves from the results of this idolatry. Mozart wrote many more than twelve masses, and his genuine Twelfth Mass is a very beautiful, if very unecclesiastical, work which is not included in our English editions of Mozart's Masses. These, however, include the spurious Twelfth Mass and four other forgeries by the same author, all of them as near rubbish as makes no difference; but whether it was or was not possible in Parry's generation for a liberal-minded musician to develop a taste for Mozart, Parry would in any case have suffered from an inveterate and deliberately developed tendency to regard all works of art as leading to something beyond. Mozart and Haydn at their best were for Parry necessary processes leading to Beethoven and destined to be superseded by him.

Now here the doctrine of Art for Art's sake becomes important, and its two cardinal errors may be for the moment left out of account. It errs in spelling Art with a capital A, as if anything existed except individual works of art; and it errs, or at all events is misapplied, by being inculcated as if it were a method instead of a result. I firmly believe that a work of art exists for its own sake, but I might not be able to put up a very strong fight against anyone who should tell me that it was a bad doctrine to put forward as practical advice. In any case, many, if not most, of the great results in art and life have been achieved by aiming at something else; or, at all events, by concentrating on the means as soon as the aim has been determined sufficiently to ensure that we do not fire in a totally wrong direction. Whether you like Mozart or not, you must understand him as if the work you are contemplating existed alone in the world.

This does not mean that you can dispense with a large mass of knowledge which could be presented in an historic form, but it means that that knowledge is of matters inside the work and only accidentally of matters outside it. If you are told that a certain aria in an opera was inserted to please a certain singer, forget it. Either the aria is the right thing in the right place, or it is not. On the other hand, the knowledge that you need in order to perform Mozart in the right style and to understand the style both of the performance and of the composition when you listen is knowledge which is often more easily conveyed in historical than in other terms; but ultimately all that is relevant in such knowledge belongs to the substance of the work, just as, to use a former illustration, ancient views as to the respectability of piracy and the importance of decorous funerals explain themselves with romantic and tragic intensity in the poetry of Homer and Sophocles.

Take again the case of the choral works of Bach. Until quite recent times it was maintained that Bach's orchestration was negligible. We now know by experiment with instruments which, if not Bach's, are capable of playing what he wrote, that under proper conditions Bach's orchestration is part of a normal and mature aesthetic system. Such knowledge is obtained through historic research into the conditions in which Bach's works were performed, but it becomes a set of purely aesthetic principles inherent in the music. And I have often had occasion to point out that some of the historic conditions do not become so absorbed, and might as well never have existed—that, for instance, the authority of Bach himself does not compel us to follow his precedent and flog the ringleaders of the choir after an atrocious performance.

A history of music, like that of all arts, falls into periods of pioneer work, of artistic maturity, of decadence, of revolution, and of renascence. Most writers on music, even when, like Parry, they are great composers, seem impelled by a strong sense of duty to put their reflections into historical form. The disadvantages of this tendency are painfully evident in the paralysis which overtakes them all as soon as they are confronted with mature works, and I cannot see any compensating advantages. We ought all to be grateful to Schweitzer for stating, as far as I know for the first time, the cardinal truth that in music of all arts perfection is essential, and that the works at periods in which it was not attainable are perishable. Far be it from me to suggest that we should allow them to perish. On the contrary, the very historians who are so helpless, so inarticulate, and so dangerously sceptical about great music, become stimulating and interesting when they are dealing with archaic and transitional works. Here, in fact, they are forced, in spite of their historical bias, to make some approach towards considering these works as things in themselves. The doctrine that such and such a composition is wonderful for the time at which it was written represents an insufferably perky and patronizing attitude if it is applied to Palestrina, Byrd, Tallis, Bach, Handel, Haydn, Mozart, and Beethoven. When we advance in the nineteenth century our patronage begins to yield to Macaulay's pride in his own enlightened age.

No mature work of art is wonderful for the time at which it was written. It is simply wonderful at all times. A naïve belief is now prevalent that all great artists have been in advance of their time. The effect of this doctrine is to make the average artist of the present day ready to believe that it is his duty to be unintelligible to his contemporaries. That is not difficult. All he need do is to be unintelligible to himself; but, as a matter of fact, it is not true that all great artists have been in advance of their time; and it is quite certain that the contemporaries of those who were in advance did not recognize the fact, even if the artists themselves did. Bach was obviously, unmistakably, and avowedly, a hundred years behind his time. He differed from his predecessors, as

Schweitzer demonstrates, in the all-important fact that his works were mature and theirs were not. That is one reason why the musical historian is so much happier in dealing with the seventeenth century instead of with the eighteenth. With the seventeenth century he is dealing with everything that led not only to Bach and Handel, but to Mozart and to all later music up to Wagner, and his tendency is to see in pioneer work the prophecy of all the glories together; nor is he necessarily or often guilty of an anachronism in this. The pioneers themselves are often deliberately aiming at what they realized in later art, and the historian is in sympathy with them just because he sees beyond the immaturity of their achievements, though he must, if he has any sense of proportion, judge that immaturity more severely than the pioneer artists could have judged it themselves without inhibiting their efforts altogether.

The danger of all this historical sympathy is manifest in many freaks of modern fashion. We get up archaic works and listen, or think we listen, with rapt attention to music, whereas we are spending, as the pioneer artists themselves no doubt did, a great deal of trouble and money upon stage accessories which are really very much more artistic and mature than the music. You will find in the *Denkmäler der Tonkunst* an opera by Marcantonio Cesti, *Il Pomo d'oro*, written for some royal wedding at Dresden. The learned editor talks of the classical perfection of its choruses in terms that would make you think that great music was in question. I hope that I am not less capable than most musicians of doing my duty to pioneer work, but I frankly own that a fleeting glance at the music is quite enough for me so long as I am not engaged in historical research, and that my entire pleasure in this publication lies in the twenty full-page engravings of the gorgeous scenery in which this otherwise very primitive opera was acted. If anyone should ever go to the expense of producing *Il Pomo d'oro*, I should consider the production an absolute fraud if, failing a reproduction of the actual scenery, a spectacle of the same calibre were not organized, with results which, I regret to say, would make the music an almost negligible feature of the whole.

Far be it from me to deny that in archaic and transitional periods, not excluding decadent periods, music has been produced that has permanent value for its own sake; and I am not prepared to maintain that an absolutely sharp line can on principle be drawn between the composers for whom no historical allowance need be made and those with whom it is necessary to consider the time at which they wrote. But I find myself in thorough agreement with Schweitzer that the distinction is much clearer in music than in other arts. Musicians, however, ought to envy the much wider standards of culture that are enforced upon the directors of picture-galleries, who are responsible for the preservation of many works of art far less important than those which we musicians will condescend to keep alive in our repertoires. Time is less elastic than wall-space, for you cannot hear a piece of music at once, and the years of man are but as threescore and ten. Few practical musicians will nowadays show much curiosity about Cherubini, whom Beethoven considered by far the greatest composer of his day since the death of Haydn and Mozart. Brahms is recorded to have praised Clementi as a master of free and vital form. Of course Brahms did not mean that this was true of a large number of Clementi's works, but it is quite worth while to search Clementi for evidence of Brahms's grounds for admiration; only I fear that most of us would be too snobbish to arrive independently at Brahms's conclusion. A year or two ago I put Clementi's beautiful little Sonata in F sharp minor into one of my pianoforte recitals, but I took the precaution of representing the composer's name by a question-mark, and divulged it only after the sonata had earned its applause in its own right; but it may safely be guessed that, if the artistic equivalent of a good Clementi or Cherubini were to be stolen from one of our national galleries or sold to America, the resulting outcry would be a front-page topic in our newspapers for months.

I am not pleading that we should devote more attention to our lesser musical masters. On the contrary, it is highly undesirable that in our short lives we should rate time as cheaply as wall-space; and most of the present argument is, in fact, devoted to a warning against the historian's tendency to lose all sense of proportion and to confuse the interest of processes with the permanent values of results. It would be easy, in fact, to turn the whole of the present argument into a diatribe against the notion of progress in art. There is no doubt that it is only in immature states of art that the term 'progress' has the same meaning as it has in science. Elsewhere the use of the term may as well be taken as a symptom of bad criticism. In practice the integrity of music has probably suffered as much from misapplying the notion of progress as from any other artistic fallacy, and certainly such a notion has never been a genuine source of inspiration.

# LECTURE V

THERE is no cheaper substitute for criticism than to call whatever we like 'inspired', and to deny inspiration to anything we do not wish to honour with our attention. We are justified in viewing with the gravest suspicion almost every use of the term as an aesthetic criterion. The suspicion should not amount to downright scepticism. Inspiration is one of the most important things in art. And we are told that one of the most fundamental criteria of Persian poetry consists in a clear separation of the spontaneous essential of poetry from the mechanical and intellectual vehicle that may or may not convey it.

In all countries, but more especially in the East, this line of criticism tends to reject all elements in art that can be paraphrased or described in terms of intellectual content and organized form. In our more self-conscious modern Western art, this tendency is beginning to recoil upon itself, for our pursuit of meaningless word-patterns and unrepresentative lines and colours, no less than our repudiations and contradictions of classical methods in music, is becoming more mechanical and self-conscious than any formalism or scholarship. The sources of inspiration lie deep within the subconscious mind, and recent developments of psychology have stimulated many artists to founding their art consciously upon the subconsciousness. Far be it from me to trespass upon the grounds of a science in which I am no expert. That is an enterprise which had better be left to artists; but there is surely no difficulty in seeing a certain inconsistency in expecting that subconsciousness will remain a source of inspiration when it has been exposed. In fact, everybody knows that the essential value of psycho-analysis consists in the fact that, as soon as the subconscious causes of a psychosis have been exposed, the whole trouble vanishes for ever.

It is unreasonable to be disturbed by the discovery that, when a drainage system is exposed, its contents are such as we normally prefer to keep out of sight. Nor, on the other hand, is it comforting to be told that a bad smell cannot be due to the drains, for there are none. But the subconscious mind is the source of the best things as well as of the worst; nor need it be any the worse for inevitably containing everything that is most shocking to our consciousness. Sanitation is one of the noblest applications of science, and its chief beauty is that its work is unseen. There may be difficulty in distinguishing the decent concealments of good sanitation from the deceitful repressions of bad, but no excuse is accepted for failure to make the distinction.

Let me admit once for all that the sources of inspiration are subconscious, but let me at once disclaim any intention of delving into them. My intention is merely to investigate the conditions in which inspiration is possible, and chiefly to remove the prejudices and scruples that arise from accepting too readily a separation between inspired work and *Verstandesarbeit*, or intellectual construction. The condition of an inspired artist working at full speed has often been noted in literature and biography, from

Shakespeare's 'poet's eye in a fine frenzy rolling', to Wagner's account of the terrific impetus which carried him through the score of *Tristan*. Recent fiction has more than once exploited this theme with the profoundly useful and interesting distinction that the inspired heroes and heroines have been described as the authors of unmitigated rubbish. E. F. Benson's *Secret Lives* and Arnold Bennett's *A Great Man*, a work which he ironically acknowledged to be autobiographical, might have been even more corrective and stimulating to artists and critics if they had appeared in time to repair or avert the damage which honest Anthony Trollope did to his own reputation by describing in his autobiography his business-like working habits. When Trollope's autobiography appeared, the artistic temperament was being discovered and its fine frenzy was a mark of respectability which could hardly be too openly displayed. Sciolists, medical and literary, had not yet taken the further step by which artists were more crassly identified with lunatics, a confusion natural enough in persons with a subnormal capacity for art, though such persons cannot be acquitted of a no less gross lack of science in their failure to see the equally profound resemblance between the philistine and the idiot.

Mr. Desmond MacCarthy has pointed out that Trollope in his autobiography confesses to nothing less than a state of inspiration in the way in which his characters occupied his mind with all the force of living experience. The first readers of his autobiography had very little excuse for their snobbery in ignoring this aspect of his work and pouncing upon the evidence that he wrote his novels much as if they were business letters. Much the same might be said of Bach, Handel, and Mozart; and these three cases are remarkable in three different ways. Bach's work is always highly organized, and nearly always evidently rich in its intellectual content: in the immense bulk of Bach's works there are few pages that can be dismissed as unimportant. Mozart's work is always highly finished, though a considerable bulk is perfunctory and unimportant. Handel's work seldom shows any apparatus at all: no great composer has written a larger proportion of rubbish, and no artist has given us so little technical means of distinguishing his rubbish from his greatest achievements.

With these three artists it is evidently quite hopeless to attempt to distinguish what is inspired from what is not inspired. Our impulse is to say that the dull work is uninspired, and that what we like is inspired. By all means let us obey this impulse, but we must not call it criticism. If there were any inherent opposition between conscious intellectual work and spontaneous inspiration we should expect to find that the bulk of Bach's work was uninspired and the bulk of Handel's inspired, but the fact remains that modern criticism finds the bulk of Bach's work inspired in itself and a source of inspiration in others, while even the great heart of the naïve British public idolizes its Handel for the sake of one-fiftieth of that master's output and is accustomed to enjoy even that with the addition of heavy sauces and seasonings.

I will skip a long process of argument, for which you have my word that I have carefully worked it out, and give you at once my own conclusion, which is that Bach, Handel, and Mozart each achieved his enormous output in a continued state of inspiration, and that the inspiration has little or nothing to do with the varying values of the output. A work of art that is merely *Verstandesarbeit*, or intellectual construction, is worthless because it is uninspired; but its lack of inspiration has nothing to do with its being a *Verstandesarbeit*. And, mysterious though the nature of inspiration may be, an inspired work is neither a *Verstandesarbeit* nor a collection of Handelian clichés with the addition of a mysterious divine spark. I find myself driven to the unpalatable and prosaic doctrine that inspiration is indistinguishable from first-rate athletic form, whether mental or physical. The highest achievements of art, of athletics, and of mechanical skill cannot be attained without practice, but are far too complex and subtle to be attained only by practice and reasoned effort. The author of an uninspired *Verstandesarbeit* is as the centipede perspiring in a ditch considering how to crawl. The centipede's inspiration, we are told, had been paralysed by a malicious snail who asked him which leg he put down first; and there is no more effective way of paralysing a skill that already exists than by calling attention to its mechanism. Nothing is easy unless most of it is habitual, and you cannot pick a habit to pieces and begin at any chance point in the middle of its action. There is much to be said for the doctrine that heredity itself is a form of habit, and there is no doubt that the more deep-set a habit is the less capable are we of analysing it, or even of noticing it.

Work that is founded on an insufficient basis of

habit can never seem spontaneous or natural. The uninspired *Verstandesarbeit* fails because all its intellectual processes are insufficient to give it the fluency of habits that have penetrated deep into the subconsciousness. The great heart of the naïve public is as susceptible as the most discerning critic to the signs of work that has attained this ease. Nothing ever became a best-seller without this quality. The best-seller may be contemptible as a work of art, but the brutal truth remains that the most valuable intellectual work will not live unless it has this quality in common with the worst of best-sellers. A work of art that will stand the tests of wholeness and consistency is an achievement far beyond conscious intellectual processes. Its achievement depends upon a mental athletic form that can be attained and preserved only by constant practice on the basis of habits which have long become unconscious. This basis ought to be too firm to be shaken by any effort of the artist to add pioneer work to his mass of ascertained habit. The difference between Bach and Handel consists largely in the fact that Bach is so continually adding pioneer work to his routine that the pioneer work itself rapidly forms into habits, whereas Handel exerts himself only where the Bible and other special circumstances rouse him. Arnold Bennett makes a shrewd critic say of the work of his Great Man that 'This author will never improve'; and the publisher of a prolific writer of best-sellers is haunted by the nightmare lest some educative accident may awaken his lucrative author's powers of self-criticism and reduce him to the condition of the perspiring, self-conscious centipede.

Obviously, the inspiration which carried Wagner through the labours of *Tristan* was a force that had grown through a long and severe process of self-criticism. Few artists have, in fact, shown so enormous a development in taste and subtlety of style as Wagner. Wagner's early musical style had a facility which might well have satisfied a less ambitious artist; and might, indeed, have even left him unconscious that anything higher could be achieved. The vulgar popular author often does not know that literature and art contain higher thoughts than his own, and, unless he is a cynical moneymaker, the discovery of this truth would probably dry up his inspiration at the source.

The most miraculous feature in Wagner's development—a feature which is quite unparalleled elsewhere in music—is that his inspiration did prevail over the inhibiting force of a self-criticism that advanced in a few years from the dangerous facility of *Lohengrin* to the uniquely rich new musical language of *Tristan*. The value of a work of art depends as much upon the self-criticism and the conscious work of the artist as upon inspiration. Men of science, such as Helmholtz and Poincaré, have given us vivid accounts of the force of inspiration that accompanied their best work. All such accounts, including the stories of work achieved in dreams, and of problems found solved after a dreamless sleep, agree in two particulars: first, that the decisive steps have eluded the conscious memory; and secondly, that the inspiration has never occurred except as the reward of strenuous work. Poincaré describes the process by the analogy of the molecules of a gas dashing about in a vessel, and he supposes that the disconnected particles of his thoughts, which are far too numerous and heterogeneous to be deliberately joined together one by one, will have their chance of finding their true alliances only when they have been stirred up into constant agitation. Helmholtz also finds that *der Einfall*, 'the thing that occurs'—or, as the excellent slang word expresses it, 'the brainwave'—never came to him if there was the slightest trace of alcohol in his system. There is nothing inconsistent with this and the fact that many persons have done their best work under alcoholic stimulus. There was a time when such persons might have learned to work much better without alcohol, and scientific experiments with work which needs attention to complex details but with no scope for original invention have shown conclusively that pipe-setters, for example, imagine that they are working better with the help of alcohol when statistics clearly show that their speed and accuracy have been reduced by it. If this is not so with inventive work, that is because the proverb *in vino veritas* is true, inasmuch as wine removes inhibitions. A sober man is afraid of making a fool of himself, and a sober artist whose self-criticism checks his inspiration will at all events start his work, if not continue it, more easily if this check is removed. But there is no reason to resort to drugs to remove the check. Beethoven has left us the record of innumerable sketches of almost all his works, from the smallest to the greatest. Nottebohm, who published selections from many of Beethoven's sketchbooks, had the wisdom to make a comment that has been neglected by other pious hero-worshippers from Sir George Grove onwards. He notices that these sketches show every conceivable variety of method: so much so that we ought to allow for the possibility or probability that in some of the cases where no sketches are to be found Beethoven went to work without making any; but Grove expresses an innocent surprise that the sketches of some of Beethoven's greatest things are often abjectly commonplace, and he fails to connect this with facts equally noteworthy to him, that the handwriting is a vile and rapid scrawl and that the sketches are exceedingly numerous; from which he infers that this admirably illustrates the infinite capacity of genius for taking pains.

Now the crux in that much-abused dictum lies in the contradiction between the idea of taking pains and the idea of an infinite capacity. If you take pains you are straining yourself, but if you have an infinite capacity nothing can be a strain to you. What Beethoven's sketches show is that he did not take pains at the wrong time. He scrawled any cliché that would mark the place where an idea ought to be, and when he had advanced to sketching whole sections of a work, as in the seven or more sketches of half the first movement of the 'Eroica' Symphony, he often found it easier to begin again from the beginning and copy out the unaltered parts of his sketch, so that the act of writing had the same continuity as the flow of his thoughts, rather than tinker at isolated passages. He wrote down what occurred to him as fast as it occurred to him. When he read it over some of it bored him, and he rewrote it easily and quickly with alterations that interested him. He is recorded to have said that this method of scribbling was a bad habit, and doubtless he may sometimes have felt that it was a drag on him. But in all its forms it is a method of a man who thoroughly knows his own mind, and who needs no alcohol to encourage him to put down a crude sketch of his thoughts before he is ready to present them accurately. Contrast this with the method of a friend of mine who long ago in our undergraduate days showed me what he called the sketch of a symphony, in which the only thing that was sketchy was that it was in full score. His process was about as practical as an attempt to construct the Forth Bridge from one rivet to the next.

Beethoven's sketches, whether for a full orchestra or for the lightest pianoforte music, were written at a pace comparable to that of the music; certainly far more rapidly than the pace at which I can dictate these lectures. My friend's symphonic sketch must have taken several hours for a few bars, and the hideous labour of achieving it in the rough could not leave the composer very ready to face the problems of reshaping it. Beethoven could cheerfully make the most radical blunders in his first sketches with the certainty that next day five minutes' work would substitute, if not the right thing, something obviously altered in the right way.

I have sometimes tried to give a lecture on the sketches for the 'Eroica' Symphony, but have found that it could not be dealt with in less than a course of six, or better still ten, lectures. Perhaps I may attempt this some day. At present I will cite the fact that Beethoven's chief difficulty in constructing the opening of this symphony was due to the persistent intrusion of a passage on the dominant for which there was no room in the exposition. Let us consider the exposition in its final form. You see that the momentary cloud which comes over the theme after it has stated its first figure is produced by a chromatic step downwards. In the counterstatement the theme replaces this by a step upwards, which is carried in further sequences till it reaches the dominant. A few bars on the dominant lead to a third statement for full orchestra, in which the theme now moves in two steps of a third which carry it on to the enhanced dominant, by means of which the home tonic is sunk beyond the horizon and the first action of the drama —that is to say, the first radical change of key—is established.

Now Beethoven wrote several sketches of this opening before he could get rid of a tiresome tendency of the main theme to appear on the dominant before its proper third statement. This idea is quite unworkable in the exposition, but the probable reason why it was so importunate in Beethoven's consciousness is that it becomes vitally necessary long afterwards in the recapitulation. The dramatic suspense which precedes the recapitulation is one of the most famous passages in all music, and the cloudy chord in the first statement of the theme is no longer a passing cloud, but the occasion for a most paradoxical modulation. This modulation has its consequences, not less inevitable than itself; and the one thing predestined by Nature to restore the balance is the passage on the dominant which was so intrusive in the first opening.

There is no *Verstandesarbeit* here, or anywhere in the sketches. Inspiration doubtless comes unsought, but it comes only to the artist who has the patience to wait for it, and while waiting to work for it. Doubtless the work is often best directed to side issues. In other words, the watched pot never boils. The astronomer and the microscopist when they wish to see very fine detail form the habit of gazing at a point somewhere to the side of what they wish to see, but their best vision will appear to an unfatigued eye.

There is no justification for saying *a priori* that the technical elaboration of this or that work renders inspiration impossible, any more than there is for saying that a work has not enough organization to be inspired. That which transcends knowledge will never come without knowledge. If the burden of knowledge is too great for the artist, his remedy is not to have less knowledge, but to have more habit and experience in the handling of it. Hence, we constantly find in the genesis of all art, bad and good, that the successful artist is always inspired in the low sense of working easily on the impetus of long habit, and that the deeper and more vivid inspiration will often first appear in matters comparatively accessory. For instance, Shakespeare's early work begins with the use of stock material which did not demand the exercise of his own powers; and to the end of his career he was so easily satisfied with such stock-in-trade devices that, as Dr. Johnson says, to censure his plots is to spend our criticism upon 'unresisting imbecility'. The power of Shakespeare's inspiration first shows itself in minor characters, such as the Nurse in *Romeo and Juliet*, and around such characters the immense and real world of Shakespeare's creation builds itself.

An artist's world must build itself of materials that he knows. A work of art is more vital than a crystal, but many conditions and apparatuses of art are to its vital organization much as a piece of string, a twig, or a twisted wire is to the crystals which will close around it and form a glorious symmetrical object when it is dipped into a saturated solution. Biology and organic chemistry have not achieved, and may perhaps never achieve, the step from crystallization to vital structures, and perhaps it is beyond any power of analysis to distinguish between what is vital in a work of art and what is merely crystalline. But it is not enough to point out that your crystalline object will retain its shape and its beauty when the string or wire round which it built itself has been dissolved or removed.

One of the most beautiful crystalline objects in all music is a certain Psalm by Sweelinck, in which the figures of the tune we know as the Old Hundredth are detached according to the grammatical sense of the words to which the tune is set, and built into a glorious little chorus. In my Deneke lecture on 'Musical Form and Matter' I cited this Psalm as an instance of the way in which matter can be quite inseparable from form. Unfortunately, I am in no position to prove that matter and form are inseparable from inspiration, for this precise crystalline structure or mechanism is used, not only by Sweelinck throughout four volumes of Psalms, but pervades the complete works of Michael Praetorius, a composer whose thirty-fourth volume has just reached me, and in whose pages I regret to say that I have not yet been able to find any inspiration whatever. Perhaps other students may have found greater patience rewarded by greater luck, and may be able to quote Praetorius as an inspired artist. I am quite certain that great inspiration is invariably accompanied by great skill. The technique of Handel's dullest work is not as great as that of his finest. In neither case does it consist in devices that are recognized as subjects of academic study, and in Bach's works the technique lies mainly in such subjects; but in the work which we can distinguish as inspired the technique differs from that of dull work in an uncanny accuracy and thoroughness.

The D sharp minor and A minor Fugues of *Das Wohltemperirte Klavier* which I quoted in an earlier lecture are, with all respect to Bach and to the textbooks which cite them with reverence, manifestly imperfect in technique, and they more than exhaust the possibilities of their subjects, because their uglinesses ought not to have existed; and I have already shown that the great B flat minor Fugue is the closest of at least eight other fugues that could have been made on the same scheme, and the work of Bach which is still supposed to be merely a technical exercise, *Die Kunst der Fuge*, is uninspired only where its technical problems are inherently those of a mere exercise. Wherever the problems are normal to the material the result is as noble as anything Bach ever wrote; and though we have every reason to think that the scheme of *Die Kunst der Fuge* is nearly complete, its actual technical possibilities are incalculably more numerous than the selections which Bach can possibly have intended to work out.

Every serious analysis of works of art reveals an uncanny accuracy and thoroughness when the work is what is called inspired. When the technical apparatus is not that by which students can be trained our analysis must not look for academic devices. Handel is undoubtedly a supreme master of counterpoint, and Shakespeare a supreme master of dramatic construction; but to analyse Handel's fugues as if they were Bach's and Shakespeare's plays as if they were French *pièces bien faites* is, to quote Johnson again, to expend criticism on unresisting imbecility. The only discoverable thread that is available for the analysis of a masterpiece of Handel is much the same as that by which you may hope to unravel the mysteries of Bach's Chromatic Fantasia, or the Organ Fantasia in G minor. These are in the main supremely accurate examples of a musical rhetoric. Stanford's favourite illustration from Handel is the aria 'Total eclipse' in *Samson*, of which Stanford has given a beautiful analysis in his little primer of composition.

It might be possible to misunderstand the conventions which are the working hypotheses of such music. Milton, of whose *Samson Agonistes* the libretto of Handel's oratorio is a ghastly travesty, would have had great difficulty in foreseeing the conventions of an art two generations later than his own; and Tennyson, who objected to song-writers who made him say twice what he had said only once, would probably have made the same objection to the symmetrical scheme which compels Handel to repeat the words; but the more intimately we know such a masterpiece the more necessary and less obtrusive its conventions appear. The repetitions present us with newer and deeper aspects of the words, and the complete impression of the whole excludes as irrelevant all the distress that we must feel at the librettist's travesty of Milton, and vindicates the authentic voice of Milton in a music as great as *Samson Agonistes* itself.

# LECTURE VI

ONE of our chief concerns to-day is to vindicate the integrity of music in opera. The student of opera can learn much from Dean Church's paradox that it is unscientific to apply the terms 'higher' and 'lower' to the criticism of poetry. The terms have a meaning which is as true within its limits as the terms 'pure' and 'mixed'. Opera is an art in which music cannot possibly be unmixed. But there is no reason why music-drama should not have its integrity. As Moth puts it in *Love's Labour Lost*, 'I am sure you know how much the gross sum of deuce-ace amounts to'. *Armado*: 'It doth amount to one more than two.' *Moth*: 'Which the base vulgar do call three.'

Let us not rest contented with the euphuistic Don Adriano de Armado's habit of leaving his elements unintegrated, and let us have no snobbish reluctance to use the language of the 'base vulgar' when it is more adequate than that of the superior person. The terms 'higher' and 'lower' are conveniently, though dangerously, applicable to conditions in which an art is free to develop in full concentration or restricted by a mixture of elements. If there is any sense in saying that a string quartet is a higher form of art than a symphony, this can only mean that a string quartet can achieve by the economic use of its four instruments music as important as that which a symphony achieves by a great number of instruments that lose their individuality in the orchestral crowd.

From this we may infer a presumption that the composer who can find his freedom in the string quartet is more capable of producing pure music—or, as I prefer to put it, that his pure music will have more integrity—than the composer who cannot satisfy himself with less than an orchestra.

We may also expect that in a census of string quartets and symphonies there will be a smaller proportion of low-grade string quartets than of low-grade symphonies—that, in fact, the prolific writer of string quartets will be a more high-minded composer than the prolific writer of symphonies; but all such statistics are troublesome work, the results of which may be unscrupulously used. The simple fact is that the composer of a string quartet has less temptations to be vulgar than the composer who deals with a more luxurious apparatus; but the dangers of a facile classification of art into 'higher' and 'lower' begin to outweigh the advantages when an art-form has obvious temptations for vulgar artists. The majority of concertos are vulgar, and there is a middle class of concertos, headed by Mendelssohn's masterpiece for the violin, which represent a very pleasant light form of art. But it is nothing less than disgraceful that critics should ever have allowed the technical needs and possibilities of the concerto to induce them to impute the resulting average vulgarities to the supreme masterpieces of concerto style.

The variation form is another case of an art-form which is contemptibly easy to handle for purposes of vulgar display, and the result is that we constantly meet persons of some musical culture who tell us that they do not like variations. This may be in some cases a matter of taste which there is no disputing, but it is far more likely to be an ignorant prejudice; and, indeed, the quasi-technical utterances of many critics and musical commentators have often displayed a radical misunderstanding of the nature of the variation form. The forms of concertos and variations are prominent among the few cases where it is advisable to have an idea of a generalized notion of a form as a thing true or false in itself. As a rule, no kind of criticism does more injustice to the integrity of art than that which objects to a work as not being a true example of the form it professes. If the work justifies its existence on its own terms its title may be regarded as an external matter; and if a large number of inherently satisfactory works are called by the name of an art-form from which they agree to differ, in the same way we must recognize their agreement by admitting that the name includes this different type. Thus, the meaning of the word 'sonata' is very different for Haydn, Mozart, and Beethoven from what it is for Bach; and both meanings are equally definite, far more definite than the original meaning of the term, which was simply the opposite of 'cantata', a piece that was sounded as distinct from a piece that was sung. But it seems legitimate, and even convenient, to talk of 'true' and 'false' forms when the name of an art-form is primarily associated with masterpieces constructed on definite lines, but has become applied to occasions for all manner of flimsiness and vulgarity. Those modern concertos which are not vulgar are for the most part in a much lighter form than that of the concertos of Mozart, Beethoven, and Brahms; but the true concertos of those three composers constitute such a mere handful in comparison with what exists for good and for evil elsewhere that it might seem rather precious to restrict the notion of a true concerto to so small a handful; yet the preciousness might be justified by the fact that these few concertos are among the sublimest achievements of pure music, whereas even the best of the lighter forms of concerto are manifestly nothing of the kind.

The case of the variation form is equally difficult, and here one of the commonest errors of criticism consists in the despising of the simpler kinds of variation. When we are told that good musicians deplore the frivolity of the choral variations in Beethoven's Ninth Symphony, we had better disregard the critic's claim to know what a good musician is. Those variations are open to criticism, but not to the charge of frivolity. The fact that variations consisting of simple embroidery of the melody can be achieved cheaply and nastily is no reason why Beethoven in the *Sonata Appassionata*, the Violin Concerto, and several other works should not achieve some of his ultimate sublimities in the terms of embroidery variation that provoke the derision of the late Monsieur Vincent d'Indy. On the other hand, variations may be based on other elements than the external melody; and so the strictest and most highly organized of variations on a deeper structural basis may be so unlike the original melody as to mislead not only critics, but composers, into the idea that where the melody is not apparent anything will do.

Two false criteria have thus arisen: one, that it

is a defect in a set of variations if the listener cannot trace the melody; the other, that where the melody cannot be traced anything may happen. It is often said that great progress has been made in the variation form since Beethoven. I have not time here to deal further with this dictum than to say roundly that it is not true. I do not know why the true variation form should be obsolete; nor is there, in fact, any reason why the neglect of an art-form by one generation of composers should prevent its rediscovery by later composers. The composer of variations is nowadays generally at a loose end, and most modern variations have little power to convince us of their reason for existing. A clear, or even a crude, notion of a real difference between true and false variations might be a great stimulus to modern composers.

Both the composition and criticism of opera are at the present day in a condition of better health and better information than the composition and criticism of pure music. When we have succeeded in excluding from our view of opera the dangerous idea that it represents a lower form of art than pure music, we still need to insist upon certain truths which have given rise to the use of that dangerous term. There is a widespread tendency, both popular and academic, to assume that the musical style of opera is more emotional than that of instrumental music. Thus, for instance, Sir Henry Hadow in the *Oxford History of Music* tells us that *Fidelio* is dramatic only as the D minor Sonata is dramatic, implying unmistakably that he thinks that instrumental music is less dramatic than opera. This is far from being the case. 'Staginess' cannot properly be a term of reproach for the stage itself. But we shall find that what is the matter with staginess off the stage is not that it seems exaggerated, but that it seems cold and flimsy. The intensity and concentration of an easel picture would be invisible on the stage, and would hardly become intelligible if the picture were magnified to the dimensions of the stage; but, conversely, stage scenery seen by daylight in a picture gallery consists of colours splashed on flat boards out of a pail, and it is only a freak of fashion that nowadays allows something almost as crude as stage make-up to conceal real human complexions in daylight.

All the intensity of Wagner's ripest style does not reach the heat of a climax in a work comparatively so statuesque as Brahms's F minor Pianoforte Quintet. I shall never forget my surprise when, being haunted by a passage in that work, I found myself trying to place it somewhere in Wagner or Verdi before I discovered where it really belonged. Mozart, the only composer who divided his time almost equally between opera and absolute music and achieved perfect integrity in both, gives us a clear illustration of the relative values of stage emotion and symphonic emotion in the fight between Don Giovanni and the Commendatore, which is perfectly represented with complete adequacy. But in one of his mature symphonies such a music would sound drily formal, and an instrumental style that does not constantly rise beyond it inadequately represents Mozart's symphonic style at the age of fifteen. This, then, is the sense in which opera may be considered a lower form of art. But we must not call that art 'low' which perfectly integrates the enormous mass of material that constitutes an opera.

With Mozart the integration is so perfect that it has had paradoxical results in the ups and downs of performance and criticism of his operas. The first thing that became obvious to the meanest capacity was that, though Mozart was doubtless a great composer, his librettists were contemptible as poets and dramatists. Hence, not only the criticism and performance, but the editors of Mozart's operas, even in what is still the standard critical edition, scorned to qualify themselves for dealing with opera at all. The standard full-scores of *Die Entführung*, of *Die Zauberflöte*, and of Beethoven's *Fidelio* appear in the so-called critical edition without any of the spoken dialogue. It is true that as literature the spoken dialogue is beneath criticism, and it is equally true that in its purely musical aspects the music is already beyond praise; but the editors and the practical improvers of the words and action ought to have known that the music which was so far beyond their praise was even farther beyond their understanding if they did not condescend to take it in its integrity— that is to say, its integrity with the words. And it was the professional musicians who were at fault in this matter. The great Mozart-lover Otto Jahn acquired his immense knowledge of music in the course of a lifetime devoted to classical scholarship. Jahn's *Persius* is a monument of Latin scholarship, even more famous among classical scholars than his Mozart biography is among musicians. He, then, of all persons might have been expected to despise and neglect Mozart's libretti; but, being a first-rate scholar, he committed no such blunder, and his accounts of Mozart's operas, including all that Mozart wrote from the age of twelve upwards, invariably begin with a thorough précis and criticism of the action.

We need not set against this the notorious fact that Jahn was a vitriolic anti-Wagnerian. A man whose affections are as strong and whose knowledge of what he loves is as profound as Jahn's may be forgiven if he has violent prejudices against what impresses not only him, but the world at large, as opposed to what he loves. But charity does not require us to forgive the iniquities committed by a tepid orthodoxy that in the editing of a great classic avowedly acts in contemptuous neglect, and even deliberate suppression, of aspects which were matters of deep concern to the composer.

The intelligent study of Mozart owes much of its impetus on the Continent to Richard Strauss, and in England to Professor Dent, who some years before the late War had a great share in an epoch-making performance of *Die Zauberflöte* at Cambridge, and whose book on Mozart's operas is one of the most important landmarks in English musical literature. The technical difficulties of Mozart's operatic roles are so great that we need not wonder that for a while progress in the renascence of Mozart was more evident in the better understanding of the libretti than in the musical standards of performance. One witty critic went so far as to write an article on da Ponte at the Old Vic in which he jibed at the imminent danger lest the librettist should be regarded as greater than the composer. That danger is past. Nothing will make da Ponte and

Schikaneder accepted as great poets; and, whatever primitive conditions we may tolerate in scenery and costumes, or even in the acting, of Mozart's operas, all regard it as self-evident that the singing must be as perfect as lies in human power. It has become as fashionable to go to Salzburg and Glyndebourne for our Mozart as to go to Bayreuth for Wagner, and at Glyndebourne and Salzburg it is taken for granted that the action of Mozart's operas must be worked out as carefully as if Mozart, like Wagner, were his own librettist. Da Ponte and Schikaneder were past-masters of stagecraft; and we may doubt whether Mozart could have been as successful with dramas of greater intrinsic value unless he had been his own librettist. There is some parallel between his case and those of Irving and Sarah Bernhardt, who in several instances won their greatest triumphs in plays, like *The Bells* and *Fédora*, that fitted them but fitted no one else, and had, indeed, but flimsy reasons for existing.

Mozart was fortunate, not only in the ready-to-hand stagecraft of his librettists, but also in the fact that they were bulliable and that he knew how to bully them. In this respect Beethoven's bad luck was almost tragic. *Fidelio* is a very much greater opera than orthodoxy is as yet ready to admit, and its defects, both in its almost impossible earlier form as the *Leonore* of 1806 and in its final form as the *Fidelio* of 1814, are not, as is still commonly thought, the result of Beethoven's habits as a purely instrumental composer, but are the defects of the important school of French opera that culminated in Cherubini, whom Beethoven regarded as the greatest composer of his time.

As a magnificent tale of heroism the plot of *Fidelio* would impress everyone as it impressed Beethoven, if only it had been reasonably clearly told. It is the chief example of several similar products of the French Revolution, being the story of a heroic wife who rescues her husband from the fate of a political prisoner. Many lectures would be needed to show how Beethoven's difficulties arose and how they spring from no fault in his music, but are the direct results of a conflict between French operatic forms and a subject which has developed a power beyond their scope; but the important conclusion reached by all study of the vicissitudes through which *Fidelio* attained its final form is that Beethoven learned by experience, what he would have learned from Mozart if Mozart's subjects had been ostensibly more serious, that music for the stage must live at a much lower temperature than purely instrumental music. The mighty overtures designed for *Leonore* in its first and second productions were inadmissible in *Fidelio*, and the modern custom of inserting *Leonore No. 3* as a prelude to the second act is a dangerous concession to musical self-indulgence.

I have used the metaphor of temperature for this question of musical values. But there are other intensities than that of temperature, and we need set no limits to the depth that is attainable in music for the theatre. While the temperature of *Fidelio* is consistently reduced at every point from that of *Leonore*, the depth is as consistently increased; and the listener need not trouble to explain the paradox that the emotional effect of *Fidelio* is point for point incomparably greater than that of *Leonore*.

Jahn is of opinion that Beethoven in 1814 was out of sympathy with the *Leonore* of 1806, that his revision of it does not do justice to the earlier ideas, and that it introduces marked discrepancies into the style. Here the philologist is too wise after the event. Nobody appreciating *Fidelio* in the light of pure instrumental enjoyment or integral musical dramatic enjoyment would ever regard as a discrepancy the fact that the most pathetic moments in this music-drama coincide with the deepest music. Still less would he impute the extra depth to a discrepancy of date, or feel the slightest concern how and why these most pathetic passages were the most beautiful. The only matter that is of interest here is a matter beyond the scope of *Fidelio*. I believe it is a measurable fact that from 1814 onwards Beethoven's purely instrumental style develops, besides its ever increasing polyphony, a certain tendency to let its moments of action occur explosively after long periods of exposition. All drama shows this tendency as it develops. However severely the dramatist may economize every word for the purposes of action, it is mainly by words that drama explains itself. Pageantry and mime without words are not more, but less, dramatic and emotionally less exciting than the drama which, relying increasingly upon dialogue, presents to us the elements of a crisis slowly and surely ripening towards the point where a sudden action explodes the whole situation.

Purely instrumental music had, as I have already pointed out, long lived consistently at a far higher temperature than theatre music; but this question of the slow incubation and explosive determination of dramatic action is not a question of temperature. After *Fidelio*, Beethoven's purely instrumental music certainly did not become more theatrical, but it did become deeper in ways which I believe he learned when he found out how to deepen the pathos of Florestan's music in the dungeon scene. It is not of the slightest importance whether my impression is a case of *post hoc ergo propter hoc*. Beethoven may have been able to increase the pathos of Florestan because his instrumental style was deepening, or the two tendencies may have merely coincided, as far as they did coincide, in time. Of course, we can cite as circumstantial evidence that the revision of *Fidelio* coincides with the production of two theatrical *pièces d'occasion*, *King Stephen* and *The Ruins of Athens*; and it is certain that an eminent critic devoted a weighty article to accusing Beethoven of a disquieting tendency to rely more and more on stage effects. The obvious correct answer to this is that staginess should not be used as a term of abuse for what belongs to the stage. Beethoven was naughty enough, as I have seen with my own eyes, to scrawl on the pages of this criticism an entirely unprintable statement as to the relative value of the critic's highest thoughts and biological waste-products, which Beethoven implicitly identifies with these insolent and perfunctory *pièces d'occasion*.

In these matters most of us know too much about drama and fiction. Drama and fiction are actually too true to life, and a man under genuine stress of emotion may possibly, though let us hope not often, be inhibited from saying what is perfectly natural to him because it is what would be said by a character in the same situation in a novel or play. In the same way, a lover of music may be less apt to misjudge the values of instrumental music if he is not experienced in opera; and as instrumental music is, speaking loosely and dangerously, much the higher and purer form of art, or, speaking accurately, much the severer in its demands on the intelligence, we shall probably find a better musical taste prevalent among lovers of instrumental music who dislike opera than among persons devoted to opera. For this very reason it is necessary to be specially on our guard against the prejudices of instrumental purists. If, when listening to a string quartet, we are so foolish as to regret that it gives us none of the thrills of opera, we shall be incapable of receiving from it the thrills that it can give to an intelligent listener. On higher grounds, we come to the fact that the string quartet is a much more ethereal and subtle medium than the symphony; and from this we can easily see that the typical vice of a bad string quartet is that it imitates an orchestra. But here, again, our knowledge may be misapplied, and we may blame a string quartet for succeeding in sounding like an orchestra. If it achieves that, it cannot have been orchestrally written at all. String-quartet writing that succeeds in sounding orchestral is magnificent, but if it were transcribed literally for the orchestra it would not sound orchestral, and I have no very clear idea of anything in earth or heaven that it would resemble. Bad orchestral writing for a string-quartet is writing that assumes that four stringed instruments scraping away in the elementary fashion which is often the noblest economy in an orchestra will sound as if the four solo players were engaged in tasks worthy of their eminence.

Similar confusions of thought arise in discussing the relation between the organ and the orchestra. The style of organ-playing and organ-composition is often ruined by an all-pervading tendency to make the organ imitate the instruments of an orchestra, a habit which destroys the noble architectural character of the genuine organ and reveals the mechanical voices of its masqueradings.

We unfortunately know that Bruckner was a great organist; and nothing is easier for the critic to detect than the organ-like habits of his orchestral compositions; but to say that he orchestrates like an organist is to say precisely the thing which is not. He orchestrates like a master of the orchestra; and, inasmuch as he succeeds in making the orchestra sound like an organ, he succeeds in producing from it the noblest sounds that he can imagine.

Jealous champions of purity should beware lest they forget that all instruments and all musical art-forms rest on the common ground of music, and that those forms and instruments which have the widest musical range can only lose their own integrity and the integrity of music by confining themselves each within the range of what no other resource can imitate. Let me repeat an illustration which I have often used: that conversation would be unnaturally restricted if the arbiters of taste were to enforce upon us that no lady should say anything that could possibly be said by a gentleman, and no gentleman say anything that could possibly be said by a lady.

# LECTURE VII

THERE is a dangerous clearness in the appearance of musical art-forms to those who can read music like books, and who can follow a technical analysis. We need not be sceptical as to the positive facts that are so easily discoverable by the analysis of individual works; but the statistical results of a large number of works are always misleading. This is partly because in art the average is always false. The only thing that matters in a work of art is the individual work, and every actuary knows that he cannot tell whether a selected individual will fall within his statistical averages, even if that individual seems already doomed by actually suffering from the causes covered by the statistics. The epicure who was assured by the doctor that his over-indulgence in lampreys would kill him promptly defeated the doctor by eating an enormous meal of the forbidden food and then throwing himself from the top of a tower in order to die from some other cause.

The apparent rigidity of musical art-forms is not merely a statistical illusion. When we are duly attending to an individual work we are in danger of drawing unsound inferences from the way in which the printed page represents symmetries that exist in time by symmetries that exist on paper. Much of our appreciation of architecture and painting depends upon the *coup d'œil*, the instantaneous and abiding impression of a thing entirely comprised in one field of vision. In architecture there are also symmetries which are not so comprised, and which demand that we should use our memory in order to appreciate the correspondence of the right side with the left; but even in these cases there is nothing to prevent us from going over the ground again; and, moreover, we are often supposed not only to do this, but to view our architecture at different distances. Our knowledge of an architectural work is an accumulation of many views, and perhaps none of these has any claim to be *the* main view. There is no point of view from which you can see all round a building, but as we approach a building we first come to a point at which a whole façade gives immediate pleasure, and at the same distance there are various views combining two sides at various angles. The architect of the Paris Opera fell into tragic despair when he found that he had miscalculated in this matter, and that his dome was not visible at the only possible first approach to the façade. There is a similar, though less fatal, defect in St. Peter's at Rome.

As we approach nearer to a building the views of whole façades extend beyond our sight, and the architect has to satisfy us with more and more detail. His art consists in contriving that at distant points of view his finer detail will not confuse his great lines, and that at nearer points of view the great lines will not be bald and tiresome. Roughly speaking, the eye will receive an impression of grand proportions in whatever is designed to fill its field, whether the view is distant or near.

There is no exact parallel to this in music. There might be, and the cinematograph might do something to develop it, if we were more in the habit of enjoying a thing which gives me personally much pleasure—the progressive change in the aspect of a building as you walk round it, the appearance of actual movement as perspectives open and close and features are gradually revealed and concealed. The symmetries of music all exist thus in motion, and the direction of that motion is unalterably fixed. There is no exact parallel in music to the mirror relation between the right and left halves of a symmetrical object. Optical symmetry demands that the right and left sides should face each other in opposition, but you cannot treat time thus. Music becomes unintelligible if you turn it backwards; and even the mis-spent ingenuity by which a musical phrase may be designed to bear the process, though it may make the backwards phrase intelligible, will not make it recognizable.

The symmetries of music are at least as powerful and necessary as those of architecture. But we must never lose sight of the fact that their real existence is in our memory, and that our power of verifying them by sight on the written page is a matter external to the music and apt to give both critics and composers misleading information. The most prominent feature in clearly constructed music is that of recapitulation. In music it is the main means of symmetry, and the musical recapitulations are at least as exact and extensive as those of architecture. They are quite without parallel in words. The symmetries of poems are omnipresent in the details of metre, but extended verbal recapitulation is quite exceptional. The correspondence of strophe and antistrophe in a Greek chorus is minute and highly musical, but is again metrical rather than topical. The parallelism of Hebrew poetry is again a matter of detail. It consists in stating a thing twice in other words. Musical recapitulation is not in other words, and is a matter of extended passages.

Much easy criticism, and some conscientiously free musical composition, has been devoted to the task of emancipating music from the conventions of recapitulation. Martyrs to this cause have been misled by the fatal ease with which musical recapitulation can be traced on paper. Such martyrs have no true idea either of the exactness or of the freedom of good musical recapitulations. In a story or drama recapitulations may be as extensive as in music, but they are not recapitulations of words. They are summaries of former events in words appropriate to a description of the past and not to an announcement of the present.

Exact verbal recapitulation would produce either an exceptional effect or none at all. You will find an exceptional effect of intense musical power towards the end of *Paradise Lost*, where Milton achieves the highest pathos and beauty in describing first how Adam and Eve resolve to go to the place where God had pronounced judgement on them and there express their penitence and pray for pardon; and then, a few paragraphs later, tells us in the same words, with only the necessary change of persons and tenses, that Adam and Eve did so. But it lies in the nature of music to recapitulate long sections note for note. Wagner proves this more conclusively than any other composer, and he proves it in spite of his own indiscreet utterances on the subject. He points out as a defect in Beethoven's Overture *Leonore No. 3* that the trumpet-call which foreshadows the climax of the opera does not fulfil its function in the overture inasmuch as Beethoven is compelled by the rules of sonata form to follow it by a formal recapitulation. It is astonishing that Wagner, who is one of the greatest masters of recapitulation in all musical history, should have allowed himself to make so cheap and unscrupulous a debating-point. He ignores the fact that in *Leonore No. 2* the trumpet-call really was the climax of the overture, in which it immediately precipitated matters and was followed by a coda that did no more than wind matters up with reasonable breadth; but in *Leonore No. 3* the trumpet-call is not the climax, either in fact or in purpose. As compared with *Leonore No. 2*, everything up to the trumpet-call has been drastically compressed to two-thirds of the original length and consistently lowered in temperature. The trumpet-call is the signal for the release of all the pent-up emotions which Beethoven feels in contemplating, not merely the incidents of the drama, but the whole character of Leonora and the glorious ideals of wedded love. The trumpet-call is not immediately followed by the recapitulation. On the contrary, it comes little more than half-way through the development; and the first great climax of the overture is the return to the home tonic, which is a much more exciting affair than any possible effect of an off-stage trumpet. The recapitulation, though spacious, provides by the contemplation of its symmetry no more than a necessary relief during which the mind recovers energy for one of the most enormous codas Beethoven ever wrote. Beethoven has, in fact, set his music free—so free that he had eventually to discard the *Leonore* Overture altogether, because it killed any conceivable stage music. Nothing could be more impertinent than to suggest that Beethoven would let a musical conventionality stand as an obstacle to a dramatic truth. The very critics who are ready to accuse him of this still cling fondly to the delusion that as an instrumental writer he inherited classical art-forms from Haydn and Mozart and broke them by subversive innovations. To believe this may be orthodox, but it shows an encyclopedic ignorance of the classical art-forms, and of what constitutes a classic. To speak of Haydn and Mozart as if they represented a single set of classical conventions is as absurd as to bracket Browning with Tennyson. I do not mean this as a parallel in any less general respect than the absurdity of supposing that the members of each pair resemble each other in habits and methods.

A further question is: Who are the classics? History, as the authors of *1066 and All That* have told us, being what you remember, we are told that the classics of sonata form are Haydn, Mozart, and Beethoven. Their contemporaries did not think so. At all events they thought of them as we think of Strauss, Elgar, and Sibelius. It is more than any living composer's reputation is worth to be accused to-day of anything more orthodox than a strictly private new aesthetic system of his own, but in the time of Beethoven correctness was the chief criterion in all the arts: and a very much better and more stimulating criterion it is than our sterilizing criteria of originality.

Surely it is obvious that the procedures of the greatest masters should not be ruled out of court in favour of averages taken from the works of artists whom we all remember, if at all, only as persons wise in their own generation. I suppose that Spohr and Hummel represent the traditions of sonata form without the disconcerting variety and range of Beethoven's methods; although, if you have the curiosity and patience to study Spohr and Hummel, you will find that both of those masters tried experiments of which the face value amounts to interesting innovations. Spohr's cloying mannerisms are not tiresome enough to destroy the affection which every violinist must feel for so great a master of his instrument; and if, as some eminent critics have been rash enough to say, it is essential to a great composer that he should be a prolific inventor of significant and beautiful themes, Spohr's rank must be high indeed. But Spohr's limitations are so obvious that many musicians whose ear for rhyme has not been cultivated are content merely to regard 'Spohr' as a rhyme for 'bore'. Still, Spohr represents, decidedly better than Mozart and infinitely better than Haydn, the only possible type of a classic if we assume that any of Beethoven's innovations represent a break from classical tradition. Fortunately, Spohr has himself given crushing evidence of the unsoundness of such a view of classical form. Joachim told me that Spohr once said to him: 'I wish some day to write a set of six string quartets all in the regular classical form.' Joachim asked in astonishment in what way Spohr's existing quartets were not regular classical examples. 'No,' said Spohr, 'I mean with shakes at the ends of the passages.'

Spohr's most affectionate friends never accused him of a sense of humour. What is the classical meaning of a shake at the end of a passage? There is nothing contemptible about the device. The sonata style is not the only one in which passages of sustained melody and of polyphonic development need to be relieved by lighter passages tending towards bravura. When your passage of more or less brilliant semiquavers has continued long enough how are you to bring it to an end? Your rapid motion must come to a climax; and you may think fit to interrupt it, or you may prefer a device by which an actual increase of movement closes it automatically. Your brilliant passage may be conventional, but the classical convention, at least in violin music, prefers rapid melody with some kind of transcendental vocal quality to arpeggio figures with no singable element. The pianoforte offers the composer temptations to devices more mechanical and glittering, and it is dreadful to see Mozart's most gifted pupil, Hummel, specializing more and more exclusively in the pianoforte, and carrying us more and more into a world filled with the musical equivalent of glass chandeliers; but, whether your style is that of a glass chandelier or that of a coloratura singer, your passage will come to its most natural conclusion by changing its forward movement to a stationary vibration, more rapid than anything else—in fact, indefinitely rapid. And this we call a trill.

The passage ending with a trill is thus a natural device, which may be expected to become a regular classical feature. The question now arises: in what classics did Spohr find it? Undoubtedly in Mozart, whom Spohr very sensibly regarded as the ideal master. But Spohr was no scholar, and long before his ideas of classical music had become settled Mozart's string quartets were known only in the last ten masterpieces. Thus we may rule out of account all Mozart's earlier works; and we must certainly rule out of account all Haydn's works of any period, for Haydn is one of the most irregular artists that ever wrote.

Now let us see what superlative lies can be told by statistics. In the only string quartets of Mozart that concerned Spohr there are nineteen opportunities for the regular passage ending in a shake. In fourteen —that is to say, in three-quarters of these cases— no such phenomenon occurs. On the other hand, it does occur in the trio of a minuet where there is normally no room for anything of the kind.

Let us return to the subject of recapitulation. Wagner's theories of dramatic declamation were put forward by him with a certain crassness intelligible to the public and suited to the crude controversies which his music provoked. And it seems self-evident that Wagner's treatment of words differs from the classics by its complete realism. You can learn from his music how his words ought to be spoken if there were no music at all. The pace of all singing tends to be slower than that of speaking, and in *Lohengrin* the declamation undoubtedly drags; but in Wagner's mature works from *Das Rheingold* onwards the slowness of the dramatic action is inherent in the huge scale of Wagner's designs, and the handling of speech is as quick as articulate singing permits. Hence, not only the naïve, but the Wagnerian listener may enjoy the works for years without noticing that recapitulations in the music are at least as extensive and exact as in any classical symphony. They happen, not according to the quasi-gravitational forces and symmetries of instrumental music, but according to the opportunities of drama. The singer usually fails to notice them, because the voice parts are with rare exceptions not the vehicles of the main musical substance, but are demonstrably invented by Wagner after the self-completed musical design in the instrumental background. This is sometimes an actual weakness in Wagner's aesthetic system and is at best a legitimate technical expedient which ought never to have been erected into a guiding principle. It does not always represent Wagner's own practice. In most of the first act of *Die Walküre* the voice parts contain the essence of Wagner's musical invention; but in a large proportion of Wagner's work, certainly in more than half, the music is in the orchestra and the voices are talking, in gloriously musical terms, but still with the effect of something written over the surface of a picture. Isolde's *Liebestod* is a magnificent piece of music; but not only singers, but commentators, have been known to analyse it into its single leitmotives without noticing that it is an exact recapitulation of the last movement of the love duet in the second act. Up to the catastrophe, a conductor could conduct the *Liebestod* from the second act with the sole difference that he has to beat four slow beats instead of two quick ones and that he takes rather slower tempi.

The *Liebestod* is a favourite concert piece for orchestra. How does the orchestral arrangement provide for the part of Isolde? It simply leaves her out. Liszt, in his wonderful arrangement of the piece as a pianoforte solo, has included six independent notes of Isolde's near the beginning. Surely the last notes of the singer in this overwhelming swan-song should be memorable. They are the right notes, and they sound supremely beautiful; but I question whether many who know Isolde's *Liebestod* by heart could quote them. As a recapitulation the *Liebestod* is quite as long as the longest in all symphonic movements, that in the first movement of Beethoven's 'Eroica' Symphony. There are plenty of other examples in Wagner's works, not self-evident lyrics like the *Preis-lied* in *Die Meistersinger*, but pages of solid dramatic development: self-explanatory in the most stupendous case of all, that in *Götterdämmerung* where Siegfried entertains his treacherous enemies with an account of his early life, and, when dying of the murderer's stab, finishes his tale with recapitulating the awakening of Brünnhilde. The fact is that Wagner is one of the supreme masters of purely musical form, but the integrity of his art makes this form arise out of the conditions of his music-drama.

We are apt to be misled as to the nature of musical recapitulation by the practical fact that it necessitates a large amount of mechanical copying. The publisher André once told Mendelssohn in shocked tones that he had seen Beethoven's Seventh Symphony in progress in manuscript, and that Beethoven was evidently composing in a manner that could not but produce disconnected results by leaving many pages blank and skipping from one part of a work to another; to which Mendelssohn replied by playing the Seventh

Symphony until André had to confess himself too delighted to criticize further. André's remarks were quite unworthy of the intelligence of a man who published a score of Mozart's *Zauberflöte* Overture distinguishing in red print the parts which a paler ink in the autograph had shown to be filled in later. It is obvious common sense to put off the mechanical labour of writing a recapitulation when you already know how to attack your coda and are anxious to get to work on it; and it is not only wasting labour, but risking serious inaccuracy, if you do not have your original statement before you when you write its recapitulation. It is extraordinary how the finest details that have occurred to you in the heat of writing will desert your memory if you have mislaid your manuscript. Moreover, the fact that most of your recapitulation can be mechanically copied is no hindrance whatever to your power of making vital changes in the finer details. On the contary, the first condition of the finest subtleties is that the rest shall be accurate. The difference between a true recapitulation and a mechanical one is precisely this, that the composer is aware of the difference between a memory and a first impression. When Siegfried describes from memory how, after tasting the dragon's blood, he understood the language of the birds, he remembers the bird's theme and message, but the orchestra does not remember the high harmonics of the violas and violoncellos.

The dull composer is often content to copy mechanically. He is perhaps more often persuaded by a stupid cleverness to do worse, and to alter for the sake of altering, regardless of the possibility that, if a passage is not necessary the second time, there may be some doubt whether it was necessary the first. The great artist recapitulates with the liveliest conscious-ness of the difference that memory and other cir-cumstances make. Sometimes it is necessary, as in that case of Siegfried, to show that the memory is a pale reflection of what had originally happened. Sometimes, and perhaps more often, the function of a recapitulation is, as it were, to make us see with two eyes what we had originally seen only with one. This is especially the case where the beauty is that of a sonata-like symmetry. Music, as I have pointed out, cannot be recognized when it is turned backwards; but music finds some analogy to the right and left opposition that we see in symmetrical objects when it recapitulates in the home tonic, or in some sym-metrically contrasted key, what had first been heard in a foreign key. In order to produce the material in the home tonic instead of a foreign key, some change is necessary in the transition between the first and second group of material. Now in binocular vision we obtain our impression of solidity through the effort unconsciously made to bring together in a single impression the retinal pictures of each eye. If these pictures were absolutely identical, the resulting impression would be flat; but they are not identical: there is a distinct parallax for nearer objects against the background of more distant ones.

With musical recapitulations, the memory com-bines its first and second impression in a way not unlike that of the parallax of binocular vision. In any case, a second impression cannot be the same as the first, and the most sensitive composer may find that the mere fact of its being a second impression provides all the difference that is needed; but I doubt whether in any vital piece of work there is such a thing as a completely flat recapitulation. The alterations may be very minute and subtle, but they almost always have in common the demonstrable fact that the second impression is more solid than the first. My favourite *locus classicus* is a single bar from the first movement of Mozart's String Quartet in E flat —the ninth bar of the recapitulation.

# LECTURE VIII

THERE is no accepted classification of musical forms, so we are saved the trouble of contradicting any received opinions in this matter, and we can proceed at once to build our own classification on a basis of fact.

In my last lecture I dealt with only one aspect of musical form. I may perhaps have given the impression that recapitulation was the only aspect to be considered. While it is true that musical recapitulation has a far greater scope, far more freedom, and a far profounder accuracy than is popularly supposed, it is not more than the antithesis to the equally important aspect of form which is conveniently called development. We may easily classify the forms of whole musical compositions into those which depend upon shape and those which depend upon texture. According to this classification, the shaped forms are those of the sonata, of which the main types are: the first-movement form, or sonata form *par excellence*; and the rondo, with the addition of the smaller lyric and dance forms that do not greatly transcend the scope of an alternation of a couple of lyric melodies. The texture forms are mainly represented by the fugue and by the structure of polyphonic motets and madrigals in sixteenth-century music. This classification is important and obvious in itself; but one of its chief consequences is that a fugue is, properly speaking, not a form at all, and most of the confusion and misinformation of the text-books on fugue results from setting up rules for the structure of a fugue as a whole without realizing that such rules, whoever designed them, exist for the sole convenience of teachers and pupils, and that the faint indications that the great composers comply with them are so rare as to be almost certainly accidental. I must leave it to more learned persons to discover the composers whose fugues anticipate or follow the precepts drawn up by Cherubini. The examples he provides specially for his treatise on counterpoint and fugue illustrate his rules with a bluff inaccuracy which may have some educational value as preparing students for the deceptions of real life; but the really noble fugue which he quotes from his own *Credo* is provided by him with an analysis which can be understood only as an attempt to avoid betraying trade secrets.

As for Bach, we all believe, and the belief is correct, that Bach's fugues are uniquely solid and consistent in their forms; yet we still persist in trying to analyse them according to the scheme of Cherubini, who strongly disapproved of Bach, while we completely ignore the clear classification and crystalline regularity of the examples drawn up with an avowed educational purpose by Bach himself in *Die Kunst der Fuge*.

The first step towards common sense in the matter is to recognize that as an integral art-form there is no such thing as *a* fugue. The term should be used mainly without an article, definite or indefinite. The only meaning of 'a fugue' is a composition written entirely in fugue. It is a medium like blank verse. There is no such thing as *a* blank verse, because you cannot tell that a verse is blank until you have heard a sufficient number of verses to convince you that the poet is abstaining from rhyme. *Paradise Lost* is *in* blank verse. A misguided contemporary of Milton thought that the poem would be more elegant and popular if it were made to rhyme, and Milton to save trouble derisively gave him permission to tag his verses. In one important sense this process obviously casts the whole poem into a different art-form; but the art-forms in question are textures, and the shape of the poem—that is to say, its plot and its theological, ethical, and descriptive contents—remains unaffected and undetermined by the textures.

For our present purpose it will be more convenient to consider the antithesis between texture and shape in the light of general means of expression available in various parts of all art-forms, and not as terms separating one form from another. Evidently recapitulation is a matter of shape, and development is a field in which we may expect a more prominent, or a higher, function for texture. From the point of view of a sonata movement a fugue consists entirely of development; by which I do not mean that fugue is a normal, or even safe, means of development in sonata works; but in a fugue anything like an extensive recapitulation has an effect rather subversive of fugue style. It is like the powerful device at the end of *Paradise Lost* which I cited in my last lecture, and it sadly distracts the attention of the orthodox analyst. Reams of fantastic speculation have been written on the provocation which Bach gives if he allows three bars of cadence in the dominant early in a fugue to be recognizable note for note in the tonic at the end. I must beg you not to expect me to treat such speculations with courtesy. The results of analysis will not be a nuisance if the analysis will only take each work on its own terms, and proceed from fact to fact instead of troubling to save Cherubini's face.

When the composer does purposely combine the procedures of texture with those of shape, he makes the savers of Cherubini's face dangerously angry. Bach's great E minor Organ Fugue, known as *The Wedge*, has the appalling effrontery to be in da capo form. I find myself in agreement with the comparatively naïve listener to whom the total effect of this fugue is magnificent just because of the da capo, and I can see no sense whatever in the criticisms directed against that feature. If Bach had produced a few more specimens of the kind, it might have been recognized as a classical form; and, similarly, if Beethoven had produced dozens of movements on the lines of the finale of the 'Eroica' Symphony, we should have had no nonsense about its being formless because its form happens at present to be unique. Unique such things are, and unique they must remain, for their form is their life which developed from within, and imitations of it cannot live if they are moulded from without; but this is also the case with living examples in forms that seem most conventional. As I have said elsewhere, a great composer's hundred specimens of a form may be as like as two peas without being as like as two buttons.

In the last resort, our analysis must condescend to details, and one curious consequence of this is that the only part of the old-fashioned teaching of fugue that is truly classical and well observed is that which is most tiresome for students: a tangle of finicking rules as to the difference between subject and answer, the delicate principles by which the answer is so often not an exact transposition of the subject, but a tonal, as distinct from a real, answer—a tonal reflection of the subject from the authentic into the plagal view of the octave, and vice versa.

It is impossible to draw up these rules without making allowances which force both the student and the teacher to recognize some of the finer aspects of a master's style. In the middle of the nineteenth century there appeared two volumes of canons and fugues, the posthumous work of an excellent musician, August Alexander Klengel, who arranged this *magnum opus* exactly like *Das Wohltemperirte Klavier*, from the scheme of which it differs in providing strict canons instead of free preludes. Hauptmann, his editor, said that Klengel 'expresses his own thoughts in the way in which Bach would have done had he lived at the present day'. This is a dangerous scheme, and those who deign to cast a contemptuous glance at poor Klengel's *magnum opus* are usually content to refute it by saying that Bach was a poet and that Klengel was a pedant. This is unfair to Klengel, who was no pedant and whose fugue subjects are always good and often charming. One fugue, on Mozart's *La ci darem la mano*, is no blasphemy on Mozart's theme, and makes witty use of the second movement of that duet. The real trouble with Klengel's work does not come from lack of poetry, but from lack of technique in a matter which ought not to be beyond the scrutiny of academic teaching. Klengel's phrases are permanently tagged, and not with the skill of a master of the heroic couplet, but with the flat-footed sententiousness of a schoolboy who can write grammar but cannot build a paragraph. An odd result of this is that the canons often sound actually more free than the fugues, because the exigences of canon prevent Klengel from coming to full closes with every clause.

If we are to get rid of the illusions produced by the apparent solidity and simplicity of the classical art-forms, we shall find it convenient to proceed on the lines of classifying modes of form universally prevalent rather than the art-forms of pieces as wholes. A fugue is a composition which, being written in fugue, has no leisure for recapitulation, but proceeds entirely by development, its very exposition being the immediate development of the fugue subject. In the forms that have shapes as wholes the effect of symmetry is produced by recapitulation; and in such forms the three principle elements are exposition, development, and recapitulation. More particular rules of form arise as convenient procedures that secure the composer against confusion, or cross-purposes, in these elements. The business of exposition is to lay the materials clearly before us, and the general rules for this are much the same in music as in drama. In the most businesslike exposition, one idea may lead argumentatively to another; and, in fact, one of the great fallacies of an over-facile analysis, and of the habits which it stimulates in composers, is the notion that a witty concatenation of the figures of one theme with those of another constitutes a trustworthy logical connexion of ideas, and that such wit is essential to all music that claims to be important. It is much more important that the ideas put forward in an exposition should be made clear by every legitimate means of contrast than that they should be connected by argumentative wit. There are no limits to the refinement and allusiveness of style permissible in an exposition, but there are limits, inexorable in music as in drama, to the amount of argumentative procedure or development for which an exposition can find room.

In exposition and recapitulation the handling of keys, and many other technical matters, will differ from what is appropriate to development; and here we often find that modern innovators are apt to ignore the consequences implicit in their new styles, and that they are far more apt to remain hidebound by irrelevant rules which they believe to be classical than to show any real sense of the freedom which they ought to find in their new world. For instance, Reger's meticulous adherence to the external features of sonata form has much the same relation to his extremely chromatic style as a high box-seat for the driver has to the purposes of a motor-car. I frankly cannot see anything in Reger's classical forms that is more to the purpose of his highly self-conscious modern ways of moving than the shape of a converted brougham was to the purpose of the earliest motor-cars. The forms of Bruckner's symphonies are a close historic parallel to the defects of the first attempt at a great Atlantic liner, the *Great Eastern*.

The criticism that treats such defects as breaches of rule is manifestly in danger of mistaking an unprecedented quality for a mere defect; but its most serious danger is in its identity with the same confusion of thought that makes the pioneer compositions fail in their purpose. The really melancholy example of this kind of confusion is to be seen in the history of a neglected work of Schumann, which cost him a great deal of trouble and which, though disappointing as a whole, contains many beautiful ideas. He published his Second Pianoforte Sonata, in F minor, Op. 14, with the title *Concert sans Orchestre*, under the naïve delusion that its style had some of the brilliance of a pianoforte concerto. In a later edition it appears as Sonata in F minor, and has an important and typically Schumannesque scherzo. I always understood that this scherzo was the most important of the improved features of the second edition. By the way, not all the other features of the second edition are improvements: Schumann's later revisions of his works are apt to show an effort to become a more conventional person. But it is really rather shocking to find that this had always been part of the sonata, and that it was extruded from the first edition because a classical concerto, which this sonata never remotely resembled, never had, and therefore ought never to have, a scherzo. If this was the notion of classical forms prevalent in what was known as the Romantic Period, no wonder that some people behaved as though the classics ought never to have occurred.

Neither in the officially recognized history of sonata form, nor in the external appearances of the distribution and derivation of sonata themes, is it possible to discover the principles of musical form in the great composers since Bach. What passes for orthodoxy in these matters is the customs of composers for whom we no longer care; and even in these composers its real merits are not discoverable by the lines of analysis which are still regarded as orthodox. The whole terminology of the sonata form is wrong. The term 'second subject', which, by the way, is an English provincialism, has perhaps done more damage to methods of musical criticism than any other blunder in musical history. If it has not done equally serious damage to composition, that is because it is almost always effective and convenient to construct a movement with two, and not more than two, important contrasted themes stated in an exposition which assigns one to the home tonic and the other to a complementary key. The two themes will not of themselves fill the necessary space. So there is always room for supplementary passages, one group of which effects the transition between the home tonic and the complementary key, while the other completes the exposition. These passages will give effective relief most easily by being rapid, and the most convenient way to bring the rapidity to a climax which automatically stops it is to end your passage with a trill. Hence Spohr's idea of strict form.

Schumann, who shared with every sane musician of his day a great admiration for Spohr, pointed out that those critics and composers were gravely mistaken in imagining that Spohr's untroubled mastery was as easy to achieve as it seemed; but the fact remains that this regular form may be cheapened until it becomes almost fool-proof, and this is what Parry means when he says that to Beethoven brilliant passages were a byword as odious as cant to Carlyle. Nevertheless, we must not judge by appearances, and the first movements of the 'Waldstein' Sonata, which contains some of Beethoven's boldest innovations, and the third 'Rasoumovsky' Quartet are externally such perfect examples of Spohr's regular form that the chief humour of the situation is in the fact that they are exceptional in Beethoven. In any case, these are pioneer works of which the originality is not for a moment in doubt. And Spohr, as he showed in his 'Historical' Symphony, regarded himself as belonging to a later generation than Beethoven.

We shall never begin to understand the sonata style so long as we take the view that it differs from earlier styles in having two contrasted themes instead of one. It may have any number of themes. Sebastian Bach has left plenty of movements externally resembling a sonata movement with several clearly contrasted themes; and Haydn tends more and more in his later works to build his second group mainly out of the materials of his first. Philipp Emanuel Bach is supposed to be the composer who bridged the gulf between the two styles, and it seems unreasonable to doubt this when early in Haydn's career he sent a personal message to Haydn to express his delight in finding a composer who really understood him; but neither Haydn nor Philipp Emanuel Bach seems aware of Haydn's own irresistible force, unique until Mozart developed it more systematically though not more persistently, as a composer to whom every process of form was inveterately dramatic: so much so that his lyric and dance forms, as in his slow movements and scherzos, became more deeply lyric as an essentially dramatic contrast to the active forms.

The only terminology which gives safe guidance to the interpretation of classical forms consists of the three words 'exposition', 'development', and 'recapitulation'; and no formal procedure can be profitably criticized as either an example or a breach of rule except in so far as it keeps these three notions inviolate. We shall do well to distrust all plausible laws of proportion that can be applied to the length and contents of sections. One of the most plausible is that which applies the canon of the golden section, the line divided in extreme and mean ratio, to musical forms. The applications are often fascinating, but are so manifold that they can be made to prove anything. We shall have more convenient occasion to deal with them in discussing the time-dimension in music and the senses in which artistic perfection is a type of infinity. At present we may conveniently consider the criteria that unquestionably arise from the nature of exposition, development, and recapitulation. Here the analogies of drama are obvious and not misleading.

Exposition should attend to its business, and not be weakened or confused by a discursiveness that may be appropriate to development. There is nothing in this to prevent a composer from using his finest wit in an exposition, and the increase in his own practice and the accumulated weight of precedents will tend to make his style more and more allusive and witty. The later works of Haydn, Mozart, and Beethoven, and every work of Brahms from the outset, all show this tendency as clearly in their expositions as anywhere else in a movement; and this gives rise to the dangerous notion that such wit constitutes the logic of music. It is extremely dangerous to suppose that it can constitute the logic of any art. Great composers themselves can be misled by it, not in their works, but in their advice to less experienced artists. When Haydn's style had become habitual to him he reproached young composers with using an extravagant amount of material instead of seeing what they could extract from one good theme. But Haydn himself extracts an abundance of good things out of his one theme, and in this he would never have succeeded if he had not in his earlier works been one of the most extravagant composers in piling up all the good things that occurred to him.

The composer whose themes are all linked together by an outwardly logical connective tissue is neither vital nor logical except in so far as there are differences in all his identities. Nothing is more childish, or for that matter more easy, than the process of inventing, or borrowing, a single pregnant figure and relying upon twisting it into different rhythms to give logical coherence to your work. It is strange to find so great a composer as Stanford giving in his treatise on composition not only the worst possible advice to young composers, but selecting the most unfortunate example for his warning against the extravagance of using a number of different themes. The early works of all great composers, Brahms's not excepted, have relied upon a large number of different themes. Not only that, but the most experienced composer will show this and many other phenomena of an early work when late in life he handles an art-form that is new to him. It is natural to write in a large hand and to make obvious distinctions before you trust yourself with small writing and subtle lines. Stanford unfortunately cites the composers of symphonic poems as representing the bad habit of using an extravagant number of different themes. Now, if there is one doctrine more prominent than any other in the pioneer Liszt's official propaganda for his symphonic poems, it is the doctrine that the whole work should be derived from one *Urkeim*, as living texture is derived from a single nucleated cell. Liszt's derivations are ingenious, but they neither help nor hinder the continuity of his works. Great impetus was given to his doctrine by the easy and fascinating analysis of the way in which the themes of Wagner's operas are associated with his dramatic events and ideas. This association is present in such minute detail that the dreadful doctrine has arisen that Wagner's music is actually built up from leitmotive to leitmotive; as, no doubt, the Forth Bridge is constructed from rivet to rivet, and the dramas are constructed from subject to predicate, if not from syllable to syllable. In the love-scene in *Tristan* the lovers do, indeed, descend to such a pathetically profound infantility as 'Dies süsse Wörtlein "und"' ('That sweet little word "and"'). Wagner carries it off quite successfully as natural lovers' babblings, but it is only a lucky accident that has saved the passage from becoming the source of an officially recognized *und-motiv*. I have already dealt with the large-scale recapitulations which are as important a feature in Wagner's forms as in any classical symphony, and all

I need insist upon here is that it is folly to suppose that the essential structure of Wagner's music is on less particular lines than that of his drama.

When we deny that Schubert is a great master of form we ought not to mean that he breaks orthodox rules. We ought not, in fact, to suppose that his mastery of form is not potentially of the highest order. His openings are magnificent, his transition to the second group primitive and abrupt, but not necessarily wrong. His second group usually falls into a weak and ill-timed process of development; a weakness which, by the way, is not present in the 'Unfinished' Symphony, though that is one of the very cases where his cadence group is derived in Haydnesque fashion from the main theme of his second group. Altogether, the first movement of the 'Unfinished' Symphony is as perfect a masterpiece as can be found anywhere; and its abrupt transition is by no means a defect.

As Schubert's expositions are ruined by premature and discursive developments, wherein Schubert differs from Dvořák in the fact that Dvořák ruins his first group and transition in the same way, so Schubert's developments are weakened, first, by the fact that too much development has already taken place, and secondly, by two compensating tendencies: (1) to develop one of his themes into a long lyric episode with no action; and (2) to aim at a cumulative effect by simply repeating whole pages of a process in another key. I believe the inspiring cause of this to be the splendid effect which Beethoven boldly produces in the development of the 'Eroica' Symphony by the recurrence of his transition theme at two different stages in preparing for two very different kinds of development.

Schubert is usually accused of repeating himself too much. Quantitatively he does not repeat himself nearly as much as the more authoritative masters, but he is in the unfortunate position of being obliged to repeat what will not bear repetition. When he comes to his recapitulation, the inconvenience of the discursive developments in his exposition becomes painfully manifest; and only in the great C major Symphony does Schubert find himself with energy left for a big coda, and here severe critics are apt to make the easy remark that the listener's energy is less than Schubert's. Still, the defects of Schubert's form are too deeply rooted in his qualities for us to accept mere shortening with a pair of scissors as a remedy. Actually, few, if any, of Schubert's movements would be too long if he had packed his material so that exposition was exposition and development was development. If Beethoven had been given Schubert's openings he would have made the works quite as long, and would have disobeyed the advice of Haydn and Stanford by using several more entirely different themes. It is a merely superficial question whether these different themes have or have not figures in common with the main themes. The exposition of Schubert's 'Unfinished' Symphony is a masterpiece, and critics who quote its cadence subject as an example of Schubert's tendency to let development intrude into exposition only show that they do not understand what development is. This cadence phrase is aesthetically a different theme from the great tune from which it is derived.

# LECTURE IX

UPON the handling of the time-dimension depends the whole sense of movement in music, from the smallest and most immediate effects of rhythm to the most extensive matters of form and contrast. In these lectures I must leave most of the immediate and detailed aspects of rhythm unexplored. The subject of rhythm as an omnipresent factor in speech and dance and everything in music that results therefrom is inexhaustible and has never been neglected. But the larger aspects of musical movement are often misunderstood in ways that give rise to methods of criticism more distinguished by strong prejudice against whole schools of classical composition than by power to stimulate and enlighten. Perhaps no general aspect of music is less understood at the present day than that of movement; and no power of classical music has been so completely lost in recent times.

According to popular prejudice, this is the age of pace. The progress of civilization, as measured in miles an hour, is alarming to some people and gratifying to business men; but the art of conveying a sense of movement in music is far more rare in our modern experiments than it is in quite conventional works on classical lines. Many of our composers and critics are quite unaware of this, and show that they simply do not appreciate a sense of movement. Others are more aware of how that sense can be stimulated, but they reject the quality of movement as representing an undignified phase through which music regrettably passed when Haydn and Mozart dramatized the art which Bach had brought to its true consummation in architectural and static majesty. Besides representing an indisputable matter of taste, this view has the advantage of being founded on fact. To a mind that has an instinctive taste for Bach and older forms of art the impact of dramatic music, if it does not come early in life, produces a disconcerting shock, and the attention is unwilling to be roused to an activity in which the sense of movement is frequently changed instead of being maintained at one steady rate. If the taste for Bach is not instinctive, but has been recently acquired, the shock may be as disagreeable as an attack upon one's religion; and if you are a composer who has discovered a knack of writing, not necessarily in Bach's art-forms, but in a style that has the same appearance of even flow, the art of Mozart, Haydn, and Beethoven, and all that is derived from those masters, may make you as furious as a tigress protecting her cubs against interference. Something like this fury inspires many intellectual fashions in music to-day. It has the weakness of all tendencies that come from being afraid of life, and such fears blind us to the deeper qualities which the things we like best share in common with all that is great and true.

Mozart is now in fashion, largely because romanticism is out of fashion. Romanticism is out of fashion because at present we are tired of the unexpected and the catastrophic, and we delight in things that are punctual, predestined, and exact. Such qualities we recognize in Bach and Mozart, and for their sake we are ready to ignore or forget Mozart's irrepressible dramatic tendencies. Before Bach attained his present popularity, the naïve listener thought him monotonous: an impression based on the indisputable fact that in Bach's forms everything reveals itself as an uninterrupted unfolding of elements already implied from the outset. It would be fair to say that in Bach much may develop, but nothing can happen. If this condition is essential to our enjoyment, the paramount symmetry and manifest system of Mozart's forms may reconcile us to the fact that in Mozart many things happen.

Before Bach became popular, the naïve lover of music had a standard of movement set by Mozart, disturbed by Haydn, raised to a higher power by Beethoven, and completely obliterated by Wagner. Bach did not reach this standard. His movement was too uniform. Current modern criticism sees that Wagner obliterated the standard, but fails to realize that he mastered a standard of his own.

Some time-elements will fill a few seconds: others will take a quarter of an hour to appear. Bach's great Organ Toccata in F ought to take eight minutes if it is not played ridiculously fast. It can be played surprisingly slowly with rather a gain than a loss to its impression of a momentum that nothing can stop; but though its whole system depends upon its having no contrasting themes, its movement constantly renews its energy by the clearest possible contrast between short phrases and long.

The sense of movement is quite independent of the sense of tempo. For artistic purposes, movement does not exist except when we have some sense of it; but our sense cannot remain enjoyable under constant irritation. It must be refreshed by being lulled to rest at times. I find it convenient to distinguish between three main types of movement. That of the highest artistic value and most immediate effect may be described as 'athletic'. Again and again, we shall find that what passes as a modern sense of pace is as unaesthetic as a millionaire snoring in his car while he leaves to the chauffeur the responsibility for evading the police. Still, we need not deny artistic value to a consciousness of movement in which we are passive rather than active. The consciousness of movement becomes impossible when the movement is on a cosmic scale. Wagner, who mastered all kinds of movement, achieved what may be called cosmic movement in his music-dramas, and such is the aspiration, conscious or unconscious, of most of the larger forms of music since Wagner. The strength of Bruckner and Sibelius lies in their attaining such movement. The weakness of Bruckner is in his uncritical and helpless retention of the externals of sonata form, for which the pace of his action is hopelessly too slow. Two things are essential to the sense of cosmic movement: firstly, it must not be reduced to lower orders of movement by the only possible kind of event that can normally give us a sense of movement at all; and secondly, it must become distinguishable from complete stagnation by the presence of the smaller forms of movement, so that we may have a standard of comparison. No catastrophe short of the Day of Judgement will make us conscious of the diurnal and orbital movements of the earth, but I for my own part owe a debt of gratitude to the excellent popular writer on astronomy, whose name I have ungratefully forgotten, who gave me an almost musical sense of cosmic movement by pointing out that, while the earth is moving in its orbit very much faster than any cannon-ball, it takes several minutes to traverse the length of its own diameter.

The movement of a masterly adagio has the same kind of momentum. Most composers fail to write slow movements, and the reason is usually because they do not realize that a phrase of given length will become four times as long if it is played four times as slowly. Slowness is bigness, immediately and constantly manifest.

The opposite mistake is still more frequent. Composers, especially nowadays, fail far more often to achieve real quickness than to flow with a dignified slowness. Mozart in the finale of his *Musikalischer Spass* already satirized his own earlier works and the common run of contemporary finales in passages which intelligently anticipate the nightmare flight of the finale of Tschaikovsky's Fifth Symphony, and of Alice with the Red Queen crying 'Faster, faster!' only to arrive at the foot of the same tree where they started. If you have not already tried this experiment, as I have suggested in my edition of Beethoven's Pianoforte Sonatas, you may be surprised to learn that in Beethoven's Sonata in D minor the single theme of the slow movement and nearly the whole exposition of the finale each fill exactly one minute. Let us proceed a little farther with the slow movement, and see how it is that Beethoven maintains in it an irresistible momentum. The opening theme closes into a transition which moves in shorter phrases. It moves to the complementary key, on the dominant of which it expands with enough dramatic suspense to delay the arrival of the second group until the right moment. The second group consists of a single self-repeating melody, moving, without change of tempo, four times as fast as the first group.[1]

Before we come to the positive elements of later styles, let us mention a few things which are impossible to Bach. We shall learn from this, amongst other things, how it was that, although Handel was by profession an opera-writer, the art of music had to wait for Gluck before opera could be reformed to genuine dramatic purpose. One of the most obvious negative features in Bach's style, and also in Handel's, is that it is impossible to end a piece of music otherwise than with a significant phrase. There is no such thing as a purely architectural feature of final chords. The nearest approach to such a feature is the Handelian interrupted cadence followed by a slow *Amen*, very rarely found in Bach. For Mozart and Haydn, when a lively piece of music ends with a theme, the effect is almost always so abrupt that it is evidently intended as a joke. Architectural final chords are so normal that a thematic feature may even be combined with them without making them the less extraneous to the real last melodic sentence. Sixteen bars of final chord are not enough

[1] Here the lecturer illustrated his point on the pianoforte by comparing the sense of movement shown in this Andante and in portions of Bruckner's Eighth Symphony.

for the Finale of Beethoven's Ninth Symphony. He needs five more—that is to say, four plus a final beat that is metrically equivalent to another four or eight—and these he accompanies with a new phrase which might quite well have been a theme in its own right. On the other hand, the first movement of the Ninth Symphony ends with extraordinary power with its most pregnant phrase; but the normal emphatic end in the Mozart-Haydn-Beethoven system is a series of themeless final chords, to which we may apply the proverb: 'it's all over but the shouting'.

Serious criticism does not begin until the critic has put away the childish habit of estimating all parts of a work of art by the prose value of their contents. It is as important for the composer as for the architect to make proper use of undecorated open spaces. One or more of our clever critics has suspected Beethoven of caricature in the final shouting of the Finale of the C minor Symphony. If I had been able to devote this whole course of lectures to discussing the time-element in music, I should have been justified in spending a whole lecture in demonstrating the perfect balance of these last chords. All that I can do to-day is to conclude with a few illustrations of the masterly handling of the time-dimension—in other words, of the sense of movement in music. I can leave Bach and earlier music out of account, because we do not suffer at the present day from any prejudices about music before 1750; but at all periods of music one of the rarest qualities has been mastery of movement, and at the present day the art of musical movement is almost entirely lost both in practice and in theory. We might as well ascribe athletic prowess to the twenty thousand spectators in a football crowd, and the energy of high speed to a passenger asleep in a motor-car, as believe that the present fashions in musical composition inculcate a sense of movement. We need no abstruse or recent science to tell us that movement and the sense of movement are relative. Whatever the actual facts of movement may be, there can be no sense of movement without change. Changes may be so frequent that the sense of interruption and obstruction may be greater than the sense of movement. You must have time to enjoy the feeling of movement at a certain pace before you are disturbed by any change, but if there is no change at all for a long time you will not have enough sense of movement to keep you awake.

The lesser masters of the sonata style were happy in the possession of an art which amounted at its lowest level to a good convention, and secured a comfortable sense of movement with enough variety to keep the listener awake. The works of Spohr and Hummel never fail to amble pleasantly, and all their paces are satisfactory. Great power they do not show; and when we descend from their dignified elevation we substitute for the genuine sense of movement the rattle-trap vivacity of Rossini's *Barbiere*, which many people consider a masterpiece of rapidity, but which represents for the most part complete stagnation. I have already cited the case of the trill at the end of a passage as a demonstration of how to stop movement by turning it into vibration, and the rattle-trap vivacity of Rossini and the Rossinians is vibration and nothing else. Rossini had a great talent for composition, which not even his complete idleness could prevent from sometimes showing itself.

Imagine that you have just heard the whole introduction to Beethoven's Fourth Symphony: that it has given you time to appreciate its slow measure. With this in mind, let us listen to the impact of the quick movement that follows. The pauses, as you see, are exactly measured, the change to a quick time is measured by subdividing the main beats in halves and quarters, and the first phrases of the Allegro combine their own varieties of length with an allusion to the first impact of the new tempo. The whole first paragraph thus gives you every means of appreciating your speed of movement. You now settle down comfortably, and need no further stimulus until the drama is ready to take fresh action. Throughout the rest of the Allegro the variety of movement seems inexhaustible. For instance, a leisurely group of three two-bar phases may lead to twice four bars, and these to a sequence unexpectedly long in itself, but of steps of only a bar and a half that proceed in cross accents and thus give a sense of breathless speed in travelling straight towards a distance horizon. In contrast to the ever-varying stimulus of this exposition, the development is a delightfully comfortable non-stop run across wide open spaces, the greatest of which is the marvellous return to the home tonic.

The question of movement is not identical with the question of tempo. The slowest and most hesitating of Beethoven's slow movements, such as the great Rondo which constitutes the slow movement of the 'Harp' Quartet, op. 74, are products of the same power of movement that produces the most rapid of prestos. When we leave the great classics, the loss of power is more evident in quick movements than in slow. Many composers can, in fact, command a true sense of movement in a slow tempo though all their quicker movements are flaccid and merely vibratory. One of the most interesting cases arises when the composer superposes a slow theme over a quick tempo. Beethoven never loses movement by this. He has changed his metre in such a way that the effect of the slow theme does not slacken the sense of pace at all. We have merely settled down in comfort while we sweep over the wide open space. If Beethoven had translated Florestan's air into three-bar rhythm to correspond with the original metre, nothing would have saved the *Leonore* Overture from sagging.

Berlioz advertises with pride the *réunion des deux thèmes* in the music of Capulet's feast; but it is evident that his only real inspiration is in the magnificent melody of Romeo's love, and that the lively themes of the feast were from the outset a far from masterly jingle which is feverishly doing goose-step and has no reason for existence except as a fumbling counterpoint to the slow theme. Wagner's *Tannhäuser* Overture only dimly foreshadows his true powers, and there is a certain Salvation Army tub-thumping in the effectiveness with which the slow pilgrims' march eventually drowns the bacchanalian orgies; but already here Wagner shows more than Berlioz's grasp of the problem by introducing the pilgrims' theme in square rhythm before it obliterates the original momentum of the allegro in three-bar rhythm. You must turn to the later Wagner to see the real power with which a slow rhythm may ride sublimely over quicker rhythms that have not lost their momentum.

# LECTURE X

THE relation between art and infinity is a subject for professional philosophers, and as such it ought to be well defined. I have no qualifications for dealing with it technically, but there are many aspects of it which I can understand well enough to treat as throwing light on the difference between great art and unimportant art, to say nothing of the difference between good and bad.

The first thing to note about infinity is that, like perfection, of which it is perhaps a special case, it is a quality that may be appreciated in samples. When Schweitzer tells us that Bach differs from his forerunners in attaining perfection and that perfection is more essential to music than to any other art, he does not commit himself to the view that all or any works of Bach are perfect, but he means that any representative specimen of Bach's style will show all the qualities that are necessary to a perfect work of art. I have already argued that there is nothing to prevent musical works of art from actually being perfect as wholes as well as in detail, a doctrine which I was brought up to fear as a heresy until the powerful authority of Robert Bridges removed my scruples.

The notion of infinity is at once burdensome and empty if it is taken to mean mere endlessness. This empty notion cannot be verified, either by experience or by reasoning. Of number and time we can only say that they provide in themselves no means of coming to an end; that no number can be conceived which you cannot add one to, or multiply by any other number, or raise to a higher power. The infinity of space has become less empty in the light of recent science. It is now said to be unbounded, but not infinite. I have no ambition to connect the art of music with the philosophical implications of space-time and an expanding universe. Somewhere in the course of my skimming readings of popular philosophy I have come across the *obiter dictum* that the infinities of number and time are unreal. The sense in which this is true is too deep for my purpose, but number presents in the simplest and most convenient way some of the phenomena by which you may recognize infinity from portions of convenient size, and may also see in it something more positive than mere endlessness.

Long before Mr. J. W. Dunne brought forward his serial philosophy, a type of infinity was found in the kind of trade-mark which consists of a picture of the patent article in question. If that picture is complete it will also have its trade-mark on its own small scale, and that trade-mark, if complete, will have its own flea on its back, and so *ad infinitum*. This is typical of the general truth that all the operations of arithmetic—addition, subtraction, multiplication and division, involution and evolution, &c. —can be applied to an infinity in quite a normal way except for the paradoxical result that they make no difference to it. Separate all the odd numbers from all the even numbers. Both classes remain infinite. Square numbers become more and more rare as we proceed in cataloguing them; yet there must be as many square numbers as plain, for every number can be squared. Properties of this kind can be seen to be infinite as soon as we have collected enough numbers to see them at all. Two of the right kind will be enough. The simplest logic will show that there is no means of limiting the field in which the relation is true.

Now such a property is present in one of the simplest lines that are known to be typically beautiful, the logarithmic curve. This is a curve, manifested by Nature in many a graceful tendril and constantly recurring in all forms of decoration and design, which has this property, that any given section of it will, if magnified, coincide with the next section. Your tendril starts with a little close curl; the radius of the curvature becomes greater in an increasing ratio as the spiral unfolds; the curvature never unfolds to a straight line; and, if you magnify any given section from the beginning outwards, you will find that it could be made to coincide with the next adjoining section.

Now it is one of the earliest discoveries in art that when an object is divided into two unequal portions, these proportions will give pleasure if the smaller portion is to the larger as the larger is to the whole—or, as Euclid puts it, if the line is divided in extreme and mean ratio. This proportion is so pleasing to the eye that it has always been known to artists as the 'golden section'. Many theorists have discovered it in the time-dimension of music. The search for golden sections in music can be fascinating; but, as I have said before, I am somewhat sceptical about its value when applied to the time-dimension, though I have often verified striking cases of it on paper. But there are so many ways of marking your sections in music that I doubt whether golden sections could not be found in all compositions, except those that are divided simply into aliquot parts. Moreover, one of the cardinal principles of rhythm, obeyed by all composers except perhaps Reger, is that a ritardando or an accelerando makes no difference to the proportions of phrases. If your phrase is too short a ritardando will not lengthen it. If your phrase is the right length no amount of rubato will damage it. Reger is fond of dissolving his final rhythms in a gradual ritardando which finally compels the conductor to beat sixteen to a bar instead of four. Far be it from me to deny that there is an aesthetic value in such a dissolution of rhythm, but it is entirely unreconcilable with the claim often made for Reger that he composes in golden sections and revives other Greek and classical notions of rhythm.

My interest is in the sound of music, and not in its appearance on paper. Far be it from me to inculcate a philistine scepticism about facts of musical proportion which are not at once evident to the ear, but I feel justified in disregarding rhythmic and proportional theories whose exponents betray that they do not hear some of the most important things in music that are not addressed to the eye. One of the less abstruse and more pestilent of these follies is a recent fashion of discovering that when Beethoven seems to shock us with an abrupt change of tempo he is in reality doing nothing of the kind—that, for instance, in the Adagio that so mysteriously interrupts the first movement of the Sonata op. 109 before the quick tempo has finished a single phrase, the semiquavers are exactly equal to the crotchets of the Vivace, so that there is no change of tempo at all. I have heard an otherwise fine and musicianly quartet party make sad nonsense of the Maestoso which begins and twice interrupts the first movement of Beethoven's Quartet op. 127. Their leader had discovered that one bar of the Maestoso ought to be exactly equal to four of the Allegro. It never occurred to him that the four-bar rhythm which Beethoven keeps up with such exceptional uniformity throughout his Allegro was specially designed to brace the Allegro up against the shocks of the Maestoso with its square but syncopated rhythm.

These readings of mysterious uniformities which thus flatten out the greatest dramatic features of classical music deserve no other epithet than 'silly'. They are natural to us only because modern music rarely has any sense of movement at all. Haydn, Mozart, and Beethoven knew quite well that one tempo could accelerate or slacken gradually into a different tempo. They had no conscious objection to the process, and there was nothing conventional in their preference for undisguised contrasts of tempo. The gradual change of one tempo to another has its merits and its purpose, but it does not express strength. On the contrary, its expression inevitably suggests loss of control. I have dealt already with some aspects of this matter in my last lecture, and need say no more about it here. If an artist uses a device which expresses loss of control, the strength or weakness of the device must depend on our impression of what it is that has lost control. In a powerful work an accelerando may suggest the force of a torrent rushing towards an abyss, or the force of Destiny stirring human passions beyond human control. In a weak work it will suggest no force at all, as if Destiny itself were merely a defective brake for a bicycle on a dangerous hill.

The weak handling of the time-dimension in music may suggest that spurious and empty infinity which is merely endless. The rhythms and proportions of great music carry their own evidence of infinity, though I believe that the discovery of golden sections in the time-dimension is too facile and naïve a procedure to give us a trustworthy clue in the matter. While it is my own conviction that the quality of infinity does exist in the proportions of great music, I confess myself quite unqualified to work on so difficult a philosophic plane; and I turn with relief to the lighter and more popular task of illustrating the infinity of music in matters of general style and emotional content.

Let us descend to a few crass illustrations of the difference between good and bad. The subject is relevant, because bad music, whatever else it can be, cannot be infinite; unless it is infinitely boring, and this it seldom is. If the truth must be faced, it is often amusing, sometimes intentionally and sometimes unintentionally. A matter perhaps more suitable for discussion over walnuts and port than in a serious lecture is the question whether bad good music is better than good bad music. Do not ask me to define without the aid of port, if not of walnuts, what these terms mean, but let us take it for granted that good bad music is infinitely preferable to bad good music. I refuse to yield to my natural impulse to abuse bad good music, by which I mean the vast bulk of honest well-schooled work without which the soil would never have become manured for any crop of great music; but good bad music is fair game. It is never infinite except in the most distressingly negative sense, but it is often inventive, and it can demonstrate with almost sublime simplicity and perfection what music ought not to be. Wagner, Meyerbeer's worst enemy, was quite generous in his praise of the really emotional duet at the end of the fourth act of *Les Huguenots*; and my own feeling towards Meyerbeer is sometimes a little wistful, like that of the daughter whose mother, having seen the folly of all such things as balls, would not let her see the folly of just one. For me this wistfulness might have survived through a whole Meyerbeer opera, had I as yet had the good luck to hear a first-rate performance. Nothing less will carry a sensitive musician through four hours, or one hour, of Meyerbeer's appalling style. And so I must content myself with enjoying its naughtiness in furtive glances at his scores. All art, says Aristotle, is imitation; and in all imitation there is an element of illusion which is more accurately called suggestion. The term 'suggestion' distinguishes what we may paradoxically call 'true' illusion from false. True artistic illusion does not deceive. False illusion deceives the unwary and exasperates everyone when it is found out.

Now you cannot accept a suggestion which you know to be false. Dr. Johnson, dealing with the grounds alleged for unity of place and other dramatic conventions, played skittles with volumes of pretentious nonsense by roundly asserting that the spectator of a drama is in his senses all the time, and is quite aware that he is in the theatre in London and not in Athens or on the sea-coast of Bohemia. Children resent a violation of their make-believe, not because it upsets their faith, but because they, being as much in their senses as Johnson's spectator, wish to play the game.

The artist must not suggest what is self-contradictory. If resources are manifestly present and implied by the circumstances, it is folly to behave as if their absence must be supplied by suggestion. Many would-be scholarly players make nonsense of Bach when they translate his harpsichord music on to the pianoforte. In the slow movement of the Italian Concerto, and many other harpsichord cantabiles, Bach writes for the harpsichord in a style that powerfully suggests the cantabile resources of a violin. The harpsichord can produce such a cantabile in a fascinatingly plaintive quality of tone with more actual sustaining power than you might expect. These elements, taken in connexion with the style of the music, will suggest many varieties of light and shade which the harpsichord is in reality not capable of giving. The pianoforte cannot give the harpsichord's quality of tone, but it can give the light and shade. The player who then argues that he must imitate the flat uniformity of the harpsichord is obviously misinterpreting, or failing to see, the suggestiveness of Bach's music.

One of the aspects of infinity in music is precisely this element of suggestion. There is no end to it, it is omnipresent, and any identifiable specimens will be a sample of the whole. Now let us use the inexhaustible, but crassly finite, Meyerbeer as our ideal awful example. In *Les Huguenots* we have soldiers and military bands galore in real presence. One of the famous choruses is the 'Rataplan', in which an unaccompanied chorus imitates in those inspiriting syllables the sound of side-drums and other military incitements to a breach of the peace. I ask whether it is possible to conceive a more impotent misuse of the device of suggestion, and I do not pause for a reply.

Do not expect a connected argument on the modes of infinity in music. I borrow from Andrew Bradley's lectures on Shakespeare an illustration of another category in which we may find infinity. Bradley ends his lecture upon that painful incident in Shakespeare, the rejection of Falstaff, by saying that Shakespeare has denied to Prince Hal and King Henry V the infinity which he gave to Falstaff. Manifestly, this kind of infinity is no less, if not more, clearly an aspect of perfection than any measurable arithmetical or geometrical matters of proportion. It means that the character is consistent from all points of view. We need not worry how this consistency has been attained. The shortest account of the matter is to say that the artist is inspired. This, as we have already seen, is inadequate, because there is a strong probability that inspiration is a state of mental athletic form which in itself gives no security whatever that the results may be artistically valuable. Modern Shakespearian criticism and research has removed many occasions for awestruck admiration by showing that Shakespeare was often using the most convenient means ready to hand without the slightest regard for the consistency of character which we are at such pains to vindicate by subtle analysis. This does not always affect the question, for the infinities of artistic perfection are not bounded by the artist's own calculations. A good action does not become less good because it is expedient, and only a vainglorious and self-righteous man will be unwilling to plead expediency as the ground or excuse for his noblest actions.

The character of Falstaff gives an excellent occasion for studying examples of perfection and infinity in music, because it forms the subject of two very great works and one faded semi-classic. The faded semi-classic is Nicolai's opera, *The Merry Wives of Windsor*, in which the straw-stuffed dummy of Shakespeare's perfunctory farce plays its part in an efficiently constructed and tolerably musical adaptation of that farce diluted in the cabbage-water of a German libretto. It is impossible to write an opera upon the real Falstaff, because, though the real Falstaff provides the quality of infinity to three plays in which the title-role is that of a man who must satisfy himself and us merely with the divine right of kings, it is round this royal person that the only coherent story is formed. But it is possible to do as Boito did: to put into the framework of *The Merry Wives* most of the speeches of the great Falstaff, reduce the farcical escapades by half, and let an element of lyric beauty into the intrigue of Anne Page and Fenton. The rest is Verdi's business, and the result is of a quality which I believe is still disputed in some quarters, but of which I have seen no adverse criticism that does not betray itself by inattention.

Perfect works of art have this quality of infinity,

that they cannot be compared. You cannot even say that an infinity of three dimensions is larger than one of two, though you may be allowed to say that it is of a higher order. You cannot say that the art of Beethoven is greater than that of Bach, or even than that of Mozart. You can only say that it has more dimensions; and so I dare not say that Elgar's symphonic poem—or, as he wisely calls it, symphonic study—*Falstaff* is greater than Verdi's opera: but I can confidently say that it is inexhaustible, and that both in relation to its programme and in its pure musical form it is a perfect example of music in full integrity.

The kind of criticism which I am attempting in these lectures is nothing if not practical, and I take occasion now to point out some obvious, but often neglected, conditions that are essential to the enjoyment of music. Many forms of irrelevant criticism arise from the judging of music under conditions which the critic should have avoided. Infinities and perfections are inexhaustible. This does not mean that the energy of listeners is inexhaustible. Unfortunately, one of the commonest forms of pious opinion assumes that the listener can treat his mind as no sane person would treat his digestion. I was once told by an extremely impressive connoisseur in such matters that you could, given time and money, enjoy in Paris a *dîner à trois cinqs*—that is to say, a meal which began with five courses, ranging from soup to dessert, which was followed by an interval employed I was not told how; after which there was another set of five courses, also ranging from soup to dessert and followed by another interval, concerning which my speculations were involuntary and regrettable: and the entertainment concluded by a third set of five courses. No doubt the whole enterprise was rendered possible by consummate art in the selection of the courses and the occupation of the intervals. At all events, I believe it to have been aesthetically a sounder proposition than that of Bülow, who on the excuse that opportunities for hearing Beethoven's Ninth Symphony were rare, performed it twice in succession to a single audience on a single occasion. The enterprise was quite unworthy of Bülow's intelligence. Few contrasts could be more inept than that provided by the beginning of such a work heard immediately after the end. Weingartner tells us from personal knowledge that neither the performers nor the audience were fit for the second performance.

Spohr, writing from London in 1820, said many severe things about English musicians and English audiences. His conclusion is that the English have no calling for music and no true sense of it; they pursue music, like everything else, seriously, but, as one sees with English tourists sightseeing in Italy, it is evidently more a task than an enjoyment to them, and they might as well say at the end of a concert, as they say after sightseeing in Rome, 'Thank God, we've done that!' The mere fact that they can listen attentively and seriously to a concert four hours long, and often five with a little interval, suffices to prove that the music does not penetrate into them, otherwise they would already be exhausted by the first half.

Evidently our musical taste has improved in the

last hundred years; but Spohr puts his finger upon one of the commonest errors to which the hardships of critics and the pressure of pious opinion makes us liable. It has sometimes been said that such-and-such a piece can remain enjoyable after the appalling test of hundreds of hearings of it in a competition festival. This is a very dangerous claim to make; and, while I am quite certain that many of the greatest things in art will fail to stand such a hideous test, I am by no means sure that bad things under such a strain will not pass quickly through a disgusting phase and become inoffensive and eventually quite amusing. Perhaps four-fifths of the bad and inattentive criticism in this world comes from the critic's neglect of the most elementary precautions in the treatment of his musical digestion. In an art that moves in the time-direction these precautions are especially necessary, and when the real existence of the art is in performance the chances of criticizing a work from a wrong point of view are multiplied indefinitely.

Many technical problems arise which have only an indirect connexion with the merits of the work. Take, for example, Glazounov's famous three types of orchestration: the first-class work which sounds well when read at sight and magnificent when properly rehearsed; the second-class work that does not sound well on a first reading, but can be made to sound well with practice; and the third-class work that cannot be made to sound well with any amount of rehearsal. Whatever perfection may be consistent with this view of orchestration, it has no touch of infinity. Every composer, from Beethoven, Wagner, and Strauss to the possessors of the merest rudiments of common sense, will agree with Glazounov and Rimsky-Korsakov that the first type of orchestration is the thing at which he should consciously and conscientiously aim; but Rimsky-Korsakov, to whom Beethoven is as contemptible as an obsolete motor-car, has not the faintest glimmering of a kind of orchestration which sounds infamous at a first rehearsal, but which, like Beethoven's, becomes magnificent when properly practised. The art by which its magnificence can be revealed is by no means capable of making good orchestration out of bad. I have more than once been rebuked for defending many errors of Beethoven's scoring by pointing out that with double wind, such as was by no means unknown to Beethoven and even to Mozart, it becomes a merely financial matter to realize Beethoven's intentions. I have been told that on these lines all bad scoring could be corrected. But this is simply not true. Bad scoring is unimaginative, and no amount of correction will make it imaginative. Moreover, there is plenty of bad scoring which is ostensibly correct. To that end the rules of part-writing have been made. If you obey the rules, you can save yourself the trouble of using your imagination at all; or, if you do not wish to indulge in so sublime a self-renunciation, you may let your imagination wallow in the self-satisfaction of a prosperous person I once heard of who, when a young artist who eventually became President of the Royal Academy was holding forth on the importance of imagination in art, broke in with the illuminating comment: 'You are quite right there, sir. It's a wonderful thing, imagination. Sometimes of a quiet evening when I've nothing better to do I sit in front of the fire imagining, and imagining, and imagining, until I feel quite stoopid.'

I am not sure that this gentleman never had a glimpse of the infinite. His frame of mind evidently included a wholesome capacity for the bewilderment which perfection and infinity must inspire. Certainly there is an incalculable element in all great art. The only danger in identifying perfection and infinity with the incalculable is that we may deny all three titles to art in which we find ourselves able to calculate at all. Herein I am compelled to join issue with one of Sir Henry Hadow's illustrations in the *Oxford History of Music*. He compares the opening of Mozart's great C major Quintet with that of Beethoven's first 'Rasoumovsky' Quartet, and says that Beethoven has added the element of the incalculable; thus denying it by implication to Mozart's opening. Now the only real resemblance between Mozart's opening and Beethoven's is that both openings agree in giving a theme to the violoncello below a long expanse of chords repeated in quaver movement. Obvious points of difference are that Beethoven is writing a tune, while Mozart is explicitly stating a formula. In its original statement, Mozart's formula must remain calculable long enough to express its meaning at all. Beethoven's opening is not a formula, but a tune. As such it is in four-bar rhythm instead of Mozart's already irregular five bars, and Beethoven's art would become painfully calculable if he allowed this tune to finish itself symmetrically. His procedure is incalculable, simple, and bold. But

I cannot see that in the long run Mozart's procedure is less incalculable. I see nothing calculable in the way in which his formula drifts into a melodic phrase which rounds off the first paragraph with a half-close; and when after an impressive pause he begins a counterstatement in the minor with the parts of violin and violoncello interchanged, no doubt I find myself saying that this is just what I expected, but I am certainly being wise after the event: and so with every later step in the music. One infinity is as great as any other, and if this example of Mozart at his highest power seems to us more calculable than Beethoven's, that is merely the illusion that comes from our being more familiar with Mozart's formulas. Note that we must not say that the difference lies in Mozart's using formulas and Beethoven's using none. The work that uses formulas is quite as incalculable as the work which places all its distinction in its themes. Mozart's three greatest symphonies illustrate this clearly. The E flat Symphony presents us with euphony in its clearest form, the G minor Symphony presents us with highly individual themes, and the last Symphony, miscalled 'Jupiter', makes a special point of presenting us with architectural formulas and decorative tags. There are plenty of works of Beethoven later than the first 'Rasoumovsky' which are as ostentatious as the 'Jupiter' Symphony in their avoidance of any but the commonest formulas in their themes.

No composer who believed, like Spohr and like our most facile critics, in the necessity for distinction as a quality in their themes would have started work at all upon what turns out to be one of the most imaginative and mysterious of all Beethoven's movements, the first movement of the so-called 'Harp' Quartet, op. 74. The one theme that shows any character in that movement is not developed at all, except for a few bars at the end of the recapitulation. If you ask in what sense the movement has any ideas, the only possible answer is that the ideas cover the whole movement. It may be possible to discover a relation between the composer's preference for such formulas and some special condition of tone-colour or romantic mystery. Certainly Mozart handles wind instruments with special affection, and writes a considerable number of important works for them. All these important works show a decided preference for formulas as distinguished from more individual themes, and we can easily infer from this that the formulas are preferred because they do not distract attention from the peculiar qualities and resources of wind tone. In this connexion it is significant that Beethoven's 'Harp' Quartet is pre-eminently a marvel of tone-colour. Of course, there is no reason why marvels of tone-colour should not also coincide with marvels of thematic invention, but I am by no means sure that a composer's thematic invention is not as much at its height when he produces formulas as when he is producing attractive melodies or pregnant figures.

One of Beethoven's most allusive works is the Overture *Zur Weihe des Hauses*. I have often produced it at Reid concerts, and have provided a single short paragraph for it in my analytical programme. When I recently collected my programme notes for the Oxford University Press I decided to make a full analysis of this overture, and was amazed at the difficulty of the task. The first four bars consist of introductory chords. And I found that quite a long argument was needed to demonstrate the exact rightness of these. I had eventually to fall back upon an awful example from the much maligned Spohr, who in the Adagio of his Ninth Concerto threw off with fatal facility some introductory chords outwardly resembling these that had probably caused Beethoven even more trouble to create than they caused me to describe.

I cannot hope to give you an impression of a coherent and well-rounded treatment of perfection and infinity but I can end these lectures with a few illustrations of a game which you may find profitable to play, either in solitude or in company. It suggested itself to me as a development of a game often played by the late Julius Röntgen, who would strike a single chord, or two chords, and ask you to guess the work of which it was the beginning. This is often easier than you might expect. There is a pathetic story of a man who had composed a great opera, and who after much wire-pulling had secured an audition limited to four hours with the intendant and the conductor of a certain theatre. He came to the audition with his skyscraper score and struck the first chord, whereupon the conductor and the intendant and the leading critics with one impulse cried '*Meistersinger!*' and therewith concluded the audition.

You may be in some doubt whether the E flat chord, struck without much percussion, is or is not the opening of Beethoven's Quartet, op. 127; but you can have no doubt that this pair of chords is the opening of Schumann's Quintet; or that the E flat triad in this position, without a fifth, is the opening of Beethoven's E flat Concerto. But a more interesting variety of the game is to proceed farther, and, instead of inquiring the title of the piece, to put yourself in the position of a naïve listener and to ask at what point you can recognize that you are dealing with an extraordinary work. With great music this will reveal itself at exactly the right time. You cannot reasonably expect a formal opening to reveal at once whether the composer is more than a master of the formula. As you listen to the opening of the 'Jupiter' Symphony, you at once recognize the formula, the typical stage gesture of the tyrant on his throne and the suppliant pleading at his feet. As the music proceeds, you recognize the excellent proportions, as of a street designed by the brothers Adam; and you also recognize in the instrumentation that the building materials are of excellent quality: but when the counterstatement begins you draw a long breath of satisfaction and evident expectation that this artist is equal to anything.

Take the opposite case of a work which begins with an obviously pregnant statement. Here what is in question will be the composer's capacity to construct anything more important than a collection of epigrams. In his early works Beethoven sometimes leaves us in doubt. The G major Quartet begins beautifully and wittily, but remains for an unusually long time without signs that it is capable of sustained effort; but even in his earliest work Beethoven never failed to overcome his nervous abruptness, and to pass from a sententious manner to a power of sustained phrasing that is evidently capable of anything.

Composers since Wagner have often emulated, with not very frequent success, his power of cosmic movement in a vast musical time-space. As the monodists already discovered at the beginning of the seventeenth century, nothing is easier than to produce a cumulative effect by dwelling on one chord and repeating a single figure *ad infinitum*. How are we to know that the creator of the opening of *Rheingold* is a wiser artist than a dear old gentleman whom my contemporary Oxonians remember as a butt of musical undergraduate wit, who came back from Bayreuth saying in his broad dialect that he did not see why they made such a fuss about the prelude to *Rheingold* being all on a chord of E flat, inasmuch as he had quite independently prefaced his own oratorio of *Jonah* with a prelude entirely on the chord of D, representing, I suppose, the interior of Jonah's whale?

Let us conclude our view of musical infinity by taking the opening of *Rheingold* and ascertaining the point at which we can see that Wagner was no fool.

PRINTED IN
GREAT BRITAIN
AT THE
UNIVERSITY PRESS
OXFORD
BY
JOHN JOHNSON
PRINTER
TO THE
UNIVERSITY

Beyond Dracula

*Also by William Hughes*

CONTEMPORARY WRITING AND NATIONAL IDENTITY (*co-editor with Tracey Hill*)

BRAM STOKER: HISTORY, PSYCHOANALYSIS AND THE GOTHIC (*co-editor with Andrew Smith*)

BRAM STOKER: A BIBLIOGRAPHY

Bram Stoker, THE LADY OF THE SHROUD (*editor*)

# Beyond Dracula

## Bram Stoker's Fiction and its Cultural Context

William Hughes
*Lecturer in English*
*Bath Spa University College*

First published in Great Britain 2000 by
**MACMILLAN PRESS LTD**
Houndmills, Basingstoke, Hampshire RG21 6XS and London
Companies and representatives throughout the world

A catalogue record for this book is available from the British Library.

ISBN 0–333–74034–3

First published in the United States of America 2000 by
**ST. MARTIN'S PRESS, INC.,**
Scholarly and Reference Division,
175 Fifth Avenue, New York, N.Y. 10010

ISBN 0–312–23136–9

Library of Congress Cataloging-in-Publication Data
Hughes, William, 1964–
Beyond Dracula : Bram Stoker's fiction and its cultural context / William Hughes.
p.   cm.
Includes bibliographical references and index.
ISBN 0–312–23136–9 (cloth)
1. Stoker, Bram, 1847–1912—Criticism and interpretation. 2. Literature and
society—England—History—19th century. 3. Popular literature—England–
–History and criticism. 4. Horror tales, English—History and criticism. 5. Gothic
revival (Literature)—Great Britain. I. Title.
PR6037.T617 Z68   2000
823'.8—dc21

99–054480

This book is printed on paper suitable for recycling and made from fully managed and sustained
forest sources.

10   9   8   7   6   5   4   3   2   1
09   08   07   06   05   04   03   02   01   00

Printed and bound in Great Britain by
Antony Rowe Ltd, Chippenham, Wiltshire

*For my Mother,*
*Emily Hughes*
*(1928–1991)*

# Contents

# Copyright Acknowledgement

Quotations from the Oxford University Press paperback editions of
*Dracula* (1996, edited by Maud Ellmann) and *The Jewel of Seven Stars*
(1996, edited by David Glover) appear by permission of Oxford
University Press. Quotations from the uncut edition of *The Lair of the
White Worm*, published in hardback with *Dracula*, appear by permission of Foulsham Press. Quotations from the second edition of *The
Snake's Pass* and from the paperback reprint of *Dracula's Guest* appear
by permission of Brandon Book Publishers, Ireland. Quotations from
the second edition of *Miss Betty* appear by permission of Hodder and
Stoughton Publishers. I would also like to express my particular gratitude to Mr Noel Dobbs for granting permission to quote from the
manuscript of Bram Stoker's *Seven Golden Buttons*, now held at the
Brotherton Library, University of Leeds.

# Acknowledgements

I began the research for *Beyond Dracula* whilst a PhD student at the University of East Anglia, Norwich, between 1989 and 1991. My return to the university was encouraged and supported by a small group of people whom I am proud to know both as true friends and as intellectual colleagues. Their consistent support gave me the courage to continue during frequently difficult times. I express my deepest thanks, therefore, to Dr Elaine Hartnell, Ms Alita Thorpe, Mr Peter Hall, Dr Clayton Mackenzie, Dr Roger Sales and Dr Victor Sage. I hope that *Beyond Dracula* fulfils their expectations.

This volume has also benefited from the many people and organisations who, over the past ten years, have responded readily to my requests for information and often scarce biographical or textual material. I am particularly grateful to David Lass of Trinity College, Dublin, who generously provided me with copies of otherwise unobtainable illustrations and textual material related to Stoker's time in Ireland, and to Professor Benjamin Franklin Fisher IV, who significantly supplemented the bibliography of this volume by tracing many of the contemporary reviews mentioned in the footnotes. Ms Diane Mason, whom I am proud to know both as a colleague and as a friend, has been a particular source of both practical help and intellectual inspiration over the past four years. I would also like to thank Dr Robert Mighall and Dr Antonio Ballasteros González for their assistance and encouragement, and Ms Charmian Hearne of Macmillan for her consistent support.

The list of friends and colleagues who have followed *Beyond Dracula* through its various stages is embarrassingly long. I hope, therefore, that they will forgive me for the necessary brevity of this acknowledgement: Peggy and Bill Burns; Rita and the late Brian Hartnell; Kim Smith; Nicholas Groves; Peter Welsh; Barry Adamson; Dr Allan Lloyd Smith; Ruth Fagg; Neil Croft; Dr Graham Ford; Dave Thorpe; Dr Jeff Rodman; Dr Marie Mulvey-Roberts; Dr Paul Edwards; Dr Andrew Smith; Dr Tracey Hill; Dr Guy Stephens; Dr Colin Edwards; Frank Shepherd; Dr Brian Griffin; Martin and Anna Wrigley; Mike Down and Estelle Corke; Dr Mary C. Lyons; Professor Lorna Sage; Dr David Seed; Dr Alan Marshall; Professor David Punter; Dennis McIntyre;

Leslie Shepard; Richard Dalby; Margaret and Gary Fagan; John Cowen; John Pritchard; Professor Geoffrey Searle; Jon Cook; Dr Albert Power; Mrs K. Greville and Eamonn Greville; Sarah Briggs; Julian Honer; Ruth Willats; D.L. Manning-Fox; Dave Colley; Miss Caroline Buddery; Karen, Nick and Jenny Baxter; Paul Withers; Simon Withers; Shirley Edwards; Dave Devlin; Dave Thackwell; the late Mrs Madge Knibbs; Dr Mark Hampton; Dr Andrew Revitt; the late Joseph James.

I would also like to acknowledge the assistance provided by the following organisations and individuals: Mrs Jean Rose (Octopus Publishing Group Library); The Rev. Canon Empey (St Ann's Church, Dublin); Jonathan Newman and The Philosophical Society of Trinity College Dublin; M. Jeremy Rex-Parkes (Christie's); Tim Fenna, Tony Walker, Bill Fenna, Nick Sperring and Maggie Patstone at Frontline Spridget; Harry Ludlam; Major A.J. Dickinson and the Royal Humane Society; Graham Snell and the National Liberal Club; William Gladstone; Snoo Wilson; Miss Pauline Adams (Somerville College Oxford); Dermot J.M. Sherlock (Trinity College Dublin).

My special thanks also go to the many librarians who gave generously of their time and expertise during the writing of *Beyond Dracula*. I am especially grateful for the assistance of Christopher Sheppard and the staff of the Brotherton Collection, University of Leeds, to Dr Judith Priestman of the Bodleian Library, and to Dr Leslie A. Morris of the Rosenbach Museum and Library, Philadelphia. Many other libraries granted me use of their facilities for research, including the Library of Trinity College, Dublin, Cambridge University Library, the British Library, and Ohio State University Library. I am grateful also for the assistance afforded by the Library of Bath Spa University College. My good friends at the University of East Anglia Library deserve a special mention for their toleration, sympathy and good humour – David Harris, Ann Wood, Sue Julier, Judith Crabtree, Caroline Onody, Fern Tranter, Carol Trollope, Elizabeth Goddard, Margaret Myhill, Jayne Coombe and Pat Rowly. Thanks.

The research for my PhD dissertation was funded through a three year studentship granted by the British Academy, which was supplemented in 1992 by an award from the Parmentergate Educational Foundation, Norwich. The Humanities Research Board of the British Academy also generously provided me with further funding in 1998, which enabled me to complete my researches at the Brotherton Library, Leeds. I have also benefited from the support of my colleagues in the Faculty of Humanities at Bath Spa University College, and would like to express my gratitude to Dr Neil Sammells, Dean of

Faculty, for the encouragement and practical assistance he has given to my work over the past five years.

William Hughes
Bath

# Introduction:
# Reading beyond *Dracula*

> Bram Stoker is to be buried to-day. The remains will be cremated at Golder's-green Crematorium. Only the friends (and they are many) who knew and loved him will be there when the last offices are done, and that will be enough. He could have desired no more and no better. The big, breathless, impetuous hurricane of a man who was Bram Stoker had no love of the limelight.
>
> Hall Caine, *The Daily Telegraph*, 24 April 1912[1]

The opening words of Hall Caine's obituary notice for his close friend and fellow author succinctly crystallise the nineteenth-century myth of Bram Stoker. In obituary tributes, Stoker is consistently portrayed as a gentleman of 'great height and fine physique' who 'seemed to give up his life' to his employer's service, so much so that his achievements as Irving's *'fidus Achates'* could only be satisfactorily discerned through the successes of the actor's long career.[2] Caine, alone, tempers the portrayal of this 'massive and muscular and almost volcanic personality' with a privileged view of Stoker's 'big heart' and an intimation of 'his humanity'. Even these, though, find their expression in the context of Irving's Lyceum Theatre: for Caine, Stoker's 'tender' nature is remembered at 'the front of a box-office, the door to the gallery, the passageway to the pit'.[3] It would seem, therefore, that the Victorian and Edwardian public viewed Stoker largely as an appendage of Irving, a mythicised figure with a symbolic as well as actual role, rather than as an individual – or as an author – in his own right.

The myth of Irving's 'faithful Bram', though a cultural commonplace by 1882, owes much of its persistence to Stoker's own autobiographical presence in his 1906 biography, *Personal Reminiscences of Henry Irving*.[4] As Stoker admits:

1

> In the doing of my work, I am painfully conscious that I have obtruded my own personality, but I trust that for this I may be forgiven, since it is only by this means that I can convey at all the ideas which I wish to impress.[5]

The two-volume biography depicts a masculine world of theatre management, after-dinner speaking, gentlemen's clubs and intimate, same-sex friendships. Stoker's relationship with Irving, which he describes as being 'as profound, as close, as lasting as can be between two men' (*PRHI* I, 33) is *the* focus of the biography, therefore: this is not a 'life' of Irving, as Stoker freely admits (*PRHI* I, vii, ix), but a study in homosocial intimacy. Caine, likewise, dwells primarily on what he calls 'the strongest love that man may feel for man', relegating Stoker's wife to a seeming afterthought in the final paragraph of his recollections.[6]

This vision of a 'clubbable' Bram, respectably married though more at home in the company of gentleman athletes and educated adventurers, is hardly exceptional in the context of the sexually divided culture of late Victorian and Edwardian London. It has its parallel in the public lives of many obscure as well as prominent members of the artistic, professional, sporting and aristocratic circles which patronised the Lyceum during the London Season.[7] When subjected to the gaze of academic criticism, however, Stoker's public life all too frequently becomes a cipher for problems of personal identity, 'repressed sexual wishes' or 'rivalrous and angry feelings' which, allegedly, the author appears reluctant to confront even in his private life.[8]

The discourse of Freudian criticism is, of course, central to the development of the view that the neurotic 'personality' of Bram Stoker is not so much consciously 'obtruded' into this one biographical volume, but is expressed in involuntary and unconscious gestures throughout the author's writings. Drawing in particular upon *Dracula* – a novel whose central activity is attractively both oral *and* penetrative – psychoanalytic critics have suggested that Stoker had difficulty resolving sibling rivalries, suffered from 'an unusually strong father fixation' or was sexually abused as a child.[9] But, where psychoanalysis may proclaim that Stoker's fiction displays a characteristic Oedipal configuration, equally compelling hypotheses of a more-conscious sexual guilt have been founded upon Daniel Farson's allegations that Stoker contracted syphilis towards the end of the nineteenth century.[10] More recent critical interpretations of the relationships between Stoker's writings, his intimacy with Irving and his public persona have suggested that the author was striving to express a culturally or psychologically repressed homosexual identity, *Dracula* in particular embodying what Talia Shaffer terms 'codes for the closet'.[11] Whether or not a particular interpretation is grounded in psychoanalysis, 'Count Dracula's sexual torment', as one popular newspaper article phrases it, is all too easily read as a synonym for 'The sexual torment of the man who created Dracula'.[12]

Such readings arguably reveal as much – if not more – about the preoccupations of the twentieth century as they do regarding the culture of the nineteenth. As Foucault argues, the common assumption that Victorian culture was repressive originates in the sexual politics of the twentieth century. It is an assumption that permits critics to distance the discourse of criticism from those present-day institutions implicated in cultural and sexual control. As a cultural practice, Foucault suggests, criticism self-consciously unites 'enlightenment, liberation and manifold pleasures': the critic does not merely perceive the sexuality that allegedly lies beneath the surface of words and gestures from the past, he or she is able also to proclaim it within the comparatively permissive, though still repressive, present. Criticism as a practice thus maintains a semblance of independence, a function in 'the revelation of truth, the overturning of global laws, the proclamation of a new day to come'.[13]

Such laudable aspirations, however, may lead to a problem of interpretation – if not to a limitation of what may be effectively said about an author whose cultural origins lie in the nineteenth century. What Foucault terms 'the singular imperialism that compels everyone to transform their sexuality into a perpetual discourse' is crucial here.[14] In the post-Victorian, post-Freudian world, sexuality as a discourse has come to eclipse other discourses. Having gained a form of cultural institutionalisation as a device by which power may be both voiced and explained, sexuality is now emphatically spoken, read and recognised at the expense of other discourses. It does not necessarily follow, though, that Stoker or his nineteenth-century contemporaries were governed by such an overwhelming need to 'voice' their sexualities. Whatever the case, any survey of recent criticism will suggest that much of the discursive context of Stoker's writings has been effectively obscured by the predominance of critical studies which emphasise the importance of sexual topics in the interpretation of the author's fiction.

Some recent studies, admittedly, have considered specific aspects of the wider cultural context of Stoker's fiction, effectively broadening the critical appreciation of the author's writings beyond its earlier focus on sexuality and sexual symbolism. Daniel Pick, Ernest Fontana and Victor Sage for example, explore the externalisation of contemporary fears of racial and physical degeneration through the medical contexts of *Dracula*, where Kellie Donovan Wixson and Colin Graham, respectively, consider the Anglo-Irish backgrounds to *Dracula* and *The Lady of the Shroud*.[15] Studies of the portrayal of the New Woman in Stoker's fiction are comparatively plentiful, as are readings of the Germanic cultural and literary contexts of *Dracula*.[16] Several significant biographical studies, which can only assist in the clarification and reconsideration of the cultural contexts of Stoker's writings, have also been published, in part as a consequence of the centenary of the first publication of *Dracula* in 1997.[17]

Such readings, though, all too frequently privilege *Dracula* in the criticism of Stoker's fiction, or make the author's 1897 novel *the* reference point through which his other writings are judged.[18] David Glover's 1996 study, *Vampires, Mummies, and Liberals*, a reading of Stoker's fiction through the tenets of Victorian Liberalism and its interface with contemporary discourses of character, nationhood and sexuality, goes an admirable distance towards redressing this balance.[19] Glover's work, though, often tantalisingly dwells on the culture at the expense of the rich textuality of Stoker's writings. A balance, as it were, needs to be struck between the context and the signifying text, between wider cultural implication and the specific detail of the works under study. Though much has been achieved by recent criticism, Stoker's fiction – always comparatively inaccessible beyond major libraries as a consequence of the reluctance of publishers to reissue the author's works beyond *Dracula* – remains underquoted, its potential both in cultural terms and with regard to its own content as narrative, unexplored. As academic criticism has moved beyond psychoanalysis, and beyond sexuality, so must it also move beyond *Dracula*.

*

In a 1990 review of Alain Pozzuoli's French-language biography *Bram Stoker: Prince des Ténèbres*, Alain Garsault queried: 'Qui ne connaît *Dracula* aujourd'hui? Qui connaît son auteur, Bram Stoker?'[20] Though, some ten years later, Stoker's life is perhaps better documented than at any time since his death in 1912, a short survey of the career of 'this most elusive subject' will serve the immediate purpose of identifying some of the cultural discourses in which Stoker – and his works – participate.[21]

Abraham Stoker Junior was born in the north Dublin suburb of Clontarf on 8 November 1847. The third of seven children, he was a sickly child who suffered a protracted childhood illness which apparently kept him bedridden for the first seven years of his life.[22] He was the second son of Abraham Stoker, a Dublin-born civil servant in the British administration of Ireland, and of Charlotte Matilda Blake Thornley of Sligo, a social campaigner whose name was linked in particular to the cause of women dependent on workhouse charity.[23] The Stoker family were Anglicans, and attended the now-ruined parish church of St John the Baptist, Clontarf, where the author was baptised according to the rites of the Church of Ireland on 3 December 1847. He adopted the shortened name of Bram in the late 1870s.

The younger Stoker was educated – it is not clear whether at home or at a day school – by an Anglican divine, the Reverend William Woods.[24] He matriculated at Trinity College, the sole constituent college of the Protestant University of Dublin on 2 November 1864. An inspection of the University's records suggests that his formal college career was not academically distinguished. Despite his later claim that he 'had got Honours in pure Mathematics' (*PRHI* I, 32), Stoker's name does not appear among the candidates for Honours (known as Moderators by the University of Dublin) or those granted the alternative distinction of Respondency. Still styled Abraham, Stoker was awarded an ordinary degree of Bachelor in Arts at the Spring Commencements on 1 March 1870. He was admitted to the degree of Master in Arts, as was customary at Trinity College Dublin, without further study at the Spring Commencements on 9 February 1875.[25]

The author, did, however, distinguish himself in less formal areas of college life, advancing his sporting achievements and skill in the debating room as integral, rather than supplementary, to the formal requirements of his scholarly environment. A successful college athlete, Stoker played competitive rugby football and was awarded several silver cups for his achievements in athletics and weight-lifting.[26] Off the sports field, he was elected President of the College's Philosophical Society in 1870 and Auditor of the rival Historical Society in 1872, the latter office being, in Stoker's own words, 'a post which corresponds to the Presidency of the Union in Oxford or Cambridge' (*PRHI* I, 32).[27] The two societies were essentially debating clubs, each organising a programme of speakers who were subsequently entertained at a formal meal or reception. Though prestigious orators such as Professor Edward Dowden and Sir John Pentland Mahaffy could readily be drawn from the College's own Fellows and former scholars, undergraduate students regularly both delivered papers and responded in debate to those of others.[28]

Stoker's maiden speech to 'the Phil', delivered on 7 May 1868 and entitled 'Sensationalism in Fiction and Society', failed to gain him either the President's Medal or one of the Society's prize certificates.[29] He subsequently delivered papers to the same Society entitled 'Shelley' (3 June 1869), 'The Means of Improvement in Composition' (23 June 1870), 'Style' (1 December 1870), and 'D.G. Rossetti's Poems' (15 December 1870), his abilities being formally recognised by the award of a Certificate in Oratory in 1869.[30] In the 1871–2 Session of the Historical Society, Stoker spoke against motions suggesting 'That the Principle of Trades Unionism is Sound', and 'That the Social and Political Disabilities of Women Ought to be Removed'. Interestingly, on two other occasions he spoke in favour of the abolition of the Irish Vice-Royalty, but against the emancipation of the British colonies.[31] He was unable – intriguingly, given his later writings on the 'Problem Novel' – to support the contention 'That the novels of the Nineteenth Century are More Immoral in their Tendency than those of the Eighteenth'.[32]

Bram Stoker, it would seem, was a willing and able participant in the masculine, common-room culture which supported undergraduate life in the University of Dublin in the nineteenth century. His experiences as an undergraduate, both formal and informal, would have introduced him not merely to the literary, social and political debates of his time, but also to many of the figures who shaped – or were later to shape – those debates: Stoker may well have been particularly influenced by the Shakespearean critic Edward Dowden, but in the debating chamber he was to encounter also Oscar Wilde's brother William, the influential journalist and populariser of Gaelic myth, Standish O'Grady, and the Dublin physician turned playwright, John Todhunter.[33]

Stoker, as was the case with other former students of the University of Dublin, maintained many of his sporting and social connections with the College after graduation. He took rooms in central Dublin, shared a house with his brothers William, Richard and George, and later occupied lodgings adjacent to those of John Todhunter.[34] Bram Stoker appears to have spent much of his time in the company of physicians: William, Richard and George all practised medicine, either in Ireland, England or as surgeons attached to military campaigns. Bram was also a frequent visitor to the Merrion Square home of Sir William Wilde, the occulist, amateur Egyptologist and father of

Oscar.[35] A general university degree, in a sense, functioned as a pass-
port to the company of educated gentlemen in the Sciences as well as
in the Arts. It was a qualification of which Stoker took full advantage.

In a broader sense, however, the collegiate culture of the University
of Dublin provided Stoker with a common core of identities and
discourses which linked him, an Anglo-Irish Protestant, to many of the
intellectual assumptions and behavioural practices shared by educated
Englishmen. Much has been made in academic criticism of Stoker's
allegedly divided sense of national identity or his self-proclaimed
support of Irish Home Rule (*PRHI* I, 343). It would be unfair, however,
to accept without question William McCormack's contention that, as
a novelist, Stoker simply 'aligns himself with the London-based exiles
... as against the home-based revivalists'.[36] Any such alignment, it
may be argued, has its origins in the author's education both before
and at Trinity College, and was certainly well established by the time
Stoker began to submit fiction to English as well as Irish periodicals in
the 1870s.[37]

Much of Stoker's early fiction was written or revised whilst he was
working as a civil servant within Dublin Castle, the seat of British
government in Ireland until 1922. During his employment in Dublin
Castle, which lasted from 1870 to 1877, Stoker also acted as unpaid
dramatic critic for the *Dublin Mail*, and, for a short time, edited a
minor daily newspaper, *The Halfpenny Press*. Through his journalistic
activities, which effectively ceased with his promotion in 1877 to the
peripatetic post of Chief Inspector of Petty Sessions, he became associated with James Knowles, editor of *The Nineteenth Century*, and – more
significantly – from 1876 (*PRHI* I, 14) with the English actor Henry
Irving.

Irving invited Stoker to become his Acting Manager towards the
close of 1878. Accepting the actor's offer with alacrity, Stoker resigned
his civil service post and brought forward the date of his marriage to
Florence Balcombe, who numbered Oscar Wilde among her former
suitors.[38] Stoker was to retain his theatrical position, which involved
him in both the financial administration of the Lyceum Theatre
during its London Season, and the practical management of the
Company's tours in the United Kingdom and North America, until
Irving's death in 1905. Eight of Stoker's novels – *The Snake's Pass*
(1891), *The Watter's Mou'* (1894), *The Shoulder of Shasta* (1895), *Dracula*
(1897), *Miss Betty* (1898), *The Mystery of the Sea* (1902), *The Jewel of
Seven Stars* (1903) and *The Man* (1905) – were thus completed effectively on a part-time basis, the research and writing often effected on

tour or in breaks between productions or rehearsals. A frequent contributor of short fiction to British and American journals, Stoker also produced a volume of stories for children, *Under the Sunset* (1882), and published a lecture on American life and manners, *A Glimpse of America* (1886), during the same period. The author's first substantial publication, a legal handbook ponderously entitled *The Duties of Clerks of Petty Sessions in Ireland*, though dated 1879, was researched and written during Stoker's employment in the Irish Civil Service.

The Lyceum Theatre, like Trinity College, was a meeting place for those who shaped the arts, or informed political and intellectual opinion. In his 1906 biography of Irving, Stoker takes an obsessive delight in listing the many celebrities he encountered either at the Theatre's productions or receptions, or whilst touring with the Lyceum Company. These included many political celebrities implicated in Irish, British and Imperial politics, including Gladstone, Disraeli, Justin McCarthy, Lord Randolph Churchill, Asquith and Balfour. Popular authors and dramatists such as Jerome K. Jerome, M.E. Braddon, the novelist of Jewish life Israel Zangwill, Thomas Hardy, Tom Taylor, Dion Boucicault and Mark Twain were frequent visitors (and often correspondents) of Stoker, as were the illustrators George Du Maurier, author of *Trilby*, and the *Punch* cartoonist Sir John Tenniel. Other acquaintances included the French physician J.-M. Charcot, the explorers H.M. Stanley and Sir Richard Burton, the zoologist and author of popular science manuals Professor Ray Lankester, and the religious writer Henry Ward Beecher (*PRHI* I, 315–26). During his later years, when his finances were at low ebb, Stoker interviewed a selection of his former Lyceum acquaintances – among them Winston Churchill and Sir Arthur Conan Doyle – for a popular London newspaper, *The Daily Chronicle*.

At the Lyceum, it may be suggested, Stoker was again in an ideal position from which to observe the current preoccupations of late nineteenth-century English society. Such matters as gender politics, religious controversy, the ethics of fiction and the integrity of national identity were almost certainly among the topics informally discussed at Stoker's clubs – the Authors', the National Liberal and The Green Room – as they had been within the debating chambers of Trinity College Dublin. Irving, too, entertained such celebrities lavishly after productions at the private Beefsteak Room within the Lyceum Theatre: as Barbara Belford suggests, 'Few Victorian memoirs fail to mention dining there.'[39]

The death of Irving, however, brought to an end such intellectual as well as culinary pleasures. The Acting Manager, in common with his employer, had seen his financial position worsen after the Lyceum was floated as a commercial company at the turn of the century. Stoker's health, already damaged by Bright's Disease, declined further as the century progressed. In early 1906 he suffered a paralytic stroke, which incapacitated him for several months and damaged his eyesight. A further illness, which Stoker explained as the consequence of overwork, occurred in 1909.[40] Stoker sought employment as a theatrical manager, as a lecturer and as an exhibition organiser, with little success.

In consequence, he became heavily dependent on his writing as a source of income, drafting the biography of Irving on his sick bed, and publishing five celebrity interviews, the short story collection *Snowbound* and the romantic novel *Lady Athlyne* in 1908. *The Lady of the Shroud* (1909), the non-fictional volume *Famous Impostors* (1910) and his final novel, *The Lair of the White Worm* (1911), followed in rapid succession. In 1910, Stoker's income totalled just £575, £166 of which was derived from his literary work.[41] Stoker was awarded a grant of £100 by the Royal Literary Fund on 9 March 1911, his application for aid having been supported by Anne Ritchie, Henry F. Dickens and W.S. Gilbert. Stoker was by this time, however, terminally ill. He died at his home in Pimlico, London, on 20 April 1912. His death certificate concludes with the telling word, 'exhaustion'.

*

*Beyond Dracula* is not a biography, though it draws upon a range of 'biographical' sources as diverse as Stoker's *Personal Reminiscences of Henry Irving*, his collected in-mail, the catalogue of his now dispersed library, and the interviews and obituaries written by his journalistic and literary contemporaries. Though it utilises these frequently personal artefacts to access a sample of the discourses which supported Stoker's education, career and writings, the volume does not seek, however, a definitive 'answer' or 'explanation' to any alleged 'problem' or dominant preoccupation which may be presumed to characterise Stoker's fiction. To do so would be to impose a closure upon the cultural and discursive plurality that supports Stoker's writings. Rather, *Beyond Dracula* argues that these works fictionalise – and at times problematise – a number of interrelated cultural issues either directly or by implication across the full range of Stoker's fictions. *Beyond Dracula* is thus a study in the culture of Stoker's fiction – and the culture *within* Stoker's fiction – a study whose unity is quite simply the acknowledgement that the author was a participant in a discursively plural society, an individual well placed with regard to, and well versed in, the issues and discourses of his day.

The four chapters which follow thus chart the way in which the cultural contexts of Stoker's fiction arguably relate to each other as well as to the novels themselves. At times, Stoker's writings unquestioningly reproduce common cultural assumptions with regard to such issues as society, gender, religion and race. On other occasions, however, the combination of discourses within a work may produce moments of unease or incongruity – effectively, crisis points at which those discourses enter into turbulent relationships with each other. These relationships hold the potential to modify meaning. At a basic level such moments may be manifested, for example, in a sentence or phrase which sits uneasily at the end of a proposition, or in the presence of a strange linguistic or moral twist to an otherwise stylistically orthodox pattern of rhetoric or narrative. More developed examples arguably engender situations which might best be described as moments of discursive reflex, effective crises in which elsewhere conventional discourses seemingly turn back in upon themselves, yielding for a compelling and intense period the very content which they would conventionally strive to repress or to contain. Thus, in Stoker's writings, the rhetoric of Christian piety may be read as yielding blasphemous possibilities as it encounters the discourses of science and occultism, just as elsewhere the allegedly comprehensive logic of medicine is made to underwrite both quackery and superstition. The fictional text thus becomes an arena in which such radical alternatives are momentarily displayed before, seemingly inevitably, the powers of orthodoxy again gain a semblance of control.

*Beyond Dracula* opens with a consideration of the religious contexts of Stoker's writings, acknowledging the importance of his Anglo-Irish Protestant upbringing and recalling also the popular theology which both author and reader would have encountered in everyday life. The first chapter begins with a detailed reading of Stoker's earliest published volume of fiction, *Under the Sunset*, a collection of short stories for children. The chapter notes how the collection utilises a well-known range of Old Testament narratives as palimpsests upon which both New Testament theology and more secular moral guidance may be inscribed. Particular attention is directed also to the interface between morality and horror in these early fictions, and to how both violence and sin are effectively employed as moral tools by the narrator who commentates upon the joys and fears of the fictional Land Under the Sunset. The chapter then moves to a reading of *The Jewel of Seven Stars*, a novel which appeared in two radically different editions during its author's lifetime. Beginning with an exploration of the novel's Orientalist and Egyptological background, the chapter then argues that the revisions to *The Jewel of Seven Stars* have a profound effect on the theological connotations of the experiment which forms the work's effective climax. The chapter concludes with a detailed comparison of the revised and unrevised conclusions to the novel, and a consideration of how science, religion and horror combine in each edition.

The second chapter examines the depiction of masculinity throughout Stoker's fiction, focusing in particular on the concept of the gentleman. Beginning with a consideration of how acceptable standards of behaviour are constructed with reference to the mythologies of a revived or 'modern' form of chivalry, the chapter moves to an analysis of how Stoker's heroes are frequently figured also as gentleman-pioneers. In *The Snake's Pass*, Stoker's first novel, such a characterisation may be said to disarm the negative associations of colonisation – a significant move as the novel is set in the frequently troubled West of Ireland. Making reference to *The Man* and to *Seven Golden Buttons*, the unpublished novella which was later rewritten as *Miss Betty*, the chapter also considers how the conquest of the wilderness may be seen to parallel the gaining – or regaining – of a personal sense of honour, itself the first step towards acceptance within the company of gentlemen. As this latter point suggests, the concept of modern chivalry may at times exclude individuals who do not visibly adhere to the criteria by which a gentleman is conventionally defined. The chapter therefore considers those men in Stoker's novels who are excluded from the company of gentlemen on account of socially or morally unacceptable behaviour, religion or race, noting how, in some cases, the signifiers of exclusion may become, unexpectedly, the very means by which a renewed and acceptable masculinity is celebrated.

The third chapter continues the exploration of the possible relationships between gender and culture through an analysis of how women are constructed in Stoker's writings. The chapter argues that Stoker's fiction is a participant in a conventional nineteenth-century discourse on gender which depicts the female as emotionally, as well as physically, distinct from the male. This discourse, which is informed by cultural debates conducted elsewhere in medicine, anthropology and religion, tempers the conventional passivity of the female with the suggestion that 'normal' women are predestined biologically towards reproductive sexuality and culturally towards marriage. Though Stoker's heroines engage in protracted courtships, usually ending in the celebration of marriage, they frequently display both a degree of personal assertion and a sexual precocity which at first sight distances them from the patriarchal ideal of female passivity and subservience. Such behaviour may, in Stoker's fiction, be attributed to the power of the other discourses which make up the individual, even though by the end of each work the suggestion is implicitly made that biological difference, the destiny invested in gender, is the most powerful force of all. The chapter first considers the relative influence exercised on female characters by religion and race through a reading of *Miss Betty* and *The Lady of the Shroud*. It then considers the erotic possibilities vested in the scenarios of potential rape and seduction which characterise *Lady Athlyne* and *The Mystery of the Sea*, arguing that conventional sexual purity is itself capable of being read as at times teasingly provocative. The chapter concludes with an exploration of Stoker's most protracted study in sexual difference and female assertiveness, *The Man*.

The final chapter begins with a consideration of the importance of blood as a signifier in Victorian and Edwardian culture. Whilst acknowledging that blood has been appropriated as a metaphor by which racial, familial and political relationships may be voiced, the chapter argues that any such relationship must be seen as being subject to the physiological laws by which the literal substance is itself governed. There is, in this sense, a 'sanguine economy' of meanings vested in the secretion, depletion and diluting of metaphorical blood to parallel the so-called 'spermatic economy' of the nineteenth century, a medical theory through which health and vitality were related to the presence of blood and semen. *Dracula*, Stoker's most famous novel, has, of course, been approached many times in criticism through the allegorical and symbolic values associated with blood. As a contrast to such readings, this chapter examines how the novel presents a detailed and consistent symptomatology for the vampire's victims, and how the medical practitioner in attendance initially misdiagnoses a physiological problem as a psychological disorder. Making reference to popular as well as clinical medical works from the nineteenth century, the chapter then charts the ambiguities supporting this misdiagnosis, and argues that the occult pathology of the vampire is structured by the same laws which govern conventional therapeutics. The chapter concludes with a consideration of how vampirism is related in *Dracula* to abnormal medical states such as hysteria, somnambulism and hypnotic sleep.

Each of the four chapters of *Beyond Dracula* may be read in isolation, either as a self-contained study of a selection of Stoker's writings, or as a contribution to knowledge in a specific area of Victorian and Edwardian cultural concern or debate. For all this, however, it will be obvious that the four chapters are unavoidably interrelated and inter-dependent because of the plurality of discourses within Edwardian and Victorian society. To move beyond *Dracula*, is, as has already been suggested, to recognise the plurality of these discourses as much as to acknowledge the breadth of Stoker's writings.

# 1
# Pity and Terror: Theology, Morality and Popular Fiction

> The rhetoric of the horror novel is demonstrably theological in character.
>
> Victor Sage, *Horror Fiction in the Protestant Tradition* (1988)

As Victor Sage argues in *Horror Fiction in the Protestant Tradition*, Christian theology conditions Western culture, providing simultaneously a common frame of reference and a series of interpretative distinctions through which political as well as sectarian difference may be proclaimed.[1] The horror novel, Sage suggests, is but one amongst many cultural forms shaped by the language, imagery and assumptions of a Christian consciousness. In British and Anglo-Irish Gothic, this consciousness is popularly constructed as being specifically Protestant, although recent criticism of the Anglo-Irish Gothic has convincingly argued that the political identities vested in sectarian difference are frequently problematic.[2] This latter is an important critical distinction, though it may be further argued that Gothic fiction articulates simultaneously a subtle sense of ontological unease, the implications of which are mobilised at a more fundamental level than that of sectarian difference.

The depiction of supernatural incidents in Gothic writing arguably tests the limits of the Deity's implicitly non-fictional power within the confines of a fictional environment. The conventional closures which characterise many Gothic works, whereby Christian and moral order are restored as the occult is banished or dispelled, may be interpreted therefore as fictionalising not merely a reassuring belief in God's continuing ascendancy, but as proclaiming also the apparent beneficence of His universe.[3] This much is tacitly acknowledged in critical readings which interpret Gothic fictions as ethical allegories or morality plays, rather than as political metaphors or fantasies.[4] For all this, however, the Gothic retains a commitment to an ongoing onto-logical dialectic in which the credible and the orthodox are presented as relative rather than Absolute, if only for a time.[5]

Stoker appears to have been aware of the moral implications associ-ated with supernatural fiction, even where he was reluctant to assign an unequivocal meaning to his own work. Interviewed by *The British Weekly* in July 1897, for example, he says of *Dracula*: 'I suppose that every book of the kind must contain some lesson ... but I prefer that readers should find it out for themselves.'[6] Stoker's apparent reluc-tance to impose a closure upon *Dracula*, however, effectively opens up the novel to alternative interpretations beyond the unspecified 'lesson' apparently envisaged by the author.[7] The near-victory of the occult forces in *Dracula* holds the potential to say as much about the negli-gence of the Deity as it does of His care and protection.[8]

Acknowledging the ambiguity of the novel's theology, a personal letter written one month earlier by Stoker to W.E. Gladstone can be read as an attempt to forestall at least one reader's objections to the supernatural and violent incidents portrayed. Gladstone was well known as a theological commentator as well as a statesman. Enclosing a pre-publication copy of *Dracula*, Stoker admits:

> The book is necessarily full of horrors and terrors but I trust that these are calculated to 'cleanse the mind of pity & terror.' At any rate there is nothing base in the book and though superstition is fought in it with the weakness of superstition I hope it is not irreverent.[9]

The letter's Aristotelian allusion frames a commitment to a stable world bounded by – as the references to 'superstition' and the 'irrever-ent' suggest – a broad Christian ontology. The tone of the letter, though, simultaneously betrays a perceptible unease at the way in which the occult and the horrific have become implicated in a tem-porary alliance with the Christian and the rational. Though a power identified as evil is ultimately defeated and a Christian soul saved from an eternity in 'paths of flame' (*D* 206), the theological discourse is effectively compromised by the events and consequences which the novel depicts. As Victor Sage suggests, in situations where the theo-logical is channelled through the fictional, theology enjoys 'the capacity to swivel and face in another direction, to present itself in another aspect, while remaining a continuing factor'.[10] Christian doctrine, in Gothic works such as *Dracula*, may thus itself be structured as alternately alien and familiar; reassuring and yet at times both disturbing and subversive.

## Moral allegories and biblical parables

This uneasy relationship between the theological and the horrific is not, however, confined to Stoker's Gothic writings. The author's first published volume of fiction, *Under the Sunset* (1882), a collection of vaguely Christian allegories for children, met with a mixed reception at the hands of contemporary reviewers. The eight stories of *Under the Sunset* take place in a fairy tale dreamscape which is bordered by a wilderness populated by the children of King Death. The Land Under the Sunset is protected from its unwelcome neighbours by two guardian angels, both named Fid-Def, who watch over the Portal which separates the two kingdoms.[11] Though bemused at times by the 'allegorical and fanciful' nature of the stories in *Under the Sunset*, *Notes and Queries* confidently advised its readers that the book's 'teachings are wholesome'.[12] The reviewer for *Punch*, however, responded to the volume's religious pretensions with a mixture of mockery and adroit Biblical allusion:

> Get *Under the Sunset* (awkward position), by Mr. BRAM STOKER, M.A. It's very pretty to look at as to binding, pictures, and general get-up. Our special child critic says, 'Oh yes, I like it, but it's rather too goody-goody. One of the stories reminds me of David and Goliath,' – ('Tell it not in Gath,' Mr STOKER) – 'and there's not very much to laugh at.'[13]

There is more at stake here than Stoker's originality as a writer. Biblical narratives, when reworked, are effectively released from the sacred and untouchable space which they customarily occupy as divinely inspired canonical texts (2 Tim. 3:16). Saints, prophets and sinners may be rescheduled as 'ordinary' people, frequently in times and places far distant from their Biblical equivalents. Narratives may be fragmented, truncated and manipulated in order to direct attention to a specific doctrinal or moral point. Interpretation and exegesis, in particular, may be worked into the very fabric of the narrative, as a form of internal rather than appended commentary. Stoker, therefore, cannot be said to be working strictly 'within the fairy tale genre', as Phyllis Roth would have it.[14] Similarly, Barbara Belford's passing dismissal of the stories in *Under the Sunset* as 'almost Biblical' fails to convey adequately how much they are implicated in and informed by an identifiably Christian discourse.[15]

Considered in this context 'The Rose Prince', the story to which the *Punch* reviewer refers, is not so much an example of plagiarism as a palimpsest in which an Old Testament story is overwritten with and through the Pauline interpretation of the New Testament. In the story, the second in the collection, the Land Under the Sunset is ruled by the magus-like King Mago. When the kingdom is threatened by a giant from the wilderness beyond the Portal the king responds by sending two successive expeditions of heavily armoured troops. Both forces are defeated. Prince Zaphir, Mago's only son, then offers to fight the giant, which he slays in the manner of the youthful shepherd boy, David. On his return to the city the narrative reverts to the fairy tale mode and Zaphir marries his childhood sweetheart, the Princess Bluebell. The tale concludes: 'They ruled well and unselfishly, ever denying themselves and striving to make others good and happy. They were blessed with peace' (*UTS* 44).

In the Old Testament, Saul initially rejects David's offer to stand as Israel's champion against the Philistine Goliath of Gath because of the shepherd boy's comparative youth (1 Sam. 17:33). It is only when David expresses his absolute faith that 'The LORD that delivered me out of the paw of the lion, and out of the paw of the bear, will deliver me out of the hand of this Philistine' that Saul commands 'Go, and the LORD be with thee' (1 Sam. 17:37). King Mago, in contrast, accepts Zaphir's offer without hesitation. Yet Zaphir's behaviour and speech appear on first sight to privilege the resourcefulness of the human over the protection of the divine. The narrator notes not merely how the prince displays 'a look of such high resolve that those who saw it could not help having a new hope', but also how his speech to the king asserts his fitness to fight the giant on the grounds that 'it is the Prince whom the people trust' (*UTS* 26).

Alone on the eve of battle, however, Zaphir prepares himself not through warlike exercises but by way of a sustained and detailed prayerful introspection and self-purgation which successfully relocates him within the standard expected of the Christian warrior. The narrator recalls:

Then, in his humility, Prince Zaphir prayed for strength.... There he knelt praying humbly, with his deep earnest eyes lit by the truth and trust that lay in his clean heart and pure soul.

> The glittering armour looked like the work of man's hands – as it was, and the work of the hands of good true men; but the beautiful boy kneeling in trust and faith was the work of the hands of God. (*UTS* 36)

With the prince's 'high resolve' at court now placed in the context of his spiritual zeal, the narrator moves to clarify the content of Zaphir's current devotions. The account continues:

> As he prayed, Prince Zaphir saw all his life in the past, from the day he could first remember till even then as he was, face to face with the Giant. There was not an unworthy thought that he had ever had, not a cross word he had ever spoken, not an angry look that had ever given another pain, that did not come back to his mind.... Prince Zaphir's heart was purified by repentance for all wrongs done in the past, and by high resolves to be good in the future.... (*UTS* 36–7)

Zaphir's prayers recall the solemn devotion of the vigil that marks the beginning of the chivalric service of knighthood. His humility is thus entirely appropriate for a Christian knight on the eve of battle.[16]

Zaphir's prayers – and his behaviour whilst at prayer – are, however, equally an expression of the story's contemporary Protestantism, albeit simplified for a junior audience. Where the Biblical David, armed by Saul with helmet, sword and mail refuses to do battle using the weapons, saying 'unto Saul, I cannot go with these, for I have not proved them' (1 Sam. 17:39), Zaphir, similarly 'doffed his splendid armour, which shone like a sun on earth, he took off the splendid helmet, and he laid by the flashing sword; and they lay in a lifeless heap beside him' (*UTS* 36). Saul clearly believes in the conventional, perceptibly secular, strength of the adult warrior and the armoured body. He does not – and cannot – trust in the implicitly Pauline armour – 'the breastplate of righteousness ... the shield of faith ... the helmet of salvation and the sword of the spirit, which is the word of God' (Eph. 6:14–17) – which is arguably adopted by both David and Zaphir. Prepared in such a way, Zaphir like David may consider that 'if the victory came to him it was not because his arm was strong or his heart brave, but that because it was willed by the One that rules the universe' (*UTS* 36).

In 'The Rose Prince' this reliance on secular rather than spiritual armour becomes associated with the phrase 'fallen in the pride of their [or his] strength' (*UTS* 26). The term is associated first with the defeat of the splendidly equipped army sent out by Mago under the command of the aptly named Captain of the Guard, Janisar. It is subsequently applied to the death of the Giant, who, like the proud Philistine Goliath, is scornful of the sling and round stones which Zaphir gathers from a brook exactly in the manner of David at Shocoh (*UTS* 41–2). As the narrator recalls:

> even as he laughed his enemy to scorn, the Giant's doom was spoken.
> Round Prince Zaphir's head swung the sling, and the whistling pebble flew. It struck the Giant fair in the temple; and even with the scornful laughter on his lips, and with his outstretched hand pointing in derision, he fell prone. (*UTS* 38)

Though the actual point of impact of Zaphir's pebble differs from that thrown by David, the accompanying illustration by the professional illustrator W.V. Cockburn recalls the wounding of the Philistine champion in the Bible, where 'the stone sunk into his forehead' (1 Sam. 17:49). Clearly, as David announces, 'the Lord saveth not with sword and spear' but rather favours those who place their confidence not in earthly weapons but in the reassurance that 'the battle is the Lord's' (1 Sam. 17:47). This is a theme common to both the childhood allegories of *Under the Sunset* and the adult Gothic of *Dracula*. Where Zaphir proclaims on his return to the city, 'Oh King my Father, and oh People! – God has been good to us, and His arm has given us the victory. Lo, the Giant has fallen in the pride of his strength!' (*UTS* 41), Quincey Morris may also say on his deathbed with similar gratitude, 'Now God be thanked that all has not been in vain!' (*D* 377).

*The Times*, whose reviewer regarded the major illustrations in *Under the Sunset* as 'mostly as theatric and obscure as the text', singled out Cockburn's illustration of the fallen Giant as 'singularly out of place in any book designed for children'.[17] Certainly, the detail of the drawing far exceeds that of the paragraph with which it is most intimate:

> At that very time, far away in the forest, the Giant lay fallen in the pride of his strength – the foulest thing in all the land – and over his dead body ran the foxes and the stoats. The snakes crawled around his body; and thither, too, crept all the meaner living things that had fled from him when he lived. (*UTS* 42)

The illustration replicates what is obviously the prelude to the consumption of the carcass first by the 'meaner living things' and later by the vultures which hover ominously in the background. The Giant lies naked upon his back, his mouth open, displaying bestial fangs which mirror his pointed finger and toe nails. The central wound to his forehead gapes, and the blood has run down, forming a deep pool on the ground between his short horns. One snake has attached itself, presumably by its fangs, to the head of the Giant, and a rat has run up his rigid right arm.

Such depth of detail is not necessarily gratuitous, however. The whole scenario echoes David's defiance of Goliath in the Bible, where he taunts his opponent with the threat that, when victorious, he 'will give the carcases of the host of the Philistines this day unto the fowls of the air, and to the wild beasts of the earth; that all the earth may know that there is a God in Israel' (1 Sam. 17:46). Where an observant child or an adult may recognise the specific Biblical allusion which lies behind the carnage, Cockburn's illustration may still be interpreted by a more general audience as an unequivocal warning of the fatal consequences of placing pride only in one's own mortal strength. Pride, literally, comes before the Giant's fall.

As the relationship between the giant's pride and Zaphir's humility suggests, 'The Rose Prince' is ripe with allegorical instruction as well as Biblical allusion. Stoker's story draws on a portion of the allegorical and metaphorical energy invested by the nineteenth century in the motif of the threatening giant – a figure common to both religious tracts and social reporting throughout the century. In such writings the giant is a figure apparently beyond the self, but whose behaviour grotesquely magnifies qualities that may lurk undiscovered or unacknowledged within the reader. Beyond the still-potent figure of Bunyan's Giant Despair may be found a range of similar leviathans adapted to a specifically nineteenth-century context. In *The Giants and How to Fight Them*, a typical work for children popular in the period, the Reverend R. Newton advises his child readers that, though David was victorious at Shochoh,

the giants are not all dead yet. There ARE giants in the earth these days. And God expects us all to engage in the work of trying to fight them. When I speak of giants now, I do not mean physical giants, but moral giants. I do not mean men with huge bodies, four or five times larger than common-sized men; but I mean GREAT SINS of different kinds, which may well be called *giants*.[18]

Three of Newton's five giants – Selfishness, Covetousness and Ill-Temper – represent 'giants made of thoughts and feelings' that afflict the individual in particular rather than society in general.[19] Such qualities, he cautions the child reader, 'may be found in our country; in our own city; in our own homes; yes, even in our OWN HEARTS'.[20]

'The Rose Prince', similarly, implies that the pride of the Giant may find its equivalent in more mundane expressions of personal vanity and self-worth. The key figures in this allegory are two emblematically named courtiers, both unduly conscious of their social position and supposed prominence at King Mago's court. The narrator provides in each case a blunt aside by which their faults are exemplified even for the most obtuse of child readers.[21]

The courtiers Skarkrou – a pun on scarecrow – and Sartorius function effectively as two poles of an argument on the relationship between external appearance and inner character. The narrator constructs Sartorius as:

> a foolish young courtier, who thought that dress was the most important thing in the world; and who accordingly dressed in the finest clothes he could possibly get. But people only smiled at him and sometimes laughed, for there is no honour due to fine clothes, but only to what is in the man himself who wears them. (*UTS* 18–19)

Similarly, Skarkrou is structured as a figure who is:

> just the opposite to Sartorius, and who thought – or pretended to think – that untidiness was a good thing; and was as proud or prouder of his rags than Sartorius was of his fine clothes. He too was despised, for he was vain, and his vanity made him ridiculous. (*UTS* 19)

The narrator goes beyond a mere echo of Christ's condemnation of the ostentation of the scribes and Pharisees, public figures who 'outwardly appear righteous unto men, but within … are full of hypocrisy and iniquity' (Mat. 23:27–8). Both descriptions simultaneously ridicule the vanities of the courtiers whilst effectively saluting the astuteness of the fictional observers who see through the superficial grandeur with which the pair surround themselves. In allegorical terms, to recognise the ridiculous and superficial in others is the first step towards preventing the development of similar vanities in the self.

This was a theme to which Stoker was to return in his later fiction for adults. For example, Arthur Markam, a wealthy cockney shop-keeper, aspires to a Scottish identity and mode of dress in Stoker's 1894 short story, 'Crooken Sands'. Duped by a Jewish supplier of replica Scottish regalia, Markam masquerades as a Scot in Aberdeenshire, meeting first with general ridicule from the local peasantry, and subsequently receiving a warning strikingly delivered in Biblical language by Saft Tammie, a wise fool in the tradition of *King Lear*:

> '"Vanity of vanities, saith the preacher. All is vanity." Mon, be warned in time!... Mon! Mon! Thy vanity is as the quicksand which swallows up all which comes within its spell. Beware vanity! Beware the quicksand, which yawneth for thee, and which will swallow thee up! See thyself! Learn thine own vanity! Meet thyself face to face, and then in that moment thou shalt learn the fatal force of thy vanity. Learn it, know it, and repent ere the quicksand swallow thee!'[22]

From this point Markam is persecuted not merely by the daily reproaches of Saft Tammie, but also by what he believes to be his *doppelgänger*, a figure he encounters at the edge of a literal quicksand. Finally seeing the figure of his *alter ego* swallowed into the abyss prophesied by Saft Tammie, Markam announces to his family his intention to dispose both of his purchased finery and of the attitudes it represents, concluding: 'I see now what a vain old fool I was' (*DG* 159). On being questioned regarding where his clothing has been sent he replies, significantly: 'In the quicksand, my dear! and I hope that my worser self is buried there along with it – for ever' (*DG* 159).

Markam himself admits that the lesson has been learned. In 'The Rose Prince', however, it is not the fictional character but the implied child reader who is manoeuvred into internalising the narrator's caution regarding human weakness. The narrator concludes his depiction of the foolish courtiers with the advice:

> Children who wish to become good and great men or good and noble women, should try to know well all the people whom they meet. Thus they will find that there is no one who has not much of good; and when they see some great folly, or some meanness, or some cowardice, or some fault or weakness in another person, they should examine themselves carefully. Then they will see that, perhaps, they too have some of the same fault in themselves –

*[margin note: ouble = doppelgänger]*

although perhaps it does not come out in the same way – and then they must try to conquer that fault. So they will become more and more good as they grow up; and others will examine them, and when these find they have not the faults, they will love and honour them. (*UTS* 20)

This is, in effect, an application of the Biblical parable of the mote and the beam, and Christ's exhortation to 'Judge not, that ye be not judged' (Mat. 7:1–5). The implication is that the child reader may discern in the self some of the faults portrayed in these simplistic and ridiculous characters, faults which in a sense are magnified beyond the point of empathy in the figure of the Giant. David opposes Goliath. But in many respects Zaphir opposes not only the Giant but also those qualities of the Giant which lie beneath the outward features of his future subjects.

## Sin and repentance

The presence of such blatant and intrusive moralising, however, arguably fails to disarm fully the reservations expressed by some reviewers regarding the frequent juxtaposition of the didactic and the horrific in *Under the Sunset*. The reviewer for *The Academy*, for example, tempers his praise for the moral excellence of the volume's teaching with the warning that a child reader might lose sight of the morality of the text through 'a kind of fascination' with the more lurid aspects of the narrative.[23] The specific focus of the reviewer's unease is the third tale in the volume, 'The Invisible Giant', the incidents of which take place in a time 'many years' after the victory of Prince Zaphir, when 'All the beautiful Country was sadly changed, and changed was the life of the dwellers in it' (*UTS* 46). The Giant in question is not a corporeal being such as that vanquished by Zaphir in the preceding tale, but rather the shadowy personification of an impending plague which appears over the city, invisible to all but the pure-hearted child heroine, Zaya. The narrator recalls, in a passage which the reviewer for *The Academy* deemed 'decidedly "creepy"', how Zaya:

> looked up from her work and gazed across the city. There she saw a terrible thing – something so terrible that she gave a low cry of fear and wonder, and leaned out of the window, shading her eyes with her hand to see more clearly.

> In the sky beyond the city she saw a vast shadowy Form with its
> arms raised. It was shrouded in a great misty robe that covered it,
> fading away into air so that she could only see the face and the
> grim, spectral hands.
> The Form was so mighty that the city below it seemed like a
> child's toy. It was still far off the city. (*UTS* 51)

The language of this description, with its suggestion of the Sublime
and emphasis on the 'grim, spectral hands' of the Giant, certainly
suggests more the literary conventions of the ghost story than the
tradition of the moral allegory. On first sight, therefore, 'The Invisible
Giant' appears distant from the pronounced theological paradigm and
essentially Christian message of humility proclaimed in 'The Rose
Prince'.

'The Invisible Giant' is, however, supported by a coherent theological discourse – albeit one which is obscured at times by the narrative's
preoccupation with the depiction of disease and death. The comparative obscurity of the tale's moral message is a consequence also of its
plot being grounded not in an immediately recognisable biblical
paradigm, but in scenes drawn at least in part from the then-
unpublished reminiscences of the author's mother.

Stoker's recent biographers, following the lead of Harry Ludlam's
1962 biography, have been consistent in linking 'The Invisible Giant'
to Charlotte Stoker's recollections of the Sligo cholera epidemic of
1832, a series of tales which she apparently told to entertain her son
during a protracted childhood illness.[24] Barbara Belford, for example,
imaginatively reconstructs an intimate scene in London in which
Stoker 'unearthed from an old trunk his Dublin notebooks, from a
time when he tinkered with drafts of fairy tales, when he tried to
dramatise his mother's Sligo stories, to capture images of the looming
cholera epidemic – or the plague, as he recreates it in *Dracula*'.[25]
Belford's coda epitomises how modern criticism has viewed *Under the
Sunset*, regarding the collection as a series of narratives whose significance rests merely in their foreshadowing of the imagery of Stoker's
later works – particularly *Dracula* – rather than as texts in their own
right.[26]

This critical approach, inevitably, obscures the textual significance
of the 'images of the looming cholera epidemic', which Belford
suggests punctuate 'The Invisible Giant'. Many of these 'images' are
fully appreciable only by an adult audience, for all their superficial
colouring of fairy-tale logic. Zaya, for example, is protected during her

stay in the plague-ridden city by the wild birds she has previously fed with the crumbs from her own frugal table. The narrator notes how:

> They pecked of her bread and drank of her cup before she touched them; and when there was danger – for the cold hand of the giant was placed everywhere – they would cry,
> 'No, no!' and she would not touch the food, or let anyone else do so. Often it happened that, even whilst it pecked at the bread or drank of the cup, a poor little bird would fall down and flutter its wings and die; but all they that died, did so with a chirp of joy, looking at their little mistress, for whom they had gladly perished. (*UTS* 65)

This touching episode, however, arguably reflects also a popular awareness of the risks of contracting cholera through impure food and drink. In a lecture published three years after *Under the Sunset*, the British physician J.S. Burdon-Sanderson echoed warnings already delivered in the majority of non-clinical medical guides by stating that cholera enters the body through 'the same channel by which the nutritious part of our food is assimilated'.[27] Significantly, the first deaths from plague in 'The Invisible Giant' take place next to the presumably contaminated water of a public fountain (*UTS* 61–2).[28] Those infected with the plague also experience abdominal pain and display the darkening of the countenance symptomatic of cholera.[29] The identification between Zaya's spectral Giant and cholera is further emphasised by Fitzgerald's illustration, which appears to draw not on Charlotte Stoker's vague description of 'a heavy sulphurous looking cloud' but on a convention in nineteenth-century cartoon art by which the contagion was represented 'as a death's head, with outstretched black skeletal arms'.[30] Such images are, again, a warning to the complacent.

Contemporary critics, such as the reviewer for *The Academy*, appear to have recognised the atmosphere of horror that surrounds the presence of contagious disease, but not the didactic possibilities which such events present. In Old Testament terms the onset of disease may signify the anger of the Deity:

> If thou wilt not observe to do all the words of this law that are written in this book.... Then the Lord will make thy plagues wonderful, and the plagues of thy seed, *even* great plagues, and of long continuance, and sore sicknesses, and of long continuance. (Deut. 28:58–9)

This much is arguably retained in the New Testament discourse which supports nineteenth-century Irish Protestantism. Charlotte Stoker, notably, suggests that the 1832 cholera epidemic was a consequence of 'deeds ... done in selfish dread, enough to call down God's direct vengeance on us' and that 'Severely, like Sodom, did our city [Sligo] pay for such crimes.'[31] The plague has become an apocalypse, made meaningful only through an association with divine displeasure.

The paradigm upon which 'The Invisible Giant' draws most heavily is not that of the New Testament Revelation, however. Rather, the narrative is an oblique reworking of the Old Testament story of the Flood, albeit one that is again informed by participation in New Testament apologetics and Protestant introspection. The Flood is represented in the Old Testament as God's reaction to human wickedness:

> And GOD saw that the wickedness of man *was* great in the earth, and *that* every imagination of the thoughts of his heart was only evil continually. [6]And it repented the LORD that he had made man upon the earth, and it grieved him at his heart. [7]And the LORD said, I will destroy man whom I have created from the face of the earth.... (Gen. 6:5–7)

The fictionalisation of plague in 'The Invisible Giant' is, similarly, a warning to the reader of how God's wrath may at any time strike the unrighteous, given that the Giant invades at a time when 'People had become more selfish and more greedy' (*UTS* 45).

Where Zaya's name temptingly recalls that of Zaphir, her companion Knoal is simultaneously the 'know-all' of curative herbalism and an elderly Noah who protects a remnant of society from the punitive act of the Deity. In the Old Testament, God saves the House of Noah alone from the Flood on account of its past behaviour: 'for thee have I seen righteous before me in this generation' (Gen. 7:1). 'The Invisible Giant', in contrast, advances a redemptive, evangelical message in which *present* repentance may overwrite the sins of the past.

Appropriately, the first victims of the plague are the violent unbelievers who threaten to duck both Zaya and Knoal in the potentially lethal waters of the public fountain:

> The hand of one who was a ringleader was already outstretched, when he gave a low cry, and pressed his hand to his side; and, whilst the others turned to look at him in wonder, he cried out in

great pain, and screamed horribly. Even whilst the people looked, his face grew blacker and blacker, and he fell down before them, and writhed a while in pain, and then died. (*UTS* 61–2)

The narrator concludes that, after the initial panic, 'for many a long day there was pain and grief and death in the Country Under the Sunset' (*UTS* 63). The sudden deaths of those who were unprepared proves a redemptive signal to others, however. Zaya and Knoal work tirelessly in the doomed city, healing the spirit as well as the body in many cases. The narrator recalls: 'Thus they saved many precious human lives, and those who were rescued were very thankful, and henceforth ever after lived holier and more unselfish lives' (*UTS* 64). The implicit nature of that thankfulness is perhaps best conveyed through the closing words of Charlotte Stoker's personal account of the Sligo cholera: 'We had great reason to thank God who had spared us.'[32]

The construction of the Giant further underlines the evangelical message of the narrative, in that he moves as an impartial agent of the Divine will rather than as an individual prosecuting his own mission. Zaya tells Knoal who, despite his wisdom and saintly asceticism, is unable see the apparition,

How the Giant was so great that all the sky seemed filled. How the great arms were outspread, veiled in his robe, till far away the shroud was lost in air. How the face was as that of a strong man, pitiless, yet without malice; and that the eyes were blind. (*UTS* 55)

The blind eyes and lack of malice are gestures akin to the conventional portrait of blindfolded Justice. In effect, the Giant facilitates the repentance of those he, on first sight, persecutes. All are judged on their inner merits rather than through the superficial appearances that characterise a society where there are 'some very rich and ... many poor' (*UTS* 45). Even the saintly Knoal succumbs, as the final victim of the Giant, though much of his parting speech to Zaya conveys the resignation of a martyr: 'I am the last victim, and I gladly die' (*UTS* 68). His redemptive and medical mission over, Knoal may at last lay down his life.

The tale concludes not with the death of Knoal, but with a last benediction, delivered by the Giant to Zaya: 'innocence and devotion save the land'. The narrator's closing words,

> Presently she saw far off the great shadowy Giant Plague moving
> away to the border of the Land, and passing between the Guardian
> Spirits out through the Portal into the deserts beyond – for ever.
> (*UTS* 71)

similarly recall the Biblical Covenant between God and Man after the
Flood: 'neither shall all flesh be cut off any more by the waters of a
flood; neither shall there any more be a flood to destroy the earth'
(Gen. 9:11). The Lesson has been taught and is now complete. The
pure have been vindicated and protected by their purity. The repen-
tant have been saved through their compliance with Divine Will. The
sinful have once again been subjugated into penitence. The seemingly
chaotic and horrific – whether it be realised in the form of sudden
death or mindless violence – is redefined in *Under the Sunset* as an
emblem of Order.

*

This paradoxical combination of chaos and order is the vehicle by
which the reader is introduced to a theological debate on sin and
repentance in *Under the Sunset*. In nineteenth-century theological writings, sin is frequently represented not merely as humanity's
characteristic disobedience to God's Will, but also as an affront to
Divine Order. Recalling the Biblical statement that 'Whosoever
committeth sin transgresseth also the law: for sin is the transgression
of the law' (1 John 3:4), one Victorian Protestant theologian
concluded, for example, that 'to a man that considers the true nature
of sin, every sin is grave, for in every sin there is lawlessness – a violation of the divine order of human life.'[33] A seemingly insignificant
action – the taking of an apple by an innocent and thoughtless adult in
the Book of Genesis, or a childish squabble in 'The Wondrous Child',
the final story in *Under the Sunset* – may thus lead to unforeseen and
disastrous consequences, by implication in life as well as in allegory.[34]

In *Under the Sunset*, as in the Bible, an idyllic prelapsarian state is
recalled, the Portal and its two Guardian Angels forming a *cordon sani-
taire* which protects the innocents within from the shadowy entities
without. The narrator recalls:

> The Country Under the Sunset was for long ages a wondrous and
> pleasant Land. Nothing there was which was not beautiful and
> sweet and pleasant. It was only when sin came that things there
> began to lose their perfect beauty. Even now it is a wondrous and
> pleasant Land. (*UTS* 2)

An identity is rapidly established for 'sin' by the narrator, who recalls how 'For long, Death and his Children stayed without the Portal and all within was Joy' (*UTS* 6). This association between death and sin is, of course, canonical in Pauline terms. The Epistle to the Romans bluntly states that 'the Wages of Sin *is* death; but the gift of God is eternal life through Jesus Christ our Lord' (Rom. 6:23).

The entry of sin into Stoker's allegorical paradise is, however, problematic in that, far from being the apparent consequence of an explicit act of disobedience, the change is not merely *permitted* but in effect *facilitated* by the All-Father, a deific though intangible presence whose beneficence in the volume is otherwise rendered as being beyond question. The 'Child-Angel', Chiaro, described by the narrator as being 'fairer than the light of the sun', initiates what is effectively an exegesis of the theology of sin during a conversation with the Guardian Angels, Fid-Def. Chiaro begins:

> 'Tell me, Fid-Def, what are those dreadful-looking Beings beyond the Portal?'
> Fid-Def answered:
> 'They are Children of King Death. That dreadfullest one of all, enwrapt in gloom, is Skooro, an Evil Spirit.'
> 'How horrible they look!'
> 'Very horrible, dear Chiaro; and these Children of Death want to pass through the Portal and enter the Land.' (*UTS* 8)

Visibly shocked, Chiaro questions Fid-Def further as to why the Children of Death wish to enter the Land Under the Sunset. Fid-Def reply simply that 'they are wicked, and wish to corrupt the hearts of the dwellers in the Land' (*UTS* 9). Chiaro's response to this statement is theologically both trusting and simplistic: 'But tell me, Fid-Def, can they get in? Surely, if the All-Father says, No! they must stay ever without the Land' (*UTS* 9). Fid-Def's rejoinder, however, qualifies the coming event by naming the benefits which it will ultimately bring to a sinful generation:

> The All-Father is wiser than even the Angels can conceive. He overthroweth the wicked with their own devices, and he trappeth the hunter in his own snare. The Children of Death when they enter – as they are about to do – shall do much good in the Land, which they wish to harm. For lo! the hearts of the people are corrupt. They have forgotten the lessons which they have been taught. They do

not know how thankful they should be for their happy lot, for of sorrow they wot not. Some pain or grief or sadness must be to them, that so they may see the error of their ways. (*UTS* 9)

The archaic syntax of Fid-Def's speech recalls the language of the Authorised Version of the Scriptures. Although the emphatic statement 'He overthroweth the wicked with their own devices, and trappeth the hunter in his own snare' is *not* a quotation from the King James Bible, it functions in 'Under the Sunset' as a sort of apocryphal Psalm, or, more pointedly, as a didactic verse in the manner of those in the Book of Proverbs.[35]

The phrase is ambiguous. The narrator has already made it clear that wrongdoing exists in a basic form in this fictional paradise, noting that even before the physical entry of sin into the land,

there came a time when all was changed. The hearts of men grew cold and hard with pride in their prosperity, and they heeded not the lessons which they had been taught. (*UTS* 6)

For all its apparent perfection, the Land Under the Sunset is *not* Eden, therefore, even though sin is scripted as entering in part through 'the snakes that crawled on the earth' (*UTS* 11). The lessons which the narrator mentions arguably relate to personal spiritual well-being as much as to the responsibilities which the Bible asserts should accompany material success – responsibilities acknowledged in 'Under the Sunset' through their eclipse by a selfish culture of 'coldness and indifference and disdain' (*UTS* 6).[36] These fortunate dwellers in a carefree paradise are in effect trapped by their unknowing self-righteousness and the purblind insularity of their spiritual vision.

But sin, personified in particular through the dark angel Skooro, is equally entrapped by the ironic purposefulness to which it is seemingly directed throughout the volume by the deific All-Father. The narrator continues:

Then when within there was coldness and indifference and disdain, the Angels on guard saw in the terrors that stood without, the means of punishment and the lesson which could do good.

The good lessons came – as good things very often do – after pain and trial, and they taught much. The story of their coming has a lesson for the wise. (*UTS* 6)

This 'lesson for the wise' is not wholly grounded in biblical doctrine, however. Rather, it represents the conjunction of popular Christian ideals with a vigorous and, in part, secular philosophy of personal development through struggle – a philosophy which Stoker was to elaborate at considerably greater length through the characters of Harold An Wolf and Rupert Sent Leger in *The Man* and *The Lady of the Shroud* respectively. Self-knowledge and self-improvement, according to this philosophy, may only be gained through experience. Hence in the sixth tale, 'Lies and Lilies', the narrator, speaking for the wise schoolmistress, simultaneously offers both fictional character and child reader some timely advice:

> 'It is ever thus, dear children. A sin cannot be wiped away till the shame comes first; for without the shame and the acknowledgement of guilt the heart cannot be cleansed from the sin.' (*UTS* 130)

The interior journey of self-scrutiny for the children and youths who people *Under the Sunset* becomes, in the sagas of the manly heroes of Stoker's later adult fiction, a physical as well as emotional purgation.

Following the explicit act by which the All-Father permits sin to enter the Land Under the Sunset, the child reader might be forgiven for voicing a problematic theological question of origins: 'Who is the author of sin?' The contemporary Protestant theologian M.G. Easton asserts that:

> The origin of sin is a mystery, and must for ever remain such to us. It is plain that for some reason God has permitted sin to enter this world, and that is all we know. His permitting it, however, in no way makes God the author of sin.[37]

Though the question of the origin or generation of sin is left, significantly, unanswered in *Under the Sunset*, the stories at least go some way towards assigning a beneficial purpose to human suffering.

This strategy arguably throws light upon many of the scenes which the reviewers of *Under the Sunset* found so disturbing when placed in the context of the volume's supposed allegorical genre. Chiaro and Skooro may effectively serve as an emblem for the whole moral logic of *Under the Sunset*. The two spirits, angel and demon, exist effectively in harness. This is, indeed, part of the sacred trust placed upon Chiaro through Fid-Def at the opening of the volume:

The Children of Death are about to enter. To you has been entrusted the watching of this dread Being, Skooro. Wheresoever he goeth, there must you be also; and so naught of harm can happen – save only what is intended and allowed. (*UTS* 10)

The All-Father, as the final sentence affirms, is still very much in control. Fid-Def continue:

You must know, dear Child, that without darkness is no fear of the unseen; and not even the darkness of night can fright if there be light within the soul. To the good and pure there is no fear either of the evil things of the earth or of the Powers that are unseen. To you is trusted to guard the pure and true. Skooro will encompass them with his gloom; but to you is given to steal into their hearts and by your own glorious light to make the gloom of the Child of Death unseen and unknown. (*UTS* 10)

Together, the names of these personifications of light and darkness make *chiaroscuro*, a pun of which a literate adult, though not necessarily a child, would be aware. The apportionment of moral and spiritual qualities to light and darkness is, of course, highly conventional here. Christ, in the Bible, is 'the light of the world' (John 8:12); Satan, in popular culture, the Prince of Darkness. In *Under the Sunset*, though, these opposing qualities are consistently portrayed as mutual and interdependent.

Light, literally as well as figuratively, *cannot be* without shade. This, certainly, appears to be the major preoccupation of 'The Shadow Builder', the fourth story in *Under the Sunset*, in which the narrator depicts a parallel kingdom of shadows and past events ruled over by a lonely demiurge. The shadows which the Shadow Builder creates reflect not merely the literal objects caught in the light of the sun or moon, but also, in more metaphysical terms, the echo of 'every act that any human being does, every thought – good and bad' (*UTS* 75).

Hence, the logic of morality cannot function when one component of the equation – in 'Under the Sunset', the negative or shadow side – is not present.[38] The value of Good is not discernible without the comparative quality of Evil; the strength of virtue will remain untested where there is no temptation. As the narrator suggests: 'When people think themselves very good they are in danger of sin, for if we are not ever on the watch against evil we surely do some wrong thing....' (*UTS*

127). *Under the Sunset*, for all its pietistic drive, is, ironically, in no way a tract that advocates the eradication of evil.

Hence, though the binary nature of *chiaroscuro* may signify, on one level, life as opposed to death, God against the Devil, or sin as the antithesis of innocence, the duality of the relationship may also be manipulated in order to carry with it a further suggestion of sin in juxtaposition to redemption. Fid-Def, again, make clear that this forms part of the purposefulness of the All-Father. Charged with the guardianship of 'the pure and true', Chiaro is instructed to withhold his light from 'the wicked, and the ungrateful, and the impure, and the untrue', so that 'when they look for you to comfort them ... they will not see you. They will see only the gloom which your far-off light will make seem darker still, for the shadow will be in their very souls.' However,

> our Father is kind beyond belief. He orders that should any that are evil repent, you will on the instant fly to them, and comfort them, and help them, and cheer them, and drive the shadow far off. Should they only pretend to repent, meaning to be again wicked when the danger is past; or should they only act from fear, then you will hide your brightness so that the gloom may grow darker still over them. (*UTS* 10–11)

There is thus a cathartic, Miltonic resonance in the struggle for the soul that this duality permits throughout *Under the Sunset*.

This struggle is at its most acute in the sixth story, 'Lies and Lilies'. Claribel, the heroine of the tale, is tempted to idle during her arithmetic lesson, drawing a lily on her slate rather than seeking the answer to the exercise. The narrator notes how Skooro is an active and ready assistant in her wrongdoing:

> In order to help her do what she ought not to do he took the shape of a lily and lay on the slate very faintly, so that she had only to draw round his edges and then there was a lily drawn. Now it is not a wrong thing to draw a lily, and if Claribel had drawn it well at a proper time she would have got praise; but a good thing may become a bad thing if it is wrongly done – and so it was with Claribel's lily. (*UTS* 128–9)

Claribel's crime, however, is not the drawing of the lily but rather the lie which she tells to the school mistress when questioned as to how she has spent the lesson: 'she answered that she had done nothing else but sums' (*UTS* 129).

Conscious of having told a lie, Claribel dreams that night of the New Jerusalem depicted in the biblical Revelation, a city from which, as both the Christian reader and Claribel know, 'whosoever loveth and maketh a lie' is excluded (Rev. 21:8, 22:15). This dream brings together Skooro and Chiaro in a battle for the future of Claribel's soul. Chiaro acts first by flooding Claribel's sleeping mind with his 'beautiful light':

> She dreamed that she saw the Angel with the golden reed measuring the city, and Claribel was so happy that she forgot all about her sin. The Child Angel knew all her thoughts, and he grew less and less till his light all died away; and to Claribel in her dream all seemed to grow dark, and she knew that she was standing without the gate of the Beautiful City. (*UTS* 131)

The Angel twice refuses to admit Claribel to the heavenly city, condemning her to 'stand without among the liars' (*UTS* 132). In the midst of her sense of pain and desperation at the prospect of eternal exclusion from the New Jerusalem, however, arises a hope for forgiveness. The narrator continues:

> Claribel saw the jasper walls before her towering up and up, and she knew that they were an eternal barrier to her, and that she must ever stand without the Beautiful City; and in the anguish and horror she felt how deep was her sin, and longed to confess it.
>
> Skooro saw that she was repenting, for he, too, could see into her thoughts, and with the darkness of his presence he tried to blot out the whole dream of the Beautiful City.
>
> But the Child-Angel crept into her heart and made it light, and the seed of repentance grew and blossomed. (*UTS* 132)

Skooro, like Milton's Satan, is granted access to man by the Deity, only to find the proposed victim ironically redeemed through her contact with evil.[39] The horrors of Hell and the threat of eternal exclusion from the presence of God become the turning point for one child, who may now regard, apparently without fear, the prospect of 'the Jasper City, which is for the pure alone' (*UTS* 132).

The Jasper City of the New Jerusalem, however, may be entered only by those whose names 'are written in the Lamb's book of life' (Rev. 21:27). Mere repentance, good works or the living of 'holier' lives (*UTS*

64) are, strictly speaking, not qualification enough in themselves, as the eleventh Article of Religion of the Church of Ireland makes clear: 'We are accounted righteous before God only for the merit of our Lord and Saviour Jesus Christ, by Faith, and not for our own works or deservings.'[40] The doctrinal vagueness of *Under the Sunset* is prevented from becoming a pitfall for the child reader only by the importance which the volume consistently attaches to life-changing decisions. When Zaphir and Zaya trust to Divine protection in the face of their respective giants, and when Claribel overcomes the lifelong temptation latent in her first act of untruthfulness, an old, sinful life is seemingly forsaken and a new beginning signalled. The power behind Skooro is rejected; that which supports Chiaro is embraced.

The broad Augustinian tenets of the Doctrine of Free Grace have thus been retained, though their theological ramifications have not been extracted to the full in *Under the Sunset*. Indeed, the volume advances a simplified version of Christian doctrine, if not one made theologically more hopeful, and thus more attractive to the child reader. Stoker's doctrinal vagueness arguably represents his participation in a lay rather than clerical appreciation of Christian theology. This position produces in the volume a broad replication of the Faith as received and transmitted publicly rather than in the privileged space of theological debate. The horror of *Under the Sunset*, in this respect, is the servant of its piety and didacticism. The experience of the horrific, for the fictional characters and, by example, for the child reader also, leads to the inculcation of a moral lesson and the purging of impiety – an outcome seemingly not acknowledged by contemporary criticism. Notably, the author made no alterations to the 'lurid passages' and retained all of the 'terribly grim' illustrations highlighted in the critical response to the first edition when revising the work for its second edition.[41]

## Unspeakable terror

Academic critics have been similarly slow to acknowledge the religious implications of Stoker's 1903 novel, *The Jewel of Seven Stars*, even where their writings explicitly consider the work's exploration of epistemological uncertainty.[42] Published initially by William Heinemann in 1903, and in a revised edition by William Rider in 1912, the novel describes the attempted resurrection of Tera, an Egyptian sorcerer-queen mummified three thousand years earlier. 'The Great Experiment', as the attempt is styled, harnesses both ancient occult ritual and Edwardian scientific observation, and is effected by a wealthy British Egyptologist, Abel Trelawny, his daughter, Margaret, an assistant, Corbeck, and the narrator, Malcolm Ross, a London barrister. The consequences of Queen Tera's successful resurrection are predicted alternately by those involved in terms of metaphysical speculation and in the anticipation of concrete technological benefits.[43]

The first fifteen chapters of both editions are identical. The second edition, however, differs from the first through the removal of the sixteenth chapter, 'Powers – Old and New', and in the substitution of a new, happier, ending to the final chapter, 'The Great Experiment'. These changes have been traditionally dismissed in both criticism and biography as being nothing more than an authorial or editorial response to a request by Rider that the novel conclude with a more conventional ending. This suggestion was first advanced – without further substantiation – in Harry Ludlam's 1962 biography of Stoker and, at first sight, appears quite plausible.[44] The 1903 conclusion, in which all but Ross die, is pervaded by a hopelessness unique in Stoker's fiction. Ross recalls:

> I found them all where they had stood. They had sunk down on the floor, and were gazing upward with fixed eyes of unspeakable terror. Margaret had put her hands before her face, but the glassy stare of her eyes through her fingers was more terrible than an open glare.... I did what I could for my companions; but there was nothing that could avail. There, in that lonely house, far away from aid of man, naught could avail.
>
> It was merciful that I was spared the pain of hoping. (*JSS* 211)

There is no suggestion here, for example, of the symbolic marriage in death by which Sailor Willy and Maggie MacWhirter are united at the end of *The Watter's Mou'*, where the narrator concludes, romantically, 'The requiem of the twain was the roar of the breaking waves and the screams of the white birds that circled round the Watter's Mou'.'[45] The 1912 edition of *The Jewel of Seven Stars*, notably, replaces the death scene with a more hopeful scenario of marriage, and an affirmation of the happiness of the wedded couple, Margaret and Malcolm.

Death, in the first edition of *The Jewel of Seven Stars*, is horrible because it is not romanticised, and because it fails to signify an acceptable message in literary or religious terms. This is not to say that death is not meaningful here. Rather, its message *is* 'unspeakable terror': fear either at the prospect of physical pain or annihilation, or the expression of dread regarding that which lies beyond and after physical death – 'unspeakable', quite simply, because the dead cannot speak, and the horror-struck narrator is unable to speak for them. Graphic descriptions such as those in the original conclusion, however, form no part of 'Powers – Old and New', a chapter in which Ross speculates on the metaphysical and ontological implications of the Experiment in which he is to participate. When, however, *The Jewel of Seven Stars* is read as the narrative of a scientific enquiry which culminates in the working of 'The Great Experiment' the cancelled sixteenth chapter falls into place as an introduction to the epistemological – and, indeed, theological – rubric by which the resurrection of Tera will be governed.

If 'The Great Experiment' and 'Powers – Old and New' are read as intimate, therefore, what is removed in the second edition of the novel is arguably not merely the scene of *narrative* horror but also the *ontological* horror that precedes and supports it, and which the experiment itself arguably verifies through its evidential process. An untenable position constructed through the rhetoric of the first edition is systematically elided in the evidential process of the second: the narrative of horror in the revised novel is, in both senses, made to *yield to* the pious.

The breakdown in signification which characterises the first edition is largely a consequence of the novel's conjunction of what may be superficially regarded as a series of cultural opposites. In Trelawny's house, and later in the experiment chamber, the foreign and exotic occupy the same space as the domestic, the past is juxtaposed with the present, and pagan beliefs claim a validity customarily reserved for the Christian and the scientific. The construction of a largely accurate backdrop of Egyptology in *The Jewel of Seven Stars* reflects Stoker's reading across the subject over a period of years. Though David Glover argues that Stoker drew primarily on the writings of W.M. Flinders Petrie and Amelia Edwards, the major technical influence on the novel would appear to be that of E.A. Wallis Budge, author of many scholarly, though frequently popular, works on Egypt.[46] Stoker owned no less than five of these, although *The Jewel of Seven Stars* appears to draw primarily on Budge's 1893 study, *The Mummy*.[47]

At times the influence of *The Mummy* is marked. In Stoker's novel, the fictional explorer Van Huyn notes how the door of Tera's tomb 'was fixed in place with such incredible exactness that no stone chisel or cutting implement which I had with me could find a lodgement in the interstices' (*JSS* 97). Van Huyn's account recalls Budge's description of the tomb of the scribe, Ani, where 'the joints between the stones are so fine that the blade of a modern penknife can with difficulty be inserted to the depth of half an inch.'[48] The contents of Tera's burial chamber are similarly prefigured in *The Mummy*; although the 'Treasurer', an automaton which protects the tomb from theft, reflects an earlier phase of Egyptology which had by 1903 become part of the non-scholarly appreciation of the discipline.[49] For all its moments of technical accuracy, *The Jewel of Seven Stars* expresses a *popular* Egyptology, that of the travel narrative and the non-academic journal. Egypt in the novel is typified by the spectacle of death rather than the drudgery of life, its focal points being the tomb and the mummy rather than the potsherd.

The detailed characterisation of Queen Tera, however, places her in high relief against this background, and allows her to function as a problematic figure in the sexual and religious politics of both archaic Egypt and twentieth-century England. Budge lists no Tera amongst the monarchs of Egypt, although *The Mummy* confirms the novel's location of the Eleventh Dynasty at Thebes, and supports Stoker's choice of Antef as a suitable name for her Theban father.[50] The Queen's name is a fabrication which enforces the structural relationship between Tera and Margaret Trelawny, the latter also 'A queenly figure' (*JSS* 55) according to Ross. 'Tera' is the inversion of the last four letters of Margaret's Christian name, though phonetically it is a tempting pointer also to *terror*.

The figure of Tera is almost certainly modelled on Budge's account of the Eighteenth Dynasty queen, Hatshepset. Corbeck, Trelawny's assistant, observes of the inscriptions in Tera's tomb:

> In one place she was pictured in man's dress, and wearing the White and Red Crowns. In the following picture she was in female dress, but still wearing the Crowns of Upper and Lower Egypt, while the discarded male raiment lay at her feet. (*JSS* 112)

Tera is styled 'Monarch of the North and the South' (*JSS* 109), echoing Budge's translation of Hatshepset's title as 'king "of the North and South...."' Budge concludes:

> Of the end of Hatshepset nothing is known. During her lifetime she wore male attire, and put on the robes and ornaments which belonged to kings only.... After her death her brother Thothmes III. caused as many traces of her rule as possible to disappear.[51]

Tera's funerary inscription similarly informs the reader that the priests, in revenge for her usurpation of their knowledge and power, 'would after her death try to suppress her name' (*JSS* 112). In this respect, the characterisation may be read as another expression of the ambivalence towards strong-willed women which arguably punctuates Stoker's writings. Tera and Hatshepset are, in a sense, condemned for their rebellion against the closely aligned secular and spiritual power of a male priesthood.

Egyptology, however, is underpinned by the broader culture of Orientalism, a mode of discourse by which Eastern civilisations and peoples are made available to Western material culture. Trelawny's assistant, Corbeck, is the novel's primary medium for the expression of the frequently negative connotations of acquisitive archaeology. These arise out of the ambivalent relationship between the quest of the explorer and the ethics of the Occident. Corbeck – the name suggests an onomatopoeic representation of some grotesque carrion bird – makes 'a living of a sort' by 'tomb hunting' on behalf of Trelawny, rather than through the academic use of his many qualifications (*JSS* 69). He attaches much importance to the discretion with which he preserves Trelawny's confidences (*JSS* 72, 90). This is an intimate part of a personal and very Western sense of honour. But Corbeck is at times visibly less sure of the methods by which he has prosecuted missions for his employer. He confides to Margaret and Ross:

> I have been several times out on expeditions in Egypt for your father.... Many of his treasures – and he has some rare ones, I tell you – he has procured through me, either by my exploration or by purchase – or – or – otherwise. Your Father.... sometimes makes up his mind that he wants to find a particular thing ... and he will follow it all over the world until he gets it. (*JSS* 69)

This hesitation is echoed later in his account of the finding of the tomb: 'when the treasures which we had – ah! – taken from the tomb had been brought here, Mr. Trelawny arranged their disposition himself' (*JSS* 118). Both evasions are ultimately to no avail. The presence of the hyphen, and the interjected 'ah!' draw attention to Corbeck's embarrassment. Though this may be an expression of Stoker's possible distaste for such private collections, it is as likely a reflection of contemporary ambivalence towards the violation of the repose of the dead, even in the cause of knowledge. The fictional Van Huyn had no such qualms.

The acquisitive attitude with which the West approaches the Orient leads further to the objectification not merely of its cultures, but of its peoples also. People, like artefacts, become objects for display, study and experiment. Tera's hand is as much a traveller's curio as the sarcophagi, tables and coffers which lie scattered about Trelawny's private museum. Significantly, Ross dwells only momentarily on the hand's status as a detached human member before moving to an abstract consideration of its texture and 'rich creamy or old ivory colour' (*JSS* 81).[52] As Corbeck suggests, such fragments of humanity may be 'disposed' about the room, and are at the disposal of the collector. For Margaret Trelawny, 'A woman is a woman, if she had been dead five thousand centuries!' However, in this archaeological context, as her father patronisingly observes, Tera is 'Not a woman, dear; a mummy!' (*JSS* 199). As such, she may have the sanctity of her sex as well as of her repose violated by the presence of men and bright lights. Her status as artefact overwrites the customary respect accorded to her as woman. The presence of the physician, Dr Winchester, at the unrolling of Tera's mummy recalls that the living, too, may be exposed to similar indignities within the permitted spaces of medicine or science.

This objectification is a point of access for the macabre, in that the unrolling of Tera's mummy represents a crisis at which the discourses of knowledge and scholarship meet head on with more popular misgivings surrounding death and decay. Where Dr Winchester is able 'to hold himself in a business-like attitude, as if before the operating table' (*JSS* 201), Ross struggles to stay within a discourse appropriate to the experimental environment. Before the unrolling begins, Ross is consistent in treating Tera as an object: 'the mummy'. He recalls:

> *The mummy* was both long and broad and high; and was of such weight that it was no easy task, even for the four of us, to lift *it* out. Under Mr. Trelawny's direction we laid *it* out on the table prepared for *it*. (*JSS* 201, my emphases)

This intimacy with the dead, however, prompts a momentary lapse in his detachment. Ross recalls:

> Then, and then only, did the full horror of the whole thing burst upon me! There, in the full glare of the light, the whole material and sordid side of death seemed staringly real. The outer wrappings, torn and loosened by rude touch, and with the colour either darkened by

dust or worn light by friction, seemed creased as by rough treatment; the jagged edges of the wrapping-cloths looked fringed; the painting was patchy, and the varnish chipped. The coverings were evidently many, for the bulk was great. But through all, showed that unhidable human figure, which seems to look more horrible when partially concealed than at any other time. What was before us was Death, and nothing else. All the romance and sentiment of fancy had disappeared. (*JSS* 201)

Reader attention is thus directed towards the realisation that what is perceived is only the surface and not the totality of the object, and that the human form lies beneath it, as yet partially revealed.

An ambiguous sense of expectation is thus generated for the reader. A well-preserved body is required for the successful completion of the Experiment. But anticipation is valorised further by the repeated descriptions of the decay of the outer coverings. Speculation arises, therefore, not as to *what* lies beneath the wrappings, but as to the condition of that which will be revealed, where sight gives a greater immediacy through not recognising the 'romance' of words and glossaries. Ross continues:

Then the work began. The unrolling of the mummy cat had prepared me somewhat for it; but this was so much larger, and so infinitely more elaborate, that it seemed a different thing ... there were the same surroundings, the same attendant red dust and pungent presence of bitumen; there was the same sound of rending which marked the tearing away of the bandages. There were an enormous number of these, and their bulk when opened was great. (*JSS* 201)

Anticipation is maintained, the sense of moving towards a conclusion conveyed in the reduction in the size of the mummy, and the corresponding growth of the pile of discarded bandages. The account begins to take on a more optimistic tone:

As the unrolling went on, the wrappings became finer, and the smell less laden with bitumen, but more pungent.... At last we knew that the wrappings were coming to an end. Already the proportions were reduced to those of a normal figure of the manifest height of the Queen, who was more than average tall. (*JSS* 201–2)

The focus here, though, remains upon the bandages and the embalming rather than the human body beneath. The use of *it* has been eclipsed by a consistent *the* which refers to both process and wrappings. Ross has, in a sense, successfully moved back into the type of detachment that characterises the discursive positions occupied by Trelawny, Corbeck and Winchester. This detachment persists, albeit momentarily, even when the perfectly preserved body of the Queen is revealed. Ross recalls:

> There was nothing of that horrible shrinkage which death seems to effect in a moment. There was none of the wrinkled toughness which seems to be a leading characteristic of most mummies. There was not the shrunken attenuation of a body dried in the sand, as I had seen before in museums. (*JSS* 203)

The rhythmic repetition of 'There was nothing.... none.... not....' echoes the syntax of the earlier rhetorical construction of anticipation, and underscores the absolute abnormality of the whole revelation. A possible expectation on the part of the perceiver is acknowledged the moment after it is violated. The apparently life-like condition of the corpse forces a question as to which discourses are appropriate to its handling. Discursive boundaries are thus broken down by the sudden intrusion of the human into the archaeological. Hence, the detached position previously occupied by Trelawny, Corbeck, Winchester and Ross collapses as the artefact – Margaret's physical double – is perceived as human: as Ross phrases it, 'This woman – I could not think of her as a mummy or a corpse' (*JSS* 204).

*

In materialistic and scientific terms, the validity of the proposition upon which the Great Experiment is founded may be said to stand or fall on the simple question of whether or not life returns to the corpse. If the experiment succeeds, science will, in theory, expand in order to accommodate the 'new' knowledge. Should the experiment fail, however, science as an empirical discipline will remain unaffected. Tera's humanity, though, confers upon her body an element of spirituality not enjoyed by the pigeons, monkeys and dogs conventionally employed in scientific or medical experimentation. As the vivisectionist Nathan Benjulia, in Wilkie Collins's *Heart and Science* (1883), notes: 'a man is a creature with a soul, and a dog is a creature without a soul.'[53] Tera's proposed resurrection is thus opened up to theological as well as physiological implications. The failure of the Great

Experiment will leave the cardinal tenets of Christian religion, like those of empirical science, unaffected. Its success, however, will effectively cast doubt on the validity of Christian doctrine in its application to the connections between death, bodily resurrection and the final Judgement foretold in the biblical Revelation.

The Christian doctrine of the Resurrection is particularly vulnerable in that it closely integrates both the resurrection of Christ and the subsequent (and consequent) resurrection of the Believer.[54] Tera's proposed resurrection is therefore immediately an action striking at the unique nature of Christ's redemptive sacrifice, 'his one oblation of himself once offered' as the *Book of Common Prayer* describes it.[55] Tera's physical condition, the Christian reader will observe, resembles that of Christ, who did not 'see corruption' (Ps. 16:10), rather than that of the Christian believer, whose body at the Resurrection is typified elsewhere by Stoker in the somewhat gruesome words of Mr Swales in *Dracula*:

> 'My gog, but it'll be a quare scowderment at the Day of Judgement, when they come tumblin' up here in their death-sarks, all jouped together an' tryin' to drag their tombsteans with them to prove how good they was; some of them trimmlin' and ditherin', with their hands that dozzened an' slippery from lyin' in the sea that they can't even keep ther grup o' them.' (*D* 65)

Swales's comment posits a further implication for the resurrection of Tera in *The Jewel of Seven Stars*. If permitted to rise from the dead, Tera will be neither Saved in the Christian sense, innocent, nor judged at her resurrection. Ross, a barrister, is careful to note the unatoned murders at the Queen's hand (*JSS* 180). Punishment fitting to her crimes during life will therefore not have been administered, and thus no gain will be apparent in conventional Faith or Salvation.[56] If Tera escapes judgement – and this again suggests a limitation of Christ's hegemony – the whole notion of Christ's Kingdom is, effectively, proved false.

It is this conception of Christianity as an Absolute that Ross comes inevitably to address in 'Powers – Old and New', and which the reader, too, is forced to consider. Ross speculates:

> The whole possibility of the Great Experiment to which we were now pledged was based on the reality of the existence of the Old Forces which seemed to be coming in contact with the New

Civilisation. That there were, and are, such cosmic forces we cannot doubt, and that the Intelligence, which is behind them, was and is. (*JSS* 158)

These 'Old Forces' are, however, ambiguously connected with science, the supposedly contemporary discourse by which Trelawny ostensibly regulates his experiment. Trelawny, indeed, asserts that the Egyptian *priests* were themselves masters in applied optics, and suggests further that the most recent of scientific discoveries may represent little more than a renaissance of ideas previously associated with a non-Christian world of occult talismans and scarabs:

This new metal, radium – or rather this old metal of which our knowledge is new – may have been known to the ancients. Indeed it may have been used thousands of years ago in greater degree than seems possible to-day. (*JSS* 161–2)

The boundaries between discourses are, again, perceptibly brittle here. A modern scientist is thus, in many respects, an occultist also. His investigation into fields not covered by scientific knowledge may be, in such instances, equally regarded as a blasphemous intrusion into the lacunae beyond the fixed canons of Christian belief, the 'secret things' which belong to God alone as Deuteronomy terms them. As one Christian apologist suggests, 'speculation on things concerning which God has not spoken (Deut. XXIX. 29) is irreverent.'[57] Trelawny notes, significantly, that such speculations have in the past 'sent the discoverers to the flames' (*JSS* 156).

The very antiquity of these 'Old Forces' is problematic for Ross. He speculates further:

Were those primal and elemental forces controlled at any time by other than that Final Cause which Christendom holds as its very essence? If there were truth at all in the belief of Ancient Egypt then their Gods had real existence, real power, real force. Godhead is not a quality subject to the ills of mortals: as in its essence it is creative and recreative, it cannot die. Any belief to the contrary would be antagonistic to reason; for it would hold that a part is greater than the whole. If then the Old Gods held their forces, wherein was the supremacy of the new? Of course, if the Old Gods had lost their power, or if they never had any, the Experiment could not succeed. But if it should indeed succeed, or if there were a possibility of success, then we should be face to face with an inference so over-whelming that one hardly dared to follow it to its conclusion. (*JSS* 158–9)

Ross, clearly, is already on the verge of accepting the notion of the Christian God as being but one deity among many. Such is the prospect before him that his closing speculations emerge as a series of questions, the answers to which may only be revealed at the climax of the Great Experiment itself:

Was there room in the Universe for opposing Gods; or if such there were, would the stronger allow manifestations of power on the part of the opposing Force which would tend to the weakening of His own teaching and designs? Surely, surely if this supposition were correct there would be some strange and awful development – something unexpected and unpredictable – before the end should be allowed to come...! (*JSS* 159)

The final sentence of this speculation is both the crowning point of a faith expressed in Christian terms, and the indicator of its rhetorical and systematic unreliability. A belief in the divine control of events represents simultaneously the supreme confidence in an ordered and non-chaotic universe, and the extent of humanity's absolute ignorance and helplessness. But the anticipation of 'something unexpected and unpredictable', while affirming the latter, reflects further the canonical inexplicability of the Christian Deity, as popularly articulated, for example, in the Creed of St Athanasius: 'The Father incomprehensible, the Son incomprehensible: and the Holy Ghost incomprehensible.'[58] As Ross suggests, the successful resurrection of Tera by non-Christian means would negate the totality of the Deity's ascribed hegemony, if not dismiss it altogether by force of logic.

But should the demiurges not triumph, nothing is proved conclusively about their plurality in earthly terms. Unless some definite sign is given beyond the mere failure of the experiment, the victory *or even participation* of the Deity cannot be proved, although to the participant within the Christian ontology it may be assumed. A sign, as St Matthew would have it, is not likely to be given (Mat. 16:1–4). Moreover, faith has become the standard of the Church after the doubts of St Thomas, and faith is that which retains belief *in spite of* rather than *through* evidence (John 20:29). As Van Helsing puts it, faith is 'that which enables us to believe things which we know to be untrue' (*D* 193), though admittedly in Protestant apologetics faith is again reinforced by testimony and personal experience.[59] The ultimate unprovability of the Christian ontology contrasts strongly with the empiricism that both verifies and modifies the material sciences. Clearly, in the first edition of *The Jewel of Seven Stars*, the narrative will have a testimonial quality from this point. The culmination of this testimony will be the Great Experiment itself.

The removal of the sixteenth chapter in the second edition of *The Jewel of Seven Stars* thus largely favours the Christian ontology. With the suppression of 'Powers – Old and New', the ontological dialectic loses its *explicit* place in the fabric of the text and is relegated to an implication – the *unwritten* place it would have in any conflict between the material sciences or the occult, and Christian theology. The notion of an act done in contravention to the dictates of the Deity may be permitted to remain, for that is the basis of the resurrection of Tera as it is the context of *Frankenstein*. But the removal of Ross's protracted exercise in ontological speculation deflects attention away from the suggestion of competing gods and back onto the human participants. The issue thus becomes implicitly one of individual, human transgression against a single divinity rather than a brave sortie into theological plurality. In the second edition of the novel, therefore, the status of theology and of the Theocracy are not so much augmented as left in their accepted position of unquestioned stability and uniqueness. As a consequence of the excision of 'Powers – Old and New' attention will arguably be directed at the theological ramifications of the Great Experiment, rather than towards the weaknesses in the theology itself.

## The Great Experiment

In both editions of *The Jewel of Seven Stars* the Great Experiment may be judged a failure. As Tera is not resurrected in any lasting form, humanity gains no new knowledge of the limits of human mortality, nor indeed is Trelawny able to 'let in on the world of modern science such a flood of light from the Old World as will change every condition of thought and experiment and practice' (*JSS* 172). However, the theological ramifications of each representation of the progress of the Experiment – and the nature of the proofs which support the theological interpretations of the two – are in almost diametrical opposition in the two editions. For, if the second edition rules out any question of the success of the Great Experiment, the first edition is not so much ambiguous as *rhetorically sure* of the possibility of the resurrection's successful completion but for the interposition of one unforeseen incident.

The text of the concluding chapter in both editions is identical – barring one or two superficial rephrasings – up to the point at which Tera's enrobed body is returned to the Experiment Chamber. From this point, however, the presence or absence of two factors, each of which functions only in one edition, modifies the theological implications which may be drawn from the outcome of the failed Experiment. These factors are the presence of Margaret's kitten, Silvio, which attends the resurrection only in the second edition of *The Jewel of Seven Stars*; and the behaviour of the wind, the strength of which varies between the two endings, outside the Experiment Chamber.

The wind is prefigured in both editions by a seemingly incidental recollection made by Ross immediately after the unrolling of Tera's mummy: 'I could hear without the roar of the wind, which was now risen to a tempest, and the furious dashing of the waves far below' (*JSS* 204). In both editions, the windows of the Experiment Chamber are closed by the observers before the Great Experiment begins. In the second edition this action is advanced as being merely part of a systematic process of overall preparation. Ross recalls:

The striking of two o'clock seemed to freshen us all up. Whatever shadows had been settling over us during the long hours preceding seemed to lift at once, and we all went about our separate duties alert and with alacrity. We looked first to the windows to see that they were closed, and we got ready our respirators to put them on when the time should be close at hand.[60]

It is only in the first edition that an explicit and overwhelmingly contextual reason is assigned to their actions:

The striking of two o'clock seemed to freshen us all up. Whatever shadows had been settling over us during the long hours preceding seemed to lift at once, and we all went about our separate duties alert and with alacrity. We looked first to the windows to see that they were closed; for now the storm raged so fiercely that we feared it might upset our plans which, after all, were based on perfect still-ness. Then we got ready our respirators to put them on when the time should be close at hand. (*JSS* 206)

The systematic nature of this excision becomes obvious when the two editions are compared further. Ross, for example, observes in the first edition:

> We waited, with our hearts beating. I know mine did; and I fancied I could hear the pulsation of the others. Without, the storm raged; the shutters of the narrow windows shook and strained and rattled, as though something was striving for entrance.
>
> The seconds seemed to pass with leaden wings; it was as though all the world were standing still. (*JSS* 208)

After revision, his account is truncated into:

> We waited with our hearts beating. I know mine did, and I fancied I could hear the pulsation of the others.
>
> The seconds seemed to pass with leaden wings. It was as though all the world were standing still. (*JSS* 1912, 301)

A further reference to the storm, and the decisive incursion of the wind into the Experiment Chamber, are omitted in the second edition.[61]

For the first edition, the incursion of the wind into the Experiment Chamber marks a theologically significant change in the progress of the Great Experiment. Up to this point the Experiment has gone well. The ritually important coffer has opened, as anticipated by all present. The apparently deliberate progress of the life-giving green vapour towards the mummy of Tera is affirmed by Ross's testimony of its catalytic effect. He recalls:

> I saw something white rising up from the open sarcophagus. Something which appeared to my tortured eyes to be filmy, like a white mist. In the heart of this mist, which was cloudy and opaque like an opal, was something like a hand holding a fiery jewel flaming with many lights. As the fierce glow of the Coffer met this new living light, the green vapour floating between them seemed like a cascade of brilliant points – a miracle of light! (*JSS* 209)

Though Ross is conscious that his vision is less than perfect, this juncture is still represented as a moment of affirmation as much as of quickening. But it is simultaneously the point of interruption or, possibly, of a disturbance which might be interpreted as *intervention*. Ross continues:

But at that very moment there came a change. The fierce storm, battling with the shutters of the narrow openings, won victory. With the sound of a pistol shot, one of the heavy shutters broke its fastening and was hurled on its hinges back against the wall. In rushed a fierce blast which blew the flames of the lamps to and fro, and drifted the green vapour from its course. (*JSS* 209)

The consequences are immediate:

On the very instant came a change in the outcome from the Coffer. There was a moment's quick flame and a muffled explosion; and black smoke began to pour out. This got thicker and thicker with frightful rapidity, in volumes of ever-increasing density; till the whole cavern began to get obscure, and its outlines were lost. The screaming wind tore in and whirled it about. (*JSS* 209)

Progress is halted. Corbeck's closing of the untethered shutter comes too late, for the 'perfect stillness' (*JSS* 206), noted earlier by Ross as an essential prerequisite of the Experiment, has been violently disturbed by the incursion of the storm. The Great Experiment concludes in confused darkness.

The reasoning here is clear. Ross's testimony advances evidence to suggest that the Experiment is effectively aborted as a direct consequence of the incursion of the wind, rather than by any fault in its internal mechanism. Equally clear is the success of the process up to the point of interruption – as testified by the sights, sounds and smells, and by the physical movement of Tera's body from inside the sarcophagus to a spot on the floor where Ross could later mistake it for the asphyxiated form of Margaret.

To return to the speculations of 'Powers – Old and New', a 'possibility of success' (*JSS* 159) *has* been suggested through the working of the Experiment, even though the ultimate aim of the project has not been effected. It is therefore both plausible that the demiurges of Ross's speculations exist, and that the Christian Deity's apparent intervention via the wind is specious. Though God may have been the 'rushing mighty wind' of Pentecost (Acts 2:2), the retributive Deity of the Old Testament was manifested to Elijah in the 'still, small voice' rather than the 'great and strong wind' (1 Kings 19:12). The Intelligence – or Intelligences – if any, that lie behind the disruption remain unidentified. The question of theological supremacy is still undecided.

A position more amenable to the theological status quo may be traced in the non-disrupted Experiment of the Second Edition. Ross again testifies:

> The coffer still continued to glow; from it began to steal a great greenish smoke. I could not smell it fully on account of the respirator; but, even through that, I was conscious of a strange pungent odour. Then this smoke began to grow thicker, and to roll out in volumes of ever increasing density till the whole room began to get obscure. (*JSS* 1912, 302)

The green smoke (*not* vapour) lacks purposeful movement. More significant, though, is that it changes condition and volume *of its own accord*, without any external influence. The evidence here points to an Experiment which fails to prove the hypothesis when allowed to proceed to its natural conclusion under what are obviously controlled conditions.

The evidence with which the second edition of *The Jewel of Seven Stars* attempts to corroborate Ross's own observations is equally damning. Margaret does not see – or does not choose to see – the supposed moment of quickening. The 'quick glint of white through the dense smoke in the fading light' (*JSS* 1912, 303) observed by Ross may as easily have been the white dress worn by Margaret as the white robe of Tera. The text notably positions Margaret adjacent to her double, the Queen being placed upon a couch rather than in a sarcophagus. In this respect, the white sheet which overlay the body of the Queen, and which was found 'thrown back, as might be when one is stepping out of bed' (*JSS* 1912, 305) could easily have been disturbed by Margaret when putting down the cat, Silvio. Only the 'sort of ridge of impalpable dust' (*JSS* 1912, 306) seems to suggest conclusively that the Queen never left the couch, though again it can say nothing about her quickening or otherwise.

Margaret's pet cat is the one factor here not present in the first edition. Silvio functions as a 'familiar' to Margaret, in much the same way as a mummified cat, also taken from the tomb by Trelawny, does to Tera. Throughout the Great Experiment, Silvio's presence is constantly recalled for the reader through the same strategy with which the text asserts the proximity of the storm in the first edition. Where, in the first edition, Ross notes how 'Doctor Winchester's eyes twinkled like stars, and Margaret's blazed like black suns' (*JSS* 208), the revised text adds a significant coda: 'Doctor Winchester's eyes twinkled like stars, and Margaret's blazed like black suns. Silvio's eyes were like emeralds' (*JSS* 1912, 301).

The cat is an ideal witness here – impartial, sensitive, giving testimony in spontaneous and non-verbal form.[62] *The Jewel of Seven Stars* draws, in addition, on the occult associations of animal sensitivity in much the same way as the narrator of Stoker's short story 'Dracula's Guest', who recalls how 'the horses … began to jump and kick about, then to scream with terror' (*DG* 12) at the approach of the vampire.[63] Throughout both editions of *The Jewel of Seven Stars*, Silvio constantly draws attention to the occult nature of his double, the mummy cat, alternately the 'Familiar' or 'pet' of the Sorcerer-Queen (*JSS* 198). Latterly, in the penultimate chapter, 'The Lesson of the "Ka"', the cat indicates for Ross and for the reader the transition between Margaret as herself, and Margaret as a phase of Tera by his alternating display of attraction and repulsion as she changes from familiar to unfamiliar, from mistress to stranger. The consistent behaviour of the cat may be taken by the reader as a 'spiritual index', a piece of evidence that may be applied later to the Great Experiment in an empirical reading. Renfield performs a broadly similar function in *Dracula* being, as Seward puts it, 'mixed up with the Count in an indexy kind of way' (*D* 248).

For much of the Great Experiment, Silvio is largely inactive. Attention is directed exclusively to the release of the smoke from the Coffer, and its effect on the participants. As the Experiment reaches its conclusion (one could not say climax), the cat makes a reappearance. Ross recalls:

> Silvio was troubled; his piteous mewing was the only sound in the room. Deeper and deeper grew the black mist…. I could still hear Silvio, but his mewing came from close under; a moment later I could feel him piteously crouching on my foot. (*JSS* 1912, 303)

The language here closely resembles that in 'The Lesson of the "Ka"', when Silvio retreats from the possessed Margaret 'with a piteous "miaou"' (*JSS* 194; *Jewel* 1912, 281) to nestle at Ross's ankles. The implication is, therefore, that Silvio has again retreated from the presence of Queen Tera whom he sees as an unwelcome counterfeit of his mistress. This behaviour may, of course, suggest that the body of the Queen has indeed been quickened, if only for a short time, by the Experiment. Given, though, that the sun has risen by the end of the Experiment (*JSS* 1912, 303), and that Tera's voluntary period of confinement within the mummy, announced in 'The Lesson of the "Ka"' (*JSS* 193) is therefore over, Silvio's behaviour may with equal ease indicate that the spiritual presence of Tera has returned one last time to the body of Margaret before the former's earthly existence is destroyed with her physical body. As Silvio hurriedly returns to his owner as soon as the smoke has cleared from the room (*JSS* 1912, 306) this latter would seem the most likely conclusion to be drawn.

The thwarting of epistemological and ontological doubt appears thus to be the whole point of the changes made between the two editions of *The Jewel of Seven Stars*. The first edition inspires religious doubt, but in its apparent drive to suppress that doubt asserts a multiplicity of contradictions. The Experiment *has* apparently succeeded, but the intervention of the wind is ambiguous. The removal of the wind is thus essentially the removal of a code of belief. Hence, in the revised text, the suppression of doubt, of contradiction, is achieved with greater effect through the substitution of a scientific code whose presentation of evidence is more clearly defined.

It is possible that Stoker was not aware of the radical theological possibilities which the outcome of the first edition of *The Jewel of Seven Stars* presented. These may well have been brought to his attention by the occultist J.W. Brodie Innes who acknowledged Stoker's gift of a presentation copy of the novel with the words:

> I think you have in some measure surpassed yourself – it is not only a good book, it is a great book.
>
> When I see you again, there are various questions I want to ask you about it. It seems to me in some way, you have got a clearer light on some problems which some of us have been fumbling in the dark after for long enough.[64]

There is no evidence to link Stoker either to Brodie Innes's occult lodge, Alpha et Omega, or to Aleister Crowley's Golden Dawn, as some biographers have suggested.[65] However, it is evident that the first edition of the novel does permit Brodie Innes to construct a subversive reading out of the fictional intersection of science and religion. The speculations of characters such as Ross and Trelawny have effectively been regarded as those of the author.

Faced with such possibilities, Stoker may well have consciously exercised the form of self-censorship and authorial self-regulation which, in 'The Censorship of Fiction', he terms 'The Necessary Reticence'. Such a practice, which he later argues ought to be exercised by authors of 'problem' novels, 'is the first line of defence against such evils as may come from imagination – itself pure, a process of thought, working unintentionally with impure or dangerous material'.[66] The second edition is thus modified in such a way as to make the theological doubt conventionally ambiguous, and therefore more easily dismissed. But the contradictions, of course, still remain; as does the theological discourse, which has, effectively, become elided under the empirical or scientific presentation of the Experiment.

*

*The Jewel of Seven Stars* and *Under the Sunset* present, therefore, two contrasting demonstrations as to how horror may combine with theological or doctrinal apologetics in a fictional text. In the allegories of *Under the Sunset*, the language and imagery of horror function as rhetorical tools which support a mythical though identifiable Christian universe, a universe whose lessons and ethics are pertinent to the non-fictional world of the child. The problematic presence of horror within a series of Christian allegories is dissipated – for the author at least – by its purposeful employment, and by its underlining of the inevitable defeat of evil at the hands of a beneficent Deity. In *The Jewel of Seven Stars*, by contrast, graphic horror is an incidental appendage of a rhetorical process which, intentionally or not, has generated a sense of ontological unease – a horror grounded in epistemology rather than mere description. The changes to *The Jewel of Seven Stars* – whether made by or at the behest of the author – intervene in and disrupt the ontological horror conclusively and, incidentally, render the final carnage unnecessary. As Victor Sage argues, in such cases theology 'plays a role at the level of cause, and of effect'.[67]

# 2

## 'Un Vrai Monsieur':
## Chivalry, Atavism and Masculinity

> Mr. Irving is fortunate in having for his manager a muscular
> Christian like Mr. Bram Stoker. Should the popular tragedian
> ever get out of his depth, he knows that his faithful Bram is
> ready to take the necessary header, and be to the rescue.
>
> The Entr'acte, 23 September 1882[1]

There is a still discernible ironic edge to The Entr'acte's response to
Stoker's attempted rescue of a Thames suicide. Through the incident,
the columnist mocks the theatrical partnership of Irving and Stoker,
holding up the latter as a sort of managerial Sancho Panza to his
employer, and suggesting further that this physical heroism may be
paralleled by equally spectacular feats of business acumen in the
future.

The satire, however, is in itself a pertinent index of the cultural
construction of positive, heroic masculinity during Stoker's lifetime.
The implication here is not so much that Stoker is literally a follower
of Charles Kingsley and Thomas Hughes, but rather that he possesses
the *directed* muscularity that characterises the Muscular Christian. For
Hughes,

> the least of the muscular Christians has hold of the old chivalrous
> and Christian belief, that a man's body is given to him to be trained
> and brought into subjection, and then used for the protection of
> the weak, the advancement of all righteous causes, and the sub-
> duing of the earth which God has given to the children of men.[2]

Read in this context, the journalist's satire is not inappropriate.
Stoker's own account of his education at Trinity College Dublin, for

example, mentions his academic achievements before moving onto an assessment of his career as 'Athletic Champion of Dublin University':

> I had won numerous silver cups for races of various kinds. I had played for years in the University football team, where I had received the honour of a 'cap!' I was physically immensely strong. In fact I feel justified in saying that I represented in my own person something of that aim of university education *mens sana in corpore sano*.[3]

An intimacy is thus forced between the educated and the physical: those who are merely muscular, Hughes argues, are nothing more than 'musclemen'.[4]

The gentlemanly caste to which Stoker was perceptibly aligned by birth, education and inclination was, as Hughes suggests, supported through images and ethical values drawn from a nineteenth-century appropriation of mediaeval chivalry.[5] As Mark Girouard argues, 'By the end of the nineteenth century a gentleman had to be chivalrous, or at least if he were not he was not fully a gentleman':

> A chivalrous gentleman was brave, straightforward and honourable, loyal to his monarch, country and friends, unfailingly true to his word, ready to take issue with anyone he saw ill-treating a woman, a child or an animal. He was a natural leader of men, and others unhesitatingly followed his lead. He was fearless in war and on the hunting field, and excelled in all manly sports; but, however tough with the tough, he was invariably gentle to the weak; above all he was always tender, respectful and courteous to women, regardless of their rank. He put the needs of others before his own ... as a landlord he took good care of his dependants. He was always ready to give up his own time to come to help of others, especially those less fortunate than himself.[6]

Stoker's writings consistently embody this conception of acceptable masculinity, no more so than where they address the relations between the sexes. Stoker states in *A Glimpse of America*, for example:

> One of the most marked characteristics of American life is the high regard in which woman is held. It seems, now and then, as if a page of an old book of chivalry had been taken as the text of a social law. Everywhere there is the greatest deference, everywhere a protective

spirit. Such a thing as a woman suffering molestation or affront, save at the hands of the criminal classes – which are the same all the world over – is almost unknown, and would be promptly resented by the first man coming along.[7]

Here is the basis of a process of exclusion. Stoker's rhetoric is suggesting that a man, for which we may here substitute *gentleman*, behaves in a certain way and affirms a certain standard. Others – and by default this includes women as well as criminals – do not.[8] America – implicitly white, Anglo-Saxon America – is thus doubly attractive to the author.[9] Chivalry has overwritten race and, in doing so, has affirmed it. The maturity and lineage of the United States as 'England's first-born child' (*GA* 47) are therefore verified through the unfeigned chivalry of what Stoker suggests are its representative classes.

In Stoker's fiction the principle of chivalric activity penetrates the concept of the hero, making him also a gentleman, his actions as well as his morals a reflection, not always explicit, of a knightly ideal. But in this balancing of the physical and the ethical there is still room for ambiguity. A hero may apparently be deficient in some quality but still be finally counted as gentlemanly. A character may, at first sight, appear a gentleman but be proved 'Other' as the novel proceeds. Further, the novels may be seen to delight as much in the physicality and sheer power of their heroes, as the author does in his auto-biographical representation of himself. The Christian moral values are thus not the only ones which count. Hence when the novels seek to impose a moral closure, creating effectively the illusion of a single discourse, the result is not always convincing because the reader has already experienced multiple and potentially *contradictory* discourses as the character oscillates between 'muscleman' and muscular Christian.

The implication is, however, that the gentleman will always retain the distinctive quantum of his station, even where it is masked for a time by circumstance. Hence, in *Lady Athlyne*, Lord Athlyne, travelling incognito, comes to the attention of a female servant, a Frenchwoman in the employ of the heroine:

She stopped to admire the tall chauffeur whom she thought the handsomest man she had ever seen. She did not know him.... She stood back and pretended to be looking in at a window as she did not care to be seen staring openly at him. Then she saw that he was no ordinary chauffeur. It was with a sigh that she said to herself:
'*Voila! Un vrai Monsieur!*'[10]

The manner in which Athlyne is outwardly presented to the servant masks his status as a nobleman and a war hero, details of which the reader is already aware but regarding which the servant has no knowledge.

This fictional situation might serve as an emblem for the reader's perception of the hero throughout Stoker's fiction. The advancing of equivocal or conflicting signifiers in the text is the unfamiliar garb which makes the hero's status at times less than clear to the perceiver. Occasionally, this uncertainty may even suggest the edge of a perversely uneasy relationship between the author and the masculine standard, in that qualities other than those conventionally associated with the gentleman may apparently be lauded through the rhetoric of a narrator. But, the argument runs, the hero (if such he is) will always be recognised, even in the most unpromising of circumstances; it will be proven, as it were, through the rhetoric of the novel that he is, unavoidably, *un vrai monsieur.*

## To introduce Patrick to his new self

Arthur Severn's chance encounter with Norah Joyce, an Irish peasant girl, in *The Snake's Pass* amply demonstrates the extent to which his status as a gentleman relies upon a readership capable of participating in the same discourse of masculinity. Severn recalls:

> She was so frank, however, and made her queries with such a gentle modesty, that something within my heart seemed to grow, and grow; and the conviction was borne upon me that I stood before my fate. Sir Geraint's ejaculation rose to my lips:
> 'Here, by God's rood, is the one maid for me!'[11]

Full cognisance of Severn's allusion demands a certain standard in literacy as much as social manners, as the novel does not supply a source for the quotation. The plot is comprehensible whether or not the reader is aware of the provenance of the remark. The reader who recognises its source, however, has access also to a series of less-explicit chivalric and literary parallels throughout the novel. Severn is quoting Tennyson's Arthurian Idyll, 'The Marriage of Geraint':

> He [Geraint] found an ancient dame in dim brocade;
> And near her, like a blossom, vermeil-white,
> That lightly breaks a faded flower sheath,

> Moved the fair Enid, all in faded silk,
> Her daughter. In a moment thought Geraint,
> 'Here by God's Rood is the one maid for me.'[12]

Though Sir Geraint and Severn initially hear rather than see the beloved, who is in both cases a girl 'Of broken fortunes', both fall in love effectively at first sight.[13] Such behaviour is typical of Stoker's heroes.[14] As the narrator of *Lady Athlyne* notes following one such encounter:

> Passion may later burn the rapture into fixed belief, as the furnace fixes the painted design on the potter's clay; but in that first moment of eyes looking into answering eyes is the dawn of love – the coming together of those twin halves of a perfect soul which was at once the conception and realisation of Platonic belief. (*LA* 72–3)

In Stoker's fiction, however, this gesture is not so much romantic as part of a complex process by which an appropriate sexual companion may be attached to the heroic male.

In part this is purely contextual, a matter of localised eugenics. The female is invariably an excellent breeding partner to complement the fictional hero. Norah Joyce is conventionally beautiful, as Arthur confirms:

> she was tall and beautifully proportioned. Her neck was long and slender, gracefully set in her rounded shoulders, and supporting a beautiful head borne with the free grace of the lily on its stem. (*TSP* 75)

This, though, is complemented by healthy blood, signified by her 'rosy' blush, and by signs of sturdy industriousness: 'Her hands were shapely, with long fingers, and were very sunburnt and manifestly used to work' (*TSP* 75). The signifiers are mixed here. 'Shapely' suggests superior breeding; 'sunburnt' and 'manifestly used to work', the peasant. The 'and' is a copula which aligns and makes seamless two opposed values. Vested in the male's choice, and in the female's frequently reciprocal and immediate response, however, may be found a further political fable.

The male in each case emblematises one component of a political or racial alliance. In *Lady Athlyne* and *The Mystery of the Sea* respectively,

Lord Athlyne and Archibald Hunter become allied to American heroines, each of whom combines distant British ancestry with a more
recent pioneer heritage. The father of Joy, the heroine of *Lady Athlyne*,
is, for example, 'a stranger to this country; though ... claiming Scottish
forbears' (*LA* 275). There is a myth in such cases of renewal, of re-
investment in the old nation, an enriching of the old blood with the
vitality of the new. Rupert Sent Leger, again, in *The Lady of the Shroud*
makes a racial match with the appropriately named Balkan princess,
Teuta, bringing peace to Eastern Europe and a further European ally for
Britain. The theme of teutonic brotherhood, of a blood relation which
embraces family, race and nation, is again notable.

As Nicholas Daly and David Glover suggest, Severn's wooing of
Norah Joyce emblematises an alliance between Britain and Ireland.[15]
However, the specific Tennysonian allusion of Severn's meeting yields
further Arthurian associations readily assimilable to the novel's political script. The selection of the name *Arthur* for the hero is significant.
The name has resonances in kingship, fraternity and national unity –
Arthur was styled as a king upon whose presence the well-being of the
land depended.[16] This latter convention combines easily in Stoker's
novel with the omnipresence of the shifting bog at Shleenanaher to
encode a projection of Anglo-Irish relations within an oblique
re-presentation of an episode from the Arthurian legend – namely, the
waste of the kingdom of the maimed Fisher King.[17]

The scene is carefully set. Two Irish estates lie barren as a consequence of the usury and obsession of a local Gombeen Man or
money-lender, and the encroachment of the sterile and unstable mass
of the shifting bog. A local inhabitant tells Arthur:

> The mountain wid the lake on top used to be the fertilest shpot in
> the whole counthry; but iver since the bog began to shift this was
> niver the same. (*TSP* 23)

Phelim Joyce, father of Norah and owner of the more prosperous of the
two farms, is, like the Fisher King, maimed. His injury is intimately
connected to his fall from prosperity, as a local inhabitant informs
Arthur:

> 'Mr Joyce borryed some money, an' promised if it wasn't paid back
> at a certain time that he would swop lands. Poor Joyce met wid an
> accident comin' home with the money from Galway an' was late,
> an' when he got home found that the Gombeen had got the sheriff

to sell up his land on to him ... an' the poor man'll to give up his fat lands an' take the Gombeen's poor ones instead.' (*TSP* 51)

The fertile land is left unworked as the Gombeen searches it for buried treasure. The Arthurian legend is disturbed at this point but survives, encoded, in a 'modern' technological form. The novel is explicit both as to how the treasure is sought, and who seeks it. Dick Sutherland, a former school fellow of Arthur, employed by the Gombeen, Murdock, explains the process to Severn:

'... we have poles on opposite sides of the bog with lines between them. The magnet is fixed, suspended from a free wheel, and I let it down to the centre from each side in turn. If there were any attraction I should feel it by the thread attached to the magnet which I hold in my hand.'
   'It is something like fishing?'
   'Exactly.' (*TSP* 62)

Murdock, though, is aided in his search by Dick *and* Arthur. The latter's participation, however, has an implicit drive towards speeding the departure of the Gombeen Man from both estates, which Arthur eventually purchases, so aiding the regeneration of the land.

For all this resemblance, the bog, rather than Joyce's injury, is the central emblem of the waste of the region. The bog in general is, in English prejudice, an overt signifier of Irish topography, and the source of derogatory racial stereotypes – the bog dweller, the 'bog trotter'.[18] In *The Snake's Pass* it is an especially rich symbol, one which encodes a reading of Irish problems and British solutions into the fabric of a supposedly local issue. As Arthur is informed when he takes shelter in the Widow Kelligan's shebeen, the shifting bog has become closely identified with Murdock and his activities through the myth of its creation – a version of the expulsion of the snakes from Ireland by St Patrick in which the King of the Snakes transforms himself into the shifting bog (*TSP* 23). In this reading, Murdock is 'a black shnake ... wid side-whishkers', his behaviour such that, as one local jokingly proclaims, 'Begorra! we want St Pathrick to luk in here agin!' (*TSP* 26).[19]

But the bog is also the source of the constant teasing of Arthur by his Irish car-driver, Andy Sullivan, who associates it with his employer's interest in Norah. On one occasion, Arthur is alone, gazing romantically out towards the Atlantic. He recalls:

Andy's voice beside me grated on me unpleasantly:
'Musha! but it's the fine sight it is entirely; it only wants wan thing.'
'What does it want?' I asked, rather shortly.
'Begor, a bit of bog to put your arrum around while ye're lukin' at it,' and he grinned at me knowingly. (*TSP* 58)

The main burden of Andy's chaffing is that women, like the shifting bog, are fickle, unpredictable, ambiguous in their relation to male power. Later in the novel, for example, he cautions Arthur to marry in youth rather than old age, warning his employer that in the latter case young wives are too often inclined to be 'wantin' – aye and thryin' too – to help God away wid ye!' (*TSP* 99–100).

When regarded as a synonym for woman – or, specifically, for Norah Joyce – the bog easily equates also to the popular visual personification of Ireland as a woman, exemplified by Sir John Tenniel's Hibernia in *Punch*, or the figure of Erin in the nationalist press. In Irish nationalist journals with a largely urban middle-class readership, such as *The Weekly Freeman* and *The Irish Pilot*, Erin is, like Norah Joyce, a noble and sorrowful maiden, beset by an invariably male power.[20] The physical elements which L.P. Curtis considers characteristic of the nationalist personification of Ireland as Erin – 'a stately as well as sad and wise woman ... her hair was long and dark, falling well down her back; her eyes were round and melancholy, set in a face of flawless symmetry' – are all present in Norah Joyce.[21] Norah has, as Arthur observes, 'a rich mass of hair as black and as glossy as the raven's wing':

> Her face was a delicate oval, showing what Rossetti calls 'the pure wide curve from ear to chin.' Luxuriant black eyebrows were arched over large black-blue eyes swept by curling lashes of extraordinary length.... (*TSP* 75)

The reader, unlike the hero, realises that this supposedly unknown girl *is* Norah, and will fully appreciate the cause of her 'deep unhappiness' (*TSP* 73), the local male power struggle between her father and Murdock. In *The Snake's Pass*, therefore, this replication of Erin is *not* beset by the occupying, English power normally associated with nationalist polemic. In this respect, Norah equates not merely to Erin but also to Tenniel's Hibernia, a passive figure characteristically portrayed as distressed by a troublesome and rebellious indigenous population, appealing in sisterhood to a Britannia of somewhat militant bearing.[22]

The consequence of this combination of two opposing visions of the Irish political impasse is that *The Snake's Pass* permits England to be personified through an emblematically named and positive male figure, while Ireland is rendered as a multiplex signifier of negative masculinity, femininity and sterile, unworkable ground. In conversation with Severn, Sutherland, an English drainage engineer, pointedly recalls the Bog of Allen at Kildare, regarded as an unsolvable Irish problem in the nineteenth century:

> He told me of the extent and nature of the bog-lands – of the means taken to reclaim them, and of his hopes of some heroic measures being ultimately taken by Government to reclaim the vast Bog of Allen which remains as a great evidence of official ineptitude. (*TSP* 56)[23]

Through the analogy of the bog *The Snake's Pass* suggests Ireland to be a victim of itself, rather than of the British presence. The 'heroic' British quantum of 'Government' is here played off against what is rhetorically rendered as Irish 'ineptitude'. Dick is suggesting Irish difference as an equivalent of Irish backwardness, Irish inability.

Murdock is central to this conceit. Immediately, the Gombeen is not a gentleman. He is thus incapable of any form of empathy with either Arthur or Dick, as the latter comes to realise:

> 'Of course I don't expect a fellow of your stamp to understand a gentleman's feelings – damn it! how can you have a gentleman's understanding when you haven't even a man's. You ought to know right well that what I said I would do, I shall do.' (*TSP* 60)[24]

As Dick's concluding remark indicates, the behaviour of the gentleman, unlike that of the Gombeen Man, is regular, reliable and bounded by ethical as well as written law. Indeed, the Gombeen Man is an embodiment of Irish difference, a social institution whose position could not be generated under English conditions. England possessed no legislative equivalent of the 1849 Irish Encumbered Estates Act, whereby the tenant of an insolvent landlord was faced with the choice, often at short notice, of purchasing his holding or risking a sharp rise in rent under a new, possibly absentee, landlord.[25] The pressing need for regular repayments generated a form of

land-based usury, which is in *The Snake's Pass* skilfully conflated with
the worst aspects of landlordism, frequently attributed by the nationalist Irish to both Anglo-Irish and English landowners.[26]

Murdock, though, is neither English nor Anglo-Irish. Indeed, the
Gombeen's powers appear to be beyond legal as well as moral control,
as Arthur discovers during a dialogue in Kelligan's shebeen. Arthur
attempts to define Murdock as 'a sort of usurer'. A local resident
responds:

> 'Ushurer? aye that's it; but a ushurer lives in the city an' has laws to
> hould him in. But the gombeen has nayther law nor the fear iv law.
> He's like wan that the Scriptures says "Grinds the faces iv the
> poor"...'(*TSP* 26–7)[27]

The financial transactions enacted between the Gombeen and his
debtors are, in the eyes of non-nationalist observers such as Arthur,
irregular, inconsistent and incompatible with the alleged regularity of
their English equivalents.[28] Murdock in this sense functions as a negative 'Other', in constant opposition to Arthur and to all that is
encoded in the latter's construction.

The moneylender in Stoker's fiction is more characteristically
portrayed through the unscrupulous and negative figure of the Jew, a
point at which race conventionally intersects with 'unacceptable'
fiscal behaviour. The Jew is typically structured as an impostor within
the community, his superficial veneer of Christian gentility beguiling
the unwary into financial ruin, as the narrator of *The Man* suggests: 'Mr
Cavendish, whose real name was Shadrach, looked so virtuous and
benignant that an inexperienced person would have really thought he
was conferring a favour.'[29] By portraying Murdock as a nominal
Roman Catholic rather than as a Jew, *The Snake's Pass* effectively
disrupts the conventional pattern of opposition between English and
Irish, Saxon and Celt.[30] The 'real' oppressor is structured as a figure
indigenous to the community, one whose practices emblematise the
stasis of that community and the choking parochialism of its organ-
isation. Conventional social, political and racial relationships are thus
inverted in order to produce a situation where the Englishman, the
gentleman who will later become the new landlord for the district, is
effectively active on behalf of the oppressed populace – bringing the
benefits of regular banking and more fertile land from the point at
which the bog and the Gombeen are swept simultaneously out to sea
as a consequence of the latter's greed and spleen.

The fictional construction of Murdock thus forecloses any potentially negative readings of Arthur's intervention that may originate in an Irish nationalist audience. Arthur's Englishness, and the colonialist code that it embodies, is diluted, made wholly positive by context. Hence Arthur may buy up land without comment because he is both less negative than Murdock and making an entry into the community through marriage to Norah, a nominal Protestant beloved of both communities, so much that 'even the nuns in Galway, where she was at school, loves her and thrates her like wan iv themselves, for all she's a Protestan'' (*TSP* 97).

For all this, the plans for the region formulated by Arthur and Dick reveal a somewhat conventional series of priorities, where the advantages gained through change will in the first instance benefit the landowner rather than the community. Dick explains to Arthur the potential of the latter's purchases:

'Why, my dear fellow ... it will make the most lovely residence in the world, and will be a fine investment for you. Holding long leases, you will easily be able to buy the freehold, and then every penny spent will return many fold. Let us once be able to find the springs that feed the bog, and get them in hand, and we can make the place a paradise. The springs are evidently high up on the hill, so that we can not only get water for irrigating and ornamental purposes, but we can get power also! Why, you can have electric light, and everything else you like, at the smallest cost.' (*TSP* 177–8)

As Dick makes clear, the proposed changes are associated with a leisured rather than agricultural future for the mountain. The entire paragraph is punctuated by the pronouns 'you' and 'we', contextually loaded so as to exclude the greater community beyond Dick and Arthur.

It is only much further into the actual purchase of the land that the question of the indigenous – that is, Irish – inhabitants is raised. Dick suspects the presence of a streak of limestone in the bedrock beneath the bog. He muses:

A limestone quarry here would be pretty well as valuable as a gold mine. Nearly all these promontories on the western coast of Ireland are of slate or granite, and here we have not got lime within thirty miles. With a quarry on the spot, we can not only build cheap and reclaim our own bog, but we can supply five hundred square miles of country with the rudiments of prosperity, and at a nominal price compared with what they pay now! (*TSP* 202–3)

Again, the sense of personal gain precedes the consideration of other beneficiaries. The 'rudiments of prosperity' advanced by Dick, now formally agent and land-purchaser to Arthur, go beyond the possession, sale and use of limestone. 'Limestone' becomes a metonym for the changes that will take place consequent to Arthur's possession of the land and draining of the bog. In part this implies the replacement of irregular Irish methods, subsistence farming almost, by the regularities of English capitalism, and a division of the productive from the commercial. Arthur notes that Dick 'had devised a plan for building houses for them – good solid stone houses, with proper offices and farmyards' (*TSP* 203). The rhetoric suggests that previous methods have been 'improper', irregular, as opposed to 'proper'. This is implicitly the reason for the region's lack of development. The imposition of English methods – the burden of Dick's somewhat paternalistic 'them' – thus becomes a catalyst which aims to force the indigenous population to cope, to develop or improve according to the rubric of the now-dominant English commercial ethos and methodology. The same logic is apparent in the granting to Andy by Arthur of regular work in place of casual employment (*TSP* 250).

The idyllic community which Arthur and Dick offer is above all *outward-looking*. This is why the novel has Dick propose a harbour whose safety will meet English standards:

> We can build a harbour on the south side, which would be the loveliest place to keep a yacht in that ever was known – quite big enough for anything in these parts – as safe as Portsmouth, and of fathomless depth. (*TSP* 178)

Coupled with the narrator's insistence on the proximity of 'the great Atlantic' (*TSP* 9), the Clare coast becomes less a border and more a gateway to the West; implicitly, the region is now a part of Imperial trade or of British expansion, rather than the limitation of dominion. Stoker was to return to the theme some seventeen years later in an essay describing an International Exhibition held on the site of the former Donnybrook Fair, near Dublin:

> The geographical position of the island, which stands as the outpost on the Western sea; its isolation, emphasised by the neglect of

many centuries; and, from the nature of its natural products, a logical lack of transport facilities – all have tended to create for its inhabitants a personal ignorance both of itself and of the outside world.[31]

The implication here, as in *The Snake's Pass*, is that the 'neglect' is a consequence of a wholly Irish problem, and that change and prosperity are only possible through incorporation rather than separation.

The mythicised past is a cultural standard within Irish nationalism that may too easily be twisted into being the foundation of a Celtic rather than British renaissance.[32] In *The Snake's Pass*, it is effectively discarded with the solution both of the mystery of the missing treasure, and the revelation of the scientific basis of the legend of the King of the Snakes. Swollen with flood water, the shifting bog finally bursts its banks and pours violently into the sea, trapping Arthur who is rescued by the strong hands of Norah Joyce. Dick afterwards connects the legend with the cataclysm: 'By George! though, it is strange! they said the Snake became the Shifting Bog, and then it went out, by the Shleenanaher! – as we saw the bog did' (*TSP* 240). Arthur, though, erects a monument to Norah's 'courage and devotion' on the mountainside previously associated only with the legends of the King of the Snakes and the lost treasure:

On the spot where she had rescued me we had reared a great stone – a monolith whereon a simple legend told the story of a woman's strength and bravery. Round its base were sculptured the history of the mountain from its legend of the King of Snakes down to the lost treasure and the rescue of myself. (*TSP* 246)

In doing so, Arthur effectively demonstrates that he has literally *over-written* the past with the contemporary discourses he embodies. The monument replaces ancient legend with a modern myth of endeavour, and valorises the English, written culture over that of the Celtic, oral culture into which Arthur is first received. Just as the 1907 International Exhibition signifies the passing away of what Stoker calls 'The days of Donnybrook Fair and all it meant, the days of the stage Irishman and the stagey Irish play, of Fenianism and landlordism' and its replacement by 'a strenuous, industrious spirit, spreading its revivifying influence so rapidly over the old country as to be worth more than historical bitterness and sentimental joys' so the palimpsest monolith and its modern legend will serve to 'introduce Patrick to his new self'.[33]

## The fighting quality

Arthur Severn's chivalric masculinity conditions the other discourses embodied in his character. In effect, the altruism and sense of honour conventionally associated with the gentleman are attached also to Arthur's activities as landlord and colonist, permitting these latter to be read as paternalistic rather than merely commercial and imperialistic. Because Arthur is a gentleman, the argument follows, his public activities will be, in Samuel Smiles's words, 'characterised by his sacrifice of self and preference of others to himself in the little daily occurrences of life'.[34] The inverse, however, is also true. The discourses which the character embodies may work reciprocally, undermining the superficial appearance of gentlemanliness as that standard is thrown into juxtaposition with personal behaviour.

Jasper Everard in *The Man* provides a particularly acute example. Emphatically a bourgeois who has recently bought himself into the gentry circles in which his family now move, Everard is represented as 'a gentleman, retired partner of a bank, who had not long before purchased a moderate estate between Norcester and Normanstand' (*TM* 41). The novel's heroine, Stephen Norman, by contrast, enjoys an ancestral inheritance emblematised by the family tombs in the parish church which depict 'an unbroken record of the inheritors since the first Sir Stephen who had his place in the Domesday Book' (*TM* 55). In contrast to Stephen's assumption of the role of Lady Bountiful to her tenants, an extension of her father's position as 'a sort of power to help them' (*TM* 85), Everard brings the 'precise, cold, exact' ethics of the urban bourgeoisie to bear upon his retainers:

> He paid all his dues to the day; and his bills the day before the time allowed for discount had elapsed. He contributed a respectable amount to local charities. His income tax return had never been queried. In his own mind he held himself as a man of honour, and in all matters of exactness fulfilled the letter of the law. But none ever looked to him for sympathy or help; and his tenants, though fairly treated, envied those who held their land from any other estate. (*TM* 196–7)

Superficially, of course, Arthur Severn might be said to be doing exactly the same in *The Snake's Pass*. However, Arthur's British, imperial alternative is rendered positive through the context of gombeenism and Irish insolvency which it strives to overwrite. In *The Man*, premised as it is upon an idealised rural world of benevolent squires and thankful tenants, Everard's behaviour signifies personal gain over and above any greater public benefit.

By implication, therefore, Everard is a 'respectable', legally bound practitioner of the same profession carried on by the 'Shadrach' partner of Cavendish and Cecil or Mr Mendoza, the Hamburg money-lender in *The Watter's Mou'*. The displaced anti-Semitism of the portrayal of the banker is subtle, and is vested primarily in how Everard's attitude to money relates to the social position – or rather, role – to which he has aspired. The mechanical precision of his dealings is here not a laudable quality but an indication of how his business behaviour is, like the speech of the Adelphian Jew in *Dracula*, 'pointed with specie'.[35] Again, the Narrator is careful to point out that Everard 'contributed a respectable amount to local charities' – the subtext to this might be, 'not a *generous* amount'. Most damning of all is the statement that the retired banker systematically 'fulfilled the letter of the law'. Clearly, Everard is at one with the Scribes and the Pharisees here – 'for the letter killeth, but the spirit giveth life' (2 Cor. 3:6). In no sense, therefore, can Everard be expected to found a dynasty which will, as is the case with the family of Stephen Norman, produce better stock through the ages. As the narrator argues:

> The children of such a man seldom improve on their father. On the contrary they deteriorate. The selfishness and the other lower qualities remain and flourish; but the coldness becomes indifference to the feelings of others, and a general want of moral tone. (*TM* 197)

The implication is that, for all his positive self-image and outward adherence to form, Jasper Everard is a fraud; his negative qualities being hardly discernible by other protagonists but visible to the reader. He is demonstrably an egotist – self-centred, self-fostering. This 'indifference' to the feelings of others is, of course, incompatible with the selfless altruism associated with the gentleman.[36]

*

Appearances, however, are not invariably reliable in Stoker's fiction. A more complex example of the intersection of class and egotism with race is presented through the characterisation of the Spaniard, Don Bernardino de Escoban, in *The Mystery of the Sea*. The first sight of the Don is far from promising. Archibald Hunter, the narrator, describes him as 'a high-bred looking, dark man' (*MS* 155). Hunter's emphasis on 'high-bred *looking*' invites the reader to view the Don's qualities from the outset as a sham. The suggestion of darkness is, further, a standard signifier of the negative in Stoker's fiction. In *The Snake's Pass* Arthur Severn recalls Murdock as having 'a dark, forbidding face', though the unbridled racism of Bat Moynahan, who describes the Gombeen as 'a nagur' and 'Black Gombeen' is perhaps closer to the sentiment behind Hunter's remark (*TSP* 30, 196). In invoking the rhetoric of race, both novels release a set of powerful connotations of exclusion and differentiation. A series of oppositions are engaged – black against white becomes in *The Snake's Pass* a conflict between the black, bilious blood of the Gombeen and the healthy bloodstock of Arthur, as testified through their colouring (*TSP* 87, 170). Similarly, the Spaniard, when angry, responds quickly with 'a swarthy flush' in contrast to the 'set white face and flashing eyes' displayed by the American heroine, Marjory Anita Drake (*MS* 194, 160).

In *The Mystery of the Sea*, though, the hostility of dark to light translates more immediately into the opposition of Anglo-Saxon to Latin, the potential conflict underlined by the tension of the Spanish-American War and the racial alliance which Hunter makes with the heroine. Marjory is a lineal descendant of Sir Francis Drake, and is herself therefore a reminder of the historical conflict between England and the Armada. With this latter in mind, there is a further religious factor – Protestant against Roman Catholic – in play, as Hunter realises:

> It was borne in upon me by flashes of memory and instinct that the man was of the race and class from which came the rulers and oppressors of the land, the leaders of the Inquisition. Eyes like his own, burning in faces of deathly white, looked on deeds of torture, whose very memory after centuries can appal the world. (*MS* 160–1)

Hunter's juxtaposition of the two adversaries is thus punctuated with his own sense of racial and religious as well as romantic alliance. Hunter recalls:

> For a period which from its strain seemed very long, though it was probably but a few seconds, they stood facing each other; types of the two races whose deadly contest was then the interest of the world. The time was at any rate sufficiently long for me to consider the situation and to admire the types. It would have been hard to get a better representative of either, of the Latin as well as of the Anglo-Saxon. (*MS* 159)

The English-speaking reader, of course, is invited to concur with the political and racial sentiments expressed in the Anglo-American alliance. Marjory, too, takes pains to undermine any empathy based on the common standard of the gentleman by recalling the blatantly unchivalric behaviour of other members of the Spanish nation during the war. For all the Don's denial that 'The Spanish nation does not make war on women!', Marjory is able to shame him with a description of the *reconcentrados*:

> 'Women and children herded together like beasts; beaten, starved, tortured, mocked at, shamed, murdered! Oh! it is a proud thought for a Spaniard, that when the men cannot be conquered, even in half a century of furious oppression, their baffled foes can wreak their vengeance on the helpless women and children!' (*MS* 160)

Such accusations underscore the suggestion that the Don is somehow not acceptable as a gentleman. For all his courtly manners, therefore, Don Bernardino cannot escape being regarded as *other*, the 'outland man wi' the dark hair' as the Scots seer Gormala MacNiel describes him (*MS* 247).

For all this, Hunter and Drake express somewhat contradictory opinions on their visitor once he has departed. Marjory remarks to Hunter:

> 'I felt it was cruel to say such things to that gentleman. Oh! but he is a gentleman; the old idea seems embodied in him. Such pride, such haughtiness; such disdain of the commoner kind; such adherence to ideas; such devotion to honour!...' (*MS* 162)

There is a point of reflex here to which the reader is not yet wholly privy. The text is permitting Don Bernardino a positive existence in spite of his apparently negative construction. Yet the encoding of this positive charge is such that the characters themselves scarcely seem aware of it at this stage in the novel.

Marjory's intimation that the Spaniard's chivalry is an 'old idea' rather than wholly contemporary provides a valuable clue, as does Hunter's own rendering of the Spaniard into racial type:

> Don Bernardino, with his high aquiline nose and black eyes of eagle keenness, his proud bearing and the very swarthiness which told of Moorish descent, was, despite his modern clothes, just such a

picture as Velasquez would have loved to paint, or as Fortuny might have made to live again. (*MS* 159)

Though the two have not previously met, Hunter confides of the Spaniard: 'there was something in his face which set me thinking' (*MS* 155). This remark alludes to an earlier scene in the novel where Hunter, who has 'second sight', experiences a supernatural vision of a procession of ghostly mariners:

> A vast number of the phantoms had passed when there came along a great group which at once attracted my attention. They were all swarthy, and bore themselves proudly under their cuirasses and coats of mail, or their garb as fighting men of the sea. Spaniards they were, I knew from their dress, and of three centuries back ... these were men of the great Armada.... They were of lordly mien, with large aquiline features and haughty eyes. As they passed, one of them turned and looked at me. As his eyes lit on me, I saw spring into them, as though he were quick, dread, and hate, and fear. (*MS* 22)

The suggestion is taken up again when Don Bernardino visits Hunter at the latter's cottage. Hunter recalls:

> So far as I remember, my thoughts were back with the time when I had seen the procession of the dead coming up out of the sea from the Skares beyond, and of the fierce looking Spaniard who walked alone in their ranks and looked at me with living eyes. I must have been in a sort of day-dream and unconscious of all around me; for, though I had not noticed anyone approaching, I was startled by a knocking at the door.... I went at once and opened the door. I recoiled in pure wonder. There, looking grave and dignified, an incarnation of the word 'gentleman' stood Don Bernardino. His eyes, though now serene, and even kindly, were the eyes of the dead man from the sea. (*MS* 191)

The encounter is seemingly uncanny. Hunter's moment of realisation, however, enforces the common identity (and, indeed, the identical religious commitments) of the two Spaniards as much as it recalls the ghostly incidents experienced earlier by the narrator. The ghostly mariner is an ancestor of the present Don.

The demonstrable presence of an ancient and noble lineage is still not enough to make the Don positive, however. Indeed, it might be argued, there is an atavism as much as a linear inheritance behind the resemblance between the ancient and modern Spaniard. Detected by Hunter in an activity which might be regarded as less than honourable, Don Bernardino responds with almost savage aggression. Hunter recalls how the Don's smile 'showed his teeth, like the wolf's to Red Ridinghood':

> As he spoke, the canine teeth began to show. He knew that what he had to tell was wrong; and being determined to brazen it out, the cruelty which lay behind his strength became manifest at once. Somehow at that moment the racial instinct manifested itself. Spain was once the possession of the Moors, and the noblest of the old families had some black blood in them. In Spain, such is not, as in the West, a taint. The old diabolism whence sprung fantee and hoo-doo seemed to gleam out in the grim smile of incarnate, rebellious purpose. (*MS* 194)

The redefinition of Don Bernardino's colouring neutralises its negative associations by investing darkness and thence difference with nobility. *The Snake's Pass* embodies a similar gesture with regard to Norah Joyce who, in a land of Celts, is a 'perfect beauty of the Spanish type' (*TSP* 75). It is apparent that this valorisation, though acknowledged, is not entirely shared by Hunter – witness both the references to the primitive religious practices of 'hoo-doo' and 'fantee', and the subtle suggestion that Spain is not 'in the West'.

The Spaniard's grimace, though, is a more complicated and problematic racial gesture for the reader. Immediately it recalls the physiognomy of Count Dracula, and with it the ancient, titled lineage, tainted blood, dubious honour and unchivalric attitude towards women expressed some five years earlier in the fictionalisation of the vampire's speech and behaviour.[37] Harker's description of his host reads physiognomy as a reflection of individual character:

> His face was a strong – a very strong – aquiline, with high bridge of the thin nose and peculiarly arched nostrils.... The mouth, so far as I could see it under the heavy moustache, was fixed and rather cruel-looking, with peculiarly sharp white teeth; these protruded over the lips.... (*D* 17)

As Victor Sage and Ernest Fontana argue, the aquiline face of the Count and his exposed canine teeth link him through the discourses of 'Scientific Criminology' to Lombroso's image of the criminal as insane, atavistic and vulpine.[38] Charles Darwin, however, views such grimaces as moments in which the primitive surfaces through the civilised veneer of modern, Western man:

> We may further suspect that our semi-human progenitors uncovered their canine teeth when preparing for battle, as we still do when feeling ferocious, or when merely sneering at or defying someone.[39]

The issue, it would seem, is thus one of self-control: degrees of cultural containment, it appears, separate the lunatic from the vampire, and indeed, from the other aquiline figures which punctuate Stoker's fiction.

Among these figures, a similar hereditary degeneracy may be traced in the Caswalls of Castra Regis in *The Lair of the White Worm*. Sir Nathaniel de Salis takes pains to note the 'dominant, masterful nature' of the family:

> The aquiline features which marked them seemed to justify every personal harshness. The pictures and effigies of them all show their adherence to the early Roman type ... the most remarkable characteristic is the eyes. Black, piercing, almost unendurable, they seem to contain in themselves a remarkable will power which there is no gainsaying. It is a power that is partly racial and partly individual.... (*LWW* 345)

Again, through an old portrait, aquiline features confirm the vindictive nature of the Hanging Judge in Stoker's short story, 'The Judge's House':

> It was of a judge dressed in his robes of scarlet and ermine. His face was strong and merciless, evil, crafty, and vindictive, with a sensual mouth, hooked nose of ruddy colour, and shaped like the beak of a bird of prey. The rest of the face was of a cadaverous colour. The eyes were of peculiar brilliance and with a terribly malignant expression.[40]

There is an ambivalence in such descriptions, a perceptible uneasiness in the relationship of each work to the conventional Victorian values of male chivalry and gentlemanliness. This uneasiness stems from the discursive componentiality of the construction of the male in Stoker's fictions. The manifest cruelty, power and sensuality of the aquiline physiognomy and the associated exposure of the canine tooth arguably signify in each both horror and a degree of fascination. More than one set of evaluative criteria are in play. The moral values of Christianity are not the only ones which may be applied. Hence, what may be deemed 'Other' by these standards may, when viewed through alternative criteria, be judged admirable.

Thus the sensuality of the Hanging Judge – like that of Count Dracula, with whom he shares a preternatural pallor and aquiline features – is unacceptable to Christian morality. The sheer spectacle of his Will, however, employed even as it is for destructive purposes, may be read as energetic, awesome, uncanny – an embodiment of the 'dominant, masterful' qualities that have ensured the survival of the Caswall race, for example. These are the qualities that permit the survival of a dynasty, that allow an individual to cross the centuries, in reputation if not in essence.[41] But the destructive Will, the egotism and self-interest of such characterisations, cannot but be incompatible with the morality of self-sacrifice – hence the turbulence which the reader may experience as the discourses clash in figures such as Don Bernardino.

In *The Mystery of the Sea* a further series of associations effectively undermines the negative connotations of Don Bernardino's grimace. Among Stoker's other characters, the Don shares his facial characteristic with the Egyptologist, Abel Trelawny in *The Jewel of Seven Stars*. Trelawny's daughter is at times ambivalent about her father's temperament. She recalls:

> 'When he is angry I can bear it much better; but when he is slow and deliberate, and the side of his mouth lifts up to show the sharp teeth, I think I feel – well, I don't know how!'[42]

Trelawny is arguably modelled upon the Orientalist Sir Richard Burton, whom Stoker met through Irving. Of two similar remarks in *Personal Reminiscences of Henry Irving*, one is particularly revealing:

> Burton's face seemed to lengthen when he laughed; the upper lip rising instinctively and showing the right canine tooth. This was always a characteristic of his enjoyment. As he loved fighting, I can fancy that in the midst of such stress it would be even more marked than under more peaceful conditions. (*PRHI* I, 355, cf. 359)

In the same volume, Stoker makes a similar observation with regard to Tennyson:

> Tennyson had at times that lifting of the upper lip which shows the canine tooth, and which is so marked an indication of militant instinct. Of all the men I have met the one who had this indication most marked was Sir Richard Burton. Tennyson's, though notable, was not nearly so marked. (*PRHI* I, 200)

Elsewhere, he remarks of Gladstone, 'there was no mistaking that eagle face' (*PRHI* I, 167). As Stoker indicates throughout *Personal Reminiscences of Henry Irving*, the three men are figures whom he holds in the highest regard, Tennyson being in particular 'a name of something more than reverence' (*PRHI* I, 197 cf. 123, 352).

The explanation for the redefinition of these elsewhere atavistic qualities may be found shortly before a comparison of Tennyson and Burton. Stoker argues:

> In a whole group of men of his own time Tennyson would have, to any physiognomist, stood as a fighter. A glance at his mouth would at once enlighten anyone who has the 'seeing eye'. In the group might be placed a good many men, each prominent in his own way, and some of whom might not *prima facie* be suspected of the quality. In the group, all of whom I have known or met, might be placed Archbishop Temple, John Bright, Gladstone, Sir Richard Burton, Sir Henry Stanley, Lord Beaconsfield ... Walt Whitman.... (*PRHI* I, 200)

The embodiment of these qualities, their association with a certain vision of manliness, is the determining factor here. The self-restraint, altruism and purposefulness associated with the conventional encoding of the gentleman ensures that these negative, atavistic qualities are restrained, the love of fighting in particular, held in check until required. These qualities become a potential, a resource upon which the gentleman may draw in the name or cause of honour. The implication is that the Spaniard is a man upon whom Hunter may depend in a crisis – although at this juncture Hunter is yet to foresee such a necessity.

As both Marjory and Hunter acknowledge in their respective descriptions of de Escoban as 'gentleman', the Spaniard is at the very least a social equal of Hunter. But this assumed equality is again problematic in

*The Mystery of the Sea.* The novel has already constructed a racial align-ment which places Hunter and Marjory in opposition to the Don. A disruption of this alliance occurs when the Spaniard effectively privileges the common standard of the gentleman above race, religion and romance – the issues which tie Hunter to Marjory. The Spaniard addresses Hunter:

> 'I come to you, Senor, because it is borne to me that you are cava-lier. You can be secret if you will, and you will recognise the claims of honour and duty, of the highest. The common people know it not; and for the dear ladies who have their own honour, our duties in such are not a part of their lives – nay! they are beyond and above the life as it is to us.' (*MS* 193)

'Cavalier' in this context means the same as '*caballero*' (*MS* 224), a Spanish term denoting both knight and gentleman. To qualify his conduct, which Hunter suggests verges at times on the dishonourable, the Don utilises a highly developed form of the rhetorical question. He explains:

> 'I am bound, despite myself, even if it were not a duty gladly under-taken for the sake of the dead. It was not I who so undertook; but still I am bound even more than he who did. I stand between law and honour, between life and death, helpless. Senor, were you in my place, would you not, too, have acted as I did?' (*MS* 196)

Don Bernardino is enforcing the notion that the treasure and its recov-ery are no longer a matter of politics or religion, but must be evaluated only through the jurisdiction of honour, and with reference to the ancestral trust which the Spaniard has embraced willingly and eagerly as an individual. Called to this bar of the common standard, Hunter can reach only one verdict: '"Sir, you are right! Any man who held to such a duty would have done the same"' (*MS* 196).

The question of priorities, however, becomes acute when the Don solicits – unsuccessfully – the assistance of Hunter in the recovery of the Papal Treasure that forms the basis of the ancestral trust. The Spaniard's rhetoric is again persuasive, based as it is on the common ground of male honour:

> '... Is there no way in which you can aid me to fulfil my trust; and let there be peace between us? ... You already know so much that I am placed almost as though the treasure has already been found.

Thereafter where am I; what am I? One who has failed in his trust. Who has allowed another to step in; and so dishonour him! A moment, Senor, and I am done,' for he saw that I was about to speak. 'It is not the treasure itself that I value, but the trust. If I could make it safe by the sacrifice of all my possessions I would gladly do so. Senor, you are still free. You have but to abandon your quest. It is not to you a duty; and therefore you sacrifice naught of honour should you abandon it....' (*MS* 197)

Hunter's refusal, though, reflects the play of the discourses that intersect in his nationality and religion:

Had the whole affair been a private or personal one; had the treasure belonged to his ancestors, I should have found it in my own heart a very difficult matter to gainsay him, and be subsequently at ease with myself. I remembered, however, that the matter was a public one. The treasure was collected by enemies of England for the purpose of destroying England's liberty, and so the liberty of the whole human race for which it made. (*MS* 198)

This Protestant consciousness, however, reflects equally the discursive interplay within the political relationship into which Hunter has entered with and through Marjory:

the treasure collected to harm England might – nay, would – be used to harm America. Spain was impoverished to the last degree.... This great treasure, piled up by the Latin for the conquering of the Anglo-Saxon, and rescued from its burial of three centuries, would come in the nick of time to fulfil its racial mission; though that mission might be against a new branch of the ancient foe of Spain, whose roots only had been laid when the great Armada swept out in all its pride and glory on its conquering essay. (*MS* 199)

The modernity of Hunter's transatlantic alliance, it appears, is potent enough to overcome Don Bernardino's appeal to the common standard of 'men of honour' (*MS* 197).

The Spaniard's response to Hunter's intransigence embodies both resignation and the restrained and cultivated suggestion of a threat:

'I trust that you will always remember that I tried all ways that I know of, of peace and honour, to fulfil my duty. Should I have to

take means other to discharge my duty, even to the point of life and
death, you understand that I have no alternative.'
'Would you take life?' I said, impulsively, half incredulous.
'I would not scruple regarding my own life; why should I, regarding that of another?' (*MS* 203–4)

This is a crucial statement about the nature of the Spaniard's egotism.
Clearly, what Don Bernardino is suggesting is that, having failed to
succeed in his quest through regular methods, he will now be thrown
upon criteria which are pragmatic rather than systematic. The explicit
lack of knowledge about the course which his future actions may take
is again a statement that he can no longer be regarded as bound by
predictable rules and etiquette. Honour and duty have, in a sense,
eclipsed the behavioural ethics hitherto associated with them.

This insistence on the all-subsuming drive towards the discharge of
duty is reminiscent of Seward's assessment of the lunatic Renfield in
*Dracula*, who he describes as 'a possibly dangerous man, probably
dangerous if unselfish':

In selfish men caution is as secure an armour for their foes as for
themselves. What I think of on this point is, when self is the fixed
point the centripetal force is balanced with the centrifugal: when
duty, a cause, etc., is the fixed point, the latter force is paramount,
and only accident or a series of accidents can balance it. (*D* 61)

The reader may judge Don Bernardino with more certainty than is
available to Seward at this juncture. Clearly, the Don is not an egotist
in the sense exemplified by Jasper Everard. His egotism is in effect the
opposite of self-interest, a sacrificing of everything – self and other –
to an external cause. This is a far less equivocal situation than that
which later pertains between Renfield and Count Dracula. But the
external cause is ancient enough to have apparently become part of
the self, part of the motivation of self, for all the Don's suggestion
that it is an imposition. It is an issue of blood, of racial as much as
familial inheritance. The Don has again fallen into a position of
opposition, of 'Otherness', in the face of Hunter and his fiancée.
Having become for a short period acceptable through his avowed
adherence to a common standard, his explicit, spoken rejection of
that standard, even for the highest and most honourable of motives,
places him in a problematic position that can only lead to his isolation in the novel.

The novel, however, immediately twists the impulse of this version of egotism back against the Spaniard by effectively forcing a definition of the cardinal tenet of masculine chivalry. Hunter has refused to restore the treasure to the Don. However, when Marjory is kidnapped it becomes necessary to solicit the Spaniard's assistance. Hunter addresses Don Bernardino:

'I have come, Sir, to ask your aid, the help of a gentleman; and I feel at a loss how to ask it.' Through the high-bred courtesy of the Spaniard's manner came a note of bitterness, as he answered:
'Alas! Senor, I know the feeling. Have not I myself asked on such a plea; and stooped in vain!'

Hunter is suitably ashamed: 'I had nothing to say in reply to this.' He presses on:

'Sir, I am aware that you can make much sacrifice: I ask, not for myself, but for a lady in peril!' He answered quickly:
'A lady! in peril! Say on Senor!' There was such hope and purpose in his quick tone that my heart instinctively leaped as I went on:
'In peril, sir; of life; of honour. To you I appeal to lay aside your feelings of hate towards me, however just they may be; and come like a true gentleman to her aid....' (*MS* 213)

The Spaniard's spontaneous reaction is in full accord with the deference towards, and defence of, the female expressed in conventional, positive chivalric manhood. It is what Stoker calls in *A Glimpse of America*, 'high regard ... the greatest deference ... a protective spirit' (*GA* 23). As Andrew Smith convincingly argues, chivalry unites the two opposing forces – Latin and Saxon, Roman Catholic and Protestant – against the common enemy of unchivalric and unrestrained behaviour.[43]

The novel, however, tests the Don's motivations further. Hunter remains suspicious following even this display of disinterested zeal, even to the point of speculating whether the Spaniard himself is the abductor. The Englishman's attempt to buy the Spaniard's assistance with the treasure is met with characteristic contempt:

He waved my hand aside with an impatient gesture as he said simply:
'I do not bargain with a woman's honour. Such comes before all

the treasures of Popes or Kings; before the oath and duty of a de Escoban.' (*MS* 214)

'Honour' is the crucial link here. 'Honour', in Stoker's rendering of the female, is a synonym for virginity – as Lord Athlyne suggests to the father of his bride-to-be: 'Joy's honour is as clear and stainless as the sunlight' (*LA* 302).[44] But 'honour' for the male is the defence of that virginity.

In *The Mystery of the Sea* such honour, such purpose, is the salvation also of the Spaniard, and marks his reintegration into the community of the conventionally honourable. He is no longer bound by conflicting loyalties, as he himself observes:

'Ah, Senor, I am happy beyond belief. I am happy as one raised from Hell to Heaven. For now my honour is no more perilled. God has been good to me to show a way, even to death, without dishonour.' (*MS* 214)

Released from the complexities and conflict that lie between personal honour and the trust, he can follow what the text asserts to be the main calling of chivalric manliness. He is a pointer to how Hunter and others like him should spontaneously behave. In taking honour to the point of death in the defence of the female – any female, even the representative of a religion he opposes and a nation he is at war with – the Spaniard purges the negative associations, political and religious as well as physical, with which the text has burdened him. The Don is 'Other' no more. Hunter, now, may recognise him truthfully and without reserve as cavalier, *caballero* – 'a noble fellow ... like a knight of old', as he later puts it (*MS* 261).[45]

## The lesson of the wilderness

Acceptable masculinity is thus, in Stoker's fiction, constructed in part through a clash of 'drives'. An 'exchange' takes place, as it were, between the conflicting demands of egotism and altruism, and between sheer strength and the controlling qualities of restraint and purposefulness. Though gentlemanliness conventionally demands the predominance of altruism and restraint, the egotistical and physical qualities are in a sense celebrated also throughout Stoker's writings. This interface between the physical and the moral is essentially part of a cultural mythology of struggle in which physical and moral fighting are made to overlap. Thomas Carlyle, for example, advises:

> Here too thou shalt be strong, and not in muscle only, if thou wouldst prevail. Here too thou shalt be strong of heart, noble of soul; thou shalt dread no pain or death, thou shalt not love ease or life; in rage, thou shalt remember mercy, justice; thou shalt be a Knight and not a Chactaw, if thou wouldst prevail![46]

The crucial phrase here is 'thou shalt not love ease'. The spectacle of physicality, the life-style based on struggle and exertion, has become a character-building exercise, one which may be conflated through nineteenth-century chivalry with a *rite de passage*, the winning of one's spurs, the achievement of manhood.

In Stoker's fiction this position frequently equates also to a 'Trial by Ordeal', a situation where the ethical state of the male has become visibly disturbed, and where manhood must be demonstrably regained or proved through a process of struggle and trial. Rafe Otwell, the hero of Stoker's eighteenth-century historical novel *Miss Betty*, and of its unpublished first draft, *Seven Golden Buttons*, provides an especially pointed example of this scenario. Exposed as a highwayman by his fiancée, Betty Pole, Otwell is in both versions of the tale sent out by the heroine, in his own words, 'to try to purge my sin and to win honour *again*'.[47]

In *Seven Golden Buttons*, Otwell dies on his quest. The novel elaborates on the perceptible changes in the former reprobate's character through the speech of a galley slave whose freedom Rafe has purchased. The narrator recalls how, on meeting Betty Pole, the former slave:

> gave his message from the dead – from his captain who after fighting for the faith and freedom against the Saracens had fallen in the fight. And Betty listened dry eyed – for it was all long past and she could glory in the regeneration of her lover who had borne himself so worthily.[48]

Through the fight against the Turk, Otwell has become again a 'man who fought for faith and honour' and a leader of men, 'a rallying point for others' (*SGB* f. H14).[49] Christianity, physical valour and honour are closely aligned here. Rafe's final message to the now elderly Betty is triumphant, even at the point of death: 'tell her that had I lived I would have gone to her and claimed my wife as not unworthy' (*SGB* f. H15).

Stoker, however, revised this ending. In the more conventional romantic reconciliation that concludes *Miss Betty*, the youthful heroine not only learns of, but herself experiences, the regeneration of Rafe Otwell. Rafe has returned and is speaking to Betty's guardian, a London Alderman. Both men are unaware that Betty is concealed in an adjoining room. The Alderman demands an explanation for the scars on Otwell's wrists, the visible evidence of the chains he has worn. Otwell replies:

> 'God knows that I have much to answer for; but though I well merited chains and prison, it was not my demerits that set these marks upon my wrists.... They were won for me in battle against the Turks, for Faith and Freedom. For a whole year I wrought in a Turkish galley. But this is not to the point; I deserved to suffer, and I do not dare to repine....' (*MB* 138)

Suffering rather than mere adventure has been the regenerating experience. Indeed, Betty's whole perception of Otwell alters with her knowledge of his suffering:

> and then Rafe spoke, but this time his voice had a new charm for Betty. It was the old voice, strong and full and mellow; but oh, how refined! Even amid her joy at such a change, Betty's heart was wrung with the thought that so much pain to him must have gone to the refining. (*MB* 141)

The ultimately beneficial purpose allocated to suffering, 'the lesson which could do good', in *Under the Sunset*, must be recalled here.[50] This message is given a more intense expression for an adult audience in *The Man*:

> Thus the circle of humanity is completed: a want, an emotion, a passion, a pain, a memory. And then the pristine dust, that has for a time been glorified by the touch of the Creator, and sullied by the touch of life, and purified by pain, goes back to dust again. (*TM* 54)

There is an echo here of the Anglican Burial Office, but the statement presupposes also a cyclical existence, an inevitable trend towards renewal, a return to the innate programming not only of honour but also the invariable qualities rhetorically vested in gender and breeding, before the final dissolution.

*

*The Man*, unlike *Miss Betty*, is not generically an historical novel. In Stoker's Victorian and Edwardian world, where the ship and the train replace the war-horse, and where cash is as ready a weapon for good or evil as the sword, the aspirant must go not to the field of battle but to the margins of civilisation, to engage in a combat where the opposition may not necessarily even be human. Stoker's rhetoric again maps over that of Carlyle in this escalation of the hero into an errant Gentleman-pioneer:

> It is ever indispensable for a man to fight: now with Necessity, with Barrenness, Scarcity, with Puddles, Bogs, tangled Forests, unkempt Cotton; – now also with the hallucinations of his poor fellow Men.[51]

This is, of course, essentially the same situation which Arthur Severn faces in his regeneration of the Shleenanaher in County Clare. It is notable that Severn's own vision of his arrival in the West of Ireland is that of a *rite de passage*:

> I felt exalted in a strange way, and impressed at the same time with a new sense of the reality of things. It almost seemed as if through that opening valley, with the mighty Atlantic beyond and the piling up of the storm-clouds overhead, I passed into a new and more real life. (*TSP* 11)

The drive towards the West is a culturally loaded motif.

Harold An Wolf, by comparison, makes his initial appearance in *The Man* in an apparently more advanced state of mental and physical completion than that suggested by the initially naïve and inexperienced Arthur.[52] At first sight Harold appears the ideal conventional hero. His qualities may easily be encoded into culturally approved signifiers of the physical:

> He was of fine stature, more than six feet two in height, deep-chested, broad-shouldered, lean-flanked, long-armed. He was big-handed, like Sir Beaumains in Prince Arthur, 'called so from the size and beauty of his hands' – signs of knightly breeding in a chivalric age, when the biggest man could wear the strongest armour and the biggest hand could hold the weightiest sword. (*TM* 3–4)

Again, through his height and build, which suggest obliquely Stoker's portrayal of himself in *Personal Reminiscences of Henry Irving*, the hero is a model of *mens sana in corpore sano*.[53] The Narrator continues:

> Altogether he had that appearance of strength, with well-poised alert neck and forward set of the head, which marks the successful athlete. His eyes were grey-blue, his straight hair brown. His high forehead was broadly developed over the eyes. The nose was fair-sized with sensitive nostrils; it was non-aquiline rather than straight. The chin and jaws were broad and massive; the lips, thick rather than thin, were marked at the corners with an iron determination. (*TM* 4)

Harold's athleticism is tempered by an approved and chivalric purposefulness, testified through the allusion to Sir Beaumains. Again, it is scripted as a 'natural' expression of his character: the 'well-poised' lines of his body contrast with those of his rival in love, Leonard Everard, whose limbs are ostentatiously 'held in some kind of suitable poise' (*TM* 134).

Most strikingly, Harold's high forehead and explicitly 'non-aquiline' features distance him from the negative associations of the aquiline physiognomy.[54] He is thus physically far less an equivocal figure than the aquiline Don Bernardino, although he shares with Sir Richard Burton 'the strong mouth and nose, the jaw and forehead' and the positive associations of the adamantine countenance of 'the man as of steel' (*PRHI* I, 352).

This latter in particular must be considered in the context of the racial qualities which Harold has inherited from his Viking ancestors. This is a potential that An Wolf senior is keen to develop in his son:

> 'There never was, my boy, such philosophy making for victory as that held by our Vikings. It taught that whoever was never wounded was never happy. It was not enough to be victorious. The fighter should contend against such odds that complete immunity was impossible. Look at the result! A handful of them from the bays and creeks of the far northern seas would conquer cities and whole lines of coast....' (*TM* 52)

The text has Dr An Wolf, an Anglican clergyman, disarm the negative associations of the Vikings, their paganism and attitude to women in particular, by attaching 'the strength and endurance and resolution of this mighty race' to participation in the morally just causes of the present. Dr An Wolf continues:

'Fight, my boy, fight!... Let your cause be ever a just one; and you need never lack such whilst sin and crime and wickedness and weakness and shame are in the world. Then fight, fight against any odds! If you go down, you go down in truth and honour! And the battle of truth and honour is God's battle!' (*TM* 52–3)

The Viking qualities have here become the equivalent of the 'warrior potential' which is manifested through the exposed canine tooth of Burton and de Escoban. These qualities are a potential, a physical resource of strength, held in check by the conditioning of the gentleman. Their tenacity may be translated into endurance of a less physical type: Quincey Morris in *Dracula* is 'a moral Viking' (*D* 173), the metaphor of Nordic strength applied here without irony to his mental suffering during Lucy's illness, as David Glover notes.[55]

But the Viking inheritance, as both Dr An Wolf and Seward make clear, is further a legacy of strong and enduring blood stock, the potential to breed dynasties (*TM* 52; *D* 173). This is a subtle theme throughout the novel. Harold is not merely a Viking. Though the text takes pains to record his ancestry as 'Gothic through the Dutch' (*TM* 52), the youthful hero is in a sense Saxon also. The correlation of his Christian name and his later eye injury suggest a racial myth symbolically enacted through the novel where the supplanted Saxon blood returns to claim and reintegrate with the stock brought over by the Conqueror, the latter suitably embodied in the emblematically named heroine Stephen *Norman*.

Harold expresses this combination of race and training through healthy, boyish activity and an unhesitating response to circumstance. The 'father's tales' of Dr An Wolf begin with stories of Harold's sporting achievements, recollections 'Of the great cricket match with Castra Puerorum when he had made a hundred not out. Of the school races when he had won so many prizes.'[56] These, though, shade subtly into the depiction of nascent deeds of heroism, including:

the swimming match in the Islam River when, after he had won the race and had dressed himself, he went into the water in his clothes to help some children who had upset a boat. How when Widow Norton's only son could not be found, he dived into the deep hole of the intake of the milldam of the great Carstone mills where

Wingate the farrier had been drowned. And how, after diving twice without success, he had insisted on going down the third time though people had tried to hold him back; and how he had brought up in his arms the child all white and so near death that they had to put him in the ashes of the baker's oven before he could be brought back to life. (*TM* 29)

The reader is given privileged access to but one such incident.

Stephen has, against Harold's wishes, ventured into the crypt in which her mother is interred. Harold enters the church above and hears 'a long, low, sobbing cry, which suddenly ceased':

It was the voice of Stephen. He instinctively knew where it came from; the crypt.... He ran towards the corner where commenced the steps leading downward. As he reached the spot a figure came rushing up the steps. A boy in Eton jacket and wide collar, capless, pale and agitated. It was Leonard Everard. (*TM* 62–3)

The motif of the ordeal in a crypt, tomb or similar chamber occurs frequently in Stoker's fiction.[57] The motif has, inevitably, a range of Gothic associations, though it is essentially a test of bravery and of purpose. This much is evidenced by thoughts of Rupert Sent Leger prior to his participation in an unknown ritual with a possible vampire in the crypt of an Eastern church:

No thought of fear really entered my mind. Every other emotion there was, coming or going as occasion excited or lulled, but not fear.... I knew not only from my Lady's words, but from the teachings of my own senses and experiences, that some dreadful ordeal must take place before happiness of any kind could be won. And that ordeal, though method or detail was unknown to me, I was prepared to undertake. This was one of those occasions when a man must undertake, blindfold, ways that may lead to torture or death, or unknown terrors beyond. But, then, a man – if, indeed, he have the heart of a man – can always undertake.... (*LS* 125)

Leonard Everard, seemingly, lacks 'the heart of a man'. His retreat signals that he has already failed the ordeal. Notably the novel enforces the point that Leonard appears as a boy, in boy's dress – the Eton jacket. In abandoning a woman in distress, he further demonstrates that he does not even possess the makings of a gentleman.

Harold, though, is impressed less by this than by his recollection of 'the white face of the boy who fled out of the crypt' (*TM* 64). The pale face enforces a convention of cowardice which Stoker utilised eleven years earlier in the short story 'The Red Stockade'. A young naval officer is singled out by his commander when he turns pale at the prospect of an impending battle:

> 'Dr Fairbrother, there is a sick man here! Look at his pale face. Something wrong with his liver, I suppose. It's the only thing that makes a seaman's face white when there's fighting ahead. Take him down to sick bay, and do something for him. I'd like to cut the accursed white liver out of him altogether!'[58]

Harold, though, enters the crypt without hesitation. By the aid of a spluttering match he locates the prone form of Stephen. The narrator continues:

> he stooped and lifted Stephen in his arms. She was quite senseless, and so limp that a great fear came upon him that she might be dead. He did not waste time, but carried her across the vault where the door to the church steps stood out sharp against the darkness, and bore her up into the church. (*TM* 63)

Explicitly, Harold thinks 'coolly' and derives no personal fear from his surroundings: his only fear is for Stephen. Her faint, though, indicates that she, like Everard, has failed the ordeal. Clearly, she cannot live up to the masculine promise of her unusual Christian name.

In a sense, though, neither can Harold live up to the overt promise of his physical masculinity. The mediation of the youthful hero primarily through the proud words of his father betrays the weakness with which the novel invests his character. Harold's manhood is incomplete in that his youth and adolescence have effectively been passive, for all his apparent activity. His education has throughout been determined by his father, his deeds of honour undertaken only in response to circumstance. There is no suggestion in the novel that Harold himself has actively sought out either adventure or greater knowledge. The deaths, first of his father and then of his guardian, Squire Norman, Stephen's father, leave him also without ready access to masculine advice.

One important consequence of this is that his regard for womankind, though idealistic, is childish rather than courtly, boyish rather than manly. This is the subtext of Harold's somewhat passive behaviour following the rescue of Stephen from the crypt:

> She did not ask Harold how she came to be out in the church instead of in the crypt when she recovered her senses. She seemed to take it for granted that Leonard had carried her out; and when she said how brave it had been of him, Harold, with his customary generosity, allowed her to preserve the belief. (*TM* 66)

Harold's 'generosity' may be read as his inability to take the sexual initiative, to manoeuvre the self to a favourable position with respect to other, predatory males, even where this concerns only an eleven-year-old child. This may be the perfect manly gesture, but Harold's naïveté does not allow him to consider any sexual advantage that may later arise for Leonard through Stephen's mistake and his own negligence.

The narrator makes the problem plain when describing Harold's relationship to Stephen:

> He knew that he was ignorant of women, and of woman's nature, as distinguished from man's. The only woman he had ever known well was Stephen; and she in her youth and in her ignorance of the world and herself was hardly sufficient to supply to him data for his present needs. To a clean-minded man of his age a woman is something divine. He may know with all his senses that she is a being compact of clay like himself, with all the limitations of the mineral, vegetable, and animal world which curb and lower poor humanity; and yet human weaknesses fade in the glamour of her womanhood. (*TM* 167–8)

'Harold's honest mind' (*TM* 186) is here a disadvantage rather than a mark of virtue. His emotional development is somehow incomplete, even where he is already physically fitted for the combat of life. Part of the struggle of manhood, it seems, must be devoted to seeing beyond the 'glamour' of others, to gaining a realistic view of human nature which is not at odds with honour. The narrator continues:

> It is only when in later life disappointment and experience have hammered bitter truth into his brain, that he begins to realise that woman is not angelic but human. When he knows more, and finds that she is like himself, human and limited but with qualities of purity and sincerity and endurance which put his own to shame, he

realises how much better a helpmate she is for man than could be the vague, unreal creations of his dreams. (*TM* 168)

It is this deficiency in particular that the novel strives to rectify when it has Stephen send Harold into exile following his abortive marriage proposal (*TM* 186). Harold's limited experience has failed to teach him that Stephen cannot be taken at face value. Hence, when Stephen expels him from her presence he takes her dismissal literally: '"... Oh, get out of my sight! I wish to God I had never seen you! I hope to God I may never see you again! Go! Go! Go!"' (*TM* 186). From this point, *The Man*, in so far as it concerns Harold, condenses the elements of both the initial proving of manhood, and the regaining of self-worth after disgrace.

*

Harold's behaviour following his dismissal by Stephen is significant. He departs immediately, literally without looking back:

> It was only when he was far on his journey that he gave thought to ways and means, and took stock of his possessions. Before he took out his purse and pocket-book he made up his mind that he would be content with what it was, no matter how little. He had left Normanstand and all belonging to it for ever, and was off to hide himself in whatever part of the world would afford him the best opportunity. (*TM* 187)

This deliberate accounting of the resources upon which he will found his future is in part a response to Stephen's earlier rebuttal of his marriage proposal:

> 'You thought, I suppose, that this poor, neglected, despised, rejected woman, who wanted so much to marry that she couldn't wait for a man to ask her, would hand herself over to the first chance comer who threw his handkerchief to her; would hand over herself – and her fortune!' (*TM* 185)

But Harold's behaviour is emblematic also of the Proppean, fairy tale logic which Stoker applies to many of his youthful heroes.

Characteristically, like Harold, the hero is an orphan.[59] His childhood, however, is usually straitened, frequently as the deliberate policy of parents or guardians. In *The Lady of the Shroud*, for example, one of Rupert's guardians informs him:

your father and [mother] had agreed that you should be brought up to a healthy and strenuous life rather than to one of luxury; and she thought that it would be better for the development of your character that you should learn to be self-reliant and to be content with what your dear father had left you. (*LS* 36)

Arthur Severn's emotionally starved childhood has been similarly manipulated, as his guardian-aunt advises him, so that 'you may find many pleasures where you thought there were but few' (*TSP* 12). This period of deprivation usually ends with the adoption and financial endowment of the hero by a parental surrogate, often a relation or family friend, an act of selection which is at times detrimental to the benefactor's more immediate – and, we may sense, less worthy – kin.[60] But at some stage after this adoption, the hero himself goes out to prove or affirm his worth and, by association, his entitlement to present or subsequent good fortune. Effectively, these novels insist that, to be whole, the hero must negotiate for himself his own terms with the world. In the words of Harold An Wolf's benefactor, Andrew Stonehouse, 'Every man, as the Scotch proverb says, must "dree his own weird"' (*TM* 318).[61]

Harold's plans emblematise the novel's overwriting of the specific cultural myth of the pioneer. The narrator confides Harold's train of thought:

As for himself, he made up his mind that he would go to Alaska, which he took to be one of the best places in the as yet uncivilised world for a man to lose his identity. As a security at the start he changed his name; and as John Robinson, which was not a name to attract public attention, he shipped as a passenger on the *Scoriac* from London to New York.... The few necessaries which he took with him were chosen with an eye to utility in that frozen land which he sought. (*TM* 189)[62]

The self is conspicuously the most basic of resources. Harold's adoption of an alias affirms this. 'Robinson' suggests not only Robinson Crusoe making the best of his wilderness, but punningly, as 'Robin's son', recalls the names of the horse which Harold rode at Normanstand under Squire Norman's tutelage – Robin Hood (*TM* 35). The name is also an emblem of the 'average', a component part of the mythical British 'middle-class' trio of 'Brown, Jones and Robinson' which Thomas Hughes mentions in the Preface to *Tom Brown at*

*Oxford.*[63] Harold is not merely seeking to lose himself: he is refusing to trade on the credit of his past, to utilise the value of his good name even through its racial signification.[64] Harold must literally *make* a name for himself.

This much is made explicit when Harold rejects an offer of an easy escape from the dishonour he has himself associated with his former name, an offer which may be read structurally as a second act of adoption and endowment. Whilst at sea, Harold saves a child from drowning (*TM* 226–91).[65] The father of the child, the wealthy iron-master Andrew Stonehouse, 'a typical product of the Anglo-Saxon under American conditions' (*TM* 277), thanks Harold in private:

'When you were in the water making what headway you could in that awful sea – when my little child's life hung in the balance, and the anguish of my wife's heart nearly tore my heart in two, I said to myself, "If we had a son I should wish him to be like that." I meant it then and I mean it now! Come to me as you are! Faults, and past, and all. Forget the past! Whatever it was we will together try to wipe it out. Much may be done in restoring where there has been any wrong-doing. Take my name as your own. It will protect you from the result of whatever has been, and give you an opportunity to find your place again.' (*TM* 312)[66]

Harold's rejection of Stonehouse's offer focuses the novel firmly on the assumption that the hero can be regenerated only by his own action, his own achievement. Stonehouse recognises Harold's motives:

'I think you are wise to go away. In the solitudes and in danger things that are little in reality shall find their true perspective; and things that are worthy will appear in their constant majesty. You will prove yourself, your manhood, your worthiness to love and be loved....' (*TM* 318)

Read in this context, the vessel upon which Harold travels into exile bears a highly emblematic name. *Scoria* is the slag or dross of metals; to scorify, to reduce to dross. On the *Scoriac*, therefore, Harold has begun the process of refining the self. Stonehouse states:

'There must be time for you both in any case. For you to regain control of yourself; for her, to purge her nature of that dross whence comes all this woe. For we all have dross in our natures, no matter what proportion of pure gold may be also in our make-up. Believe me that God who knows both you and her has some high purpose in this doing.' *(TM* 317)[67]

Significantly, Harold's return to Stephen is via Canada, on the twice aptly-named vessel, *Dominion.* He leaves his exile by way of a land over which Britain exercises dominion. He has mastered both the wilderness and himself.

*The Man* charts Harold's voyages exhaustively. The narrative, however, is less forthcoming with details of his sojourn in Alaska beyond one protracted scene in which the narrator recounts the background to the rheumatic fever suffered by Harold whilst prospecting *(TM* 395). This incident, though, is rendered largely so as to anticipate the blindness which Harold suffers on his ultimate return to England.[68]

Beyond this incident, the details of Harold's prospecting and success are extremely compressed. Two pages suffice to chart Harold's discovery of an Alaskan goldfield. The climax of this episode is similarly economic:

It is not purposed to set out here the extraordinary growth of Robinson City, for thus the mining camp soon became. The history of Robinson City has long ago been told for all the world. *(TM* 351)

Effectively, of course, the history of Robinson City *has* been told before. It is the cultural myth emblematised in the popular phrase, 'Go West, Young Man!', the expectation that a man who 'goes west' can, if he be resourceful enough, make his fortune. It is in a sense the story also of Andrew Stonehouse.

The voyage west is a frequent signifier of self development in Stoker's fiction, though seldom does it carry the explicit fiscal resonances of Harold's case. Rupert Sent Leger, for example, persistently travels further and further west:

He had gone as a cabin-boy on a sailing ship round the Horn. Then he joined an exploring party through the centre of Patagonia, and then another up in Alaska, and a third to the Aleutian Islands. *(LS* 16)[69]

Such voyages, however, may also be read as racial and imperial myths. The hero – and this is especially true of Harold, and of Seward and

Holmwood through their connection with Quincey Morris – has joined a body of pioneers, the descendants of his own race, a branch of the racial stock demonstrably purified through experience, struggle and challenge.

The myth is one of constant expansion, tempered with a Darwinian underscript of racial improvement and adaptation – as the American heroine Marjory Anita Drake recognises:

> Our nation is so vast, and it expands so quickly, that there is nearly everywhere a family separation. In the main, all the children of one generation become the heads of families of the next. Somehow, the bulk of our young people still follow the sunset; and in the new life which comes to each, whether in the fields or in the city or in the reclamation of the wilderness, the one thing which makes life endurable is this independence which is another form of self-reliance. (*MS* 82)

To follow the sunset is, in a sense, to journey towards an ever-retreating boundary, to seek a horizon whose limits may never truly be reached. The boundaries of civilisation are thus constantly pushed further westward, and each new outpost is shaped on the model of the established west that has been left behind. There is a suggestion of this in Dick's remodelling of the Irish farming community at the Snake's Pass.[70] But in Harold's quest for identity, the order imposed on Robinson City may be read as synonymous with the mastery the hero has brought to bear upon own his internal, mental wilderness. The real point of the condensed narrative of Harold's two years in exile is that 'The Lesson of the Wilderness' – Stoker's emblematic title for the chapter – has been learned. Renewed, chastened and purified by the wilderness he is ready to return. Acceptable to himself, he is now prepared to make himself again acceptable to those he has left behind.

In consequence of his regeneration, however, Harold may be regarded as being equally acceptable to those among whom he currently lives, whether these be the miners and prospectors of Robinson City, who had 'claimed him as their chief' (*TM* 352), or the sailors on the *Dominion*:

> He was able to take his part freely amongst both the passengers and the officers of the ship. Even amongst the crew he soon came to be known; the men liked his geniality, and instinctively respected his enormous strength and his manifest force of character. Men who

work and who know danger soon learn to recognise the forces which overcome both. (*TM* 355)

Such force of character transcends class and affirms race. In *The Lady of the Shroud* the Balkan mountaineers will not respect Rupert Sent Leger's noble though cowardly cousin, Ernest Melton, who 'dropped to his knees in a state of panic' when faced with the prospect of death by beheading. They will, however, acknowledge the 'genuine pluck' of Melton's valet, a stage Cockney who nevertheless confronts his employer's assailants 'in boxing attitude'. The courage behind this defiance is spontaneously acclaimed by those present: 'The mountaineers recognised his spirit, and saluted with their handjars' (*LS* 200).[71] When acknowledging similar qualities in Rupert, however, the mountaineers make a further distinction:

> the men around closed in upon the Gospodar like a wave of the sea, and in a second held him above their heads, tossing on their lifted hands as if on stormy breakers. It was as though the old Vikings of whom we have heard, and whose blood flows in Rupert's veins, were choosing a chief in old fashion. (*LS* 161)

Harold, similarly, is proclaimed chief and captain by the men of Robinson City and the sailors of the *Dominion*: 'to them he was a born Captain whom to obey would be a natural duty' (*TM* 356). For all the irony of the sailors' belief – Harold's distinctive qualities have been achieved as much as inherited – the implication of such scenarios is clear. The acclaim of strong men, of whatever class or race, is a standard to be sought. For Rupert, the acclaim is especially acute in that the Mountaineers are Teutons in the East, new allies for the West.[72] Such situations represent, even within a context of imperial and racial fantasy, the reception into knightly fellowship following the successful completion of the Ordeal and period of errancy.

*

One final example will suffice in conclusion. This is the encounter in *The Shoulder of Shasta* between the American mountain dweller, Grizzly Dick, and the 'calm and gallant' English artist, Reginald Hampden. Dick is effectively outclassed when he gains admission to a San Francisco drawing room, the circle of 'the smartest young people in San Francisco society'.[73] The Narrator reports how Dick:

> with his native taste and daring selected out the prettiest girl in the room ... Dick had opened his conversation with a piece of

complimentary pleasantry such as he would have used to a barmaid in a dancing saloon, nothing coarse, nothing unpleasant, but altogether familiar and out of place in a conventional assembly. The young lady was not offended ... but she saw her opportunity, and led him on. (*SS* 216–17)

This is a tense moment, in that Dick's established and creditable qualities of strength and virility, his 'simplicity and manhood' (*SS* 235), momentarily sit uneasily against his gaucherie. The potential of this juncture is successfully foreclosed by the narrator. Dick, explicitly, is not being 'coarse'. He is not so much a fraud in his social relations as out of his social depth. As is the case with Harold An Wolf and Arthur Severn, Dick had hitherto 'only been tested in ways that brought out his natural force and left it triumphant' (*SS* 223). The integrity of the hunter's manliness, though, is revealed when his version of sexual honour, that most basic standard of the masculine, is challenged. Esse, the object of the mountain dweller's affection, pleads with Dick, who is delivering a marriage proposal:

'Oh, Dick, Dick! not before all these people! They'll think you are making game of me.' One of the smart young men here said:
    'Making game of her! He is a hunter! Good!' Dick turned on him like lightning:
    'Dry up there, mister! I don't make game of no female of her sex; and I don't allow no man to say I do, see?...' (*SS* 222)

Dick may be regarded as socially presumptuous, but there is no doubt from 'his very simplicity, and the honesty of his purpose' (*SS* 218) that his intentions are honourable. It is the relationship between his intentions and the context in which he has been placed that is faulty.

The situation fully revealed, Dick reacts violently, first threatening one of the men present, and subsequently demonstrating his immense physical strength in a dramatic display of anger and shame:

As he spoke he lifted his arm, and with a mighty downward sweep hurled down his bowie knife, so that it stuck inches deep into the oaken floor, where it quivered. (*SS* 228–9)

As a cultivated and manly Englishman, Hampden must rise to the occasion where the American males present have already explicitly failed:

With a sharp jerk, and with a force which made his arm tingle from wrist to shoulder, and sent the blood up into his head, he plucked it from the floor amid a buzz of approval, and a responsive 'Good!' from Dick ... '... Shake! Ye're a man, ye are; and I wish you and Little Missy all the happiness in the world!' (*SS* 230–1)

This is a rich passage which condenses almost the entirety of Stoker's literary vision of the hero. Immediately, there is a chivalric content. The gauntlet is thrown down, and is unhesitatingly picked up by the champion and accepted suitor of the distressed 'Little Missy'. The woman is satisfactorily defended. But the gauntlet here is also emblematically the Arthurian sword in the stone, which can be drawn out only by the rightful leader. Dick, of course, recognises the ascendancy embedded in Reginald's response, and willingly defers to it. The right to lead, as Carlyle would have it, is recognised by those who are themselves a worthy counterpart to the chief.[74] Dick's abdication is a final closure of the problem his presence creates in the drawing room. His positive qualities and his gauche manners can combine successfully only when he is viewed in his own environment. Hampden subsequently takes the penitent Dick out of the salon, introducing him again to the company 'clad in a hunter's outfit' amid 'a buzz of admiration through the room' (*SS* 235). The leader and the led are racially homogeneous, and an alliance is cemented, both through marriage and through an accord with strong men. But through all this is the constant subtext of an inbuilt superiority which permeates Stoker's whole presentation, striving to contain the uneasiness which pertains between the powerful and the ethical. The master of lesser men, the gentleman-hero is the physical equal of the pioneers among whom he moves. But the positive qualities that define him as a gentleman also serve emblematically to assert his superiority, the granting of greater – if not absolute – purposefulness to the muscular. And for Stoker, the Englishman is invariably the most complete of Gentlemen.

# 3
# The Taming of the New: Race, Biological Destiny and Assertive Womanhood

> I do not think that there would be the *remotest* chance of my getting any sale and I should do neither you nor myself any good by putting it on the market. As a slight sketch of a pure and amiable girl *it is* rather pretty – although 'a girl of the period' would hesitate to do what she *seems to think* quite the thing to do – but this of itself won't sell a book.
>
> J.W. Arrowsmith to Bram Stoker, 8 October 1894[1]

The rejection of *Miss Betty* by the publisher J.W. Arrowsmith provides a telling index to the play of discourses which construct women throughout Stoker's fiction. In his role as reader, Arrowsmith has brought into play two opposed late Victorian stereotypes. His terminology is highly technical. The adjective 'pure' signifies a physical and moral as well as mental and spiritual state. As one commentator on female behaviour suggested in 1890, 'a true maiden' should be

> pure and modest, not seeking but being sought, – found out, like the violet among the leaves, rather by her sweetness than her beauty – a maiden of whom all good men would say, 'that is a woman I could love and honour as my wife; a woman I could trust with the happiness of my home and the bringing up of my children.'[2]

By a process of cultural agglomeration, to be 'pure' is thus also to be passive, 'not seeking but being sought'. Conforming to standards imposed and required by a patriarchal establishment, the ideal woman is thus a commodity, '*my* wife', owned alongside '*my* home' and '*my* children'.

In Arrowsmith's rhetoric, this figure functions in diametric opposition to the highly specific concept of the 'Girl of the Period', whose assertive behaviour conventionally suggests a corresponding looseness of morals which 'assimilate her as nearly as possible to a class of women whom we must not call by their proper – or improper – name'.[3] In Arrowsmith's opinion, therefore, the reader's expectation has been violated by the novel. The character and the plot of *Miss Betty* are disjunctive, the novel committing the eponymous heroine to actions which clash with how she is constructed adjectivally. Arrowsmith accepts the 'purity' of the heroine, but dismisses its conjunction with her assertiveness as improbable.

The publisher, however, has failed to acknowledge the limits which the novel places upon Betty Pole's apparent radicalism. The assertive behaviour of Betty, like that of Stoker's other heroines, is contained by a textual structure which consistently returns the female to a conventional passivity by the close of the novel. Stoker's fictions participate in a biologistic and deterministic view of humanity, in which the female is perceived as emotionally and mentally as well as physiologically discrete from the male. In the foreclosed rhetorical space of Stoker's fiction the woman will, after any emotional disturbance, invariably return to the most basic of standards, the difference vested in her sex. Even where her behaviour is for a time modified through the powerful influence of discourses such as race or religion, she cannot escape *being* a woman – nor indeed can she avoid behaving ultimately in a manner prescribed culturally as appropriate for those of her sex.

## The fighting blood of her race

The rhetoric of cultural approval in which Stoker's writings participate clearly echoes the anti-feminist polemic of the time. Writing in *The Illustrated London News* in 1892, Elizabeth Lynn Linton systematically juxtaposes the behaviour of 'Sweet Mistress Dorothy', a supposedly representative girl of 1792, with her equally emblematic counterpart in 1892, claiming that the former 'found her restricted life both pleasant and sufficing; and was content to wait in patience for the day of her social emancipation', before concluding:

> Pure, fair, and innocent, sweet Mistress Dorothy understood, like her mother, the uses of time and the fitness of knowledge to age. She knew that her life's business was to be a good housekeeper, an amiable wife, a devoted mother, a just and well-ordering mistress.[4]

Miss Betty is a close rhetorical cousin of sweet Mistress Dorothy, as their personal titles suggest. Stoker's novel adopts the adjective 'sweet', utilising Linton's positive standard some twenty-eight times during the narrative to signify approval of the heroine. This is in a sense a marked anachronism. Nineteenth-century rhetoric is voiced through eighteenth-century characters such as Betty's fiancé, who describes her as 'a pure, sweet, noble young thing'.[5] A more intensive use of the adjective, and of its derivatives 'sweetness', 'sweetly', 'sweeter' and 'sweetest', is to be found in the interjections of the Narrator.[6]

Through the use of 'sweet', the narrator conditions and maintains the continuity of Betty Pole's manner from the 'sweet, old-fashioned' speech of her childhood to the mild and almost asexual romantic attentions of her majority, where her fiancé's hand is taken and 'pressed ... to her side in the sweet old fashion of her childhood' (*MB* 11, 152). The novel's usage here is an amalgam of Linton's nostalgia and the contemporary construction of the female in both law and culture as an 'adult child'.[7] But the main thrust of the rhetoric is legal-istic and behavioural rather than psychological. Betty willingly defers to male power – to grandfather, father, guardian or husband – throughout the novel. Whatever personal and material advantages the novel has her possess, whatever disruptions she may face and disperse, she remains a vindication of Linton's ideal, the woman who will 'wait in patience for the day of her social emancipation' through marriage, through submission to male power.

This convention of passivity, however, becomes problematic in its particular application to female initiative and resourcefulness. In Stoker's fiction, female initiative is at once laudable and subject to further conditional bounds. It is generated not from the approved encoding of the feminine, but through the presence of the other discourses with which the novel endows the characters. Betty Pole, for example, is inspired not only by the self-interest of love, but also by a purgative and introspective Protestant zeal when she determines to disrupt Otwell's career as a highwayman. The narrator's rhetoric again recalls the role of pain in purification, here as much in the anguish of Betty's prayers as in the physical struggle undertaken by Otwell:

> The burnt offering of charred flesh is poor indeed before the renun-ciation of the soul that pain has burned and purified and made a worthy gift to the Creator of Mankind! (*MB* 93)

*Miss Betty* is an acutely religious text. The moral reform of Otwell is equally the regeneration and purification of his spiritual self. The narrator makes this much clear by observing how, after Betty unmasks and shames Rafe, 'the manhood of him seemed triumphant again, and all the nobler part of the soul within stood revealed without dross' (*MB* 125). Though the point is made more forcibly through the death of Rafe in *Seven Golden Buttons*, the unpublished first draft of *Miss Betty*, it is in both versions this loading of action onto faith, this vision of the woman as redeemer of the dissolute male, that permits Betty to commit the actions which Arrowsmith deemed unacceptable. Her role is thus completely conventional. Woman's mission is, in the words of one commentator,

> To help [man] to overcome evil, to subdue the baser and fouler part of his nature and to rise to the higher altitude of honour, honesty, and unblemished purity.... Her help thus given has saved many an outcast from despair, has lifted many a life from a pit of sensuality and foulness to hopeful usefulness and spiritual blessedness.[8]

It is the extent to which Betty takes her mission – the exposing of the self to danger, the *pursuit* of the highwayman – that is disturbing.

*

The combination of religious zeal with a personal romantic interest is motivation enough for Betty to challenge, albeit for a short time, the bounds of female modesty and passivity. Her unchaperoned meeting with the highwayman functions effectively as an act of closure in that, once her mission is over, she is able to discard assertiveness forever, slipping back easily into the conventional roles of fiancée and wife. A more problematic situation, however, is presented when the forces that support female assertiveness are essentially open-ended and ongoing – innate qualities such as race and family lineage which, in effect, run parallel to, and at times in rivalry with, the biological workings of sex.

In Stoker's fiction, racial qualities are frequently scripted as the retention of an aggressive past. Harold An Wolf in *The Man*, for example, finds the heritage of his Viking ancestors, 'the old Berserker spirit, which had drowsed through ten peaceful centuries', revived by a sea voyage in stormy weather.[9] Such racial qualities, which allow the landsman Harold instinctively to pace the vessel's deck 'like a ship-master' (*TM* 280), are fully appropriate to the hero who may be, at various times, gentleman, knight and pioneer. They sit uneasily, however, against the socially approved submissiveness associated with the female who is, in theory, predestined biologically to motherhood and culturally to marriage.

In *The Lady of the Shroud*, the Voivodin Teuta is, like Harold An Wolf, constructed as the inheritor of Viking blood. The only child of a Balkan warlord, she is sufficiently confident to initiate an unchaperoned meeting with the hero, Rupert Sent Leger, with a racial and class-based imperiousness well beyond his western, bourgeois experience. Rupert, shocked not merely by her presence but by the paucity of her clothing, protests: 'But surely – the convenances! Your being here alone at night! Mrs Grundy – convention – the –'.[10] The 'incomparable dignity' of Teuta's response to Rupert's outburst both silences him and makes him feel 'a decided inferior':

> 'What are convenances or conventions to me! If you only knew where I have come from – the existence (if it can be called so) which I have had – the loneliness – the horror! And besides, it is for me to *make* conventions, not to yield my personal freedom of action to them. Even as I am – even here and in this garb – I am above convention. Convenances do not trouble me or hamper me.' (*LS* 72–3)

The 'convenances' are conventional behavioural proprieties. The garb of which Teuta speaks is a shroud, whose presence permits Rupert to believe his nocturnal visitor to be a vampire. There is thus a double irony in her rebuff; that of the ruler who makes etiquette, and of the dead who do not have to observe it.

The racial investment in Teuta's character permits her further to take up arms with a Teutonic militancy which echoes her name, literally minutes after Rupert has released her from a band of kidnappers:

> The Voivodin held up her tied hands. Again the handjar flashed, this time downwards, and the lady was free. Without an instant's pause the Gospodar [Rupert] tore off the gag, and with his left arm round her and handjar in right hand, stood face toward his living foes. The Voivodin stooped suddenly, and then, raising the yataghan which had fallen from the hand of one of the dead marauders, stood armed beside him. (*LS* 160)

For all this, however, Teuta plays no further part in the ambuscade. The sexually transcendent role which has been generated through the discourses of her racial construction is effectively terminated through a gesture of submission to the man who saved her when she could not save herself. The novel's representation of a fictional local custom arguably betrays an Occidental fantasy of female submission and subservience. Kneeling before Rupert, the Voivodin speaks:

> 'Gospodar Rupert, I owe you all that a woman may owe, except to God. You have given me life and honour! I cannot thank you adequately for what you have done....'
> This was so sweetly spoken, with lips that trembled and eyes that swam in tears, so truly womanly and so in accord with the custom of our nation regarding the reverence that women owe to men, that the hearts of our mountaineers were touched to the quick. (*LS* 161)

Sexual biology here overcomes the imperatives of both race and class, the adverb 'sweetly' standing significantly as the indicator of the triumph of the culturally and biologically 'normal'. From this point, Teuta's actions are secondary to, and conditioned by, those of Rupert Sent Leger, her husband: she is no longer able to act on her own initiative. Royal heir though she is, Teuta must become the conventional chattel of Rupert, 'Teuta Sent Leger', as she ultimately styles herself, rather than the 'Voivodin' (*LS* 211).

Her marriage, though, cannot erase the militant heritage which she bears through her embodiment of 'the fighting blood of her race' (*LS* 168), however. The novel, therefore, forecloses any further threats to her new-found wifely status through the working of a sexual component into the fabric of the racial discourse. Teuta addresses the National Council of her nation in what is effectively her speech of abdication:

> 'We women of Vissarion, in all the history of centuries, have never put ourselves forward in rivalry of our lords.... My lord does not, I fear, know as you do, and as I do too, that of old, in the history of this Land, when Kingship was existent, that it was ruled by that law of masculine supremacy which, centuries after, became known as the *Lex Salica*. Lords of the Council of the Blue Mountains, I am a wife of the Blue Mountains – as a wife young as yet, but with the blood of forty generations of loyal women in my veins. And it would ill become me, whom my husband honours – wife to the man whom you would honour – to take a part in changing the ancient custom which has been held in honour for all the thousand years, which is the glory of Blue Mountain womanhood. What an

example such would be in an age when self-seeking women of other nations seek to forget their womanhood in the struggle to vie in equality with men! Men of the Blue Mountains, I speak for our women when I say that we hold of greatest price the glory of our men. To be their companions is our happiness; to be their wives is the completion of our lives; to be mothers of their children is our share of the glory that is theirs.' (*LS* 224)

The principle of separate spheres of male and female existence is thus explicitly affirmed by a strong woman, who seeks to be an exemplar to her sex and people, to impose this domesticity upon them also. Teuta's words echo those of Katie Cowper who, in 1890, lamented the apparent collapse of discrete gender roles and the consequent withering of 'those womanly virtues which are the glory of a civilised country'.[11] This abdication speech is, further, not a denial of Teuta's race, but its ironic affirmation. The use of 'blood' to signify race and ancestry is pointed. The reworking of the sexual through the addition of the racial in Teuta's speech parallels, for example, the rhetoric of an earlier attack by Linton on politically active women:

> these insurgent wild women are in a sense unnatural. They have not 'bred true' – not according to the general lines on which the normal woman is constructed.[12]

To depart from 'normal' behaviour is thus, in cultural terms, to deny both race and ancestry, to enter into decadence.[13] The Land of the Blue Mountains, in effect, demonstrates to Edwardian Britain that twentieth-century modernity is not incompatible with nineteenth-century values.

## A bonnie bit lassie in the power o' wicked men

The woman actively and willingly taking the initiative is, however, too easily the woman unable to display the culturally desirable quantum of passivity in any conventional way. To maintain a sense of sexual difference, therefore, she must be made to suggest at least a degree of vulnerability and, indeed, availability for the accepted sexual transaction of marriage, before the closure of the novel brings her into conventional relations with the proprietary hero. Notably, Stoker's novels valorise female passivity in part through an association with the premarital state. Stoker consistently constructs his heroines as virgins, capitalising on the tension that exists between the physical condition of virginity and the at times different male and female responses to it. This construction has a functional basis in the transactive nature of patriarchal society. For Stoker's contemporaries, virginity could be read metonymically as a codification of approved behavioural standards for the female. This perception is accelerated into a position in which the female comes to view the self in terms of the desirable quantum of virginity; a position in which the heroine is conscious that it is not the self but the *quality* of the self that is threatened during the course of the text.

Innocence, though, does not necessarily imply ignorance. For the female to acknowledge the importance of virginity is arguably for her to admit also to a degree of knowledge regarding the sexual basis of marriage. This awareness is most often expressed in Stoker's fiction through the heroine's public avoidance of all matters connected with the progress of courtship – in effect, by having her react to the proposal as if it were the consummation. Betty Pole, for example, systematically forestalls Rafe Otwell's attempts to propose marriage, though her efforts ironically kindle her lover's passion still further (*MB* 43–6). The same might be said of the interrupted meetings and lovers' trysts which punctuate *The Snake's Pass*, *The Mystery of the Sea* and *The Lady of the Shroud*.

More provocative, though, is the response of Norah Joyce in *The Snake's Pass*. Arthur Severn has proposed sending his fiancée to finishing school prior to their marriage and eventual honeymoon in Italy. At the suggestion, 'the delicate porcelain of her shell-like ear became tinged with pink':

> As I looked I saw the pink spread downward and grow deeper, till her neck and all became flushed with crimson. And then she put me aside, rose up, and with big brave eyes looked me full in the face through all her deep embarrassment, and said to me:
> 'Arthur, of course I don't know much of the great world, but I suppose it is not usual for a man to pay for the schooling of a lady before she is his wife – whatever might be arranged between them afterwards. You know that my dear father has no money for such a purpose as we have spoken of, and so if you think it is wiser, and would be less hardly spoken of in your family, I would marry you before I went – if – if you wished it. But we would wait till after I came from school to – to – to go to Italy,' and whilst the flush deepened almost to a painful degree, she put her hands before her face and turned away. (*TSP* 157–8)

Arthur's description here fulfils primarily an erotic and immediate purpose, rather than any development of plot. Attention is directed wholly onto the body and reactions of the woman, the male – as character, and as reader reading through the narrator – becoming an observer first of her, and then more subtly of the interest progressively aroused through the act of observation, encoded into reading, itself. The proposal of marriage has already been made and accepted. But Norah Joyce's stammer, blush and reluctance to pronounce even the name of their honeymoon destination both indicates, and draws reader attention to, her adoption of 'Italy' as a mental synonym for defloration. Though *virgo intacta*, Norah Joyce like Betty Pole, is not ignorant of sexuality, though she still stands in direct and positive contrast to Linton's 'emancipated Dolly', who 'shows neither fear nor bashfulness, neither nervous tremor nor maidenly hesitation'.[14]

The signifiers of Linton's approval are here inverted, their conventional import eclipsed by the sexual expediency of the novel. The signs of modesty become the signs of arousal. The description of Norah's involuntary blush is in particular protracted by the narrator, becoming a cogent indicator of the sexual potential that she is forced both to confront and, physiologically at least, to admit to. Her behaviour is both provocative and biologically 'normal'. The anthropologist J.M. Allan, for example, asserts:

> Every normal woman desires to be married, and yearns for children, although from a sublime deceit (also characteristic of feminine nature) she professes indifference and unwillingness to fulfil the great end of her existence. A feigned disinclination to celebrate the nuptial rites, and a simulated repulse, which increases the desires of the male, is common to almost all females of the higher mammalia, and constitutes another very remarkable point of resemblance between the human species and other animals.[15]

Ironically, therefore, the blush and Norah's futile, and indeed provocative, attempts to conceal it behind her hands are potent reminders of her cultural 'normality' – Linton refers elsewhere to what is in effect the opposite of Norah's modesty, the 'unblushing honesty' of the demimonde 'queens of St. John's Wood'.[16] In Norah's case, the hiding of the blush is thus a testimony of the necessity of reconciling sexual feeling with convention. It is a form of 'blushing honesty'. Norah is undeniably sexual in her 'innocence', tempting on account of the very knowingness of her state. Marriage, therefore, is the final gesture in the reconciliation of desire to convention – the granting of a privileged yet still circumscribed and conditional space for the private exercise of 'immodesty'.

*

Like bashfulness, virginity is provocative. It is transient, irrecoverable and therefore desirable. Its removal confers ownership, possession and the modification of perceived worth to other competing males. Stoker's fiction constructs the female as a form of erotic currency constantly in transmission between one male and another, and always before the eye of an implicitly male reader. Stoker's heroines pass from father to suitor, from false lover or potential seducer to 'true' husband, but always in such a way that they are displayed – emotionally and physically – to a male audience of reader, narrator or fictional character. The late Victorian modesty of Stoker's fiction is shot through with a commitment to the eroticisation of the female body, a prurience which the novel itself must strive to contain and control.

Bearing this prioritisation of virginity in mind, *all* incidents in which a female passes between one proprietary male and another are essentially periods of risk, where the threat originates in other predatory males. This threat enables incidents linked to the sanctity of marital ownership, such as the extra-marital affair between Henry Mortimer and Loo Haliday in 'A Star Trap', the fourteenth tale in *Snowbound*. But it is more strongly expressed, and with a greater compulsion for the male reader in particular, through its reworking of the rhetoric of moral outrage when the incident is based not on consent, but on an act of violence or coercion against the woman herself – and thus indirectly against her male 'owner', current or future.

The threat of rape is present in virtually all of Stoker's novels. Like marriage, rape is a transaction whereby ownership and value are modified as a result of male power. Its enactment of possession through force rather than through legality enables it to pre-empt marriage, or to subvert ownership already gained through marriage – a devaluation of the female through the modification of her value in implicitly male eyes. The threat of rape, though, provides an opportunity also for display and titillation. Such is its frequent function in the Gothic tradition – whether in the uncertainty of the relationship between Ann Radcliffe's Emily and Montoni, or in the actual violence inflicted by M.G. Lewis's Ambrosio on his sister Antonia. Stoker's most compulsive and protracted scenes of attempted or potential rape appear in his first-person narratives, where the immediacy of the writing permits the reader to identify with a sense of outrage based more on the portrayed emotions of the proprietary male than on those of the threatened woman herself.

Stoker's constant return to the theme of sexual coercion – in *Miss Betty*, *The Snake's Pass*, *The Lady of the Shroud*, *Dracula* and *The Mystery of the Sea* – signals an uneasy interface between outrage and prurience for both author and reader. Clearly, the signifiers of outrage, like those of cultural approval, are capable of semiotic inversion. Appreciation of the *display*, upon which both outrage and prurient enjoyment are based, opens up the reader – the male reader – to further possibilities of erotic gratification, and to possible identification with the exposed desire to violate – or to *see* violated.

In Stoker's fiction the threat of sexual coercion typically arises when recently engaged or married couples are temporarily separated from each other. This, with the assumed virgin state of the female participants, creates a tense period of transmission – an artificial and dangerous deferral of the marriage celebration or of the honeymoon – a period in which proprietary sexual consummation may be pre-empted by an outsider or outsiders. It is this threat, under the euphemism 'honour', which empowers the abduction of the Voivodin Teuta by Turkish brigands, and equally the kidnap of Norah Joyce by Murdock in *The Snake's Pass*.[17] But the combined tension and titillation are at their greatest in the abduction of Marjory Anita Drake by a group of kidnappers, or as Stoker's novel euphemistically puts it, 'blackmailers'.

Drake has legally married Archibald Hunter, the Narrator of *The Mystery of the Sea*, in secret. The marriage, however, remains unconsummated by mutual consent. As Hunter suggests to Marjory:

> 'Later on – and this shall be when you choose yourself and only then – we can have a real marriage, where and when you will; with flowers and bridesmaids and wedding cake and the whole fit out.' (*MS* 124)

There is a wealth of sexual desire beneath the apparent restraint of this proposal. 'A real marriage' clearly implies more than the external trappings which Hunter lists in his speech. Significantly, Hunter later muses on the wedding night as a time when lovers may 'love each other unfettered' (*MS* 128). Marjory is equally aware of the greater significance of the ceremony as a prelude to sexual activity. On being presented with a wedding, rather than engagement, ring by Hunter she responds:

'But I am too surprised to think. What does it all mean? I thought that this – this sort of thing came later, and after some time was mutually fixed for – for – *it*!' (*MS* 123)

'*It*', and the hesitation which adds emphasis to Marjory's perturbation, carry similar connotations to Norah's use of 'Italy' in *The Snake's Pass*. The wedding service and the wedding night are closely aligned here. This is an intensely sexual relationship, even before actual *coitus*. The novel emphasises throughout that it is Marjory *herself* who must determine when to yield up her virginity, when to advance to the sexual rather than sacerdotal altar. As Hunter himself suggests:

'Remember, dear ... it is only on your account, and to try to meet your wishes at any sacrifice, that I suggested the interval of comradeship. As far as I am concerned I want to go straight to the altar – the real altar – now.' (*MS* 124)

The obvious sexual interest expressed by Marjory, who blushes throughout the scene, and her determination to surrender her virginity on her own terms, add *piquancy* to the rape scenario that follows.

Marjory is kidnapped and is taken out to sea by her captors. In a supernatural premonition Hunter sees the course of events on the ship on which Marjory is held captive. Marjory herself 'looked pale and wan':

But there was resolution in her mouth and nostrils; resolution fixed and untameable. Knowing her as I did, and with her message 'I can die' burned into my heart, it did not need any guessing to know what was in the hand clenched inside the breast of her dress.... (*MS* 252)

The captive has a steel bonnet pin concealed beneath her dress, manifestly as a suicide weapon rather than as a defensive tool.[18] Implicitly Marjory, like the Scots seer Gormala, is aware of the potential dangers faced by 'A bonnie bit lassie in the power o' wicked men!' (*MS* 247). Hunter, though, is forced to watch helplessly as the situation deteriorates, bringing Marjory's fears closer to reality:

my eyes beheld, as though it were through the sides of the ship, a boat pass out from a watercave in the cliffs behind the Rock of Dunbuy. In it I saw, with the same seeing eye which gave me power in aught else, seven men some of whom I knew at a glance to be those whom Marjory had described in the tunnel. All but one I surveyed calmly, and weighed up as it were with complacency; but this one was a huge coal-black negro, hideous, and of repulsive aspect. A glimpse of him made my blood run cold, and filled my mind at once with hate and fear. (*MS* 252–3)

The party boards the ship, and begins to transfer a cargo of stolen bullion from the boat to the hold. The Narrator's eyes are all for the negro, however. Compulsively, Hunter follows his actions:

At a moment, when all others were engaged and did not notice him, I saw the great negro, his face over-much distorted with an evil smile, steal towards the after hatchway and disappear. With the growing of the fog and the dark, I was losing the power to see through things opaque and material; and it came to me as an actual shock that the negro passed beyond my vision. With his going, the fear in my heart grew and grew; till, in my frantic human passion, all that was ethereal around me faded and went out like a dying flame.... (*MS* 253)

Hunter's vision ceases at the apex of tension, the point where the negro begins to move towards his passive and unknowing white, female, virginal victim.

The implied male reader is being manipulated here. The strength of the vision lies not in Marjory's sleep, but in the helplessness of Hunter. He knows – and can do nothing. His vision has ceased at the point where wild imaginings – implicitly, distortions of desires held within the self – take over. The risk is again to property. Virginity is synonymous with the self and its value. By this time, both the reader and Hunter are in possession of a cipher message from Marjory: '... Frightful threats to give me to the negro if any trouble, or letters to friends. Don't fear, dear, shall die first. Have sure means....' (*MS* 235).[19] This is the nature of the 'blackmail' levied upon Marjory, in her guardianship of a self-image based as much upon race as on Hunter's proprietorship. The potential of the situation is thus geared to its effect on the male proprietor – Hunter grinds his teeth 'at every new thought of fear and horror' (*MS* 222).[20] Effectively, though, Marjory strives to retain her virginity as much for Hunter's benefit as for her own.

The novel prolongs the agony even beyond the tortured and intense recollection of Hunter's interrupted vision. Both Hunter and the reader believe temporarily in the immediacy of the event. But Hunter's second sight – like that of the appropriately named Scot Janet MacKelpie in *The Lady of the Shroud* – has consistently been presented as premonitory.[21] The agony begins again, therefore, when Hunter retraces his visionary route, this time in person, with the tortured expectations of the uncompleted vision still obviously in his mind. The threat imposed by the negro is evidenced by Marjory's instinctive reaction as the cabin door opens:

> When I opened the door she started up; the hand in her bosom was whipped out with a flash, and in an instant a long steel bonnet pin was ready to drive into her breast. My agonized whisper:
> 'Marjory, it is I!' only reached her mind in time to hold her hand. She did not speak; but never can I forget the look of joy that illumined her poor, pale face. I put my finger on my lip, and held out my hand to her. She rose, with the obedience of a child, and came with me. I was just going out into the cabin, when I heard the creak of a heavy footstep on the companion way. So I motioned her back, and drawing the dagger from my belt, stood ready. I knew who it was that was coming; yet I dared not use the pistols, save as a last resource. (*MS* 259)

The novel's rendering of Marjory's childlike obedience to Hunter's gesture affirms how totally her racial initiative has been eclipsed. She is made subservient not by the crisis itself, throughout which she has demonstrated her resourcefulness, but by an instinctive – and we are meant to read here, *intrinsically feminine* – yielding to the superior power of the male when present in such situations. Hunter continues:

> I stood behind the door. The negro did not expect anyone, or any obstacle; he came on unthinkingly, save for whatever purpose of evil was in his mind. He was armed, as were all the members of the blackmail gang. In a belt across his shoulder, slung Kentucky fashion, were two great seven shooters; and across his waist behind was a great bowie knife, with handle ready to grasp. Moreover, nigger-like, the handle of a razor rose out of the breast pocket of his dark flannel shirt. He did not, however, manifestly purpose using his weapons – at present at any rate; there was not any sign of danger or opposition in front of him.... Every minute now the wind was rising, and the waves swelling to such proportions that the anchored ship rocked like a bell-buoy in a storm. In the cabin I had

to hold on, or I should have been shot from my place into view. But the huge negro cared for none of these things. He was callous to everything, and there was such a wicked, devilish purpose in his look that my heart hardened grimly in the antagonism of man to man. Nay more, it was not a man that I loathed; I would have killed this beast with less compunction than I would kill a rat or a snake. Never in my life did I behold such a wicked face. In feature and expression there was every trace and potentiality of evil; and these superimposed on a racial brutality which made my gorge rise. Well indeed did I understand now the one terror which had in all her trouble come to Marjory, and how these wretches had used it to mould her to their ends. I knew now why, sleeping or waking, she held that steel spike against her heart. If –

The thought was too much for me. (*MS* 259–60)

Here is outrage. In cultural terms, the negro as rapist is an opponent physically but not racially superior to his victim. His action is implicitly the violation of the superior race by the inferior, the human by the animal, the child by the adult, the mistress by the slave. Again, this is the rhetoric of outrage, but for the reader it carries beneath it the compulsion of pornography.

Despite the perspective of the narrator, the reader is compelled to follow the negro in his painfully slow and deliberate movement across the restricted space of the cabin, his progress emphasised by his facial anticipation and the pathetic fallacy of the rising wind and tide. The male reader, too, anticipates – even relishes – the negro's intent. The whole encounter is a fantasy based on compulsion through strength. It carries within it the notion of the negro male as stud animal, his genitals monstrously magnified beyond western dimensions through the Narrator's meticulous detailing of the weapons and associated adjectives of size. But it is also a pornography of bondage and humiliation – based on the display and absolute humbling of the assertive female before the male, here safely disguised within the 'degenerate' mould of the vengeful 'nigger'.

The force of Hunter's final reminder that the violator is a negro as well as – or rather *instead* of – an individual is the point of reflex which permits the rhetoric of outrage to reassert itself. Hunter states:

Never in my life did I behold such a wicked face. In feature and expression there was every trace and potentiality of evil; and these superimposed on a racial brutality that made my gorge rise. (*MS* 260)

The civilised and chivalric white male reader is reminded here that he cannot safely empathise with the bestial negro. This textual gesture, which attempts to justify the racist violence of Hunter's attack – itself a sexualised thrill to parallel the 'unspeakable wrong' anticipated by the reader through the negro – is an eleventh-hour opportunity for the reader to retreat, transferring his allegiance back to Hunter, his reading of the signifiers of outrage back to their conventional resonance:

> With a bound I was upon him, and I had struck at his heart; struck so truly and so terrible a blow, that the hilt of the dagger struck his ribs with a thud like the blow of a cudgel. The blood seemed to leap out at me, even as the blow fell.... Never before did I understand the pleasure of killing a man. Since then, it makes me shudder when I think of how so potent a passion, or so keen a pleasure, can rest latent in the heart of a righteous man. It may have been that between the man and myself was all the antagonism that came from race, and fear, and wrongdoing; but the act of his killing was to me a joy unspeakable. It will rest with me as a wild pleasure till I die. (*MS* 260)

The blood which Hunter so pleasurably sheds is both a substitute for the aborted defloration – a sort of poetic justice – and an assertion of the mastery of the male – of the white male – in the power of determining life and death. The turning point for the male reader, though, is the forced viewing of *himself,* rather than any deference towards the feelings of the female.

## Wild desires, vague and nebulous as yet

The virginal heroine, though, may herself pose a threat to her own virginity as dangerous as that of any kidnapper or seducer. In *Lady Athlyne*, Joy Ogilvie unknowingly sleeps in an unlocked room adjoining that of her lover, Lord Athlyne, who is travelling under the alias of Richard Hardy. The narrator allows the reader privileged access to Joy's thoughts at the moment of awakening from sleep, a time implicitly when cultural safeguards of self-repression are but partially operative:

> For what seemed a long time, Joy lay in a sort of languorous ecstasy whilst memory brought back to her those moments of the previous day that were sweeter even than her dreams. Again she heard the footsteps of the man she loved coming up rapidly behind her. Again

she saw as she turned, in obedience to some new impulse which swayed her to surrender, the face of the man looking radiant with love and happiness. Again, she felt the sweet satisfaction of living and loving when his arms closed round her and her arms closed round him and they strained each other strictly. Again there came to her the thrill which seemed to lift her from her earthly being as his mouth touched hers and they kissed each other in the absolute self-abandonment of reciprocated passion – the very passing memory of which set her blood tingling afresh; the thrill which set her soul floating in the expanse of air and made all conventions of the artificial world seen far below seem small and miserable and of neither power nor import. Again she was swept by that tide of wild desires, vague and nebulous as yet, inchoate, elusive, expansive, all-absorbing, which proclaimed her womanhood to herself. That desire of wife to husband, of sex to sex, of woman to man, which is the final expression of humanity – the love song of the children of Adam. It was as though memory and dreaming had become one.

The narrator concludes, simply, 'In such receptive mood Joy awoke to life.'[22] The physical intensity of Joy's semiconscious reminiscences is far more erotic than the earlier descriptions of the incidents which she recalls. Memory has not so much become one with dreaming but, rather, has joined with a sexual desire which may only be modestly expressed through its association with Joy's uncontrolled, semiconscious state. The reader is aware also of Athlyne's ironic presence in the adjoining room. Again, the thrill of anticipation, of the seemingly inevitable coming together of the proposed sexual participants, is made available.

The use of 'languor' is highly significant in this context. In *Dracula*, Jonathan Harker succumbs to 'a languorous ecstasy' at the culmination of a highly sexualised vampire attack.[23] In Harker's misreading of vampirism as seduction, 'languor' encodes a body in repose, a morality in abeyance, a sexual appetite no longer dormant.[24] For Joy Ogilvie, 'languor' is the uncontrolled and uncontrollable sexual world of the dream, of the unconscious mind. Joy, though, is clearly perpetuating its relaxed conditions into waking existence, to the inevitable detriment of conventional restraint. The model of personal psychology constructed here is one of perpetual sexual volatility held in check by the wakeful mind. This volatility or sexual assertiveness is a force akin to other compulsive influences such as race. The narrator's reference to Adam – the first of several – is significant. The Bible portrays Eve as the agent in Adam's downfall, and consequently in the Fall of Mankind (Gen. 3:12–19). Joy, too, is a woman temporarily unrestrained by convention or interdiction. The risk here is clearly again that of temptation – of Eve holding out for a second time the sexual apple to Adam.

As Joy enters Athlyne's darkened chamber, the focus switches to his own volatile condition – an unconscious preoccupation with the emotional hinterland 'between memory and expectation' which produces an unmistakably sexual, if not masturbatory, physical reaction. The Narrator notes how

> the imaginative power of the mind had worked on the nerves – and through them on the body – till he too lay in a languorous semi-trance – the mind ranging free whilst the abnormally receptive body quivered in unison. It was a dangerous condition of being in which to face the situation which awaited him.

Significantly, Athlyne knows 'that his love was reciprocated' and that 'his call to his mate had been answered – answered in no uncertain voice' (*LA* 252). The 'situation' which awaits him is, of course, the discovery of the almost unclad and equally aroused figure of Joy in his bedchamber. The danger, encoded again through 'languor', is of a sexuality not wholly under the control of the conscious mind, of the dream erupting into reality for both participants.

The discrete conventions which restrain the sexes are thus simultaneously brought under threat. Awakened by the opening of the window shutter, Athlyne perceives 'a figure between him and the window'. He steps immediately from his bed:

> At the sound of a step on the floor Joy turned. The light streaming in through the unshuttered window showed them in completeness each to the other. The light struck Athlyne full in front. There was instant recognition, even in the unaccustomed garb, of that tall lithe form; of those fine aquiline features, of those dark flashing eyes. As to Joy, who standing against the light made her own shadow, Athlyne could have no doubt. He would have realized her presence in darkness and silence. As she stood in her fine linen, the morning light making a sort of nimbus round the opacity of the upper part of her body, she looked to him like some fresh realization – some continuation in semi-ethereal form – of the being of his dreams. There was no pause for thought in either of the lovers.... Delight had sealed from within the ears of Doubt. Unhesitatingly

they ran to each other, and before a second had passed were locked tightly in each other's arms. (*LA* 252–3)[25]

Their reciprocal vision of completeness is wholly sexual. Athlyne must be viewed in direct light, so as to show to Joy the obvious stigmata of his sexual arousal, the erect phallus being discreetly embedded within 'that tall lithe form' by the narrator. But Joy, also, must be presented in silhouette, with the light at her back – a teasing illusion of nudity which arouses the male again through partial concealment, and which leaves implicit the visibility of her parted legs within the nimbus through an insistence on the opacity of her torso.[26] The Narrator's defensive suggestion that Athlyne 'would have realised her presence in darkness and silence' is merely conventional, therefore. It cannot neutralise the sexual energy already invested in the encounter.

This episode represents an obvious discursive crisis in the novel. At times the narrator even appears to approach a justification of pre-marital sexuality, a denial of the control customarily exercised by church and morality:

But Dame Nature has her own church and her own ritual. In her case the blessing comes before the Service; and the Benediction is but the official recognition that two souls – with their attendant bodies – have found a perfect communion for themselves. (*LA* 254)

This daring suggestion, though, is rapidly retracted as the narrator derides

the believers in natural religion and natural law – those that do not hold that personal licence, unchecked and boundless, is an appanage or logical result of freedom. To these, freedom is in itself a state bounded on all sides by restrictive laws – as must ever be, unless Anarchy is held to be the ultimate and controlling force. (*LA* 254)

Mutual sexual attraction is here seen as part of what the narrator terms 'Cosmic law – that systematised congeries of natural forces working in harmony to a common end' (*LA* 254). Endowed with the racial and eugenic implications that punctuate Stoker's writings, 'love at first sight' is an emblem of order, and encounters such as that between Joy and Athlyne may be viewed as signifying more than mere lust. The formal marriage sacrament thus functions as a religious and legal acknowledgement of the multidiscursive harmony already expressed in the encounter between the British peer and the American heiress. Later, the novel further disarms criticism of its moral integrity through a correct interpretation of Scottish Law, which recognises marriage effected by intention followed by cohabitation or *copula*.[27] Mutual recognition of sexual compatibility permits the apportionment of blame for present amorality equally between the two: 'Shame was not for them, or to them, who loved with all their hearts – whose souls already felt as one' (*LA* 255). Their embrace is, again, the more dangerous because of its spontaneous nature:

> Their circumstances but intensified the pleasure of the embrace. Athlyne and Joy had both felt the same communion of spirits when they embraced at their first meeting out of Ambleside when their souls had met.... Now it was completed in this meeting, unexpected and therefore more free and unhampered by preparatory thoughts and intentions, when body met body in a close if tentative communion. The mere paucity of raiment had force and purpose. They could each feel as they hung together closely strained, the beating of each other's heart; the rising and falling of each other's lungs. Their breaths commingled as they held mouth to mouth. (*LA* 255)

The final consequence of this prurient conjunction, though, remains Unspeakable. The Narrator continues:

> For seconds, in which Time seemed to stand still, they stood body to body and mouth to mouth. The first to speak was the man:
> 'I thought you were in England by late in the evening – and you were there all the time!' He indicated the direction by turning his eyes towards her room. His words seemed to fire her afresh. Holding him more closely to her, she leaned back from her hips and gazed at him languorously; her words dropped slowly from her opened lips:
> 'Oh-h! If we had only known!' What exactly was in her mind she did not know – did not think of knowing – did not want to know. Perhaps she did not mean anything definite. It was only an expression of some feeling, of some want, some emotion, some longing – some primitive utterance couched in words of educated thought, as sweet and spontaneous as the singing of a bird in its native woods at springtime. (*LA* 256)

'Sweet' is not a morally problematic term here. The equivocal potential of Joy's languor is temporarily contained by its expression within a relationship which will later receive the convenient sanction of Scots law. Moreover, as Joy considers Athlyne 'as already her husband' (*LA* 257), there is no suggestion that this is a casual, transient encounter. The novel does not wholly disarm the sexual potential of Joy's languorous condition, however. Though she speaks innocently and unfeignedly, she is at her most natural and primitive in her response to Athlyne's presence. Effectively, her womanly qualities of modesty and restraint are being tested to their limits.

The same is true, of course, of her lover. Athlyne's rapid return to self-control is as much an indication of his distance from the 'primitive' component of his own character, as it is of the superiority of a discrete masculine psychology:

> An educated man, accustomed to judgement and action in matters requiring thought, thinks, perhaps unconsciously, all round him, backward as well as forward; but mainly forward. Present surroundings form his data; consequences represent the conclusion. Himself remains neutral, an onlooker, until he is called on for immediate decision and consequent action.
> So it was with Athlyne. His instant ejaculation:
> 'Thank God we didn't know!' would perhaps have been understood by a man. To a woman it was incomprehensible. Woman is, after all, more primitive than man. Her instincts are more self-centred than his. (*LA* 256–7)

Athlyne is able to view the social consequences – as well as the personal pleasures – of what might have happened had they known of each other's presence. He thus returns to the masculine prerogative of control and assertion, applying the culturally positive ideals of male society onto the at times dangerous and tempting primitive 'Other' of the female.

Of necessity, Athlyne must suppress the outward display of Joy's sexual precocity. The act of suppression, though, is further an act of *possession*, and as such forms part of the transfer of power between the two contracting male parties who have an interest in the disputed female territory. Joy's father, Colonel Ogilvie, has questioned Athlyne on whether *copula* has taken place:

> 'That, sir,' said Athlyne interrupting with as fierce and truculent aspect as had been to the Colonel at any moment of the interview

'is a subject on which I refuse to speak, even to you.' Then after a pause he added:

'This I will say to you as her father who is entitled to hear it: Joy's honour is as clear and stainless as the sunlight. Whatever has taken place has been my doing, and I alone am answerable for it.' (*LA* 302)

Athlyne's reply, of course, is ambiguous enough to be read as an admission of rape or seduction, of the exercise of a purely male force.

Joy, up to this moment of the interview a model of wifely submission, even to her 'downcast eyes', intervenes:

'Father what he says is God's truth. But there is one other thing which you should know, and you must know it from me since he will not speak. He is justified in speaking of my honour, for it was due – and due alone – to his nobility of character that I am as I am. That and your unexpected arrival. For my part I would have –'

'Joy!' Athlyne's voice though the tone was low, rang like a trumpet. Half protest it was, half command. Instinctively the woman recognised the tone and obeyed, as women have obeyed the commands of men they loved, and were proud to do so, from Eden garden down the ages.

'Speak on, daughter! Finish what you were saying.' His voice was strangely soft and his eyes were luminous beneath their shaggy white brows. Joy's answering tone was meek:

'I cannot, father. My ... Mr. – Lord Athlyne desires that I should be silent.' (*LA* 303)

This is one of the closing gestures in a transaction which has already almost been settled by combat rather than treaty. As the Colonel states, conventionally '"It's my place to look after my little girl – till such time as you have registered your bond-rights"' (*LA* 307). However, once the right of ownership has been conceded, the danger of her sexually aware nature becomes contained by the overwhelming – and 'natural' – desire of wife to husband.

When the concept of the female as erotic currency is acknowledged, the gesture in which proprietorship is handed formally from father to husband becomes more than, as Phyllis Roth terms it, 'an awkward image of which unfortunately Stoker was especially fond'.[28] There is a touch of masculine solidarity in such gestures, of the striking of a business deal, the transfer of cash or property, even the signing of a treaty or alliance:

The two men shook hands as do two strong men who respect each other. Joy stepped forward and took the clasped hands between her own. When the hands parted she kissed her husband and then her father; she had accepted the situation. (*LA* 308)

The same triadic gesture, with the same proprietorial resonance, is enacted in *The Snake's Pass, Miss Betty, The Jewel of Seven Stars* and *The Lady of the Shroud*.[29]

Even beyond this formal transfer of proprietorship, the sexuality of the female may still remain titillating for the male reader. Conflating cohabitation with *copula*, for example, Athlyne's Irish nurse asks Joy 'mayn't I have the nursin' av yer childher, the way I had their father before them?' Joy responds:

'But dear Mrs. O'Brien, isn't it a little soon to think – or at any rate to speak – of such things?'
'Wasn't ye married yesterday?' interrupted the old woman. But looking at her lady's cheeks she went on in a different tone:
'But me darlin' – Lady, it's over bould an' too contagious for me to mintion such things, as yit. But I'll take, if I may, a more saysonable opportunity to ask ye to patthernise me. Some time whin ye're more established as a wife thin ye are now!' (*LA* 319)

Given the context, of which Mrs O'Brien knows nothing, her closing remark is doubly ironic. Predictably, Joy is made to blush as she makes her affirmative reply.

The closing sequence of *Lady Athlyne* illustrates the triumph of the novel's attempts to make Joy Ogilvie all things to all men. Moral, Anglican, honour is satisfied by the promise of a second formal marriage and later solemnisation in church, to ratify the Scottish 'irregular marriage' – the latter a source of terminological jokes in the novel.[30] Joy, unlike Norah Joyce, approaches defloration without fear – she may 'gaily' anticipate three honeymoons in accordance with the three marriages effected between her and Athlyne (*LA* 310).

Joy is enabled also by the marital and legal complexities of the novel to remain the nubile virgin in her firm resistance to the institution-alised trappings of matronhood. Preparing for the second marriage, Joy's aunt whispers:

'Joy, you must come to your room and let me dress you properly. I have brought a dress with me.'

'What dress dear?' she asked.

'The tweed tailor-made.'

'But, Judy, dear, I have on a white frock, and that is more suitable for my wedding.'

'That was all right yesterday, dear. But to-day you shall not wear white. You are already a married lady; this is only a re-marriage.' A beautiful blush swept over Joy's face as she looked at her husband writing away as hard as his pen could move.

'I shall wear white to-day!' she said in the same whisper, and stood up. (*LA* 314–15)

Colonel Ogilvie's momentary glimpse of a 'bed with clothing in disarray' (*LA* 258) has already teasingly evidenced a sexual encounter which the reader knows has not taken place.[31] Later, though, the narrator approaches the same topic as explicitly as he dares, presumably for the benefit of male readers still seemingly unsatisfied with the earlier self-exposure of Joy's desire.

In a complete inversion of the deferred honeymoons that characterise the betrothals and weddings of Teuta, Norah Joyce and Marjory Anita Drake, Joy rejects the interval between the second marriage in Scotland and the Anglican marriage in England proposed by her father, and elects instead for an immediate consummation of the relationship. Joy states:

'No! Daddy, that won't do; I'm going with my husband!' She took his arm and clung to him lovingly, her finger tips biting sweetly into his flesh. 'But, Daddy dear, we'll come over to-morrow and lunch or breakfast with you, if we may. Call it early lunch or late breakfast. We shall be over about noon. Remember we have to come from Bowness!' (*LA* 329)

The reader, of course, may be satisfied that there is more than the six miles' distance to account for the late hour of dining. On arrival, their clothing recalls Judy's earlier words to Joy on the eve of the remarriage:

When they came into the room they made a grey pair, for with the exception of Athlyne's brown eyes and hair and a scarlet neck tie, and Joy's dark hair and a flash of the same scarlet as her husband's on her breast, they were grey – all grey. (*LA* 330)

Joy has worn white 'today'. Her adoption of grey is an explicit indicator of her sexual standing, of her recent participation in *copula*.

The narrator takes pains to show that Joy has in no way changed following the loss of her virginity. There is 'a brilliant colour in her cheeks', and her 'scarlet lips' and pearl-like teeth blend the image of the threatening female vampires of *Dracula* with the 'perfect Cupid's Bow' of Norah Joyce's womanly and modest visage (*TSP* 75). Sexuality, once contained, does not cease to exist. Indeed, it becomes part of a more general vivacity which signifies personal fulfilment:

> She was in a state of buoyancy, seeming rather to float about than to move like a being on feet. She was all sweetness and affection, and flitted from one to another, leaving a wake of beaming happiness behind her. (*LA* 330)

The signifier 'sweet' is again conspicuous. Within the relationship there is no ambiguity, no threat of promiscuity. For Joy, poised in the uneasy space between vamp and passive heroine, the change is one of legitimation, of the granting of an arena which sanctions as well as sanctifies the female's physical desire towards the male.

## At one with the grandeur of nature around her

The assertive behaviour of Norah Joyce, Marjory Anita Drake, the Voivodin Teuta and Joy Ogilvie is, in effect, as 'natural' as the 'feminine' passivity to which they eventually return. These heroines demonstrate what might be termed a centripetal view of human nature in which gender is prioritised over and above equally natural racial and familial drives. The situation, however, is markedly different in *The Man*, Stoker's most protracted study of assertive womanhood, where the disruptive force is not innate to the self but imposed from outside. *The Man*, indeed, is Stoker's most direct approach to the question of the relative ascendancy of nature over nurture.

Education is the disruptive influence here. Through the expedient death in childbirth of Stephen Norman's 'sweet and beautiful' mother (*TM* 11), the novel constructs a situation in which the individual whims of the surviving parent may be paramount. This is in itself dangerous. As Elizabeth Lynn Linton suggests in 'Modern Mothers II', mothers 'are the artificers who give the initial touch that lasts for life'; indeed, 'they bring up their daughters on their own pattern.'[32] Stephen is so-named in compensation for the son desired by her father. She is inducted at an early age into prototypically male pastimes and pursuits. The Squire 'never ... quite lost the old belief that Stephen was indeed a son':

> This belief tinged all his after-life and moulded his policy with regard to his girl's upbringing. If she was to be indeed his son as well as his daughter, she must from the first be accustomed to boyish as well as to girlish ways. This, in that she was an only child, was not a difficult matter to accomplish. Had she had brothers and sisters, matters of her sex would soon have found their own level. (*TM* 20–1)

Squire Norman's inclinations are eccentric rather than iconoclastic. Stephen's isolation, though, permits her father to make the assumption that the male and female psychologies are identical rather than discrete and distinctive.[33] As one medical writer argued in 1916, 'It is the training which girls receive which accentuates their female qualities, just as the training which boys receive accentuates their manly characteristics.'[34] Acknowledging that Squire Norman is at odds with much late Victorian and Edwardian psychological thought, the novel may thus be seen as an experimental space for the testing of a hypothesis based on the alleged mental congruence of the sexes, and the value of gendered training.

The dialectic begins almost immediately, and the earliest evidence presented in the novel emphatically supports the conservative rather than radical cause. The novel's omniscient narrator takes pains to ensure that the innate feminine qualities that *should* be present in Stephen are suitably acknowledged. This is in part achieved through occasional narratorial asides which recall the conventional viewpoint:

> But sex is sex all through. It is not, like whiskers or a wedding ring, a garnishment of maturity. Each little item of humanity gurgling in the cradle, or crowing when tossed in brawny arms, has a method of its own. For one sex there are thumpings; for the other tears and such like blandishments. Not that either sex has an absolute monopoly of these means of accomplishing a wished-for end. But averages rule life. (*TM* 19)

The narrator underlines the alleged fundamental difference vested in gender: innate gender identity lies behind the learned responses of maturity. Prototypically, therefore, these responses should reflect that basic identity. The closing equivocation implicitly signals that race, class or other forces may distort the harmony of this overall picture. Arguably, though, it prefigures also Stephen's apparent undermining of difference not merely through the education which she receives, but also through her *conscious* adoption of the mannerisms of the other sex.

As a relatively untutored child, though, Stephen displays what are imaged as unfeigned reactions which link her both to her mother and to her sex. The narrator recalls how, for her father,

> The pretty little ways, the eager caresses, the graspings and holdings of the childish hands, the little roguish smiles and pantings and flirtings were all but repetitions in little of the dalliance of long ago. (*TM* 20)

Again, the narrator emphasises Stephen's instinctive, as opposed to consciously adopted, behaviour – for example, through her deference to Harold An Wolf who has rescued her from a fearful ordeal in her mother's crypt:

> She lent herself unconsciously to the movement, holding fast with her arm round his neck as she used to do. In her clinging was the expression of her trust in him. The little sigh with which she laid her head on his shoulder was the tribute to his masculine power, and her belief in it. (*TM* 65)

Stephen's 'almost hysterical' agitation (*TM* 66), and her fainting in the crypt is, similarly, a textual reminder of her sex by way of an allegedly characteristic female reaction to danger.[35]

Stephen's deference to Harold – at this juncture a surrogate brother, though later to become a legitimate sexual suitor – is characteristic of her present fitness for sexual transaction, even where this is expressed only in the limited sense of dominance and submission in youthful incidents. The narrator has previously noted a seemingly 'unfeminine' dominance exercised over her playmates by the heroine (*TM* 39). Immediately following the crypt incident, however, the central male and female characters in *The Man* are complementary. The narrator's later suggestion that 'like speaks to like in other ways than in words' (*TM* 301) arguably echoes the popular opinion that 'in friendship and in love, individuals seek their opposites and contrasts, not their copies'.[36] For all this, the relationship between the two is sustained during Stephen's adoption of masculine prerogatives not by the signifiers of sexual dissimilarity, which her behaviour at times eclipse, but by underlying similarities of race and breeding.

Stephen's conventionally feminine qualities are subsequently overwhelmed by her eager response to parental approval: 'as he seemed to be pleased when she did anything like a little boy, the habit of being like one insensibly grew on her' (*TM* 24–5).[37] The narrator employs a series of natural metaphors to prefigure Stephen's transition from adolescence to adulthood. The emphasis is on force and inevitability:

> From the nature of her feeling and her peculiar surroundings she could make confidence with no one, and so was being eternally thrown back upon herself. With each throwing back of the little waves of feeling the object at which they aimed was advanced. It was just like when at the incoming of the tide some little piece of wood or seaweed which lay upon the shore is lifted a little with each lapping wavelet, itself the forerunner and symbol of the coming force behind it. The waves spend their effort and fall back into the advancing tide; but with each effort the burden they have carried is moved a little, now and again backward with the recoil, but in the moving with a tendency mainly onward and shoreward on its destined course. (*TM* 108)

Arguably, her unique circumstances can only lead to the further development of her rebellion. The dynamism vested in the image of the waves, though, is related intimately to other signifiers of the inescapability of the innate, as opposed to constructed, human condition. The novel renders this at first briefly:

> The process of nature is one of shocks. The rigour of the nut and the bud has to give way to the swelling force within; and the yielding is only accomplished with somewhere the exercise of dynamic force. (*TM* 20)

The assertion is subsequently made with more direction:

> Nature, in all her various and multitudinous workings, has in all some common principles of procedure. The process by which, enveloped in its own darkness, the seed cell swells, bursts outward and upward towards the light, has doubtless its counterpart in the growth of a mind, a soul. (*TM* 71)

The wave advances and retreats, tending forward but always being drawn back. The 'swelling force', however, 'bursts' and ruptures, leaving the shattered and irreparable past behind. This imagery of dynamic and inevitable forces in opposition draws part of its rhetorical energy from the contemporary debate on women's mental and social equality. Similar images punctuate late Victorian feminist polemic. Frances Power Cobbe, for example, writes of the awareness that 'has stirred an entire sex':

> Like the incoming tide, also, it has rolled in separate waves, and each one has obeyed the same law, and has done its part in carrying forward all the rest ... every one of these waves, great and small, has been rolled forward by the same advancing tide.[38]

If *The Man* is read as a conventional, if not reactionary, gesture against sexual equality, the wave metaphor is, in effect, semantically inverted. The tide is thus not an unequivocal image of sexual equality in *The Man*: though its *tendency* is forward, it fails to signify absolute or comprehensive progress. The bud and the seed are ostensibly smaller, but seemingly more powerful. The rhetorical energy of the wave metaphor is thus turned back in upon itself, asserting through Stephen's experience the opposing viewpoint of the inevitable triumph of the doctrine of sexual *inequality*, the continual necessity of feminine submission in a world that is rightly structured by and for the male.

The narrator grafts upon these images of growth a further erotic text that teasingly charts the inevitable development of Stephen's distinctive sexual characteristics, 'the slender lines of youth and the soft swelling curves of budding womanhood' (*TM* 247). Effectively, the narrator suggests, as Stephen is developing physically as she should, her mind will inevitably follow the lead of her body. This notion of 'rightful' or appropriate development again echoes the anti-feminist polemic of the time:

> Quite as disagreeable as the bearded chin, the bass voice, flat chest, and lean hips of a woman who has physically failed in her rightful development, the unfeminine ways and works of the wild women of politics and morals are even worse for the world in which they live.[39]

In effect, Stephen's cultural rebellion is undermined from its outset by the narrator's constant return to the involuntary, instinctual gestures made by the heroine, and his attention to the physiological changes which she is unable to avoid.

*

Despite the timely intervention of Stephen's explicitly Victorian maiden aunt, Laetitia Rowly – whose function is as much an archaism for the young Edwardian to rail against, as a model to be emulated – the heroine reaches adolescence resembling Linton's 'Girl of the Period', the woman who 'makes between the sexes no distinctions, moral or æsthetic, nor even personal; but holds that what is lawful to the one is permissible to the other'.[40]

However tempting first appearances may be, it is important to note that Stephen Norman is emphatically neither a 'Girl of the Period' nor a 'New Woman' in the popular and iconographic senses of these terms. She does not smoke, for example, in emulation of masculine freedom.[41] Unlike Linton's 'Emancipated Dolly', Stephen has no desire to ride a bicycle.[42] Her participation in sport and 'boyish games' such as cricket is curtailed during childhood on the grounds of social decorum as much as gender – her aunt objecting to a team made up of 'lads from the stable and the garden' (*TM* 39).[43] Even Stephen's hair is *naturally* auburn, linking her to the race whose name she bears as a patronymic, and to popular iconographic notions of volatility of temper, rather than to the 'false red hair and painted skin' of the 'Girl of the Period'.[44]

Where Stephen *does* concur with the external trappings of the emancipated stereotype, her inability to maintain the expected radical image serves to emphasise what she is *not* rather than what she *is*. This is again largely the consequence of the ironic relationship between the reader and the narrator. The narrator makes available to the reader an instinctive drive towards conformity within Stephen Norman, not readily visible to the other characters, and for much of the novel hardly acknowledged or comprehended by the heroine herself.

Hence, Stephen's attempt to become a bluestocking – at Somerville rather than the more evocative Girton – is confounded not by intellectual inability, but by the seemingly uncontrollable tendency of her mind to wander from the *conscious* activity of being a female intellectual.[45] The narrator confides:

> During her visit she had had no one to direct her thought, and so it had been all personal, with the freedom of individuality at large. Of course her mother's friend, skilled in the mind-workings of average girls, and able to pick her way through intellectual and

moral quagmires, had taken good care to point out to her certain intellectual movements and certain moral lessons; just as she had in their various walks and drives pointed out matters of interest – architectural beauties and spots of historic import. And she had taken in, loyally accepted, and thoroughly assimilated all that she had been told. But there were other lessons which were for her young eyes; facts which the older eyes had ceased to notice, if they had ever noticed them at all. The self-content, the sex-content in the endless tide of young men that thronged the streets and quads and parks; the all-sufficing nature of sport or study to whichever their inclinations tended. The small part which womankind seemed to have in their lives. Stephen had had, as we know, a peculiar training; whatever her instincts were, her habits were largely boy habits. Here she was amongst boys, a glorious tide of them; it made now and again her heart beat to look at them. (*TM* 77–8)

The novel is explicit here about nature and nurture, which the narrator calls 'instinct' and 'habit'. Stephen, it is suggested, has been left to her own devices at Oxford and has found her mind straying naturally and inevitably to conventional sexual interests. The narrator is quick to highlight also the differences between Stephen and her elderly academic mentor. The inability of the older woman to appreciate the sexuality invested in the Oxford environment distinguishes her not only from the instinctive portion of Stephen, exposed here, but also from the conservative maiden aunt Laetitia Rowly, who is visibly pleased when Stephen attracts male attention (*TM* 203). The academic female is culturally the sexually indifferent or sterile female, the woman unavailable for sexual transaction in any conventional sense.[46]

Stephen's palpitating heart is more, therefore, than a mere romantic convention. It represents equally a physiological reaction, an involuntary, instinctual indicator of nascent sexual arousal. As the narrator confides, 'it was as a girl that men looked at her, not as an equal' (*TM* 78). Stephen, though, responds to the attention of the undergraduates not with a demand for intellectual recognition but with an emotional reverie which recalls her deference to Harold following her fit in the crypt:

somehow, unconsciously at first, but afterwards more, if not quite, consciously, she found in herself a tendency to look up, to admire. There was some strange want in her; something which she did not know, which was new to her; which was full of delicious, languorous negation of self; not pain, not joy, not sorrow nor regret, not longing; but whose prolonged sensation was ended in tears. A sort of divine dissatisfaction with self which comes when sex begins to stir. (*TM* 78)

Stephen's 'dissatisfaction' here has nothing to do with the cultural disabilities which she has customarily faced, 'the little self-repressions which go to make up the habit of a well-bred woman' (*TM* 70). The 'strange want' is not a desire for a man's rights or privileges. Rather, it is expressive of a notion of the self as incomplete without the conventional coupling of sex to sex. Her languor, though, lends an ominous tone to this newly surfaced consciousness.

This perceived sense of dissatisfaction is extended to the female academic community itself, again inverting the positive and egalitarian resonances of a well-known feminist aspiration. Stephen discards the idealised portraits of intellectual debate presented by progressive educationalists in favour of 'fragments of common-room gossip' and 'half confidences of scandals, borne on whispered breaths' (*TM* 78–9). In consequence,

The glimpse which she had had of her own sex had been an awakening to her; and the awakening had not been to a pleasant world. All at once she seemed to realise that her sex had defects – littlenesses, meannesses, cowardices, falsenesses. (*TM* 79)

Her horrified conclusion, 'Surely, I am not like that!' and subsequent resolution are again rendered as heavily ironic:

If, indeed, she was a woman, and had to abide by the exigencies of her own sex, she would at least not be ruled and limited by woman's weakness. She would plan and act and manage things for herself, in her own way. She had some good models of manhood within the circle of her own life, and she would take from them example and all the lessons of the nature of man which she could get. (*TM* 79–80)

Again, Stephen has valorised her sex through implicitly male criteria. Her dismissive portrait of the lifestyle of progressive womanhood, to which she ostensibly aspires herself, is permeated by the trivialising and marginalising prejudices of contemporary masculine rhetoric, from 'gossip' and 'scandal' to the inferences of hypocrisy – a supposedly biological trait of the female – embedded in whispering and the granting of '*half* confidences'.[47] But she *is* 'like that'. Extremes blur essential issues. In rejecting the 'exigencies of her own sex', Stephen pointedly ignores the instinctive investment in her earlier reaction to male company. Physically, too, her sense of embarrassment at the limitations of womanhood is conveyed through the blush, 'A flood of shame' (*TM* 79) which she instinctively hides behind her hands, a gesture common to almost all of Stoker's bashful heroines.

*

The revelations at Oxford are crucial to the incidents which follow. Having disposed of the distracting eccentricities of the New Woman, and in constructing a virago who is not physically menacing but demonstrably attractive to the male, the novel is in a strong position from which to attack the insistence on equality of action and opportunity which characterises Edwardian feminism. Though a strong case has already been made that Stephen's unique training has eclipsed – though not overwritten – the instinctual qualities associated with her sex, absolute proof is still required that her rebellion can, in the end, only come to nothing.

Significantly, this proof is obtained through a consideration of the question of marriage – a major point of sexual and social interest at which the biological, erotic and culturally radical forces may be said to intersect. Stephen's conscious radicalism places her, arguably, beyond conventional understanding. During an argument on the contemporary position of married women, Stephen's aunt queries:

> 'But what if a woman does not get the opportunity of being married?' Stephen looked at her a moment before saying with conviction:
> 'It is a woman's fault if she does not get the opportunity!'
> The old lady smiled superiorly as she answered:
> 'Her fault? My dear, what if no man asks her?' This seemed to her own mind a poser; as she spoke she raised her lorgnon to look at its effect.
> 'Still her own fault! Why doesn't she ask him?' The lorgnon was dropped in horrified amazement. (*TM* 89–90)

The conclusion of this exchange reduces the sacrament of marriage to a primarily contractual liaison. Stephen continues:

'Marriage is a union. As it is in the eye of the law a civil contract, either party to it should be at liberty to originate the matter. If the twain are to be as one flesh, as the Bible says, and if as we are taught, there should be equal understanding and communion between them, how else is this to be done? If a woman is not free to think of a man in all ways, how is she to judge of the suitability of their union? And if she is free in theory, why not free to undertake if necessary the initiative in a matter so momentous to herself?' (*TM* 90) [48]

Free to think of a man *in all ways*. Free to *undertake the initiative*. Stephen's reference to the flesh in the midst of her tissue of rhetorical questions underscores the sexual possibilities of such freedom in so far that the contract will have physical as well as legal repercussions. All this, though, may be lost behind the assertive rhetoric of sexual politics. When it does come, the proposal thus becomes, first and foremost, an opportunity for Stephen 'to test her own theory; to prove to herself, and others, that she was right' (*TM* 109).

*

The proposal itself is a carefully regulated exercise in bathos, an encounter calculated to contrast with the marriage proposals by women in the so-called 'hilltop' novels and in *fin-de-siècle* works such as Sarah Grand's *The Heavenly Twins*.[49] Demonstrably unable to communicate with her aunt on the subject of marriage, Stephen is further ridiculed as being unable to make her intentions understood by her prospective bridegroom.

Stephen selects for her experimental subject Leonard Everard, a man whose selfishness and egotism she has from infancy misread as independence and mastery (*TM* 41–2). The reader is aware of both this and of Everard's sexual indifference towards Stephen – though there is a titillating potential for change in this latter direction through an oblique reference which links Leonard to the seduction of a servant girl in Oxford.[50] The contractual tone of the letter summoning Everard to the tryst gives no intimation of Stephen's supposedly romantic intentions towards its recipient:

'Dear Leonard, – Would it be convenient for you to meet me to-morrow, Tuesday, at half-past twelve o'clock on the top of Cæster Hill? I want to speak about a matter that may have some interest to you, and it will be more private there than in the house. Also it will be cooler on the shade on the hilltop.
– Yours sincerely, STEPHEN NORMAN.' (*TM* 116)

Indeed, as she later admits, 'he had often been summoned in similar terms and for the most trivial of social purposes' (*TM* 125).

The absolute and complementary ignorance of the protagonists permits a situation where prior anticipation, internal monologue, and external incident may run parallel but with jarring discordancy. Stephen awaits Leonard at a place she herself describes as a *hilltop*:

> very early she became conscious of a distant footstep. Ordinarily she could not have heard it so far off, and this fact came filtered through imagination so that she attributed the additional power to the existence of love. The thought made her blush, and for a little while she sat still in a silent ecstasy. She was awaiting her lover, and it was he whose feet she heard crushing the débris of the wood which lay below. Since Eve waited in the Garden the waking of her lord, down all the ages in every country and under all conditions, this has been a sound to quicken a woman's pulses and to thrill her with delight. (*TM* 126)

On the occasion of this most radical of proposals, Stephen is again emblematised through the conventional romantic signifiers of the blush and the racing pulse. Eve awaits her master: but, the question follows, will she tempt him? The Narrator protracts her obvious expectation, paralleling Stephen's heightened emotion with the approach of the lover:

> To Stephen's straining ears the footsteps seemed wondrous slow, and more wondrous regular; she felt instinctively that she would have liked to have listened to a more hurried succession of less-evenly marked sounds.... the sound of the coming feet brought great joy to Stephen's heart. For, after all, they were coming; and coming just in time to prevent the sense of disappointment at their delay gaining firm foothold. It was only when the coming was assured that she felt how strong had been the undercurrent of her apprehension lest they should not come at all. (*TM* 126–7)

The closing sentence conveys how fragile Stephen's self-confidence actually is. The Narrator though, moves quickly to reassure the reader that Stephen really is a woman who will physically and emotionally complement a worthy suitor:

Very sweet and tender and beautiful Stephen looked at this moment. The strong lines of her face were softened by the dark fire in her eyes and the feeling which glowed in the deep blushes which mantled her cheeks. The proudness of her bearing was no less marked than ever, but in the willowy sway of her body there was a yielding of mere sorry pride.... In all the many moods which the gods allow, to good women there is none so dear or so alluring, consciously as well as instinctively, to true men as this self-surrender. (*TM* 127)

Leonard, however, is neither receptive nor the 'true' man – the latter here a close connotation of the 'true' or fitting husband. His reaction is an emphatic and brutish anticlimax:

As Leonard drew near, Stephen sank softly into a seat, doing so with a guilty feeling of acting a part. When he actually came into the grove he found her seemingly lost in a reverie as she gazed out over the wide expanse in front of her. He was hot after his walk, and with something very like petulance threw himself into a cane armchair, exclaiming as he did with the easy insolence of old familiarity:
  'What a girl you are, Stephen! dragging a fellow all the way up here. Couldn't you have fixed it down below somewhere if you wanted to see me?' (*TM* 127)

Stephen's 'acting' is a complex gesture. She is rehearsing the role of an assertive woman. But she is doing so in a manner and location that retain all the trappings of a conventional lovers' tryst. Again, she is behaving in such a way as to suggest to Leonard that she is not stirred by his approach, or by what his arrival may herald.

Characteristically and instinctively, Stephen misreads Leonard's peevishness as an expression of his masculinity rather than of his individual temper:

Strangely enough, as it seemed to her, Stephen did not dislike his tone of mastery. There was something in it which satisfied her. The unconscious recognition of his manhood, as opposed to her womanhood, soothed her in a peaceful way. It was easy to yield to a dominant man. (*TM* 127)

Again, the novel scripts Stephen's internal yielding as a rather obvious reversal of her previous assertiveness and refusal to adhere to convention. If Leonard were a 'true' man, a fitting partner, then this *would* be the appropriate deference due to his masculinity in the conventional marital relationships prescribed by Allan, Linton, and others.[51] Stephen's unknowing suitor remains obviously unaffected, his casual and unfeigned repose in direct contrast to the agonies of modesty Stephen has suffered in arranging the tryst, her current artifice, and the formality demanded of such an auspicious occasion.

The mockery continues, however. Hot and thirsty, Leonard comments:

> 'I say, Stephen, it wouldn't be half bad if there were a shanty put up here like those at the Grands Mulets or on the Matterhorn. There could be a tap laid on where a fellow could quench his thirst on a day like this!' (*TM* 128)

This passing remark is internalised and developed by Stephen into a 'momentary vision' of

> a romantic châlet with wide verandah and big windows looking over the landscape; a great wide stone hearth; quaint furniture made from the gnarled branches of trees; skins on the floor; and the walls adorned with antlers, great horns, and various trophies of the chase. And amongst them Leonard, in a picturesque suit, lolling back just as at present and smiling with a loving look in his eyes as she handed him a great blue-and-white Munich beer mug topped with cool foam. (*TM* 128)

The romantic investment in this fantasy is wholly the product of the supposedly business-like and contractual mind of Stephen. She has overwritten the casual product of Leonard's temporary, selfish appetite with an edifice of lasting and mutual significance. Further, though, she has failed to note that he has neither smiled nor given the slightest suggestion of a 'loving look' in her direction during his speech. Leonard, in fact, seldom even turns his face towards Stephen during their sojourn on Cæster Hill.

For all her preparation, Stephen has lost control of the situation. Once proposed, the shanty becomes a tool by which Stephen desperately seeks to lead Leonard onto the subject of marriage. As a bargaining tool it becomes associated with her attempts to manipulate Leonard into proposing to her before she proposes to him. This has been an understated element of her plan all along:

In the depths of her heart, which now and again beat furiously, she had a secret hope that when once the idea was broached Leonard would do the rest. And as she thought of that 'rest' a languorous dreaminess came upon her. (*TM* 113)

Stephen's 'languor' is again a danger sign, a suggestion of the sexual possibilities that may arise during the tryst. Leonard, though, fails to appreciate the significance of the shanty:

'It would be for you I would have it built, Leonard!' The man sat up quickly.
   'For me?' he asked in a sort of wonderment.
   'Yes, Leonard, for you and me!' She turned away; her blushes so overcame her that she could not look at him. When she faced round again he was standing up, his back towards her. She stood up also. He was silent for a while; so long that the silence became intolerable, and she spoke:
   'Leonard, I am waiting!' He turned round and said slowly, the absence of all emotion from his face chilling her till her face blanched:
   'I don't think I would worry about it!' (*TM* 135–6)

Her expectation of his performing in response to what she sees as a recognisable and prototypical engagement scenario is stressed *seven* times during their encounter, destabilising both Stephen's avowed intention to propose and the myth of her control over her own destiny.

Ultimately, Stephen is carried forward not by her feminism, but by her own strength of character, a biological or innate force, the inheritance of pride, race and breeding. Frustrated, she muses:

Was it all worth so much? why not abandon it all now?... Abandon it! Abandon a resolution! All the obstinacy of her nature – she classed it herself as firmness – rose in revolt. (*TM* 129)

The proposal, when it does come, ruptures completely the atmosphere of farce which has maintained reader anticipation from Stephen's arrival at the hilltop:

'Leonard,' she said softly, 'are you sure there is no mistake? Do you not see that I am asking you,' she intended to say 'to be my husband,' but she could not utter the words, they seemed to stick in her mouth, so she finished the sentence: 'that I be your wife?' (*TM* 136)

Stephen's hesitation draws attention to her inability even to phrase the proposal in an assertive manner. Essentially, her words are a passive request, an offering of the self rather than a proposal to the other. The question is a revelation to her as much as it is to the dumbfounded and angry Leonard:

> The moment the words were spoken – the bare, hard, naked, shameless words – the revulsion came. As a lightening flash shows up the blackness of the night the appalling truth of what she had done was forced upon her. The blood rushed to her head till cheeks and shoulders and neck seemed to burn. Covering her face with her hands she sank back on the seat behind her, crying silently bitter tears that seemed to scald her eyes and her cheeks as they ran. (*TM* 136)

The involuntary gestures of virginity are again manifested through blood, and in the need to conceal the shame of blood exposed to the world in the heat of the blush. Again, the blush is the icon of self-knowledge. This is the crossing of the impossible Rubicon between theory and practice. And yet it is not a crossing which fulfils the full promise of its potential. Leonard's priggishness is again the inhibitor of what *might* have happened:

> Young men are so easily shocked by breaches of convention made by women they respect! And his pride was hurt. Why should he have been placed in such a ridiculous position! (*TM* 136–7)

In *The Woman Who Did*, Herminia Barton propositions her lover by saying: 'I am yours this moment. You may do what you would with me.' Like Leonard, the lover is too shocked to act: 'he drew back ... He scarcely realised what she meant.'[52] The shock to Leonard's pride and egotism, as the narrator confirms, is all that has prevented him from taking up the 'magnificent possibility' (*TM* 137) presented to him by her body as much as her fortune.

*

The experiment has now effectively concluded. The novel has made its point about Stephen's inability to carry out the promise of her unique education. A man's education, the implied argument runs, does not make a man. The final phase of *The Man* – Chapters XIII to XL – thus shows Stephen in her progress towards a reconciliation with her 'natural' sex and a conventional goal in marriage. The process is one of *re-education*: 'She was learning to be patient in these days' (*TM* 245). Significantly, the renaissance of Stephen Norman is rendered as a parallel to the regeneration of Harold An Wolf, in that it embodies the same strenuous philosophy where personal pain, mental as much as physical, is a regenerating power. The Narrator states:

> But thought and purpose, and the resourcefulness to carry them into being and if necessary into action, are born of anguish. The motherhood of pain is a factor in the making of a strong life.... (*TM* 142)

It is in their comparative struggles that it becomes completely clear that Harold, rather than Stephen, is 'The Man' of the novel's title, and that the racial resonance of Stephen's surname is underscored further by her status as *No-man*.[53]

By the time Stephen assists in the rescue of Harold, travelling incognito, from a shipwreck off the coast of fictional Angleshire, she is in a state of conventional readiness for sexual transaction. She may discern between the 'true' and false suitor. Her racial heritage intact but no longer misdirected, she is now complementary to the 'true' male rather than his unworthy rival. The narrator is careful to embed this change in an appreciation of Stephen's emotions when Harold willingly exposes himself to danger:

> This was indeed a man! a brave man; and all the woman in her went out to him. For him, and to aid him and his work, she would have given everything, done anything; and in her heart, which beat in an ecstasy of anxiety, she prayed with that desperate conviction of hope which comes in such moments of exaltation. (*TM* 360–1)

The spontaneity and 'correctness' of her unfeigned reaction is in effect the crowning of her re-education.

The betrothal of Harold and Stephen, when it does come, mirrors the unfulfilled promise of the impasse on Cæster Hill. Stephen is no longer acting: 'She was a woman! A woman who awaited the coming of a man!' (*TM* 434). Harold, too, is suitably purposeful. He is coming specifically for *her*, not for some unspecified matter of interest:

And through all her thoughts passed the rider who even now was thundering over the green sward on his way to her. In her fancy at first, and later in her ears, she could hear the sound of his sweeping gallop.

It was thus that a man should come to a woman! (*TM* 435)

The parallel with the earlier encounter is carried to the final approach of the suitor:

The sound stopped. With all her ears she listened, her heart now beginning to beat furiously.... And then she saw suddenly a pillar of shadow beyond the line of the cliff. It rested but a moment, moved swiftly along the edge, and then was lost to her eyes.

But to another sense there was greater comfort: she heard the clatter of rolling pebbles and the scramble of eager feet. Harold was hastening down the zigzag. (*TM* 435)

With a furiously beating heart which contrasts with the mildly quickened pulse of the earlier proposal, Stephen's reactions fall into accord with the cosmic law of mutual attraction. The narrator confides:

Oh! the music of that sound! It woke all the finer instincts of the woman. All the dross and thought of self passed away. Nature, sweet and simple and true, reigned alone. Instinctively she rose and came towards him. In the simple nobility of her self-surrender and her purpose, which were at one with the grandeur of nature around her, to be negative was to be false....

When the two saw each other's eyes there was no need for words. Harold came close, opening wide his arms. Stephen flew to them.

In that divine moment, when their mouths met, both knew that their souls were one. (*TM* 435–6)

The 'dross' of egotism has evaporated. Her sex has prevailed.

\*

This prioritisation of biological gender over and above all other drives may be said to hold true throughout Stoker's fiction. The woman, no matter how successful she is in taking the initiative for a time, can only find her destiny in her sex – and in all that it commits her to, culturally. Stoker's construction of women, though, consistently traces a fine line between outrage and prurience. The assertive heroine is always, at heart, modest and virginal, even though she knows the significance of sexuality in social and emotional engagements. The dangerous or compromising situations in which she finds herself are crisis points in which she discovers her vulnerability, and in which the male regains control, bringing order to her troubled life. The emotions the heroine expresses, with blushing face and hesitant words, convey embarrassment, shame, regret and self-abasement for sexual events which have not happened. The reader may thus access the thrill of impropriety whilst remaining morally assured that the heroine has no taint of salaciousness. Whether headstrong or saintly and passive, Stoker's heroines are constantly on display, a source of gratification to the male in their purity, in their eroticism, and in their final and inevitable return to the desired state of sexual subservience through marriage.

# 4
# The Sanguine Economy: Hysteroid Pathology and Physiological Medicine

Blood is an item of multidiscursive significance, a cultural concept as much as a literal physiological substance. It is the icon of common identity, of alliance: one is 'of the same blood', to quote Foucault.[1] The nation, the race, the family are all structured metaphorically and/or metonymically in terms of blood relations, the individual functioning as a blood-bearing synecdoche of the greater unity in which he – and his blood – circulate.

Such encodings punctuate Stoker's writings. In *Personal Reminiscences of Henry Irving*, for example, Stoker applauds the seamen of the American warship *Chicago* who, in defiance of the official neutrality of the US Navy, rescued the crew of a British gunboat from defeat at the hands of the Chinese. When an explanation was demanded for the crew's action, the ship's commander responded: 'Blood is thicker than water.'[2] The rhetorical energy of a proverb customarily used to indicate the binding ties of family kinship is here seamlessly redirected into a myth of common racial identity. The identities invested in blood, in other words, are more compelling than a political dogma which, if adhered to, would have allowed fellow Anglo-Saxons to be massacred by the representatives of another race.

These sentiments of racial brotherhood, which unite 'the English on both sides of the Atlantic' and which distinguish the Anglo-Saxon from all other races, are, of course, central to *The Mystery of the Sea*, *The Man* and *Lady Athlyne*.[3] As familial as well as racial myths they are arguably engaged in every marital transaction in Stoker's fiction. Equally, though, such relationships form part of the background to every scenario in which a virginal heroine is exposed to sexual danger. The fluid nature of blood makes both the substance and the meanings encoded in it peculiarly vulnerable. Blood, as Foucault argues, is 'easily spilled, subject to drying up, too readily mixed, capable of being quickly corrupted'.[4] Unmingled, it is the guarantor of purity and thus of the strength or integrity of the qualities which it encodes. Even when mixed with the blood of other racial identities, some qualities will arguably remain as vestiges of former greatness. This much is evidenced by Harold An Wolf's father, who says of his Viking ancestors:

> Go where you will throughout this country, or any seaboard of Europe, and you will find that where the old type remains they dominate their fellows. Ay, even where the passing of centuries has diluted their blood with that of weaker races.[5]

Sentiments such as these effectively expose the economic basis of the significations vested in blood. In cultural terms, modifications to the composition or quantity of blood affect its ability to proliferate meaning. When the integrity of the literal fluid is compromised, the multiple meanings it embodies subtly change.

The release of blood from an internal economy, or its introduction as a possible contaminant into another circulation, is simultaneously a medical crisis. As blood is gained, lost or transferred, physical vitality is affected. In this sense, the physiological logic which governs the secretion, depletion and transfer of blood forms what may be termed a 'Sanguine Economy', a discursive phenomenon which aligns both the literal and figurative qualities of blood. Individual and racial health are dependent on pure and plentiful blood: depletion or contamination brings both personal illness and racial decline. Each crisis point in the Sanguine Economy thus permits an exchange of meaning between several overlapping cultural encodings, as well as a conventional medical consequence.

The Sanguine Economy, in this respect, may be regarded as a counterpart to the Spermatic Economy – a popular nineteenth-century quasi-medical discourse in which semen is regarded as a product of the blood.[6] In both economies there is an equation between a bodily fluid – blood or semen – and the quantum of personal vitality. When semen is discharged or 'spent', the consequent generation of fresh spermatozoa 'drains from the blood all its purest and most strengthening qualities', leaving the patient drained and exhausted.[7] Likewise, when the blood is, from another cause, deficient in quality or lacking in quantity, the patient is physically depressed, his circulation frequently being described as 'languid'.[8] The physiological crisis, however, has moral and social implications also. In nineteenth-century medical and religious writings, the masturbator, the pallid male who 'spends' his seminal vitality unwisely and unproductively, is frequently depicted as an enemy to society as much as to himself.[9] Likewise, the pale countenance and physical lassitude of the bloodless body signifies a future of decadence, an invaliding of the self and a legacy of weakness for one's descendants.

The pale body is, in this respect, always disturbing and threatening when the moral or figurative as opposed to literal implications of blood loss are emphasised. This much is evidenced in *Dracula* through Seward's pointed rendering of the vampiric Lucy's behaviour in the Hampstead churchyard. Academic criticism has to date emphasised primarily the symbolic possibilities of this scene, reading Lucy's behaviour as a form of sexual predation.[10] Seward recalls the incident:

> She still advanced, however, and with a languorous, voluptuous grace, said:-
> 'Come to me, Arthur. Leave these others and come to me. My arms are hungry for you. Come, and we can rest together. Come, my husband, come!'[11]

Seward translates what is essentially a medical problem into a sexual – and thus moral – threat. Lucy seemingly demands sperm, but wants blood. Her languor is as much that of a depleted circulation as it is the signifier of sexual abandonment proposed by Seward.[12] The penetration proposed here is an intervention into the economy of the male's body, the only craving expressed by Lucy her desire to feed.

The ambivalent relationship between cause and symptom in *Dracula* is, for the characters, an invitation to misdiagnose. For the reader, however, the position is one of continual rediagnosis – of reconciling a range of competing pathologies and causalities, any one of which may claim to the right to make authoritative statements on a highly systematic and consistent pattern of symptoms. *Dracula* is a novel preoccupied with pathology rather than health, and in particular with morbid and abnormal states whose boundaries become increasingly nebulous as the narrative progresses.

## Unconscious cerebration

The major pathological study in the novel is that of Lucy Westenra. The choice of name is significant. Symbolically, *Lucy* correlates easily to *Lucis*, light. Hence, her character is an embodiment of the positive feminine qualities of 'sweetness and light' which, for commentators such as Elizabeth Lynn Linton, emblematise a racial and sexual 'ideal of womanhood ... of home birth and breeding.'[13] Linton's allusion to breeding suggests, again, how such characteristics may, through race, be easily transferred to an encoding in blood. To drain the blood of Lucy is, arguably, to deprive her of these qualities and of the cultural identities which they signify. Lucy's surname is equally significant in this context. Stoker was to make use of it again in *Lady Athlyne* as one of the Christian names of Lord Athlyne, where its symbolic value signals the teutonic marital alliance that the British nobleman seeks to make with the American heiress, Joy Ogilvie.[14] In infecting this synecdoche of the British race, Dracula is not only colonising the West, but is also modifying its cultural identity by sapping its moral and physical energy.

Lucy's descent into vampirism is structured as a medical case, the progress of her 'illness' being observed and investigated by a variety of participant characters including the patient herself. The diagnostic processes of the novel draw heavily on the physiologically biased practice which dominated British medicine in the later nineteenth century. *Dracula* locates itself within this tradition through repeated references to the process of Unconscious Cerebration, a physiological model of mental activity formulated by the British physician W.B. Carpenter in the 1860s.[15] The unconscious mind, Carpenter argued, was able to produce logical conclusions '*below the plane* of consciousness, either during profound sleep, or while the attention is wholly engrossed by some entirely different train of thought.'[16] Seward, for example, notes in his observation of the lunatic Renfield:

> There is a method in his madness, and the rudimentary idea in my mind is growing. It will be a whole idea soon, and then, oh, unconscious cerebration! you will have to give the wall to your conscious brother. (*D* 69)

The process is frequently rendered also in a less explicit form. Elsewhere, Van Helsing describes figuratively his own mental processes to Mina:

> here is a lesson: do not fear ever to think. A half-thought has been buzzing often in my brain, but I fear to let him loose his wings. Here now, with more knowledge, I go back to where that half-thought come from, and I find that he be no half-thought at all; that he be

a whole thought, though so young that he is not yet strong to use his little wings. (*D* 340)[17]

As a physiological process within the brain, unconscious cerebration is particularly dependent upon the supply of blood to the cerebrum. Depletion of blood, as Carpenter observes, causes a consequent decline in cerebral activity. The introduction of impurities into the bloodstream may similarly pervert the processes of cerebration.[18] Mental integrity – and thus cultural identity – are, therefore, literally dependent upon the economics of blood.

Nominally, provision is made in the novel to include the reasoning of both popular and clinical interpretations of the pathological symptoms, the lay observation of Mina and self-diagnosis of Lucy being supplemented by the consultative role played by Seward and Van Helsing. The patient's 'condition' at the start of the novel is first mentioned as a trifling detail in the record of an enjoyable and crowded holiday visit. Mina writes in her diary on 1 August:

> Lucy was looking sweetly pretty in her white lawn frock; she has got a beautiful colour since she has been here. I noticed that the old men did not lose any time in coming up and sitting near her when we sat down. She is so sweet with old people; I think they all fell in love with her on the spot. (*D* 64)

The innocuous pleasantry of Mina's comment regarding Lucy's complexion conveys a muted suggestion of less robust health in the past, evidently observed by the diarist herself prior to the Whitby visit. Lucy's enhanced colour supersedes an unhealthy pallor which is acknowledged only in its eclipse.

Her present state, though, is a potent euphemism for a feature of both physiological and moral significance. Lucy, clearly, retains the ability to blush. Morally, this emphasises her modesty, which is also underscored by the virginal white of her dress, and Mina's conventional use of the adjective 'sweet'. As with Norah Joyce, though, a responsive complexion may signal equally the sublimated sexual curiosity of a young woman recently engaged and anticipating marriage. Notably, the elderly mariners on the cliff top are attracted to the outwardly passive and demure Lucy rather than to the businesslike and inquisitive Mina.[19] Physiologically, though, Lucy's complexion is an index to the literal presence of blood, of a healthy circulation responsive to physical as well as emotional changes.[20] In the light of

Harker's earlier conclusions regarding Dracula's sanguine diet (*D* 51), this latter proposition is likely to be noted with interest as a relevant detail by the reader.

The recurrence of a congenital and hereditary complaint in Lucy, though, brings a ripple of disquiet to the tranquillity of the visit. Writing on 26 July, Mina notes in her diary:

> Lucy, although she is so well, has lately taken to her old habit of walking in her sleep. Her mother has spoken to me about it, and we have decided that I am to lock the door of our room every night. Mrs Westenra has got an idea that sleep-walkers always go out on roofs of houses and along the edges of cliffs, and get suddenly awakened and fall over with a despairing cry that echoes all over the place. Poor dear, she is naturally anxious about Lucy, and she tells me that her husband, Lucy's father, had the same habit; that he would get up in the night and dress himself and go out, if he were not stopped. Lucy is to be married in the autumn, and she is already planning out her dresses and how her house is to be arranged. (*D* 72)

Though fancifully expressed, Mrs Westenra's fears are largely in accord with the physiological model of mental action. Carpenter argues that actions or gestures, once learned, may be 'habituated' within the self and thus become

> not less automatic than the act of walking; as is shown by the fact that, when once set going, they will continue in regular sequence, not only without any Volitional exertion, but whilst the Attention is wholly directed elsewhere....[21]

Carpenter further asserts that somnambules tend to climb during their trance wanderings, and assigns their ability in this activity to a retention of those motor skills practised volitionally, though usually unconsciously, whilst awake:

> the sufficiency of the Muscular sense, when the Mind has no consciousness of the danger, and when the visual sense neither affords aid nor contributes to distract the attention, is remarkably illustrated by the phenomena of Somnambulism; for the sleep-walker traverses, without the least hesitation, the narrow parapet of a house, crosses narrow and insecure planks, clambers

roofs, &c. – But how soon a new coordination of this kind can be acquired is shown, (as Mr H. Mayo pointed-out), by what happens to a landsman on first going to sea. 'It is long before the passenger acquires his "sea-legs". At first, as the ship moves, he can hardly keep his feet.... In a short time, he learns to disregard the shifting images and changing motions, or acquires facility in adapting himself (like one on horseback) to the different alterations in the line of direction in his frame.'[22]

The same process is teasingly demonstrated in *Dracula* through Seward's behaviour during his proposal to Lucy. Lucy recalls the event in a letter to Mina:

> He was very cool outwardly, but was nervous all the same. He had evidently been schooling himself as to all sorts of little things, and remembered them; but he almost managed to sit down on his silk hat, which men don't generally do when they are cool, and then when he wanted to appear at ease he kept playing with a lancet in a way that made me nearly scream. (*D* 56)

This is a significant point of discursive intersection. The lancet is a metonym of surgery.[23] But the instrument is metonymically linked also to the sanguine economy through its role in the opening of the veins for transfusion or blood letting.[24] Seward's nervousness affects his social behaviour. But in the handling of his customary surgical tool, he may safely trust to habit, diverting his attention fully elsewhere. Lucy's suitor is perfectly safe, in so far as he remains within the physiological parameters of the sanguine economy, within the play of material factors anticipated by physicians such as Carpenter. Lucy, too, is safe in her somnambulism – but only while the door remains literally and figuratively locked, where no unprecedented factors may be introduced to disturb the equilibrium of her neurosis.

It is this medical tradition, therefore, that Mina draws upon when she awakes to find Lucy absent from the bedroom which they share in their holiday lodgings at Whitby's Royal Crescent:

> The room was dark, so I could not see Lucy's bed; I stole across and felt for her. The bed was empty. I lit a match, and found that she was not in the room. The door was shut, but not locked, as I had left it. I feared to wake her mother, who has been more than usually ill lately, so threw on some clothes and got ready to look for her. As I

was leaving the room it struck me that the clothes she wore might give me some clue to her dreaming intention. Dressing-gown would mean house; dress, outside. (*D* 89)

Lucy, however, has left the house clad only in her night-dress, an inappropriate – if not immodest – garment for a lady to wear in a public street. This detail appears at first sight to militate against the suggestion that Lucy's somnambulism is an automatic or unconscious reflection of the walking trips of her waking hours. Arguably, a truly habituated sleepwalker would dress before leaving the house, as Lucy's father does.

Academic critics have been quick to suggest that Lucy's behaviour occurs solely in response to a summons issued by the vampire through some occult power sympathetic to her somnambulism.[25] Count Dracula, though, is occupied draining the crew of the *Demeter* in the Bay of Biscay when Lucy begins her adult somnambulism at Whitby, seven days before she encounters the vampire in the churchyard. In this respect, the Count's alleged involvement in the early phases of Lucy's mental condition is by no means certain.

Mina's behaviour, rather, suggests that Lucy's wandering is being treated as if it were a function of habituation originated in repeated waking practice. Mina clearly *expects* Lucy to take the path which the pair use daily to reach a favoured vantage point in the churchyard, rather than to wander aimlessly around the town itself:

> The clock was striking one as I was in the Crescent, and there was not a soul in sight. I ran along the North Terrace, but could see no sign of the white figure which I expected. At the edge of the West Cliff above the pier I looked across the harbour to the East Cliff, in the hope or fear – I don't know which – of seeing Lucy in our favourite seat.... Whatever my expectation was, it was not disappointed, for there, on our favourite seat, the moon struck a half-reclining figure, snowy white. (*D* 89–90)[26]

Mina does not make a mistake here in looking for Lucy initially on the North Terrace, the road which lies at the seaward end of the Royal Crescent. This would have been a logical and scenic daytime route from the Royal Crescent by way of the West Cliff, steps and pier to the Drawbridge and thence via Church Steps to St Mary's Church Yard on the East Cliff, the location of 'our favourite seat' (*D* 90). Prototypically, the somnambulist *climbs* the Church Steps to reach the seat.

Mina, notably, admits elsewhere that it was *her*, rather than the 'sensitive' Lucy, who chose the seat initially, ignorant not only of its status as the grave of a suicide, but also of the significance of that factor to Dracula, of whom she is aware only as a business correspondent of her fiancé:

> If I hadn't gone to Whitby, perhaps poor dear Lucy would be with us now. She hadn't taken to visiting the churchyard till I came, and if she hadn't come there in the daytime with me she wouldn't have walked there in her sleep; and if she hadn't gone there at night and asleep, that monster couldn't have destroyed her as he did. Oh, why did I ever go to Whitby? (*D* 257)[27]

Mina's speech demonstrates the extent to which the physiological model of mental habituation has penetrated the fabric of the novel. Simultaneously, though, her words confirm that all attempts to assign the choice of seat solely to occult design are specious. The location of the seat, as Mina suggests, *ought* to appeal to the Romantic or sensitive nature:

> Right over the town is the ruin of Whitby Abbey, which was sacked by the Danes, and which is the scene of part of 'Marmion,' where the girl was built up in the wall. It is a most noble ruin, of immense size, and full of beautiful and romantic bits; there is a legend that a white lady is seen in one of the windows. (*D* 62)

The novel assails the reader here with the signifiers of the Sublime and the Gothic, the 'white lady' prefiguring Lucy's own later presence beneath those very windows, the reference to *Marmion* a reminder of an act of victimisation. But the character who mouths these signifiers is constructed as a practical woman, a stenographer, a collector and cataloguer of facts. The major irony is that it is *she* who should inflict all this potential upon her sensitive friend – although, as Mina notes earlier, the view *from* the seat savours more of the picturesque, while they sit with their *backs* to the sublimity of the ruined Abbey, gazing instead upon a picture postcard view of the red-roofed town.

The seat is therefore not advanced as a pathetic fallacy for Lucy's sensitive nature. Lucy's mental state, and that of Mina, become important in the relationship with Dracula later in the novel: they are not a factor before Lucy is bitten in the churchyard. It appears that the vampire's first victim is encountered purely by chance, and not by design. Indeed, it is only from the time of this meeting that the vampire becomes part of Lucy's pathology, that the investment in her of the sanguine economy, in all its senses, moves towards imbalance – the depletion of her blood adversely affecting both her personal vitality and, apparently, her moral character also.

Mina's lay observation of Lucy's condition following the initial attack is heavily biased towards physiological disturbance as the most obvious and conventional cause for her friend's discomfort. She recalls:

> When I bent over her I could see that she was still asleep. Her lips were parted, and she was breathing – not softly, as usual with her, but in long, heavy gasps, as though striving to get her lungs full at every breath. As I came close, she put up her hand in her sleep and pulled the collar of her nightdress close round her throat. Whilst she did so there came a little shudder through her, as though she felt the cold. I flung the warm shawl over her.... I feared to wake her all at once, so, in order to have my hands free that I might help her, I fastened the shawl at her throat with a big safety-pin; but I must have been clumsy in my anxiety and pinched or pricked her with it, for by-and-by, when her breathing became quieter, she put her hand to her throat again and moaned. (D 90–1)

The ambiguous black figure which Mina momentarily glimpses at Lucy's side, having left no immediate evidence of its presence, is rapidly discarded as an agent in Lucy's prostration. Mina similarly dismisses the significance of what she believes to be 'a good-sized bird', discovered next to the sleeping Lucy, later in the novel (D 94).

Mina, therefore, sees no component in Lucy's state that is not compatible with the effects of cold – the shudder – or of disturbed sleep – the breathing and moaning. The two punctures in Lucy's neck are similarly dismissed as insignificant:

> I was sorry to notice that my clumsiness with the safety-pin hurt her. Indeed, it might have been serious, for the skin of her throat was pierced. I must have pinched up a piece of loose skin and have transfixed it, for there are two little red points like pin-pricks, and on the band of her nightdress was a drop of blood. (D 92)[28]

Seward also dismisses the punctures as having nothing to do with Lucy's bloodlessness when he makes his own professional examination of the case (*D* 123–4). With Lucy apparently none the worse for her adventure, Mina has nothing to report of in her journal other than one further incidence of somnambulism, the evening merely being encapsulated in the reference, 'her sleep-walking adventure' (*D* 92).

It is because of this misreading of the events of the night of 11 August that Mina is unable to attribute Lucy's subsequent – and consequent – atrophy and lethargy to any medical cause. On 14 August Mina writes:

> She looks so sweet as she sleeps; but she is paler than is her wont, and there is a drawn, haggard look under her eyes which I do not like. I fear she is fretting about something. I wish I could find out what it is. (*D* 94)

There remains, however, the suggestion of a concern already implicitly in process within Mina's own unconscious cerebration:

> I trust her feeling ill may not be from that unlucky prick of the safety-pin. I looked at her throat just now as she lay asleep, and the tiny wounds seem not to have healed. They are still open, and, if anything, larger, than before, and the edges of them are faintly white. They are like little white dots with red centres. Unless they heal within a day or two, I shall insist on the doctor seeing about them. (*D* 95)

The further development of Mina's concern is disrupted not so much by her departure for Budapest, but through an ironic and unexpected improvement in Lucy's condition.

Mina takes comfort, for example, from Lucy's revival following the night of 17 August:

> Lucy is ever so much better. Last night she slept well all night, and did not disturb me once. The roses seem coming back already to her cheeks, though she is still sadly pale and wan-looking. If she were in any way anaemic I could understand it, but she is not. She is in gay spirits and full of life and cheerfulness. All the morbid reticence seems to have passed from her.... (*D* 97)

Mina's turn of phrase is, admittedly, a cliché. Norah Joyce at her most nubile is noted by Arthur Severn to have 'blushed rosy red'.[29] The metaphor, though, has a multidiscursive significance. The phrase has a place in popular medicine – here, for example, in an article on the physiological benefits of gardening by 'Medicus' [Dr Gordon Stables] in *The Girl's Own Paper*:

> The consequence is that the heart is strengthened, and the blood rendered far more pure, so that every organ of the body is strengthened and regenerated. The roses return to the cheeks of the delicate, the carmine to the lips....[30]

Stables's words, and in particular his drawing of the reader's attention to the lips and the cheeks, illustrate again the physiological material with which both the moral and occult encodings interact. Seward, significantly, notes that the vampirised Lucy 'was ghastly, chalkily pale; the red seemed to have gone even from her lips and gums' (*D* 120). The full irony of Mina's words, therefore, will not become apparent to the reader until after the death of Lucy, when Van Helsing describes the vampire's victim as 'a woman who have not change only to be more rose and more beautiful in a whole week after she die' (*D* 202).

The signs of health have been reworked into the indicators of danger. Conventional medical logic testifies that the corpse of Lucy cannot of itself secrete the blood whose presence, as in her lifetime, is manifested through her complexion. The laws of internal circulation still seemingly apply after Lucy's apparent death, although their edges have become undeniably permeable. Lucy's encounter with the vampire is something more substantial than a conventional transfusion of blood, although it maps over, in part at least, the economic logic of that surgical operation. It is not merely the physiological but the moral also that is ruptured through the multidiscursive irony of these elsewhere positive symptoms of vitality.

For the moment, though, the reader will correlate Lucy's improved condition on the morning of 18 August with Dracula's migration from Whitby to London on the same night – communicated through the preceding correspondence between the solicitor, Billington, and Carter, Paterson & Company.[31] Lucy is, for the moment, out of danger, and indeed rapidly recovers much of her lost vitality, as she wryly observes in a letter to Mina, dated 30 August:

> This strong air would soon restore Jonathan; it has quite restored me. I have an appetite like a cormorant, am full of life, and sleep well. You will be glad to know that I have quite given up walking in

my sleep. I think I have not stirred out of my bed for a week, that is, when I once got into it at night. Arthur says I am getting fat. (*D* 106)[32]

It is the newly secreted blood and its capacity to transport oxygen, rather than the 'strong air' alone, that has 'restored' her.[33] Lucy appears as much uncertain as unconcerned as to whether or not she is still sleepwalking. But although the text advances no evidence as to the present intervention of the vampire, the reader will view as ominous Lucy's subsequent diary entry, written as it is at her *London* home, Hillingham.[34]

Though Lucy attempts self-diagnosis, her analysis is again restricted by her tendency to comprehend symptoms only through the frame of physiological medicine. Her diary entry for 25 August reads:

This morning I am horribly weak. My face is ghastly pale, and my throat pains me. It must be something wrong with my lungs, for I don't seem ever to get air enough. (*D* 109)

Her words, therefore, serve only to convey to the reader a sense of a worsening situation whose whole compass at present may be comprehended only by those outside the novel. For Mina and Seward, the worsening pathology of Lucy may make sense only in retrospect.[35]

## Obscure diseases

It is at this point that Seward is brought in to examine Lucy by her fiancé, Arthur Holmwood. Seward's misdiagnosis, based as it is upon observation and conventional physiological reasoning, is forgivable given his ignorance of the journals of Jonathan Harker and Mina Murray, and of the fragmentary secondary sources which, to the reader, may be seen to link their salient points. Writing to Holmwood shortly after his visit, Seward reports:

I could easily see that she is somewhat bloodless, but I could not see the usual anaemic signs, and by a chance I was actually able to test the quality of her blood, for in opening a window which was stiff a cord gave way, and she cut her hand slightly with broken glass.... I secured a few drops of the blood and have analyzed them. The qualitative analysis gives quite a normal condition, and shows, I should infer, in itself a vigorous state of health.

With such contradictory symptoms, Seward can turn only to the possibility of a mental illness, a trauma rather than a lesion:

> In other physical matters I was quite satisfied that there is no need for anxiety; but as there must be a cause somewhere, I have come to the conclusion that it must be something mental. She complains of difficulty in breathing satisfactorily at times, and of heavy, lethargic sleep, with dreams that frighten her, but regarding which she can remember nothing. (*D* 111)

It is curious that Seward – a mental health specialist who, as Lucy herself notes, 'has an immense lunatic asylum all under his own care' (*D* 55) – immediately considers recourse to a foreign consultant. Seward clarifies his decision to Arthur:

> I am in doubt, and so have done the best thing I know of: I have written to my old friend and master, Professor Van Helsing, of Amsterdam, who knows as much about obscure diseases as anyone in the world. (*D* 111)

Seward's remark, 'I am in doubt', conveys a suggestion that there is a part-diagnosis already formulated following his recent examination of Lucy. Seward is not so much positing the presence of an obscure disease as engaging in a calculated act of duplicity, a deliberate concealment of the tentative diagnosis from the concerned fiancé.

Clearly there is a hidden script here which defines the perceived basis of a condition which Seward tantalisingly suggests may be 'something mental'. Seward is deducing from symptoms. It is apparent, therefore, that he is fearful of giving utterance to his diagnosis without further qualification or verification. The possibility of an act of evasion on the part of the physician may be projected yet further into a consideration that Seward would prefer to announce the presence of a purely physiological complaint – an alternative to the anaemia which his test results have been unable to substantiate – rather than that which he apparently suspects to be the case.

Lucy is not insane, however. Rather, she appears to be suffering from a debilitating and intermittent emotional disorder which, though frequently accompanied by physical symptoms, is normally regarded as being 'largely a mental malady'.[36] She is, in short, hysterical. Seward, who is constructed as a physician well-versed in the work of contemporary theorists of the mind such as Charcot, would know that

British medical thought prioritised the role of sexual passion over that of physical dysfunction in the development of hysteria.[37] He would know also that, in previous centuries, hysteria was frequently associated with female salaciousness. Seward thus has two compelling reasons – scientific doubt and personal diplomacy – for being doubly sure before voicing his suspicions to Lucy's fiancé, his own close friend.

The symptomatic evidence with which Seward is presented at this early stage of the case appears largely to support this diagnosis, although its correlation is to the generalisations of contemporary medicine rather than to any physical examination or second opinion conducted with regard to the individual patient. As Seward observes, Lucy displays no physical disorder or lesion which could account for her lassitude and bloodlessness. Such an absence is a common feature of hysterical neuroses, as one popular medical manual from the period affirms. In hysteria

> no visible diseased condition is discovered in any particular organ; the brain and nervous system generally show no evident changes in their structure, and the disease must therefore be classed amongst those which we have described as functional diseases, the functions of the nervous system being those chiefly at fault.[38]

Seward is also aware of Lucy's earlier somnambulism, as he informs Arthur:

> She says that as a child she used to walk in her sleep, and that when in Whitby the habit came back, and that once she walked out in the night and went to the East Cliff, where Miss Murray found her: but she assures me that of late the habit has not returned. (*D* 111)

There is an ominous subtext to this superficially comforting report. The cessation of Lucy's somnambulism conveys to the reader not an improvement in her condition, but the possibility that Dracula is now able to visit her at home. Seward's report, though, rehearses also the correlation frequently made between somnambulistic states and hysteria in medical casework. Carpenter, for example, provides one such study:

> The subject of it was a young lady of highly nervous temperament; and the affection occurred in the course of a long and trying illness,

in which all the severest forms of hysterical disorder had succes-
sively presented themselves. The state of Somnambulism usually
supervened in this case upon the waking state; instead of arising, as
it more commonly does, out of the condition of ordinary sleep.[39]

In contrast to Carpenter's patient, Lucy follows the normal pattern of
somnambulism contracted in sleep: under medical precedent, she is
again a non-exceptional case. Through such corroboration the misdiagnosis becomes concretised.

Charcot voices a similar opinion regarding the susceptibility of
hysterical patients to hypnosis.[40] The novel is thus asserting by implication the sympathy of the vampire with such 'abnormal' mental
states. The lunatic, Renfield, is similarly a locus of vampiric activity (*D*
107–8, 248). Yet, as is also the case with Lucy's somnambulism,
Renfield's psychosis cannot be said to have been *originated* by Count
Dracula: rather, both conditions are eclipsed, overwritten, by another
pathology.[41]

Though certain pathological conditions – most notably anaemia and
goitre – were associated with the production of hysteria, *Dracula*
constructs a corroborative network for Lucy's complaint primarily
from the non-medical context of her recent personal history. Lucy's
susceptibility – to hysteria and to the vampiric contagion, for both are
engendered through the text's symptomatology – is therefore incidental, individual rather than racial.[42] In support of his hypothesis,
therefore, Seward may draw immediately upon the raw data of Lucy's
age – which the text takes pains to communicate to the reader as nineteen – 'twenty in September' (*D* 56). This detail is in accord with
contemporary thought, expressed here in popular form by *Cassell's
Family Doctor*, published, like *Dracula,* in 1897:

Hysteria is almost entirely seen in women, although rare cases occur
in very impressionable men. It most commonly shows itself at an
early age, between the fifteenth and twentieth years.[43]

If Lucy were younger, her contemplation of marriage would appear
neither credible nor modest; if older, she would be a marginal case and
the diagnosis – or misdiagnosis – would not be as conclusive as it
appears by the logic of the medical discourse.

Lucy's approaching marriage is in itself an event which may have
implications for her mental condition. Mina notes twice how her
friend is preoccupied with the practicalities of the approaching

marriage and the arrangement of the marital home (*D* 67, 72). An understated core of *sexual* curiosity, however, may be detected in Lucy's apparently light-hearted though tearful aside to the narrative of her three marriage proposals: 'Why can't they let a girl marry three men, or as many as want her, and save all this trouble?' (*D* 59). 'Want' in this context arguably embodies a sexual as well as social significance. To speak openly of such things, as Stephen Norman discovers in *The Man*, is to behave in a manner contrary to that conventionally expected of a pure-minded, unmarried woman. Because her proposal of marriage to Leonard may be interpreted by others as a sexual invitation, Stephen regards herself as subsequently having 'a secret to keep, an appearance to preserve'. Indeed, as the narrator comments, the shame is such that, in her own mind, 'it was as though her virginity had left her' (*TM* 142).

The cultural as well as personal pressures which demand the concealment of sexual emotions are a frequent cause of neurosis. Robert B. Carter, author of *On the Pathology and Treatment of Hysteria* (1853), explains:

> when sexual desire is taken into the account, it will add immensely to the forces bearing upon the female, who is often much under its dominion; and who, if unmarried and chaste, is compelled to restrain every manifestation of its sway.... from the modern necessity for its entire concealment, it is likely to produce hysteria in a larger number of the women subject to its influence, than it would do if the state of society permitted its free expression.[44]

Lucy's slip thus functions as a strategic, and indeed teasing, exposure of the awareness of sexuality within in the heroine. As with Norah Joyce's embarrassed blush in *The Snake's Pass*, and Marjory Anita Drake's perturbation at the sight of a wedding rather than engagement ring in *The Mystery of the Sea*, the sexual knowingness of the heroine is obvious: it is not equivocal. For Lucy, though, such knowingness signals tension as much as the erotic.

Unlike Stephen Norman, Lucy cannot be said to be engaged in a conscious sexual rebellion. Stephen, notably, destroys the drafts of her letter inviting Leonard to the tryst even though they contain nothing which suggests 'any sense of overweening ardour' (*TM* 114). Lucy, however, does not excise her discussion of polygamy from her letter to Mina. Lucy's expression of sexual precocity may thus be unconscious or unacknowledged by the heroine herself, though apparently present as a symptom available to the medically aware gaze of the reader. Emphatically, the reader lacks the reliable stigmata of the blush, which is the index of similar sexual perturbation in Norah Joyce, Stephen Norman and Joy Ogilvie. The whole question has been kept vague. The novel suggests – but holds back from allowing the heroine full access to – an unreservedly *conscious* sexuality. The presentation of Lucy's allegedly mental as well as physical illness, though, is a proleptic gesture which will ultimately assist the contrast between this, the supposedly 'true' and innocent Lucy, and that which usurps her form.

With Lucy's apparent sexual curiosity in mind, both Seward and Mina may ironically concur on the role played by the fiancé, Arthur Holmwood, in the generation of Lucy's supposed neurosis. With an understated concern for Lucy's health which contrasts with her friend's present physical condition, Mina notes in her diary on 27 July, twelve days prior to Count Dracula's arrival at Whitby:

> Mr Holmwood has been suddenly called to Ring to see his father, who has been taken seriously ill. Lucy frets at the postponement of seeing him, but it does not touch her looks; she is a trifle stouter, and her cheeks are a lovely rose pink.... I pray it will all last. (*D* 72)

Seward, too, is aware of the serious nature of the Lord Godalming's complaint, and of Holmwood's prolonged sojourn at his father's seat, *Ring*, the name of which again acknowledges symbolically the forthcoming marriage.[45] With the thesis of hysteria established in Seward's mind, such a threat to the rapid effecting of the nuptials is likely to be regarded medically as the exciting cause of an attack of self-induced or 'tertiary' hysterical symptoms. Carter, again, explains:

> The emotions likely to be secretly dwelt upon as a consequence of the pleasures derived from them are thus reduced to a very small number; and it is evident that a young woman whose chief enjoyment rests either upon a complacent contemplation of her own perfections, mingled with an angry sense of the neglect shown to them by her associates, or else upon an imagined gratification of her sexual desires, is not in the best possible frame of mind for withstanding the pressure of a new temptation; such as is held out by the discovery that she can, at will, produce an apparently serious illness, and thus make herself an object of great attention to all around her, and possibly, among others, to the individual who has been uppermost in her thoughts.[46]

Lucy herself provides an insight for the reader into her egocentricity and vanity with regard to Seward, just before his unsuccessful marriage proposal to her:

> He has a curious habit of looking one straight in the face, as if trying to read one's thoughts. He tries this on very much with me, but I flatter myself he has got a tough nut to crack. I know that from my glass.... He says that I afford him a curious psychological study, and I humbly think I do. (*D* 55)

For a medico-jurist (*D* 244) such as Seward the case would appear almost conclusive. Holmwood, whose access to specific medical precedent and the clinical data of the case is more restricted, would probably not even consider it. Precedent – written and theoretical precedent – confirms hypothesis. This is again an important component in a process that can in *Dracula* lead only to misdiagnosis.

The acknowledgement of Lucy's sexual curiosity, however, casts the consultative role of Van Helsing into a new light. Because of his earlier sexual aspirations towards Lucy, and his long-standing amicable relationship with Holmwood, Seward cannot himself ethically undertake the full examination which Lucy's condition demands – and which the medical conventions of hysteria suggest that she may likely herself *desire*. There is more at stake here than nudity. Carter, for example, notes the frequency with which female hysterical patients demanded a pelvic examination, where a speculum would be admitted to the vagina by a *male* doctor.[47] The presentation of Lucy's neurosis, when taken in cultural context, may thus suggest a drive towards surrogate sexual gratification, a desire to be masturbated on the part of the female.[48] The consulting room, significantly, is Lucy's *boudoir*. A tasteful though compelling veil is drawn over the scenario – and Seward's feelings – as the alienist strolls smoking in the garden, his father-mentor in attendance within.

*

Lucy Westenra is not conventionally hysterical though, according to the medical logic of the novel, she *ought* to be. Rather, she is subject to an occult pathology which progressively overwrites a series of conventional medical symptoms. Lucy's symptoms effectively signify twice: first in the moral and medical construction of hysteria; second, in their relevance to the physiological and apparently moral implications of vampirism.

Carter, among the most influential of writers on hysteria, posits three main factors in the aetiology of the neurosis – the emotional temperament of the subject; the event which triggers the initial attack; and the degree to which the subject is compelled to repress this latter 'exciting cause'.[49] These factors are replicated without parody or comment in the embodiment of both occult and conventional pathologies in *Dracula*. The genetic inheritance which Lucy receives from her valetudinarian mother – 'who has been more than usually ill lately' (*D* 89), as Mina euphemistically puts it – and somnambulistic father, should, according to Carter's thesis, predispose her through temperament to hysteria. There is a tacit reference to this in Mina's fear that Lucy is 'of too supersensitive a nature to go through the world without trouble' (*D* 87).

Lucy's temperament appears to generate her somnambulism. The novel, however, does not allow this condition, which is again associated with hysteria, to develop uncomplicatedly into the latter neurosis. Lucy's somnambulism is superseded, rather, by the alternative though still hysteroid pathology of the vampire. Somnambulism, rather than hysteria, is the abnormal mental condition through which the vampire annexes Lucy. To annex in the novel through hysteria itself, with its popular sexual associations, would take the work too close to the cruder stereotype of sexuality which is safely dissipated throughout by Stoker's symbolism.

The novel's rendering of the initial attack, Carter's second factor, is more equivocal. Rhetorically, it may be construed that Lucy has experienced her initial hysterical paroxysm in childhood, prior to her infantile sleepwalking. In any case, the paroxysm itself may have itself escaped the attention of those in attendance.[50] The novel thus appears to suggest that Lucy's first encounter with Count Dracula, which prostrates her, is a *secondary* attack, based on her predisposition. Carter notes that a patient may indeed find the sympathetic attention that follows such attacks a temptation in itself:

> Under such circumstances, it cannot but become a matter of observation to the patient, that the recollection of a certain event, or train of thought, is usually followed by the fit, and it perhaps occurs to her to ascertain by experiment, whether the association be invariable, or only accidental.[51]

Lucy suffers a further, unequivocal, secondary attack of hysteroid distraction later in the novel when the movement of the sunlight on the windows of a church acts as an 'exciting cause' in recalling the red eyes of the vampire. Mina recalls how Lucy suddenly enters 'a half-dreamy state' and murmurs to herself 'His red eyes again! They are just the same.' Following her friend's eyes she notes:

> She appeared to be looking over at our seat, whereon was a dark figure seated alone. I was a little startled myself, for it seemed for an instant as if the stranger had great eyes like burning flames; but a second look dispelled the illusion. The red sunlight was shining on the windows of St. Mary's Church behind our seat, and as the sun dipped there was just sufficient change in the refraction and reflection to make it appear as if the light moved. (*D* 94)

The 'dark figure' may not necessarily be the Count. The implication of Lucy's abstraction, however, is that it *is*, and that she is lost in a reverie similar to that experienced during her sleepwalking adventure – a state of mind triggered by an image that recalls to her mind the earlier episode.

Away from the vampire's occult or apparent presence, Lucy will arguably be compelled by her own bourgeois modesty to repress her recollections of this 'exciting cause' and its supposedly sexual content. An engaged woman, she has been alone with a man in an isolated spot. The ambivalent, bittersweet emotions which Lucy recollects following the incident, therefore, can only be safely communicated to Mina through images of mental disturbance or hallucination – experiences that she suggests could not really have happened to her (*D* 98). Certainly Lucy has good reason to repress details of her nocturnal adventure. Though her fiancé may take account of her recurrent somnambulism, it is likely that the provincial society of Whitby would not judge her actions with such lenience.

The same hysteroid process occurs in Mina, who sees a vision of 'two red eyes, such as Lucy told me of' (*D* 259) during what she believes to be a dream in disturbed sleep. Mina is approached by the vampire not during an attack of hysteria, to which she has shown no apparent predisposition, but during the confused semi-unconsciousness associated with the first stages of sleep. Like Lucy, Mina is reluctant to recall the event other than by rendering it as a dream in her diary entry for the day. Here, though, her motivation is an apparently conscious fear of alarming her compatriots.

Neither of the Count's female victims is clinically hysterical, therefore. In each case, the victim is first attacked at a time in which the conscious mind is seemingly in abeyance, a condition associated with sleep and the unconscious. The victim is subsequently prostrated by recurrences of the event, or distracted by images which recall the ambivalent emotions and sensations associated with it. An act of repression takes place in both cases – a fear to speak of the incident in public, lest others misunderstand, is seemingly paralleled by a distracted state of mind which can only partially rationalise the significance of what has happened. The vampirised state is, in effect, a counterfeit of conventional hysteria.

*

Conventional hysteria, however, is to be found within the novel, though only in the symptomatology of two of the men involved in the pursuit of the vampire. The novel thus emphatically discards the essentially British consensus that hysteria is a complaint suffered only by women and effeminate men, and adopts in its place a continental hypothesis popularised by Charcot which acknowledges the potential for hysteria 'just like a woman' in men who are 'well developed, not enervated by an indolent or too studious mode of life ... never before emotional, at least in appearance'.[52]

Jonathan Harker suffers a secondary attack of hysteria when he encounters his former host in London.[53] Mina recalls the attack, which she euphemistically describes elsewhere as a consequence of 'brain fever':

> 'I believe it is the Count, but he has grown young. My God, if this be so! Oh, my God! my God! If I only knew! if I only knew!' He was distressing himself so much that I feared to keep his mind on the subject by asking him any questions, so I remained silent. (*D* 172)[54]

The 'exciting cause' of Harker's seizure, as he suggests, is his recollection of finding the encoffined vampire 'looking as if his youth had been half-renewed' (*D* 51). It is this vision that affirms the collapse for Harker of the scientific and theological absolutes invested in death. As Mr Swales argues, 'death be all that we can rightly depend on' (*D* 74). Harker, who admits to being 'encompassed about with terrors that I dare not think of' (*D* 34) can only keep his sense of ontological panic safely in check by repressing its 'exciting cause', by sealing up the apocalyptic book – which Mina does as a sign of her trust – in which what can only be reconciled as madness is written. As Harker tells his wife:

'I have had a great shock, and when I try to think of what it is I feel my head spin round, and I do not know if it was all real or the dreaming of a madman. You know I have had brain fever, and that is to be mad. The secret is here, and I do not want to know it.' (*D* 104)

To do otherwise is to invite the return of the neurosis. Harker is released from his neurotic state only when Van Helsing confirms that his experiences are objective, that the impossible has in effect happened. Returning to his diary, he is now able to write: 'It was the doubt as to the reality of the whole thing that knocked me over.... But, now that I *know*, I am not afraid, even of the Count' (*D* 187–8). He is, essentially, cured from the point at which repression becomes unnecessary.

Arthur Holmwood is similarly prostrated by conventional hysteria following his ordeal in Lucy's tomb. Mina recalls how:

> In an instant the poor dear fellow was overwhelmed with grief. It seemed to me that all he had of late been suffering in silence found a vent at once. He grew quite hysterical, and raising his open hands, beat his palms together in a perfect agony of grief. He stood up and then sat down again, and the tears rained down his cheeks. I felt an infinite pity for him, and opened my arms unthinkingly. With a sob he laid his head on my shoulder and cried like a wearied child, whilst he shook with emotion. (*D* 230)

The location of Arthur's collapse betrays the 'exciting cause' of his neurosis. Holmwood's hysteria is associated with the rupture of his conception of the female, the result of his recent meeting with the vampiric Lucy, whose gestures may be perceived as an expression of a previously unacknowledged – by Arthur at least – libido.

Of course, the physical constitution of the vigorous English nobleman militates against the hysteria becoming chronic. But the novel has provided for Arthur a further explicit release of the tension associated by Carter with the repression of the 'exciting cause' of the hysterical paroxysm and, through Mina's spontaneous, 'unthinking', action, access to the sexual component of the aetiology. Mina recalls:

> We women have something of the mother in us that makes us rise above smaller matters when the mother-spirit is invoked; I felt this big, sorrowing man's head resting on me, as though it were that of

the baby that some day may lie on my bosom, and I stroked his hair as though he were my own child. I never thought at the time how strange it all was. (*D* 230)

This scenario is reassuringly non-sexual. Mina as mother is the antithesis of Lucy as seductress. Despite Mina's belief to the contrary, it isn't really that 'strange' at all. Her love is selfless and innocent. Most significantly, however, it is instinctive. Mina does not resist the impulse of her 'mother-spirit'. Even her sexuality is contained in marriage and by the procreative function: she is not a personified libido. With this reassurance of the persistence of a treasured credo – a belief in the innate purity of the female which corresponds with Harker's need to believe in the evidence of his own eyes – life for Holmwood may go on. He has no further compulsion to repress the exciting cause of his seizure.

*

It is clear that Van Helsing's treatment of Lucy is defeated only by unforeseen human circumstance – the removal of the garlic wreath on two occasions by Lucy's mother – rather than by any fault in its reasoning. The physician's use of garlic as a prophylactic in the sick room, however, puzzles Seward:

> The Professor's actions were certainly odd, and not to be found in any pharmacopoeia that I ever heard of. First, he fastened up the windows and latched them securely; next, taking a handful of the flowers, he rubbed them all over the sashes, as though to ensure that every whiff of air that might get in would be laden with the garlic smell. Then with the wisp he rubbed all over the jamb of the door, above, below, and at each side, and round the fireplace in the same way. (*D* 131)

Seward's gallant attempt to reconcile Van Helsing's actions with conventional medicine by suggesting that his mentor is adopting inhalation as a therapeutic practice is unconvincing, even though several references have already been made to Lucy's recurrent breathing problems.[55]

Van Helsing's methodology, rather, echoes the rubric of both Hippocratic and late Victorian responses to hysteria. The pungent wreath of garlic flowers which Van Helsing places around Lucy's neck reflects the use of the plant in a more ancient pharmacopoeia. In ancient Egyptian and Græco-Roman medicine, aromatic substances were applied to the upper body to drive the so-called *Globus Hystericus*

– the floating and mobile uterus – from the throat, where it character-istically restricts breathing, and back to the abdomen.[56] Garlic, in this context, has both an occult and a quasi-medical significance.

The wreath, though, emblematises the crisis points of the two possi-ble diagnoses of Lucy's disorder. It is simultaneously both a bridal bouquet and a funerary tribute. It is only after death that conclusive action may be taken to eradicate the persistence of the vampiric complaint. Hysteria – explicitly that which has a sexual aetiology – may be cured, according to Carter, through the transaction of marriage or engagement in sexual intercourse.[57] This former is obliquely provided for in the proposed union of Holmwood and Lucy. But when death, the alternative pathology, threatens to intervene, Van Helsing substitutes the transfusion of blood for sexual consummation, making the equation between blood and semen that Sigmund Freud was later to popularise. Arthur, ignorant that he has been but one among many donors to Lucy's depleted circulation, regards his transfusion of blood as an act of marriage. Van Helsing, though, sees the irony in the fiancé-cum-widower's remark:

> 'But there was a difficulty, friend John. If so that, then what about the others? Ho, ho! Then this so sweet maid is a polyandrist, and me, with my poor wife dead to me, but alive by Church's law, though no wits, all gone – even I, who am faithful husband to this now-no-wife, am bigamist.' (*D* 176)

This polygamous marriage, of course, realises both the presumed sublimated sexual desires of Lucy and the gentlemanly intentions of three of the four male blood donors.

Sexual activity posits both literally and figuratively, through race and heredity, the exchange of bodily fluids, the mingling of bloods. It is notable, therefore, that the final 'operation' performed on Lucy's body is described by Seward in the language of sexual intensity rather than through the more detached vocabulary of the clinic. As the stake penetrates 'the white flesh' of Arthur's fiancée:

> The body shook and quivered and twisted in wild contortions; the sharp white teeth champed together till the lips were cut and the mouth was smeared with a crimson foam. But Arthur never faltered. He looked like a figure of Thor as his untrembling arm rose and fell, driving deeper and deeper the mercy-bearing stake, whilst the blood from the pierced heart welled and spurted up around it. His face was

set, and high duty seemed to shine through it; the sight of it gave us courage, so that our voices seemed to ring through the little vault. (*D* 216)

The compulsion of the thrill of rape is clearly available to the male reader here, from the detailing of the receptive whiteness of Lucy's flesh through to the repetitive movements which Holmwood makes in his attempt to penetrate, to rupture, to draw blood from the prone body. The quasi-orgasm which Lucy experiences, a *grande mort* rather than a *petite mort*, is similarly the fulfilment of a male sexual fantasy. The veil cast by the 'mercy-bearing stake' is thin indeed.

The ritual staking is arranged in particular for Arthur's benefit, as Van Helsing twice makes clear (*D* 202, 215). It must be noted, though, that the Dutch physician earlier proposes a more restrained and conventionally surgical procedure towards the same end, an operation more appropriate to the clinical treatment of the dead than of the living. Asked by Van Helsing to provide a set of post-mortem knives, Seward queries 'Must we make an autopsy?' Van Helsing replies:

'Yes, and no. I want to operate, but not as you think. Let me tell you now, but not a word to another. I want to cut off her head and take out her heart. Ah! you a surgeon, and so shocked! You whom I have seen with no tremble of hand or heart, do operations of life and death that make the rest shudder. Oh, but I must not forget, my dear friend John, that you loved her; and I have not forgotten it, for it is I that shall operate, and you must only help.' (*D* 164)

This plan is again thwarted by unforeseen human circumstances – the theft by Lucy's servant of the golden crucifix that would have prevented the victim's condition reaching an active and contagious phase after death.[58]

Arthur's actions in the tomb therefore 'become' the sexual cure of the hysterical neurosis, as advanced by Carter. The operation itself is constructed so as to unite the two medical scripts, the two diagnoses, of the novel. The parallel to the clinical operation first proposed by Van Helsing is obvious, particularly in the light of Seward's response to his mentor's actions:

Van Helsing, in his methodological manner, began taking the various contents from his bag and placing them ready for use. First he took out a soldering iron and some plumbing solder, and then a small-oil lamp, which gave out, when lit in a corner of the tomb, gas which burned at fierce heat with a blue flame; then his operating knives, which he placed to hand; and last a wooden stake, some two and a half or three inches thick and about three feet long.... With this stake came a heavy hammer, such as in households is used in the coal-cellar for breaking the lumps. To me, a doctor's preparations for work of any kind are stimulating and bracing, but the effect of these things on both Arthur and Quincey was to cause them a sort of consternation. (*D* 214)

As his reactions indicate, Seward is viewing the surgical instruments of the occult pathology through the filter of the medical. For the alienist, but not for Quincey or Arthur, there is a congruence between the two views of Lucy's disorder. A parasitic growth is to be removed through the skilled application of these conspicuously domestic implements.

Though Arthur is seemingly enacting his *jus primae noctis* for a second time, he, like the reader, is compelled now to dissociate the disease from its embodiment. Though anger and indignation may harden his purposefulness, he must maintain the disinterestedness of the surgeon. Seward may state on viewing the possessed corpse that 'there was no love in my own heart, nothing but loathing for the foul Thing which had taken Lucy's shape without her soul' (*D* 213–14), but the fact remains that this is still the exact semblance of Lucy's body. The novel, again, is permitting the reader to have it both ways sexually, simultaneously exposing both prurience and moral outrage. This is the effect of Seward's rhetoric of high morality and moral purpose, as it is the background to the Alienist's portrayal of Arthur as Thor, or his earlier vision of Van Helsing entering the tomb, saturated as it is with Seward's own prurience:

> Van Helsing went about his work systematically. Holding his candle so that he could read the coffin plates, and so holding it that the sperm dropped in white patches which congealed as they touched the metal, he made assurance of Lucy's coffin. (*D* 197)

Seward narrowly skirts the obscene here through the convenient conflation of 'sperm' with both *spermaceti* and *spermatozoa*. His sexual interest is obvious throughout. Arthur, though, is portrayed as comparatively sexless by Seward. Arthur's satisfaction must only be spiritual: he cannot permit his own enjoyment of the violation of Lucy's body. Such would be contrary to his explicit Christian faith, and to his underplayed and somewhat etherealised vision of love. Prurient to the last, Seward unwittingly encodes a sexual and economic resonance to Arthur's supposedly moral satisfaction. In Seward's words, Arthur withdraws from the prone body, exhausted:

> The hammer fell from Arthur's hand. He reeled and would have fallen had we not caught him. Great drops of sweat sprang out on his forehead, and his breath came in broken gasps. It had indeed been an awful strain on him.... (*D* 216)

Explicitly, he is drained of another vital fluid, the saline content of sweat encoding easily into that of both blood and semen.[59]

Arthur is simultaneously the pious widower venerating the memory of his pure-minded fiancée, and the enraged rapist violating the erotic being which, in Seward's words, has 'taken Lucy's shape without her soul' (*D* 214). Lucy is thus, in occult (and, indeed, erotic) terms, 'possessed' by the vampire. Though modern criticism has tended to conclude that the dormant sexuality of Lucy is somehow 'awakened' by her induction into vampirism, it may argued with equal force that her character is progressively overwritten by the growth of a parasitic organism within her body.[60] In life and in death Lucy is absolved from complicity in her eroticised vampiric behaviour by the trance condition in which it was contracted. As Van Helsing points out when examining her vampirised corpse:

> 'Here, there is one thing which is different from all recorded: here is some dual life that is not as the common. She was bitten by the vampire when she was in a trance, sleep-walking ... and in trance could he best come to take more blood. In trance she died, and in trance she is Un-Dead too.... this so sweet that-was when she not Un-Dead she go back to the nothings of the common dead. There is no malign there, see, and so it make hard that I must kill her in her sleep.' (*D* 201)

Commonplace in conventional hysteria, somnambulism as part of vampirism both complicates the diagnosis and releases the victim from conscious complicity in her condition – and in its sexualised propagation. Lucy's feet are saved from 'paths of flame' by the intervention of devoted and resourceful men. In a sense, though, she is 'saved' also by the reflex action of the conventional hysterical complaint. Lucy both *is* and *is not* hysterical. The pseudo-Lucy that

Holmwood despatches does not necessarily represent the release of her hitherto repressed libido, as modern readers frequently assume: it is equally the excrescence of the alien pathology.[61] The disease has become separated from the host-victim, and it is the disease that is treated, not the patient. There are a whole series of Lucies – the bitten Lucy, subject to the occult pathology; the hysterical Lucy; and Arthur's idealised Lucy – and they are not wholly congruent. Hence, in *Dracula*, hysteria has become a strategy employed to make a moral point about the innateness of feminine purity, *not* the innateness of female lust.

## Into the very soul of the patient

The multidiscursive nature of blood is central also to the presentation of the pathological case of Mina Harker. Like Lucy, Mina manifests what may be interpreted as a moral as well as physical deterioration following the draining – and, indeed, contamination – of her blood by the Count. Mina's medical treatment, however, differs from that previously applied to Lucy in that both the patient and her associates are fully aware of the presence and likely progress of the vampiric disorder with which she has been infected. Mina is, in a sense, a lay participant in the systematic observation of her condition, a knowing index of her own relative well-being in occult as well as physiological terms.

The clinical response to Mina's disorder is complicated through the intersection in the novel of the *fin-de-siècle* therapeutics of Seward and Van Helsing with an earlier – and, by the 1890s, discredited – pseudo-medical practice. At the patient's own suggestion, Van Helsing investigates the progress of her disorder through hypnotism. Though popularised towards the close of the century by Charcot's work at the Salpêtrière, clinical hypnotism frequently remained associated in the public eye with charlatanism and with the 'occult' practices of mesmerism and magnetism.[62] Such associations arguably form the subtext of Van Helsing's protracted questioning of the parameters of Seward's beliefs just before Lucy is revealed as the victim of a vampire. Dismissing Seward's empirical approach as 'too prejudiced', Van Helsing asks:

'... I suppose now you do not believe in corporeal transference. No? Nor in materialization. No? Nor in astral bodies. No? Nor in the reading of thought. No? Nor in hypnotism –'
'Yes,' I said, 'Charcot has proved that pretty well.' He smiled as he went on: 'Then you are satisfied as to it. Yes? And of course then you

understand how it act, and can follow the mind of the great Charcot – alas that he is no more! – into the very soul of the patient that he influence. No? Then, friend John, am I to take it that you simply accept fact, and are satisfied to let from premise to conclusion be a blank? No? Then tell me – for I am student of the brain – how you accept the hypnotism and reject the thought-reading...?' (*D* 191)

As a physician cast in the mould of Carpenter, Seward is able to accept the hypnotic findings of Charcot because these are apparently supported by supplementary proofs tenable within physiological logic.[63] Van Helsing, though, insistently couples the epistemologically acceptable work of the emphatically 'great' Charcot with a range of phenomena which Carpenter, among others, consistently refutes through the application of physiology to mental action.[64] The Professor's rather patronising remark, 'of course then you understand how it act', embedded within his tissue of rhetorical questions, arguably refers not to Seward's understanding of the *process* of hypnotism but to the perceived logic upon which its veracity is founded. Van Helsing seeks to shift the basis of this logic from the primarily physiological to a more transcendentally spiritual stance not tenable under Seward's materialism.

Van Helsing is thus not proposing an unquestioning adherence to Charcot's assertions. Indeed, the hypnotic component of *Dracula* cannot be said to be unequivocally founded on Charcot's technique, nor on the popular understanding of his theories of hypnotism and hysteria. The name and achievements of Charcot are merely tools within Van Helsing's rhetoric. Quite simply, to persuade Seward into a reconsideration of unproven phenomena such as thought reading, Van Helsing posits first that Charcot holds but part of the perceived 'truth'; and, second, that the 'medical' proposition that Seward accepts is founded upon essentially the same principles which support the 'occult' phenomena whose existence he rejects. The 'blank' between premise and conclusion is crucial here. Effectively, this is the epistemological space in which the familiar assumptions of physiological medicine meet with the nebulous possibilities which Van Helsing finds within Charcot's theories of the mind. Seward's trusting acceptance of what Van Helsing calls 'fact' indicates, in effect, the Alienist's unwillingness to face a possible fracture in his supposedly comprehensive understanding of modern mental diagnostics.

Significantly, Van Helsing's hypnotic technique differs from the methodology popularly associated with Charcot. Harker describes in detail the Professor's initial attempt to hypnotise Mina:

Looking fixedly at her, he commenced to make passes in front of her, from over the top of her head downward, with each hand in turn. Mina gazed at him fixedly for a few minutes, during which my own heart beat like a trip hammer, for I felt that some crisis was at hand. Gradually her eyes closed, and she sat stock still; only by the gentle heaving of her bosom could one know that she was alive. The Professor made a few more passes and then stopped, and I could see that his forehead was covered with great beads of perspiration. (*D* 312)

Charcot's customary technique, in common with that employed by the Scottish physician James Braid, directs the attention of the subject away from the hypnotic operator and towards an object upon which the attention must be fixed. The practice, as an anonymous contributor to *The Times* suggests, is thus effectively one of *self*-hypnosis:

a patient is placed before an intense light – *e.g.*, the electric – and requested to look at it. In a few seconds or minutes she becomes motionless in a state of catalepsy. The eyes are fixed, the limbs are supple, and will keep any position given them. In this state the physiognomy seems to reflect to some extent the expression of the gestures ... but beyond such modifications from attitude the patient remains impassive, fixed, and insensible to the outer world.[65]

The fixed gaze of the patient, which Harker observes, maintains the most tenuous of methodological links to accepted hypnotic practice. For, where Carpenter's thesis suggests that the patient *herself* (and gender is again an important component of susceptibility to hypnotism here) induces the trance, the novel is asserting through Van Helsing's gestures and the obvious stigmata of his effort that *the Professor*, as hypnotic operator, has *caused* the change in Mina's consciousness.[66] To recall Van Helsing's earlier interpretation of Charcot's therapy, Harker's rendering of this incident suggests that the operator himself has journeyed 'into the very soul of the patient that he influence'.

For all Van Helsing's harnessing of Charcot's name as an authority, however, such intimacies are clearly not part of contemporary medical discourses in so far as these touch upon clinical hypnotism. Rather, they reflect the presence in *Dracula* of less orthodox theories addressing the hypnoid state, and the persistence of these in fiction generally as a popular (though misleading) signifier of contemporary clinical practice. Harker's inclusion of two key terms – 'passes' and 'crisis' – in his description of Van Helsing, is significant. Both recall the magnetic treatment popularised initially in the eighteenth century by Mesmer – the 'crisis' which Carpenter associates with the 'hysteric fit'; the 'passes' which Mayo asserts as being fundamentally identical in the practice of Mesmer and in contemporary hypnotism – which Mayo patronisingly describes as 'disguised Mesmerism'.[67] Stoker is well aware of the provenance of these terms. He recalls their mesmeric associations in *Famous Impostors*, where he also suggests that Mesmer's findings, having been 'tested and employed in therapeutics for a century', are now 'accepted as a contribution to science'.[68]

Herbert Mayo's *On the Truths Contained in Popular Superstitions, with an Account of Mesmerism*, which Stoker lists among the sources for *Dracula*, is probably the most important single source for the novel's fictionalisation of the hypnoid state. Van Helsing, certainly, is styled as a mesmerist after the model displayed by Mayo in his exploration of the subject:

> the two hands of the operator may be held horizontally with the fingers pointed to the patient's forehead, and either maintained in this position, or brought downwards in frequent passes opposite to the patient's face, shoulders, arms; the points of the fingers being held as near the patient as possible without touching.[69]

Beyond this superficial resemblance, however, *Dracula* draws heavily on the equation which Mayo makes between mesmeric practice and contemporary hypnotism. Mayo tempers this equation with a persistent polemical drive in favour of the odylic theories propounded by Baron von Reichenbach in 1845.[70] Von Reichenbach proposed the existence of an 'intangible force' vested in magnets, crystals and in the nature of certain sensitive manipulators and subjects. Mayo is quick to equate this force with the similarly intangible *fluid* of Mesmer's theory of mental influence.[71] Stoker is, as we have seen, committed to fluid economy in *Dracula*; and, though the novel does not explicitly embrace the assertions of Mayo, it appears safe to assume that it draws on the rhetoric through which Mayo's contentions are mobilised – particularly in the insistence by both Mayo and Van Helsing that unprecedented phenomena as well as contemporary scientific knowledge may be explained with reference to discarded ideas and the investigation of a substance whose nature is regarded as a fluid.

Stoker's choice of hypnotic technique is dictated in part also by a readership which vested its consciousness of hypnoid states neither in clinical practice nor in Mesmer but in fictional characters such as Du Maurier's Svengali – like Van Helsing a man of curious speech:

> Svengali told [Trilby] to sit down on the divan, and sat opposite to her, and bade her look him well in the white of the eyes.
> 'Recartez-moi pien tans le planc tes yeux.'
> Then he made little passes and counterpasses on her forehead and temples and down her cheek and neck. Soon her eyes closed and her face grew placid.[72]

Svengali's mesmerism (for so it is termed in Du Maurier's *Trilby*) is initially employed as a cure for the heroine's ocular neuralgia.[73] The association with Svengali, however, generates an additional negative charge of manipulation by the hypnotic operator, a risk which always formed an undercurrent in the debate on hypnotism, and an uneasy complement here to Van Helsing's obvious altruism.[74]

With the Professor's practice so readily identifiable as modern mesmerism, the implicitly hypnotic technique earlier employed by Count Dracula on Mina appears even more problematic in so far as the latter closely resembles the orthodox method of Charcot. Mina recalls her encounter with Dracula, which she interprets as a dream:

> The gas-light which I had left lit for Jonathan, but turned down, came only like a tiny red spark through the fog, which had evidently grown thicker and poured into the room. Then it occurred to me that I had shut the window before I had come to bed. I would have got out to make certain on the point, but some leaden lethargy seemed to chain my limbs and even my will. I lay still and endured: that was all.... [The mist] got thicker and thicker, till it seemed as if it became concentrated into a sort of pillar of cloud in the room, through the top of which I could see the light of the gas shining like a red eye.... the fire was in the red eye, which at the thought got a new fascination for me; till, as I looked, the fire divided, and seemed to shine on me through the fog like two red eyes, such as Lucy told me of in her momentary mental wandering when, on the cliff, the dying sunlight struck the windows of St. Mary's Church. Suddenly the horror burst upon me that it was thus that Jonathan had seen those awful women growing into reality through the whirling mist in the moonlight,

and in my dream I must have fainted, for all became black darkness. (*D* 258–9)

Mina stares fixedly at a point some distance from her body, and effectively hypnotises herself in a manner reminiscent of the description of Charcot's practice in *The Times*. Her dream-like state is, again, crucial. Immediately, it enables her to dismiss the whole event as a dream, and thus unworthy of the attention of her preoccupied guardians. The notion that the will may be in abeyance in sleep as much as in trance, though, is of vital importance in the novel's consistent drive to clear the victims of the vampire from any charge of complicity in their spiritual downfall.

Count Dracula, however, is constructed under the same hypnotic rubric as that which empowers Van Helsing. The resemblance between his trance-inducing behaviour and clinical practice is superficial and misleading, for orthodox hypnotism could not generate nor support the full range of hypnotic or hypnoid phenomena presented in *Dracula*. The logic here is emphatically that of Mayo and Mesmer, and not that of Carpenter or Charcot. It is a logic that the reader may access, albeit with modifications, through characters such as Du Maurier's Svengali or the mesmeric operator who preserves the corporeal existence of Poe's Monsieur Valdemar.

The extent to which hypnotism as portrayed in *Dracula* has departed from the findings of Charcot and Carpenter is betrayed by the relationship between the subject or patient and the hypnotic operator. An intimation of the problematic nature of this relationship in conventional medical terms is given prior to Van Helsing's treatment of Mina. Lucy is implicitly initiated into a trance by Count Dracula on the occasion of her sleepwalking to the Whitby churchyard. Her trance state becomes intermittent, though the hypnotic operator is not always himself physically present when it supervenes upon conventional sleep. Seward observes of Lucy:

Towards dusk she fell into a doze. Here a very odd thing occurred. Whilst still asleep she took the paper from her breast and tore it in two. Van Helsing stepped over and took the pieces from her. All the same, however, she went on with the action of tearing, as though the material were still in her hands; finally she lifted her hands and opened them as though scattering the fragments. (*D* 152)

The blurring of boundaries between abnormal and non-conscious states of mind – sleep, trance, hysteria, somnambulism, insanity – is again significant here. As Lucy is in a state analogous to trance she may of course perform such an action at the behest of her hypnotic operator. Count Dracula is not present. The reader is led to believe, though, that Lucy is, during her trance, attempting to destroy the written evidence of the vampire's visitation, the *Memorandum* of 17 September which the reader will have already read prior to Seward's journal entry of 18 September, in which the Alienist recalls this incident. The reader is clearly supposed to believe that Lucy has been instructed to destroy the document from a distance.

As Carpenter explicitly states, however, the logic underpinning contemporary hypnotism cannot support such an action when the operator himself is not present to initiate it. Carpenter argues:

It is affirmed, however, that proof of this agency is furnished by the power of the 'silent will' of the mesmeriser to induce the sleep in 'subjects' who are not in the least aware that it is being exerted, and, further, to direct from a distance the actions of the somnambule.... it has been repeatedly found that mesmerisers who had no hesitation in asserting that they could send particular 'subjects' to sleep, or could affect them in other ways, by an effort of silent will, have utterly failed to do so when these subjects were carefully kept from any suspicion that such will was being exerted.[75]

The reader, therefore, is forced to consider the possibility of a telepathic or sympathetic link between the two, something akin to, but more directed than, Renfield's nocturnal sensitivity. This is an option not permitted by Carpenter's thesis, but well attuned to Mesmer's magnetism and Mayo's odylism.

The novel stops short of explicitly defining the nature of this link. However, the process by which the channel of communication is opened advances sufficient information from which the reader may formulate a hypothesis. Seward's vision of the vampire's attack on Mina has frequently been regarded as an encoding of fellatio and violent sexual practices.[76] Seward describes the scene:

On the bed beside the window lay Jonathan Harker, his face flushed, and breathing heavily as though in a stupor. Kneeling on the near edge of the bed facing outwards was the white-clad figure of his wife. By her side stood a tall, thin man, clad in black.... With his left hand he held both Mrs Harker's hands, keeping them away with her arms at full tension; his right hand gripped her by the back of the neck, forcing her face down on his bosom. Her white night-dress was smeared with blood, and a thin stream trickled down the man's bare breast, which was shown by his torn-open dress. The attitude of the two had a terrible resemblance to a child forcing a kitten's nose into a saucer of milk to compel it to drink. (*D* 281–2)

Mina is displayed at the front of the marital bed, within sight of her impotent husband, for the benefit of the male reader, and through the expedient frame of the fascinated gaze of the prurient Alienist. This representation of the scene, however, is in many ways of secondary importance.

The central implication of the incident is arguably made elsewhere, in Mina's own recollection of the event. Mina recalls Dracula's words and actions immediately prior to the group's incursion into her bedchamber:

'"You have aided in thwarting me; now you shall come to my call. When my brain says 'Come!' to you, you shall cross land or sea to do my bidding; and to that end this!" With that he pulled open his shirt, and with his long sharp nails opened a vein in his breast. When the blood began to spurt out, he took my hands in one of his, holding them tight, and with the other seized my neck and pressed my mouth to the wound, so that I must either suffocate or swallow some of the – Oh, my God, my God! what have I done?' (*D* 288)

It is obvious from Mina's description of the blood as 'spurting', and from her reluctance to name the substance which she has been forced to swallow while kneeling before the Count 'in that terrible and horrible position' (*D* 284), as Seward calls it, that the blood/semen equation persists here, becoming also a *mesmeric* equation.[77]

*Dracula* advances a vision of infection not through contact, not through the bite alone, but by way of a process analogous to *osmosis*. Count Dracula is not merely taking sustenance from Mina, he is implanting his own spiritual poison within her by the same physical channel. His actions with respect to Mina are an amplification and exaggeration of those which he inflicts upon Lucy. In a sense he is more obviously *inseminating* Mina, passing to her through contagious pathology the seed of her own vampirism and that of a future generation of vampires. The oral and the vaginal are as closely identified here as their respective fluid economies were in the case of Lucy. With this incident in mind, a series of remarks regarding contamination of the blood, from Harker, as reported by Sister Agatha of the Buda-Pesth hospital:

'He has had some fearful shock – so says our doctor – and in his delirium his ravings have been dreadful; of wolves and poison and blood; of ghosts and demons; and I fear to say of what.' (*D* 99)

from Seward, in his private journal:

I suppose it is some of that horrid poison which has got into her veins beginning to work. The Count had his own purposes when he gave her [Mina] what Van Helsing called 'the Vampire's baptism of blood.' Well, there may be a poison that distils itself out of good things; in an age when the existence of ptomaines is a mystery we should not wonder at anything! (*D* 322)

and latterly, from Mina herself:

'There is a poison in my blood, in my soul, which may destroy me; which must destroy me, unless some relief comes to us. Oh, my friends, you know as well as I do, that my soul is at stake....' (*D* 330)

become totally meaningful and obviously systematic.[78] In *Dracula*, spiritual disorder is a consequence of fluid contamination, as both Seward and Mina acknowledge. Ptomaines are amine compounds, often toxic, in putrefying animal matter.[79] The Count is, in physiological terms, dead animal matter, his 'rank' breath (*D* 18) hinting of interior putrefaction.[80] Mina has effectively consumed the vampire's morbid pathology, and his corruption is multiplying, bacteria-like, within her own circulation.

Though the novel draws heavily here on the eugenic implications of mingling bloods, and the suggestion that such relationships invariably result in the decline and dilution of the healthier stock, the whole issue has a moral and spiritual resonance also.[81] Mina's Christian spirit faces a progressive undermining by that of the vampire, who has, like Christ, purchased her through his blood. Van Helsing's depiction of the incident as a 'baptism of blood' is, similarly, a point of intersection with the religious script. It will take the shedding of Quincey Morris's innocent and freely given blood to repurchase Mina adequately.[82] The blood clearly is not only that of earthly life, but of the Life Everlasting also.

Blood thus forms the basis of the supposedly intangible telepathic connection between Mina Harker and Count Dracula, overwriting the equivalent channels in both mesmerism and hypnotism. Mina, like Charcot, may undertake a spiritual journey 'into the very soul' of another being, following the suggestive questions posed to her by Van Helsing, her second hypnotic operator. In Van Helsing's initial hypno- tising of Mina the 'great beads of perspiration' stand in place of blood as the sign of communication, drawing again on the common saline content of the two bodily fluids.[83] Mina's interpretation of what she experiences when in mental communion with the vampire's dormant body is succinct and utterly convincing: when the Professor asks 'What are you doing?' she replies, simply 'I am still – oh, so still. It is like death!' (*D* 313). The baleful stare of the vampire may still paralyse; but, as Dracula makes clear as he opens his vein to Mina, it is blood, the mingling of bloods, the entering into communion through blood, through which the commands of his brain are transmitted to her limbs, and her sensations back to his consciousness – 'and to that end, this!' (*D* 287–8).

Hence, Mina, like Lucy, displays a tendency to involuntary sympa- thetic movements when placed in the hypnotic state. Seward recalls the termination of a later hypnotic session induced by Van Helsing:

> Here she stopped. She had risen, as if impulsively, from where she lay on the sofa, and raised both her hands, palms upwards, as if lifting a weight. Van Helsing and I looked at each other with under- standing. (*D* 344)

The two physicians, of course, understand not only that Mina is repli- cating Dracula's emergence from his coffin, but also the psychological and spiritual process that makes the duplication of that action possible at a distance of several miles. But it is Mina who, in requesting hypno- tism at the hands of Van Helsing, suggests that her own hypnotic condition may be reciprocal, and not the mono-directional chain of command between operator and subject prototypically encountered in Charcot's work. Mina is a participant in her own salvation, twisting the logic of science to her own advantage. Clearly, as her recollection of the vampiric baptism suggests, she appreciates the symbolic as well as the physiological meaning of blood. The novel has reasserted not only the presence of the spiritual in the material; at the same time it has recalled the fluid to its former place in the aetiology of hypnoid states. It is only through such a medium that the fictional hypnotic subjects could engage in the exoneural activities which form the distinctive feature of their trance existence. Blood is as close to the mesmeric Fluid in *Dracula* as it ever could be.

*

The relationship between the novel, the reader and the cultural archive upon which both draw is a complex one in *Dracula*. The text is an extended play upon the multiple connotations of blood, literal and symbolic; it charts their economic relations to the body, and their potential for exchange and coexistence with each other. Demonstrably, the medical script is not included merely to function as a convenient authority for occasional statements that draw on conventional therapeutics or surgery. Nor, again, is the novel a polemic against one or more traditions in medical or psychological thought: the failure, as we have seen, is that of the practitioner, not that of the discipline. The discipline – and under this heading we might include physiology, diagnosis, toxicology and surgery – has been itself represented as a discursive economy in the text, subject to exchange, and with boundaries that shift in response to the ebb and flow of symptom and hypothesis.

Hence the medical script is a persistent and integral component of the fabric of the novel, saturated with mythic as well as literal value, a prime motive force in the construction and interaction of both human and supernatural character. The medical language does not yield at all easily to the occult script. Rather, through its ability to reflex, to twist its own meaning to another purpose, the medical script demonstrates an unforeseen potential with which it may subvert the occult, forcing further the adherence of the supernatural to the more mundane laws of economics, the physiological concepts of secretion and depletion. The occult cannot be said therefore to be the only source of instability in the novel: the medical content enjoys a markedly similar function throughout. The rhetorical strategy of *Dracula* therefore is one of realignment, an assertion of coexistence rather than of an Absolute. Boundaries become blurred as the Christian and the scientific move to accommodate the occult, and as the demarcations between pathological conditions, pharmacopoeias and techniques break down. Causes and consequences are no longer assignable with ease to *either* the material *or* the spiritual.

# Afterword

*Beyond Dracula* has argued that the crude evaluative criteria which allow Stoker's writings other than *Dracula* to be dismissed merely as the emphemera of a 'hack writer' are clearly no longer adequate.[1] It is apparent that the concerns of *Dracula* – be they religious, racial, social or epistemological – are equally the concerns of the author's other writings. Moreover, the manner in which these concerns are presented in Stoker's fiction, whether through plot, character or scenic backdrop, are again in no respect unique to *Dracula*. It might be argued, in response to such an assertion, that the frequent recurrence of such devices as the knightly vigil, the aquiline countenance or the blushing face confirms Stoker's writings to be characterised by an unimaginative or obsessive repetitiousness. It should be evident, however, that such recurrences are, in essence, *reworkings* rather than simply replications. Each fresh occurrence, as it were, is modified by its contiguity to other issues, other signifiers and other texts. Though certain features of Stoker's fiction at times appear markedly *reminiscent* of each other, they are seldom truly *congruent* in terms of their contextual effect on the reader.

A cultural analysis of this type also calls into question the whole place of biographical detail in criticism – particularly here in the acknowledgement that much of the biographical commentary available on Stoker is either ambiguous or riddled with inacuracy.[2] For the purpose of this volume, therefore, biographical details have been significant not in themselves but in so far as they constitute multi-discursive moments, points of visibility for the cultural assumptions and preoccupations of Stoker's time. Likewise, the details of specific fictional incidents or characters have not been viewed as covert auto-biographical gestures, however tempting this may be. What the

178

volume has done, is to suggest the presence of the cultural coherences behind such details, and to chart at least some of the tensions that may exist between them.

# Notes

### Introduction: Reading beyond *Dracula*

1 Hall Caine, 'Bram Stoker. The Story of a Great Friendship', *The Daily Telegraph*, 24 April 1912, p. 16.

2 'Death of Mr. Bram Stoker. Sir H. Irving's Manager', *The Daily Telegraph*, 22 April 1912, p. 6; Caine, 'Bram Stoker', p. 16; 'Obituary. Mr. Bram Stoker', *The Times*, 22 April 1912, p. 15. A *fidus Achates* is a faithful companion or bosom friend, the allusion being to Virgil's *Aeneid*. The term is used to describe Bram Stoker by *The Times* and recurs in a further obituary: 'Bram Stoker', *The New York Times*, 23 April 1912, p. 12.

3 Caine, 'Bram Stoker', p. 16.

4 'Merry-go-Round', *The Entr'acte*, 23 September 1882, p. 4.

5 Bram Stoker, *Personal Reminiscences of Henry Irving*, 2 vols (London: William Heinemann, 1906) Vol. 1, p. ix (Hereafter *PRHI*).

6 Caine, 'Bram Stoker', p. 16.

7 Stoker records an eclectic selection of guests at Lyceum First Nights in the first volume of his biography of Irving. The list, which is arranged throughout in two columns, occupies an astonishing eleven single-spaced pages. Though a few women – most notably Genevieve Ward, Lady Gregory, Sarah Bernhardt and the Baroness Burdett-Coutts – feature in their own right, the majority are listed merely as the partners of their distinguished husbands (*PRHI* I 315–26). For information on the masculine culture of London in the period see Pamela Horn, *High Society: The English Social Élite 1880–1914* (Stroud: Alan Sutton, 1992) pp. 24–9, 147–51.

8 Maurice Richardson, 'The Psychoanalysis of Ghost Stories', *The Twentieth Century* 166 (1959) 419–31 at p. 427; Joseph Bierman, 'A Crucial Stage in the Writing of *Dracula*', William Hughes and Andrew Smith, eds, *Bram Stoker: History, Psychoanalysis and the Gothic* (Basingstoke: Macmillan, 1998) pp. 151–72 at p. 169.

9 Joseph Bierman, '*Dracula*: Prolonged Childhood Illness, and the Oral Triad', *American Imago* 29 (1972) 186–98; Richardson, 'The Psychoanalysis of Ghost Stories', p. 429; Daniel Lapin, *The Vampire, Dracula and Incest* (San Francisco: Gargoyle, 1995) p. 31.

10 Phyllis Roth, *Bram Stoker* (Boston: Twayne, 1982) p. 23; Daniel Farson, *The Man Who Wrote Dracula* (London: Michael Joseph, 1975) pp. 233–5; cf. David Skal, *V is for Vampire* (London: Robson, 1996) p. 186. For an opposing viewpoint, based on a reading of recent and nineteenth-century medical textbooks, see Peter Haining and Peter Tremayne, *The Un-Dead* (London: Constable, 1997) pp. 179–82.

11 Skal, *V is for Vampire* p. 183; Talia Shaffer, '"A Wilde Desire Took Me": The Homoerotic History of *Dracula*', *English Literary History* 61/2 (1994) 381–425 at p. 397.

12 Daniel Farson, 'The Sexual Torment of the Man who Created Dracula', *The*

*Mail on Sunday*, 3 January 1993, pp. 35, 43.

13  Michel Foucault, *The History of Sexuality: An Introduction* (London: Penguin, 1984) pp. 6–7.

14  Foucault, *The History of Sexuality*, p. 33.

15  Daniel Pick, '"Terrors of the Night": *Dracula* and "Degeneration" in the Late Nineteenth Century', *Critical Quarterly* 30 (1989) 71–87; Ernest Fontana, 'Lombroso's Criminal Man and Stoker's Dracula', *Victorian Newsletter* 66 (1984) 25–7; Victor Sage, *Horror Fiction in the Protestant Tradition* (Basingstoke: Macmillan, 1988) pp. 180–5; Kellie Donovan Wixson, '*Dracula*: An Anglo-Irish Gothic Novel', Elizabeth Miller, ed., *Dracula: The Shade and the Shadow* (Westcliff-on-Sea: Desert Island Books, 1998) pp. 247–56; Colin Graham, 'A Late Politics of Irish Gothic: Bram Stoker's *The Lady of the Shroud*', Bruce Stewart, ed., *That Other World* (Gerrards Cross: Colin Smyth, 1998) 2 vols, Vol. 2, pp. 30–9.

16  Matthew Brennan, 'Repression, Knowledge and Saving Souls: The Role of the "New Woman" in Stoker's *Dracula* and Murnau's *Nosferatu*', *Studies in the Humanities* 19 (1992) 1–10; Carol A. Senf, '*Dracula*: Stoker's Response to the New Woman', *Victorian Studies* 26 (1982) 33–49; David B. Dickens, 'The German Matrix of Stoker's *Dracula*', and Diane Milburn, '"For the Dead Travel Fast": Dracula in Anglo-German Context', in Miller, ed., *Dracula: The Shade and the Shadow*, pp. 31–41 and pp. 41–53, respectively.

17  Though Barbara Belford's biography *Bram Stoker* (London: Weidenfeld and Nicolson, 1996) was the major focus of public attention during 1997, *The Un-Dead* (1997) by Peter Haining and Peter Tremayne presents considerably more detailed information on the movement, education and relationships of the Stoker family. See also Leslie Shepard, 'The Library of Bram Stoker', *The Bram Stoker Society Journal* 4 (1992) 28–34.

18  See, for example, J. Gordon Melton, 'Stoker, Abraham "Bram"', *The Vampire Book* (Detroit: Visible Ink Press, 1994) pp. 583–7 at p. 584; Clive Leatherdale, *Dracula: The Novel and the Legend* (Brighton: Desert Island Books, 1993) p. 74.

19  David Glover, *Vampires, Mummies, and Liberals* (Durham, NC: Duke University Press, 1996).

20  Literally, 'Who today does not know *Dracula*? Who knows its author, Bram Stoker?' Alain Garsault, 'Pozzuoli (Alain): *Bram Stoker: Prince des Ténèbres*', *Positif*, 353 (1990) 128.

21  The phrase is David Glover's, though Barbara Belford expresses similar sentiments in the introduction to her 1996 biography. See Glover, *Vampires, Mummies, and Liberals*, p. 1; Belford, *Bram Stoker*, p. xi.

22  Harry Ludlam, *A Biography of Dracula* (London: Foulsham, 1962) p. 11.

23  Charlotte Stoker was the author of two minor published works, one considering female emigration from the workhouse, the other on the education of the deaf and dumb. See Haining and Tremayne, *The Un-Dead*, p. 46.

24  Stoker may also have been educated by a Mr Moore, according to the details published in the author's record as a member of the University's First Fifteen in the period 1869–70. See *Dublin University Football Club 1854–1954*, published on behalf of the Committee of Dublin University Football Club (Dublin: Montford Publications, 1954) p. 50.

25  I would like to express my gratitude to Dermot J.M. Sherlock, Recorder of

Alumni at Trinity College Dublin, for granting me access to information on Stoker contained in the Muniment Records and Catalogue of Graduates of the University of Dublin.

26  See Farson, *The Man Who Wrote Dracula*, p. 18.

27  The Historical Society granted honorary membership to 'The Fellows of Trinity College, Dublin; the Members of the Oxford Union; Members of the Cambridge Union; the Members of the Speculative Society, Edinburgh.' Bram Stoker was one of two candidates sharing the Society's silver medal for History in 1870, and was awarded a silver medal for Composition in his own right in the same year. *Appendix to the College Historical Society Address, 1872* [National Library of Ireland P1399(20)] pp. 37, 40, 41.

28  Dowden, the author of author of *Shakspere: His Mind and Art* (1875), was Professor of Oratory and English Literature at the University of Dublin and, as a champion of Walt Whitman's verse, reputedly became a role model for the young Stoker. J.P. Mahaffy – whose influence on Oscar Wilde is recalled in Oliver St John Gogarty's 1950 autobiography *Intimations* (London: Sphere, 1985) pp. 32–4 – was a noted Classical historian who later transferred his attention from Greece to Egyptian papyri.

29  *Dublin Philosophical Society Minutes*, Fourteenth Session, dated 11 June 1868, preserved by the Philosophical Society, Trinity College Dublin.

30  *Dublin Philosophical Society Minutes*: Fifteenth Session (Shelley); Sixteenth Session (Composition); Seventeenth Session (Style and Rossetti). These papers have not survived, though Stoker's *The Necessity for Political Honesty* was published in 1872 by the Historical Society in a limited – and now scarce – edition. Stoker's 'Second Certificate in Oratory', as it was titled, was awarded by the Philosophical Society on 25 November 1869, the Vice Chancellor of Ireland being the Chair for the opening of the Sixteenth Session.

31  *Appendix to the College Historical Society Address 1870* [National Library of Ireland P1399(20)], pp. 53, 54, 56.

32  Bram Stoker, 'The Censorship of Fiction', *The Nineteenth Century and After*, 66 (1909) 974–89; *Appendix to the College Historical Society Address 1870* [National Library of Ireland P1399(20)], p. 51.

33  Standish O'Grady was an active member of both Societies and was awarded the President's Medal for Composition by the Philosophical Society on 26 November 1868 (*Dublin Philosophical Society Minutes*: Fifteenth Session). William Wilde was elected to the Philosophical Society on 10 February 1870, and delivered an address laconically entitled 'Moliere' on 26 November 1870 (*Dublin Philosophical Society Minutes*: Seventeenth Session). Stoker seconded the election of Todhunter as an Honorary Member of 'The Phil' on 9 February 1871 (*Dublin Philosophical Society Minutes*: Seventeenth Session).

34  Haining and Tremayne, *The Un-Dead*, pp. 88, 91.

35  Haining and Tremayne, *The Un-Dead*, pp. 62–3; Richard Ellmann, *Oscar Wilde* (London: Hamish Hamilton, 1987) p. 99.

36  W.J. McCormack, 'Irish Gothic and After, 1820–1945', Seamus Deane, ed., *The Field Day Anthology of Irish Writing* (Londonderry: Field Day Publications, 1991) pp. 842–6 at p. 845.

37  Stoker's first recorded publication, 'The Crystal Cup', was printed in *London*

*Society* in 1872. Another short story, 'Jack Hammon's Vote', now lost, was rejected in turn by *The Cornhill Magazine*, *Macmillan's Magazine*, *Temple Bar*, and *Blackwood's* as a letter from Stoker, dated 6 October 1874 and now held at the National Library of Scotland, notes (MS4325 f. 240). The author returned to print with three serial novellas – 'The Primrose Path', 'Buried Treasures' and 'The Chain of Destiny' – all published in *The Shamrock*, an Irish journal, in 1875. Stoker's subsequent short fiction was published either in anthologies or in journals originating in England or the United States.

38  The Stokers were married at St Ann's Church, Dublin, on 4 December 1878. For information on the relationship between Wilde and Balcombe, see Ellmann, *Oscar Wilde*, pp. 55–6, 99–100, 353; Oscar Wilde, *A Letter from Oscar Wilde* (Dublin: The Tragara Press, 1954).

39  Belford, *Bram Stoker*, p. 125.

40  See Stoker's letter to the Committee of the Royal Literary Fund dated 25 February 1911, filed as Case 2841 in the Fund's archive (British Library M1077/117).

41  This figure almost certainly included any advance royalties paid in respect of *The Lair of the White Worm*. See Stoker's case file in the archive of the Royal Literary Fund (British Library M1077/117).

## 1. Pity and terror: Theology, morality and popular fiction

1  Victor Sage, *Horror Fiction in the Protestant Tradition* (Basingstoke: Macmillan, 1988) p. xvi.

2  See, for example, Colin Graham's reading of Julian Moynahan in 'A Late Politics of Irish Gothic: Bram Stoker's *The Lady of the Shroud* (1909)', Bruce Stewart, ed., *That Other World* 2 vols (Gerrards Cross: Colin Smythe, 1998), Vol. 2, pp. 30–9 at pp. 30–1.

3  See Fred Botting, *Gothic* (London: Routledge, 1996) pp. 7, 8. Gothic tales, of course, are not invariably bound by such closures. Stoker's short story 'The Judge's House' (1891; reprinted in *Dracula's Guest*) constitutes, as Antonio Ballasteros Gonzáles suggests, 'a deterministic and negative victory of the forces of evil over those of good'. The Gothic, in such circumstances, arguably draws on the energy of the Godwinian novel of persecution rather than the comfortable fiction of the moral tale. See 'Portraits, Rats and Other Dangerous Things', in Stewart, ed., *That Other World*, Vol. 2, pp. 18–29 at p. 27.

4  For example, C.G. Raible, 'Dracula: Christian Heretic', *Christian Century*, 96 (1979) 103–4 at p. 103.

5  Sage, *Horror Fiction in the Protestant Tradition*, p. 233.

6  'Lorna', 'Mr. Bram Stoker. A Chat with the Author of "Dracula"', *The British Weekly*, 1 July 1897, p. 185. Stoker was interviewed on 28 June 1897.

7  Such possibilities are acknowledged in Stoker's 1908 essay 'The Censorship of Fiction', the rhetoric of which is primarily directed against authors who knowingly exploit the 'sex impulses' of a prurient readership. Stoker concedes, however, that 'In all things of which suggestion is a part there is a possible element of evil.' See Bram Stoker, 'The Censorship of Fiction', *The Nineteenth Century and After*, LXIV (1908) 479–87 at p. 482.

8   Consider, for example, Van Helsing's despairing speech after the revelation that Mrs Westenra has removed the garlic wreath from her daughter's neck: Bram Stoker, *Dracula* (Oxford: Oxford University Press, 1996) p. 134 (Hereafter *D*).

9   Bram Stoker to William Ewart Gladstone, 24 May 1897 (British Library ADD MSS 44525 f. 221).

10  Sage, *Horror Fiction in the Protestant Tradition*, p. xiv.

11  Bram Stoker, *Under the Sunset* (London: Sampson Low, Marston, Searle and Rivington, 1882) p. 7 (Hereafter *UTS*). The name Fid-Def has an obvious Protestant resonance, being an abbreviation of Henry VIII's title 'Defender of the Faith', formalised in 1544 after his break with the Church of Rome. It is used on British coinage as a royal title to the present day.

12  'Notes on Books, & C.', *Notes and Queries*, 12 November 1881, p. 399.

13  'Christmas Books', *Punch*, LXXXI (1881) 261. The reviewer alludes to David's lament at the death of Saul and Jonathan: 'Tell *it* not in Gath, publish *it* not in the streets of Askelon; lest the daughters of the Philistines rejoice....' (2 Sam. 1:20).

14  Phyllis Roth, *Bram Stoker* (Boston: Twayne, 1982) p. 64.

15  Barbara Belford, *Bram Stoker* (London: Weidenfeld and Nicolson, 1996) p. 139.

16  The vigil was a popular subject in the genre painting of the period, particularly in its association with the purity of Sir Galahad. See D.N. Mancoff, *The Return of King Arthur* (London: Pavilion, 1995) pp. 123–4.

17  'Christmas Books', *The Times*, 15 December 1881, p. 11.

18  R. Newton, *The Giants and How to Fight Them* (London: S.W. Partridge, n.d.) p. 5.

19  Newton, *The Giants*, p. 13. The other two giants, which represent social rather than strictly personal evils are Heathenism and Intemperance.

20  Newton, *The Giants*, p. 12.

21  Two further courtiers are depicted, albeit at shorter length, by the narrator. The first, Tufto, is openly despised for his obsequiousness. The second, Gabbleander, 'who did nothing but talk from morning till night', 'was laughed at, for people cannot always talk sense if they talk much. The foolish things are remembered, but the wise ones are forgotten; and so these talkers of too many things come to be considered foolish' (*UTS* 19). Children, it appears, should be seen and not heard – that is, if they wish to be taken seriously.

22  Bram Stoker, 'Crooken Sands', reprinted in *Dracula's Guest* (Dingle: Brandon, 1990) pp. 145–6.

23  *The Academy*, XX (1881) 431.

24  Charlotte Stoker's memoirs are quoted at length in Harry Ludlam, *A Biography of Dracula* (London: Foulsham, 1962) pp. 25–32. Cf. Peter Haining and Peter Tremayne, *The Un-Dead* (London: Constable, 1997) pp. 44–5.

25  Belford, *Bram Stoker*, p. 139.

26  See, for example, Haining and Tremayne, *The Un-Dead*, p. 45; David Skal, *Hollywood Gothic* (New York: W.W. Norton, 1991) pp. 20–1.

27  J.S. Burdon-Sanderson, 'Cholera: Its Cause and Prevention', *Contemporary Review*, 48 (1885) 183.

28  Dr John Snow's investigation into the Soho cholera outbreak of 1854 linked the epidemic to a public pump, contaminated with the faeces of the earliest victims, from which most of those affected drew their drinking water. See Michael Howell and Peter Ford, *The Ghost Disease* (Harmondsworth: Penguin, 1986) pp. 160–1. Thomas Willis observed similar conditions in the North Dublin water supply in 1845. See J.F. Fleetwood, *The History of Medicine in Ireland* (Dublin: Skellig, 1983) p. 137.

29  J. M'Gregor-Robertson, *The Household Physician* (London: Blackie, n.d.) pp. 188–9.

30  Ludlam, *A Biography of Dracula*, p. 29; Christopher Wills, *Plagues* (London: HarperCollins, 1996) pp. 116–17. Wills reproduces a mid-century cartoon in which the shrouded figure of 'Cholera' hovers over the New York skyline while a sentinel labelled 'Science' slumbers at his post. The attitude and dress of the giant strongly resembles the figure in Fitzgerald's illustration.

31  Ludlam, *A Biography of Dracula*, p. 26.

32  Ludlam, *A Biography of Dracula*, p. 31.

33  R.W. Dale, *Christian Doctrine* [1894] (London: Hodder and Stoughton, 1903) p. 198.

34  In a commentary on the 'Thirty-Nine Articles' by which the doctrine of the Anglican Church (including the Church of Ireland) is popularly defined, G.F. Maclear and W.W. Williams argue that the Reformed Churches regard Adam's disobedience as the origin of 'a corruption, more or less entire, of human nature in its spiritual aspect, inclining man to evil and disinclining him to good'. See G.F. Maclear and W.W. Williams, *An Introduction to the Articles of the Church of England* (London: Macmillan, 1896) p. 145.

35  Van Helsing makes use of the same quotation (*D* 343). Three passages conveying similar implications, though through different syntax, occur in Ps. 9:15, Ps. 10:2 and Prov. 21:13.

36  Matt. 25:34–46. Newton makes a similar point with regard to his third 'Giant', Covetousness. See Newton, *The Giants*, p. 20.

37  M.G. Easton, *The Illustrated Bible Dictionary* (London: Nelson, 1893) p. 632. Cf. Dale, *Christian Doctrine*, p. 215.

38  A similar situation arises in 'How 7 Went Mad', the fifth story in *Under the Sunset*. When the raven, Mr Daw, eats every occurrence of the number seven in a school room, the logic of mathematics breaks down, to be restored only as the bird drops the numbers back into the room (*UTS* 116–17).

39  See William Empson, *Milton's God* (London: Chatto and Windus, 1961) p. 42.

40  Cf. Gal. 2:16: 'a man is not justified by the works of the law, but by the faith of Jesus Christ'.

41  *The Academy*, XX (1881) 431–2; Richard Dalby, *Bram Stoker: A Bibliography of First Editions* (London: Dracula Press, 1983) p. 10.

42  See, for example, David Glover, *Vampires, Mummies, and Liberals* (Durham, NC: Duke University Press, 1996) pp. 81–8; Robert Edwards, 'The Alien and the Familiar in *The Jewel of Seven Stars* and *Dracula*', William Hughes and Andrew Smith, eds, *Bram Stoker: History, Psychoanalysis and the Gothic* (Basingstoke: Macmillan, 1998) pp. 96–115 at pp. 98–112.

43  Bram Stoker, *The Jewel of Seven Stars* (Oxford: Oxford University Press, 1996), pp. 145, 158 (Hereafter *JSS*).

44  Ludlam, *A Biography of Dracula*, p. 128. Ludlam's lead has been followed by many subsequent critics. See David Glover's 'Introduction' to the Oxford University Press edition of the novel (*JSS* ix); Carol A. Senf, *'Dracula, The Jewel of Seven Stars* and Stoker's "Burden of the Past"', Carol Davison, ed., *Bram Stoker's Dracula* (Toronto: Dundurn Press, 1997) pp. 77–94 at p. 78.

45  Bram Stoker, *The Watter's Mou'*, reprinted in Charles Osborne, ed., *The Bram Stoker Bedside Companion* (London: Victor Gollancz, 1973) pp. 166–224 at p. 224.

46  Glover, *Vampires, Mummies and Liberals*, p. 90. Senf acknowledges Petrie, but points also to Stoker's personal acquaintance with Sir Richard Burton and Sir William Wilde as possible sources. See Senf, *'Dracula, The Jewel of Seven Stars* and Stoker's "Burden of the Past"', pp. 87, 88.

47  Stoker's private library, sold at Sotheby's on 7 July 1913 included Budge's *Egyptian Ideas of the Future Life* (1900); *Egyptian Magic* (1899); *Easy Lessons in Egyptian Hieroglyphics* (1899–1902); *The Mummy* (1893); *The Book of the Dead: The Papyrus of Ani in the British Museum* (1895); *A History of Egypt ...* (9 vols, 1902) as well as Flinders Petrie's 1895 *Egyptian Tales Translated from the Papyri* (British Library: SC SOTHEBY 7/7/1913). Trelawny's explanation of the 'Ka' (*JSS* 150) is lifted almost verbatim from Budge's *Egyptian Ideas of the Future Life* (London: Kegan Paul, Trench, Trübner & Co., 1900) pp. 163–4.

48  E.A. Wallis Budge, *The Mummy* (Cambridge: at the University Press, 1893) p. 173.

49  Budge, *The Mummy*, p. 170–2. A device similar to that imagined by Stoker is described in R.A. Proctor, 'The Mystery of the Pyramids', *Belgravia*, XXXII (1877), 434–52 at p. 451.

50  Budge, *The Mummy*, p. 18.

51  Budge, *The Mummy*, p. 31.

52  See also: *JSS* 204. Budge also describes ivory artefacts in terms of human skin colouring. See Budge, *The Mummy*, p. 171.

53  Wilkie Collins, *Heart and Science* [1882–3] (Peterborough: Broadview, 1996) p. 188.

54  See J. Pearson, *An Exposition of the Creed*, ed. Bradley (London: Valpy, 1870), p. 344, p. 529. Cf. also John 11:25.

55  'The Prayer of Consecration' in 'The Order of the Ministration of the Lord's Supper', *The Book of Common Prayer* (Dublin: A.P.C.K., 1927) p. 223.

56  John 5:29; John 3:16.

57  John Ritchie, *Contested Truths of the Word* (Kilmarnock: Ritchie, 1917) p. 3.

58  This Creed was recited daily in the Anglican office of 'Morning Prayer' in Ireland up to the revision of the Irish *Book of Common Prayer* in 1877. See G.J. Cuming, *A History of Anglican Liturgy* (London: Macmillan, 1969) p. 207.

59  Sage, *Horror Fiction in the Protestant Tradition*, p. 133.

60  Bram Stoker, *The Jewel of Seven Stars* (London: William Rider, 1912) p. 229. The Oxford Popular Fiction edition of *The Jewel of Seven Stars* reproduces only the final four pages of the 1912 ending as an appendix, and does not detail the many other differences between the two editions. Further references to the Second (or Rider) Edition are given in the text as *JSS* 1912.

61  *JSS* 209, cf. *JSS* 1912, 302.

62  Compare Sherlock Holmes's analysis of the behaviour of the dog in 'Silver

Blaze', in Arthur Conan Doyle, *The Memoirs of Sherlock Holmes* [1894] (Harmondsworth: Penguin, 1952) p. 28.

63 See also: *D* 10. The occultist John Silence makes similar use of a cat in Algernon Blackwood's 1908 short story 'A Psychical Invasion'. See Blackwood, *John Silence* (London: Richards, 1962) pp. 36–7.

64 J.W. Brodie Innes to Bram Stoker, 29 November 1903 (Brotherton Collection, Leeds University Library). Letters held in the Brotherton Collection also reveal that Stoker presented Brodie Innes with copies of *The Mystery of the Sea* (20 July 1902), *Lady Athlyne* (26 February 1909) and *The Lady of the Shroud* (14 July 1909).

65 Ludlam, *The Man Who Wrote Dracula*, p. 207; Alain Pozzuoli, *Bram Stoker: Prince des Tenénèbres* (Paris: Librairie Séguier, 1989) pp. 49–53. The association between Stoker and the Golden Dawn appears to stem from a highly questionable list of literary and celebrity members of the Order first published in Louis Pauwels and Jaques Bergier, *Le Matin des Magiciens* (Paris: Gallimard, 1960) p. 270.

66 Stoker, 'The Censorship of Fiction', p. 482.

67 Sage, *Horror Fiction in the Protestant Tradition*, p. xiv.

## 2. *'Un Vrai Monsieur'*: Chivalry, atavism and masculinity

1 'Merry-go-Round', *The Entr'acte*, 23 September 1882, p. 3. Stoker was awarded the Bronze Medal of the Royal Humane Society for his efforts, becoming Case 21,808 in the Society's *General List of Cases*.

2 Thomas Hughes, *Tom Brown at Oxford* [1861] (London: Macmillan, 1880) p. 99.

3 Bram Stoker, *Personal Reminiscences of Henry Irving*, 2 vols (London: Heinemann, 1906) Vol. 1, pp. 31–2 (Hereafter *PRHI*).

4 Hughes, *Tom Brown at Oxford*, p. 99.

5 Bram Stoker's entry in the Baptismal Register of St John the Baptist, Clontarf, renders his father's profession simply as 'Gentleman' (Entry 62, 3 December 1847). The record of his marriage at St Ann's Church, Dublin, gives the author's 'Rank or Profession' simply as 'M.A.', and his father's as 'Esq.' (Entry 120, 4 December 1878).

6 Mark Girouard, *The Return to Camelot* (New Haven: Yale University Press, 1981) p. 260.

7 Bram Stoker, *A Glimpse of America* (London: Sampson Low, Marston and Company, 1886) p. 23 (Hereafter *GA*).

8 Women have their own, separate, code of honour. See Bram Stoker, *The Mystery of the Sea* [1902] (Stroud: Sutton Publishing, 1997) p. 193 (Hereafter *MS*).

9 Stoker places tramps and Negroes outside of community: *GA* 14–15.

10 Bram Stoker, *Lady Athlyne* (London: William Heinemann, 1908) p. 188 (Hereafter *LA*).

11 Bram Stoker, *The Snake's Pass* [1890] (Dingle: Brandon, 1990) p. 77 (Hereafter *TSP*).

12 Alfred, Lord Tennyson, 'The Marriage of Geraint' [1857], *The Marriage of Geraint, Geraint and Enid* (London: Macmillan, 1892) p. 11, ll. 363–8.

13 Tennyson, 'The Marriage of Geraint', p. 10, ll. 326–44; p. 1, ll. 12–13; *TSP* 44, 73.

14   Other examples in Stoker's fiction include *MS* 44; *The Lady of the Shroud* [1909] (Stroud: Sutton Publishing, 1994) p. 74 (Hereafter *LS*); *The Lair of the White Worm* [1911], bound with *Dracula* (London: Foulsham, 1986) p. 358 (Hereafter *LWW*).

15   Nicholas Daly, 'Irish Roots: The Romance of History in Bram Stoker's *The Snake's Pass*', *Literature and History* 4/2 (1995) 42–70 at p. 53; David Glover, *Vampires, Mummies, and Liberals* (Durham, NC: Duke University Press, 1996) p. 53.

16   See Alfred Nutt, *Studies on the Legend of the Holy Grail* (London: The Folk-Lore Society, 1888) pp. xi–xiv.

17   See R.S. Loomis, *The Grail* (Princeton: Princeton University Press, 1991) pp. 36–8, 40.

18   Dick rather pointedly lists Giraldus Cambrensis, Edmund Spenser and Gerard Boate among those who have written historically about the problems of Ireland's topography (*TSP* 56). For further examples see Liz Curtis, *Nothing but the Same Old Story* (London: Information on Ireland, 1988) pp. 53, 89; Edith Somerville and Martin Ross, *Some Experiences of an Irish R.M.* [1899] (London: Longmans, Green and Company, 1903) p. 56.

19   Murdock's 'side whishkers' are another component of the Irish stereotype. See 'Reciprocity', the cover cartoon of the Irish comic journal *Pat*, 7 February 1880.

20   L.P. Curtis, *Apes and Angels* (Newton Abbot: David and Charles, 1971) pp. 68, 75. A representative example of Erin may be seen in the anonymous cartoon 'Ha! Ha!! Revenged!!!', a supplement to *The Weekly Freeman*, 23 May 1885.

21   Curtis, *Apes and Angels*, p. 75.

22   See John Tenniel, 'Two Forces', *Punch*, 29 October 1881, p. 89; 'The Fenian Pest', *Punch*, 3 March 1866, p. 89.

23   See 'Allen. Bog of', J.M. Ross, *The Illustrated Globe Encyclopædia*, 12 vols (London: Thomas C. Jack, 1882) Vol. 1, p. 66.

24   Murdock confirms his lack of gentlemanliness later in the novel by striking Norah (*TSP* 226), an act of brutality which parallels that of the 'unknightly' Earl Doorm who strikes Enid in Tennyson's 'Geraint and Enid', the companion piece to 'The Marriage of Geraint'.

25   See J.S. Donelly, 'Landlords and Tenants', W.E. Vaughan, ed., *A New History of Ireland* V (Oxford: Clarendon Press, 1989) pp. 346–9.

26   Nationalist political cartoons in this period portray the Anglo-Irish landlord as insolvent, exploitative and frequently backed up through the presence of British soldiery. See Thomas Fitzpatrick, 'On the Ass's Back, Once More', *The Weekly Freeman*, 4 December 1886, Supplement; Anon., 'The Irish Juggernaut', *United Ireland*, 22 September 1888, Supplement.

27   The allusion is to Isa. 3:15.

28   See Samuel Smiles, *Self-Help* [1859] (London: John Murray, 1902) pp. 285–7 on 'the general probity of Englishmen' as the foundation of the success of British commerce; and p. 382 on 'consistency' and character.

29   Bram Stoker, *The Man* (London: William Heinemann, 1905), p. 226 (Hereafter *TM*). Similar figures appear in *Dracula*, *The Watter's Mou'* and in the short story 'Crooken Sands'.

30   Murdock does, however, embody a range of vulpine and vampire-like

characteristics which link him to the fictional portrayal of the Jew in late-Victorian culture. See *TSP* 26, 87.

31  Bram Stoker, 'The Great White Fair in Dublin', *The World's Work*, IX (1907) 570–6 at p. 571.

32  See John Hutchinson, *The Dynamics of Cultural Nationalism* (London: Allen and Unwin, 1987) pp. 115–16, 119.

33  Stoker, 'The Great White Fair in Dublin', pp. 570, 571. Notably, the exhibition favoured Italian Renaissance architecture rather than structures of indigenous design for most of the major exhibition buildings. See William Hughes, '"Introducing Patrick to his New Self": Bram Stoker and the 1907 Dublin Exhibition', *Irish Studies Review* no. 19 (Summer 1997) 9–14.

34  Smiles, *Self-Help*, p. 407. The fictional public, of course, are unaware of the true focus of Dick's plans for Arthur's Irish estate (*TSP* 177–8).

35  Bram Stoker, *Dracula* [1897] (Oxford: Oxford University Press, 1996) p. 349 (Hereafter *D*). Everard senior also appears to favour his son's withholding of money set aside to pay off debt in order to gain interest: *TM* 199.

36  See Girouard, *The Return to Camelot*, pp. 4, 260.

37  This is an important context. The title-page of the first edition of *The Mystery of the Sea* (London: William Heinemann, 1902) bears the legend 'By Bram Stoker, Author of "Dracula"'.

38  Victor Sage, *Horror Fiction in the Protestant Tradition* (Basingstoke: Macmillan, 1988) pp. 180–2. Fontana quotes Lombroso's observation that in criminals 'the nose is often *aquiline* like the beak of a bird of prey': Ernest Fontana, 'Lombroso's Criminal Man and Stoker's *Dracula*', *Victorian Newsletter* 66 (1984) 25–7 at p. 26.

39  Charles Darwin, *The Expression of the Emotions in Man and Animals* [1872] (London: Watts and Company, 1934) pp. 123–4.

40  Bram Stoker, 'The Judge's House' [1891], *Dracula's Guest* (Dingle, Brandon, 1990) p. 37 (Hereafter *DG*).

41  Count Dracula, significantly, boasts of his descent from Attila the Hun: *D* 28–9.

42  Bram Stoker, *The Jewel of Seven Stars* (Oxford: Oxford University Press, 1996) pp. 9–10 (Hereafter *JSS*).

43  Andrew Smith, 'Bram Stoker's *The Mystery of the Sea*: Ireland and the Spanish-Cuban-American War', *Irish Studies Review*, 6/2 (1998) 131–8 at pp. 132, 137.

44  Similar uses of the term may be found in *LS* 192 and, as 'an honest woman', in *TSP* 171.

45  This recognition is the more compulsive in that Hunter has received 'The Accolade' of knighthood from Marjory in the Treasure Cave: *MS* 168.

46  Thomas Carlyle, *Past and Present* [1843] (Oxford: Clarendon Press, 1927) p. 172.

47  Bram Stoker, *Miss Betty* [1898] (London: New English Library, 1974) p. 141, my emphasis (Hereafter *MB*).

48  Bram Stoker, *Seven Golden Buttons*, MS dated 1891, f. H15 (Brotherton Collection, Leeds University) (Hereafter *SGB*).

49  Similar anti-Turkish sentiments are expressed in the Edwardian political fantasy of *The Lady of the Shroud*. See *LS* 152, 185.

50  Bram Stoker, *Under the Sunset* (London: Sampson Low, Marston, Searle and

Rivington, 1882) p. 6.

51  Carlyle, *Past and Present*, p. 172.

52  Severn appears particularly ignorant of how social class may modify the permitted social relations between a gentleman and a lady from more humble stock: *TSP* 77–8, 85.

53  Stoker's obituaries frequently mention his physical achievements. See 'Death of Mr. Bram Stoker. Sir H. Irving's Manager', *The Daily Telegraph*, 22 April 1912, p. 6; Hall Caine, 'Bram Stoker. The Story of a Great Friendship', *The Daily Telegraph*, 24 April 1912, p. 16.

54  Cesare Lombroso, *The Man of Genius* (London: Walter Scott, 1891) p. 14.

55  Glover, *Vampires, Mummies and Liberals*, p. 74.

56  There is a pun vested in the name *Castra Puerorum*. The Latin *puer* translates as 'boyish' or 'childish'. Harold, in exile, erects 'castles in the air', the recrudescence of childish hopes, now matured (*TM* 346). The *Islam* River recalls a 'historical' opponent against which Christian manhood could be proven, as much as it acknowledges the crusader ancestry of Stephen Norman.

57  See *D* 47–8, 213–16; *MS* 174–8; *JSS* 196–211; *LWW* 428–9.

58  Bram Stoker, 'The Red Stockade', *Cosmopolitan Magazine*, 17 (1894), 619–30 at p. 627. The use of 'white-livered' as a signifier for cowardice may be traced back at least as far as *The Merchant of Venice* (III. ii. 83–6).

59  This is true of Arthur Severn in *The Snake's Pass*, Rupert Sent Leger in *The Lady of the Shroud*, and Adam Salton in *The Lair of the White Worm*.

60  See *D* 154; *TM* 50; *LS* 36; *LWW* 338.

61  This proverb is used also in *LS* 38 and *MS* 186. James Hogg uses the phrase in *The Private Memoirs and Confessions of a Justified Sinner* [1824] (Harmondsworth: Penguin, 1987) p. 102.

62  The name is used as an alias in Arthur Conan Doyle's 'The Adventure of the Blue Carbuncle', *The Adventures of Sherlock Holmes* [1892] (New York: Belmont Tower Books, 1974) p. 168.

63  Hughes, *Tom Brown at Oxford*, p. viii, cf. p. ix.

64  The same may arguably be said of Lord Athlyne, who distinguishes himself through his bravery and courts the heroine while keeping her ignorant of his title.

65  The narratorial voice betrays at times an autobiographical strain in the depiction of the rescue. Similar rescues occur in the posthumous short story 'Greater Love', *The London Magazine*, 33 (1914–15), 161–8 at p. 168, and in the pastiche heroism of 'The 'Eroes of the Thames', *The Royal Magazine*, October 1908, pp. 566–70.

66  Two of Stoker's characters are, in common with their creator, medallists of the Royal Humane Society. Both, however, receive the Gold rather than Bronze Medal: *TM* 411; *LA* 8.

67  Stephen's own 'dross' explicitly evaporates in her self-surrender to Harold at the close of the novel: *TM* 435.

68  The symptomatology of Harold's Retrobulbar Neuritis is accurately described in the novel. See G.A. Berry, *Diseases of the Eye* [1889] (Edinburgh: Young J. Pentland, 1893) pp. 233–4.

69  The Aleutian Islands lie between Alaska and Asia. Of Stoker's other heroes, Athlyne travels to the Rockies; Seward, Morris and Holmwood have visited

the Prairies and Titicaca; Severn journeys to the West of Ireland; and Salton, a colonist in Western Australia, has visited Comanche country.

70  Dick Sutherland compares the proposed limestone quarry to 'a gold mine', an allusion to prospecting in the *American* West (*TSP* 202). A similar allusion may be found in the title of the article 'Pioneering on the West Coast' by 'Pat', which appeared in the May 1907 issue of *The World's Work* alongside two pieces by Stoker.

71  The Handjar, a short cutlass, is the national weapon of the fictional Land of the Blue Mountains.

72  The Land of the Blue Mountains is described by one Briton as 'a friendly land now beyond the outposts of our Empire, but which had been one with her in the past, and might be again.' (*LS* 211).

73  Bram Stoker, *The Shoulder of Shasta* (Westminster: Constable, 1895) pp. 227, 216 (Hereafter *SS*).

74  Carlyle, *Past and Present*, p. 74.

## 3. The taming of the new: Race, biological destiny and assertive womanhood

1  J.W. Arrowsmith to Bram Stoker, 8 October 1894 (Brotherton Collection, Leeds University Library).

2  Amy Marryat, 'On Sweethearts', *Half-Hours with My Girls* (London: Rivingtons, 1890) pp. 97–8.

3  Elizabeth Lynn Linton, 'The Girl of the Period', *The Girl of the Period and Other Social Essays*, 2 vols (London: Bentley, 1883) Vol. 1, p. 7.

4  Elizabeth Lynn Linton, '"In Custody" and "Emancipation"', *The Illustrated London News*, 6 February 1892, pp. 172–3 at p. 172.

5  Bram Stoker, *Miss Betty* [1898] (London: New English Library, 1974) p. 142 (Hereafter *MB*). For similar instances of 'sweet' see Stoker's *The Snake's Pass* [1890], (Dingle: Brandon, 1990), pp. 128, 130, 165 (Hereafter *TSP*); *The Lady of the Shroud* [1909] (Stroud: Alan Sutton, 1994), pp. 36, 126 (Hereafter *LS*); George Du Maurier, *Trilby* (London: Osgood, McIlvaine and Company, 1895), pp. 253, 257.

6  *MB* 31, 69, 99, 102, 112.

7  See J. McGrigor Allan, 'On the Real Differences in the Minds of Men and Women', *Journal of the Anthropological Society*, 7 (1869) cxcv–ccxix at p. ccxix.

8  Joseph Johnson, *Noble Women of Our Time* (London: T. Nelson and Sons, 1886) p. 16.

9  Bram Stoker, *The Man* (London: William Heinemann, 1905), p. 280 (Hereafter *TM*).

10  'Mrs Grundy' is a character referred to, though never seen, in Thomas Morton's play, *Speed the Plough* [1800]. She is regarded in the play as the embodiment of English respectability, the phrase gaining a cultural currency during the nineteenth century.

11  Katie Cowper, 'The Decline of Reserve among Women', *The Nineteenth Century*, 27 (1890) 65–71 at p. 70. Stoker was associated with James Knowles, editor of *The Nineteenth Century*, and contributed sporadically to the journal from June 1890.

12 Elizabeth Lynn Linton, 'The Wild Women: No. 1 As Politicians', *The Nineteenth Century*, XXX (1891) 79–88 at p. 79.

13 Linton compares the 'Girl of the Period' to the 'savage', 'negress' and 'maniac': *The Girl of the Period*, Vol. 1, p. 4.

14 Linton, '"In Custody"', p. 173.

15 Allan, 'On the Real Differences', p. cci.

16 Linton, *The Girl of the Period*, Vol. 1, p. 7. St John's Wood was a favoured domicile for mistresses and illicit second households during the nineteenth century.

17 A contemporary review coyly suggests that Murdock entices Norah out onto the bog 'for the purpose of possessing himself of her person': 'New Books and Magazines', *Labour World*, 29 November 1890, p. 15.

18 Betty Pole admits to carrying a dagger for the same purpose when she meets Rafe Otwell in his highwayman guise (*MB* 122).

19 A less-threatening use of 'give' occurs in Stoker's romantic short story, 'Greater Love', *The London Magazine*, 33 (1914–15) 161–8 at p. 166.

20 Stoker made frequent use of this melodramatic gesture to signify male outrage. See *TSP* 19, *MB* 121, *LS* 154.

21 A Kelpie is a Scots water spirit. Stoker owned a copy of J.G. Campbell, *Superstition and Witchcraft and Second Sight in the Highlands and Islands of Scotland*, 2 vols. [1902]. See British Library: SC SOTHEBY 7/7/1913.

22 Bram Stoker, *Lady Athlyne* (London: William Heinemann, 1908) pp. 250–1 (Hereafter *LA*).

23 Bram Stoker, *Dracula* [1897] (Oxford: Oxford University Press, 1983) p. 38 (Hereafter *D*).

24 The un-dead Lucy, similarly, uses the language of conventional sexual seduction and displays 'a languorous, voluptuous grace' when attempting to lure her fiancé into vampirism (*D* 211).

25 Athlyne's aquiline features and melodramatically flashing eyes may in themselves hint of a sexual threat.

26 The couple are wearing underclothes, *not* night-shirts. For similar garments see R.T. Wilcox, *The Dictionary of Costume* (London: Batsford, 1969) pp. 357, 378. Hunter is similarly able to appreciate 'the ease and poise of [Marjory's] beautiful figure' when she is dressed in the trousers of a footman's livery: *MS* 132.

27 For a popular view of Scots marriage law, see 'Bringing in the New Year in Scotland', *The Illustrated London News*, 30 December 1876, p. 637. David Glover quotes a letter from the Rt. Rev. John Dowden, Bishop of Edinburgh, to Stoker, dated 20 January 1901, in which the former clarifies the distinction between regular and irregular marriages. Stoker also corresponded on the subject of special marriage licences with the Rt. Rev. William Boyd-Carpenter, Bishop of Ripon. Though Boyd-Carpenter's advice is probably more relevant to the fictionalisation of Hunter's elaborate arrangements in *The Mystery of the Sea*, one sentence is worthy of quotation in the context of *Lady Athlyne*: 'Of course, you know that in Scotland the mere act of saying in the presence of a couple of witnesses I take you as my wife, etc. – would probably be held a valid wedding' (Brotherton Collection, Leeds University). See also: David Glover, *Vampires, Mummies, and Liberals* (Durham, NC: Duke University Press, 1996) pp. 130, 184.

28   Phyllis Roth, *Bram Stoker* (Boston: Twayne, 1982) p. 23.

29   *TSP* 147, *MB* 158, *LS* 179, Bram Stoker, *The Jewel of Seven Stars* (Oxford: Oxford University Press, 1996) p. 138.

30   *LA* 290, 317, 318.

31   Hunter anticipates a similar risk from Marjory's use of his drawing room as a dressing room (*MS* 192).

32   Elizabeth Lynn Linton, 'Modern Mothers II', *The Girl of the Period*, Vol. 1, pp. 19–26 at pp. 25–6.

33   This view was still current as late as 1916. Bernard Hollander argues that, though men tend to be deductive and intellectual, where women are intuitive and emotional, 'woman is mentally not inferior to man, she is only dissimilar'. Bernard Hollander, *Nervous Disorders of Women* (London: Kegan Paul, Trench, Trubner and Company, 1916) pp. xv, xvi–xvii.

34   Hollander, *Nervous Disorders of Women*, p. xx.

35   'A Medical Man', *Cassell's Family Doctor* (London: Cassell and Company, 1897) pp. 535, 389.

36   Allan, 'On the Real Differences', p. ccii, cf. Otto Weininger, *Sex and Character* [1906] (New York: A.M.S. Press, 1975) p. 29.

37   This response, as Glover argues, is in itself gendered. See Glover, *Vampires, Mummies, and Liberals*, p. 114.

38   F.P. Cobbe, 'Introduction', Theodore Stanton, ed., *The Woman Question in Europe* (London: Sampson Low, Marston, Searle and Rivington, 1884) pp. xiii–xviii at p. xiv, cf. J.E. Butler, ed., *Woman's Work and Women's Culture* (London: Macmillan, 1869) p. xv.

39   Linton, 'The Wild Women: No. 1', p. 79.

40   Elizabeth Lynn Linton, 'The Wild Women as Social Insurgents', *The Nineteenth Century* XXX (1891) 596–605 at p. 596.

41   Linton, 'The Wild Women as Social Insurgents', p. 597.

42   Linton, '"In Custody"', p. 173.

43   Linton, '"In Custody"', p. 173.

44   Lady Callcott, *Little Arthur's History of England* (London: John Murray, 1888) p. 51; Linton, *The Girl of the Period*, Vol. 1, p. 9. Marjory Anita Drake *does* ride a bicycle, although Hunter reassures the reader that it is 'a lady's wheel' (*MS* 126).

45   Hermina Barton, the New Woman heroine of Grant Allen's *The Woman Who Did* (1895) is a 'Girton Girl'. Stoker's selection of Somerville would thus serve to further distance his heroine from the example of her sexually active counterpart in Allen's novel.

46   See the opinion of Alexander Walker, cited in Allan, 'On the Real Differences', p. cciii.

47   Allan, 'On the Real Differences', p. ccix.

48   The correspondence column of the *Girl's Own Paper* states unequivocally that such unconventional proposals are incompatible with 'maidenly reserve and delicacy': 'Church Bells', *The Girl's Own Paper* XVIII (1896) 144.

49   Sarah Grand, *The Heavenly Twins* [1893] (London: William Heinemann, 1897) p. 321. Grand was personally acquainted with the Stokers, dining with them on several occasions and corresponding with Florence Stoker. See S. Grand to F.A.L. Stoker, 4 August 1906 (Brotherton Collection, Leeds University).

50  *TM* 73, 111–12. Tom Brown rejects a similar temptation whilst an under-graduate at Oxford: Thomas Hughes, *Tom Brown at Oxford* (London: Macmillan, 1880) pp. 156–7, 183.

51  Allan, 'On the Real Differences', p. ccxi; Linton, 'The Wild Women: No. 1 as Politicians', pp. 81, 82–3.

52  Grant Allen, *The Woman Who Did* [1895] (Oxford: Oxford University Press, 1995) p. 41.

53  It should be noted, however, that the title is first applied to Harold by Pearl, the child he saves from drowning on his outward voyage. See *TM* 296.

## 4. The sanguine economy: Hysteroid pathology and physiological medicine

1  Michel Foucault, *The History of Sexuality: An Introduction* (London: Penguin, 1984) p. 147.

2  Bram Stoker, *Personal Reminiscences of Henry Irving*, 2 vols (London: William Heinemann, 1906) Vol. 1, p. 327 (Hereafter *PRHI*).

3  Bram Stoker, *A Glimpse of America* (London: Sampson, Low, Marston and Company, 1886) p. 47.

4  Foucault, *The History of Sexuality*, p. 147.

5  Bram Stoker, *The Man* (London: William Heinemann, 1905) p. 52 (Hereafter *TM*).

6  For a general overview of the economic basis of medicine in the nineteenth century, see Ben Barker-Benfield, 'The Spermatic Economy: A Nineteenth-Century View of Sexuality', *Feminist Studies*, 1 (1972) 45–74.

7  Edward Bliss Foote, *Home Cyclopedia of Popular Medical, Social and Sexual Science* (London: L.N. Fowler, 1901) p. 167.

8  W.H. Bennet, 'Blood-Letting', Christopher Heath, ed., *Dictionary of Practical Surgery*, 6 vols (London: Smith, Elder and Company, 1886) Vol. 1, p. 163; Spencer Thomson and J.C. Steele, *A Dictionary of Domestic Medicine and Household Surgery* (London: Charles Griffin and Company, 1899) p. 27.

9  See Arthur N. Gilbert, 'Doctor, Patient, and Onanist Diseases in the Nineteenth Century', *Journal of the History of Medicine*, 30 (1975) 217–34 at pp. 217–18; Lesley A. Hall, 'Forbidden by God, Despised by Men: Masturbation, Medical Warnings, Moral Panic, and Manhood in Great Britain, 1850–1950', John C. Fout, ed., *Forbidden History* (Chicago: University of Chicago Press, 1992) pp. 293–315 *passim*. Similar sentiments punctuate the twentieth-century writings of Robert Baden-Powell (1857–1941), founder of the Boy Scout movement. See R. Baden-Powell, *Scouting For Boys* [1932] (London: C. Arthur Pearson, 1947) p. 154; *Rovering to Success* [1922] (London: Herbert Jenkins, n.d.) pp. 104–6.

10  See, for example, Andrew Smith, *Dracula and the Critics* (Sheffield: Pavic, 1997) pp. 50–1; Anne Cranny-Francis, 'Sexual Politics and Political Repression in Bram Stoker's *Dracula*', Clive Bloom, Brian Docherty, Jane Gibb and Keith Shand, eds, *Nineteenth Century Suspense* (Basingstoke: Macmillan, 1988) pp. 64–79 at pp. 67–8.

11  Bram Stoker, *Dracula* (Oxford: Oxford University Press, 1996) p. 211 (Hereafter *D*).

12  See L. Humphry, *A Manual of Nursing: Medical and Surgical* [1889] (London:

Charles Griffin and Company, 1900) pp. 160–1.

13 Elizabeth Lynn Linton, 'The Girl of the Period', *The Girl of the Period and Other Social Essays*, 2 vols (London: Bentley, 1883) Vol. 1, p. 1.

14 Stoker may well have discovered the name either through its connections with the Anglo-Irish Barons of Rossmore, or through a reading of the supernatural legends associated with the family. Its resonance in *Dracula*, though, would appear to be primarily symbolic. See Mark Pinkerton, 'Why Westenra?', *The Bram Stoker Society Journal*, no. 7 (1995) 12–15.

15 According to Whyte, the concept entered popular usage around 1870. See L.L. Whyte, *The Unconscious before Freud* (London: Social Science Paperbacks, 1967) pp. 155, 163, 169–70.

16 W.B. Carpenter, *Principles of Mental Physiology* (London: Henry S. King, 1874) p. 516, Carpenter's emphasis.

17 Similar displays of mental activity occur in several of Stoker's other works. See *The Shoulder of Shasta* (Westminster: Constable, 1895) p. 215; *Lady Athlyne* (London: William Heinemann, 1908) p. 250.

18 W.B. Carpenter, 'The Unconscious Action of the Brain', *Science Lectures for the People*, Third Series (1871) 1–24 at pp. 9–10; *Principles of Mental Physiology*, pp. 385, 636–52.

19 Indeed, Mr Swales, the 'Sir Oracle' of the mariners, does not contradict Lucy's contentions but compensates by giving Mina a 'double share instead' (*D* 64).

20 Carpenter, *Principles of Mental Physiology*, p. 127.

21 Carpenter, *Principles of Mental Physiology*, pp. 217–18. This functional, rather than purely ideational, aspect of unconscious cerebration resembles the process outlined under the same name by Charcot. See A.R.G. Owen, *Hysteria, Hypnosis and Healing: The Work of J.M. Charcot* (London: Dennis Dobson, 1971) p. 114.

22 Carpenter, *Principles of Mental Physiology*, p. 215. Mayo's *On the Truths contained in Popular Superstitions – With an Account of Mesmerism* (Edinburgh: William Blackwood and Sons, 1851) is listed among the sources for *Dracula* in the manuscript notes to the novel, held at the Rosenbach Museum and Library, Philadelphia.

23 Witness the title of the elder journal of the British medical profession, *The Lancet*, founded in 1823, seventeen years before the *British Medical Journal*.

24 W.H. Bennet, 'Arteriotomy', in Heath, *Dictionary of Practical Surgery*, Vol. 1, p. 97.

25 See Burton Hatlen, 'The Return of the Repressed/Oppressed in Bram Stoker's *Dracula*', M.L. Carter ed., *Dracula: The Vampire and the Critics*, (Ann Arbor: U.M.I. Research Press, 1988) pp. 117–35 at p. 123.

26 Haining and Tremayne suggest that Lucy lodges in the East Crescent, a smaller terrace situated at the junction of Hudson Street and East Terrace. If this were the case, Mina would have had to retrace her steps along the East Terrace after seeking Lucy on the North Terrace, a manoeuvre which is not mentioned in the novel. See Peter Haining and Peter Tremayne, *The Un-Dead* (London: Constable, 1997) p. 140. A map of Whitby in 1859 is reproduced in Andrew White, 'The Victorian Development of Whitby as a Seaside Resort', *The Local Historian*, 28 (1998) 78–93 at p. 84.

27 The Count uses the suicide's grave as a resting place during his stay in Whitby (*D* 240).

28   There is an ironic *double-entendre* here, vested in Mina's use of the word 'transfixed' – meaning, popularly, to pierce or impale, and, more technically, to exorcise and 'stake' a vampire.

29   Bram Stoker, *The Snake's Pass* (Dingle: Brandon, 1980) p. 147. For similar examples, see *The Lady of the Shroud* (Stroud: Sutton Publishing, 1994) p. 194; 'Greater Love', *The London Magazine* 33 (1914–15) 161–8 at p. 166.

30   'Medicus', 'When Bud and Burgeon Come Again', *The Girl's Own Paper*, XVIII (1897) p. 295.

31   Carter Paterson were hauliers to Sidgwick and Jackson at the time Stoker was writing *Famous Impostors*. See Bodleian Library: Sidgwick & Jackson MS.11 f. 223.

32   Anne McWhir suggests that Lucy's use of 'cormorant' is an acknowledgement of her subjection to the 'animal' power of Dracula. See A. McWhir, 'Pollution and Redemption in *Dracula*', *Modern Language Studies*, 17 (1987) 31–40 at p. 39, n. 4.

33   See John Thornton, *Elementary Practical Physiology* [1904] (London: Longmans, Green and Company, 1919) pp. 85–7.

34   Despite initially plotting the dates of the fictional incidents on a blank calendar, Stoker does not appear to have revised his copy carefully here. Lucy is at Hillingham on 24 August, but again at Whitby on 30 August, without explanation. Hillingham, logically, must be close to central London, given that it is possible for the wolf, Bersicker, to escape from Regent's Park Zoo, visit Hillingham, and return to his keeper's lodge within the zoo, all in the space of two days at most. See The Rosenbach Library, MS. Notes to *Dracula*, f. 29.

35   Cf. David Seed, 'The Narrative Method of *Dracula*', *Nineteenth-Century Fiction*, 40 (1985) 61–75.

36   Charcot's preface to Pierre Janet's *The Mental State of Hystericals* [1892] states that the volume's studies 'confirm a thought often expressed in our lectures, namely, that hysteria is largely a mental malady'. See Owen, *Hysteria, Hypnosis and Healing*, p. 161.

37   Robert Brudenell Carter, *On the Pathology and Treatment of Hysteria* (London: John Churchill, 1853) p. 34. Carter – mindful no doubt of the social standing of both his patients and professional colleagues – argues that, though sexual disorders are most likely to be at the root of hysteria 'among the poor and ignorant', 'many other kinds of feeling' may account for its presence 'in the higher glasses' [*sic*] of society (pp. 34–5).

38   'A Medical Man', *Cassell's Family Doctor* (London: Cassell, 1897) p. 534.

39   Carpenter, *Principles of Mental Physiology*, p. 597.

40   See R.E. Fancher, *Pioneers of Psychology* (New York: W.W. Norton, 1979) p. 194.

41   Renfield's psychosis is at a highly advanced stage eighteen days before the Count's arrival at Whitby (*D* 70–1). Victor Sage suggests that Renfield 'tries to imitate his Satanic Master's annexations', although it may be argued that the lunatic's neurosis is systematically encouraged by Seward for experimental purposes. See Victor Sage, *Horror Fiction in the Protestant Tradition* (Basingstoke: Macmillan, 1988) p. 54; cf. William Hughes, '"So unlike the normal lunatic": Abnormal Psychology in Bram Stoker's *Dracula*', *University of Mississippi Studies in English*, New Series 11–12 (1993–5) 1–10.

42 Carter associates both struma (i.e. scrofula, goitre) and anaemia with the tendency to hysteria: Carter, *On the Pathology*, p. 92. Goitre was associated with cretinism in Romania, though the complaint was, allegedly, scarcely encountered in Great Britain. See F. Henschen, *The History of Diseases* (London: Longmans, 1986) pp. 187, 189. As Harker notes, 'goitre was painfully prevalent' in Transylvania (*D* 7). The frequency of the complaint in the Count's homeland arguably suggests both the 'degenerate' status of its inhabitants and their racial susceptibility to vampiric contagion.

43 'A Medical Man', *Cassell's Family Doctor*, p. 535. This view of male hysteria contrasts with that of Charcot – an example of coexistence. See J.-M. Charcot, 'Hysteria in the Male Subject' [1873], L.T. Benjamin ed., *A History of Psychology* (New York: McGraw-Hill, 1988) pp. 129–35 *passim*.

44 Carter, *On the Pathology*, pp. 33–4.

45 Holmwood is summoned to Ring to attend his sick father shortly after he requests Seward to make a medical examination of Lucy (*D* 110).

46 Carter, *On the Pathology*, p. 52.

47 Carter, *On the Pathology*, pp. 67, 68–9. For an account of the position of women in nineteenth-century medicine, see F.E. Hoggan, 'Women in Medicine', T. Stanton, ed., *The Woman Question in Europe* (London: Sampson Low, Marston, Searle and Rivington, 1884) pp. 63–89.

48 For a comprehensive review of the medico-moral debate on female masturbation in the nineteenth century, see Diane Mason, 'Un-like a Virgin: Female Masturbation and Virginity in *Fin-de-Siècle* Medical Advice Literature', Nickianne Moody and Julia Hallam, eds, *Medical Fictions* (Liverpool: MCCA, 1998) pp. 213–25. Masturbation, as Mason suggests, was frequently regarded as a likely cause of hysteria in young women: p. 218.

49 Carter, *On the Pathology*, pp. 4, 21–2, 26, 31–2, 33.

50 Carter himself acknowledges this as a problem in diagnosis. See Carter, *On the Pathology*, p. 29.

51 Carter, *On the Pathology*, p. 42.

52 Charcot, 'Hysteria in the Male Subject', p. 130.

53 There is no evidence in the novel to support Christopher Craft's contention that Harker was attacked by the three female vampires following the Count's departure. Indeed, Harker's decision to scale the wall at the close of Chapter Four (*D* 53) appears to be prompted by his desire to avoid such a fate. Harker's neurosis, therefore, can be considered medically conventional rather than occult in its origins. See C. Craft, '"Kiss Me with Those Red Lips": Gender and Inversion in Bram Stoker's *Dracula*', *Representations*, 8 (1984) 107–33.

54 Though the term 'Brain Fever' conventionally indicated meningitis in British medical practice, as *Cassell's Family Doctor* pointed out in 1897, 'it is used in a popular sense to include all feverish diseases accompanied with brain symptoms' (p. 312). Its use here serves primarily to indicate the lack of precision in non-western medical diagnoses. For a further exploration of the subject, see Elaine Hartnell, 'Thoughts Too Long and Too Intensely Fixed on One Object: Fictional Representations of Brain Fever', Moody and Hallam, eds, *Medical Fictions* pp. 201–12.

55 Inhalation was frequently used in the treatment of conventional bronchial difficulties. See 'A Medical Man', *Cassell's Family Doctor*, p. 331.

56    For a popular nineteenth-century description of the *Globus Hystericus*, see
      J.M. Ross, ed., *The Illustrated Globe Encyclopædia*, 12 vols (London: Thomas
      C. Jack, 1882) Vol. VI, pp. 464–5. Carter suggests that the inhalation of
      'stimulating vapours' frequently results in the worsening of the hysterical
      paroxysm. See Carter, *On the Pathology*, p. 91. See also Ilza Veith, *Hysteria:
      The History of a Disease* (Chicago: University of Chicago Press, 1965) pp. 3,
      5, 23, 25, 136.

57    Carter, *On the Pathology*, pp. 36, 102.

58    Anne Williams argues, however, that 'Ironically, Van Helsing understood
      Lucy's vampire condition at her death, but failed to do what was necessary
      before burial ...': A. Williams, *Art of Darkness: A Poetics of Gothic* (Chicago:
      University of Chicago Press, 1995) p. 125.

59    A.E. Housman uses a similar image in the seventh stanza of 'The True
      Lover' [1896], *A Shropshire Lad* (New York: Dover, 1990) p. 38.

60    See, for example, Carol A. Senf, '*The Lady of the Shroud*: Stoker's Successor
      to Dracula', *Essays in Arts and Sciences*, 19 (1990) 82–96 at p. 87.

61    Cf. the opinion of Burton Hatlen: 'The Return of the Repressed', pp. 123–4.

62    See, for example, Foote, *Home Cyclopedia of Popular Medical, Social and
      Sexual Science*, pp. 343–5.

63    See, for example, W.B. Carpenter, 'Mesmerism, Odylism, Table-Turning
      and Spiritualism Considered Historically and Scientifically: Lecture 1',
      *Fraser's Magazine* 95 (1877) 135–57 at p. 141.

64    W.B. Carpenter, 'Spiritualism and its Recent Converts', *Quarterly Review* 131
      (1871) 301–53; 'Electrobiology and Mesmerism', *Quarterly Review* 93 (1853)
      501–57.

65    Anon., 'Demonstrations of Some Abnormal Nervous States', *The Times*, 23
      January 1879, p. 3, col. 3. Cf. Carpenter, *Principles of Mental Physiology*,
      p. 601; Mayo, *On the Truths Contained in Popular Superstitions*, pp. 237–9.

66    Carpenter, *Principles of Mental Physiology*, p. 601.

67    Carpenter, 'Mesmerism, Odylism, Table-Turning and Spiritualism', p. 139;
      Mayo, *On the Truths Contained in Popular Superstitions*, p. 151, see also
      pp. 149, 150. 'Crisis' is also used to describe the hypnotic state induced by
      Charcot's method, reflecting again the popular association between
      mesmerism/magnetism and hypnotism: Anon., 'Demonstrations of Some
      Abnormal Nervous States', p. 3, col. 3.

68    Bram Stoker, *Famous Impostors* (London: Sidgwick and Jackson, 1910) p. 95.

69    Mayo, *On the Truths Contained in Popular Superstitions*, p. 151.

70    Mayo, *On the Truths Contained in Popular Superstitions*, p. 239. Von
      Reichenbach's theories were published in English translation some five
      years later. For a short discussion of the influence of Von Reichenbach on
      Victorian hypnotism, see Ronald Pearsall, *The Table-Rappers* (London: Book
      Club Associates, 1973) pp. 19–22.

71    Mayo, *On the Truths Contained in Popular Superstitions*, p. 151.

72    George Du Maurier, *Trilby* (London: Osgood, McIlvaine and Company,
      1895) p. 67. Beerbohm Tree produced a dramatisation of *Trilby* in London
      in 1895. See M. Bingham, *The Great Lover: The Life and Art of Herbert
      Beerbohm Tree* (New York: Athenaeum, 1979) pp. 70–6.

73    Du Maurier, *Trilby*, p. 72.

74    Mayo, *On the Truths Contained in Popular Superstitions*, pp. 242–4.

75 Carpenter, *Principles of Mental Physiology*, p. 144.

76 Modern sexual interpretations of the two representations of this scene include: C.F. Bentley, 'The Monster in the Bedroom: Sexual Symbolism in Bram Stoker's *Dracula*', *Literature and Psychology*, 22 (1972) 27–34 at p. 30; Daniel Lapin, *The Vampire, Dracula and Incest* (San Francisco: Gargoyle, 1995) p. 41; Jerrold E. Hogle, 'Stoker's Counterfeit Gothic: *Dracula* and Theatricality at the Dawn of Simulation', William Hughes and Andrew Smith, eds, *Bram Stoker: History, Psychoanalysis and the Gothic* (Basingstoke: Macmillan, 1998) pp. 205–24 at pp. 220–2; and Sage, *Horror Fiction in the Protestant Tradition*, p. 180. The incident is presented in this light in F.F. Coppolla's 1992 film adaptation, *Bram Stoker's Dracula*.

77 'Spurted' is used in a similar manner in the description of the transfixing of Lucy – *D* 216. Compare also Roland Barthes's correlation of the liquefaction of the mesmerised Monsieur Valdemar with his 'awakening' from the hypnotic trance. See 'Textual Analysis: Poe's "Valdemar"', David Lodge, ed., *Modern Criticism and Theory* (Harlow: Longman, 1989) pp. 172–95 at p. 193.

78 In a later work vampires are described as beings 'who live on the blood of the living, and bring eternal damnation as well as death with the poison of their kisses!' See Bram Stoker, *The Lady of the Shroud* (Stroud: Sutton Publishing, 1994) p. 113.

79 For a nineteenth-century view of ptomaines, see J. M'Gregor-Robertson, *The Household Physician* (London: Blackie and Son, n.d.) pp. 599, 1014.

80 Clive Leatherdale reads the Count's foul breath as another example of the novel's xenophobia. See C. Leatherdale, *Dracula: The Novel and the Legend* (Brighton: Desert Island Books, 1993) p. 229.

81 Eugenic fears reached a climax in following the revelations regarding the condition of volunteers for service in the South African War. See A. White, *Efficiency and Empire* [1901], in E.J. Evans, ed., *Social Policy 1830–1914* (London: Routledge and Kegan Paul, 1978) p. 224; G.R. Searle, *The Quest for National Efficiency* (Oxford: Basil Blackwell, 1971) pp. 60–1.

82 Leatherdale, in contrast, interprets the death of Morris in 'nationalistic' terms, configuring the Texan as a sort of 'failed Englishman'. See Leatherdale, *Dracula: The Novel and the Legend*, p. 228.

83 Compare here Victor Sage's argument, based on a reading of Lombroso's *The Man of Genius*, that the Count and the Professor share a common heritage, emblematising degeneration and genius respectively. See Sage, *Horror Fiction in the Protestant Tradition*, pp. 182–3.

## Afterword

1 Clive Leatherdale, *Dracula: The Novel and the Legend* (Brighton: Desert Island Books, 1993) p. 74.

2 Among other curious attributions, Stoker has been recorded as becoming 'a professor of English' and (admittedly through an act of mistaken identity, corrected in a later reprint) the proprietor of a bookshop appropriately named 'The Vault of Horror'. See Basil Copper, *The Vampire in Legend and Fact* (New York: Citadel, 1973) p. 72; John Nicholson, 'Scared Shitless: the Sex of Horror', Clive Bloom, ed., *Creepers* (London: Pluto, 1993) pp. 123–46

at p. 132. Nicholson's error is corrected in a later reprint in Clive Bloom, ed., *Gothic Horror* (Basingstoke: Macmillan, 1988) pp. 249–77 at p. 259.

# Bibliography

Allan, J.McGrigor, 'On the Real Differences in the Minds of Men and Women', *Journal of the Anthropological Society*, 7 (1869) cxcv–ccxix.

Allen, Grant, *The Woman Who Did* (Oxford: Oxford University Press, 1995).

Anonymous, 'Bringing in the New Year in Scotland', *The Illustrated London News*, 30 December 1876, p. 637.

Anonymous, 'Demonstrations of Some Abnormal Nervous States', *The Times*, 23 January 1879, p. 3, col. 3.

Anonymous, 'Merry-go-Round', *The Entr'acte*, 23 September 1882, p. 4.

Anonymous, 'Death of Mr. Bram Stoker. Sir H. Irving's Manager', *The Daily Telegraph*, 22 April 1912, p. 6.

Anonymous, 'Obituary. Mr. Bram Stoker', *The Times*, 22 April 1912, p. 15.

Anonymous, 'Bram Stoker', *The New York Times*, 23 April 1912, p. 12.

Anonymous, *Dublin University Football Club 1854–1954*, published on behalf of the Committee of Dublin University Football Club (Dublin: Montford Publications, 1954).

Auerbach, Nina, *Our Vampires, Ourselves* (Chicago: University of Chicago Press, 1995)

Baden-Powell, Robert, *Rovering to Success* (London: Herbert Jenkins, n.d.).

Baden-Powell, Robert, *Scouting For Boys* (London: C. Arthur Pearson, 1947).

Barber, Paul, *Vampires, Burial, and Death: Folklore and Reality* (New Haven: Yale University Press, 1988).

Barker-Benfield, Ben, 'The Spermatic Economy: A Nineteenth-Century View of Sexuality', *Feminist Studies*, 1 (1972) 45–74.

Barthes, Roland, 'Textual Analysis: Poe's "Valdemar"', David Lodge, ed., *Modern Criticism and Theory* (Harlow: Longman, 1989) pp. 172–95.

Belford, Barbara, *Bram Stoker: A Biography of the Author of Dracula* (London: Weidenfeld and Nicolson, 1996).

Benjamin, Ludy T., ed., *A History of Psychology: Original Sources and Contemporary Research* (New York: McGraw-Hill, 1988).

Bennet, W.H,.'Arteriotomy', in Christopher Heath, ed., *Dictionary of Practical Surgery*, 6 vols (London: Smith, Elder and Company, 1886) Vol. 1, p. 97.

Bennet, W.H. 'Blood-Letting', Christopher Heath, ed., *Dictionary of Practical Surgery*, 6 vols (London: Smith, Elder and Company, 1886) Vol. 1, p. 163.

Bentley, C.F., 'The Monster in the Bedroom: Sexual Symbolism in Bram Stoker's *Dracula*', *Literature and Psychology*, 22 (1972) 27–34.

Berry, G.A., *Diseases of the Eye* (Edinburgh: Young J. Pentland, 1893).

Bierman, Joseph, '*Dracula*: Prolonged Childhood Illness, and the Oral Triad', *American Imago*, 29 (1972) 186–98.

Bierman, Joseph, 'The Genesis and Dating of *Dracula* from Bram Stoker's Working Notes', *Notes and Queries*, 222 (1977) 39–41.

Bierman, Joseph, 'A Crucial Stage in the Writing of *Dracula*', William Hughes and Andrew Smith, eds, *Bram Stoker: History, Psychoanalysis and the Gothic* (Basingstoke: Macmillan, 1998) pp. 151–72.

Bingham, M., *The Great Lover: The Life and Art of Herbert Beerbohm Tree* (New York: Athenaeum, 1979).

Blackwood, Algernon, *John Silence* (London: Richards, 1962).

Bloom, Clive, ed., *Gothic Horror* (Basingstoke: Macmillan, 1988).

Botting, Fred, *Gothic* (London: Routledge, 1996).

Brady, J.C., 'Legal Developments 1801–1877', W.E. Vaughan ed., *A New History of Ireland* V (Oxford: Clarendon Press, 1989) pp. 451–81.

Brander, Michael, *The Victorian Gentleman* (London: Gordon Cremonesi, 1975).

Brennan, Matthew, 'Repression, Knowledge and Saving Souls: The Role of the "New Woman" in Stoker's *Dracula* and Murnau's *Nosferatu*', *Studies in the Humanities* 19 (1992) 1–10.

Brereton, Austin, *Henry Irving: A Biographical Sketch* (London: David Bogue, 1883).

Brereton, Austin, *The Life of Henry Irving*, 2 vols (London: Longmans, Green and Company, 1908).

Brodie, Fawn M., *The Devil Drives: A Life of Sir Richard Burton*, (London: Eyre and Spottiswoode, 1967).

Budge, E.A. Wallis, *The Nile: Notes for Travellers in Egypt* (London: Thomas Cook, 1892).

Budge, E.A. Wallis, *The Mummy: Chapters on Egyptian Funereal Archaeology* (Cambridge: at the University Press, 1893).

Budge, E.A. Wallis, *Egyptian Magic* [1899] (London: Routledge and Kegan Paul, 1979).

Budge, E.A. Wallis, *Egyptian Ideas of the Future Life* (London: Kegan Paul, Trench, Trübner & Co., 1900).

Budge, E.A. Wallis, *The Gods of the Egyptians* [1904] 2 vols (New York: Dover, 1969).

Budge, E.A. Wallis, *Osiris and the Egyptian Resurrection,* 2 vols (London: Philip Lee Warner, 1911).

Bunson, Matthew, *Vampire: The Encyclopædia* (London: Thames and Hudson, 1993).

Burdon-Sanderson, J.S., 'Cholera: Its Cause and Prevention', *Contemporary Review*, 48 (1885) 183.

Burton, Isabel, *AEI – Arabia Egypt India* (London: William Mullen and Son, 1879).

Butler, J.E., ed., *Woman's Work and Women's Culture* (London: Macmillan, 1869).

Byron, Glennis, ed., *Dracula*, Macmillan New Casebooks (Basingstoke: Macmillan, 1999).

Caine, Hall, 'Bram Stoker. The Story of a Great Friendship', *The Daily Telegraph*, 24 April 1912, p. 16.

Callcott, Lady, *Little Arthur's History of England* (London: John Murray, 1888).

Carlyle, Thomas, *Past and Present* (Oxford: Clarendon Press, 1927).

Carpenter, W.B., 'Electrobiology and Mesmerism', *Quarterly Review* 93 (1853) 501–57.

Carpenter, W.B., 'Spiritualism and its Recent Converts', *Quarterly Review* 131 (1871) 301–53.

Carpenter, W.B., 'The Unconscious Action of the Brain', *Science Lectures for the People*, Third Series (1871) 1–24.

Carpenter, W.B., *Principles of Mental Physiology* (London: Henry S. King, 1874).

Carpenter, W.B., 'Mesmerism, Odylism, Table-Turning and Spiritualism Considered Historically and Scientifically: Lecture 1', *Fraser's Magazine* 95 (1877) 135–57.

Carter, Robert Brudenell, *On the Pathology and Treatment of Hysteria* (London: John Churchill, 1853).

Charcot, J.-M., 'Hysteria in the Male Subject', L.T. Benjamin ed., *A History of Psychology* (New York: McGraw-Hill, 1988) pp. 129–35.

Charcot, J.-M., 'The Faith-Cure', *The New Review*, January 1893, pp. 18–31.

Cobbe, Frances Power, 'Unconscious Cerebration. A Psychological Study', *Macmillan's Magazine*, November 1870, pp. 24–37.

Cobbe, F.P., 'Introduction', Theodore Stanton, ed., *The Woman Question in Europe* (London: Sampson Low, Marston, Searle and Rivington, 1884) pp. xiii–xviii.

Collins, Wilkie, *Heart and Science* (Peterborough: Broadview, 1996).

Copper, Basil, *The Vampire in Legend and Fact* (New York: Citadel, 1973).

Cowper, Katie, 'The Decline of Reserve among Women', *The Nineteenth Century*, 27 (1890) 65–71.

Craft, Christopher, '"Kiss Me with Those Red Lips": Gender and Inversion in Bram Stoker's *Dracula*', *Representations*, 8 (1984) 107–33.

Cranny-Francis, Anne, 'Sexual Politics and Political Repression in Bram Stoker's *Dracula*', Clive Bloom, Brian Docherty, Jane Gibb and Keith Shand, eds, *Nineteenth Century Suspense* (Basingstoke: Macmillan, 1988) pp. 64–79.

Cuming, G.J., *A History of Anglican Liturgy* (London: Macmillan, 1969) p. 207.

Cunningham, Gail, *The New Woman and the Victorian Novel* (London: Macmillan, 1978).

Curtis, L.P., *Apes and Angels* (Newton Abbot: David and Charles, 1971)

Curtis, Liz, *Nothing but the Same Old Story* (London: Information on Ireland, 1988).

Dalby, Richard, *Bram Stoker: A Bibliography of First Editions* (London: Dracula Press, 1983).

Dale, R.W., *Christian Doctrine* (London: Hodder and Stoughton, 1903).

Daly, Nicholas, 'Irish Roots: The Romance of History in Bram Stoker's *The Snake's Pass*', *Literature and History* 4/2 (1995) 42–70.

Daniel Lapin, *The Vampire, Dracula and Incest* (San Francisco: Gargoyle, 1995).

Darwin, Charles, *The Expression of the Emotions in Man and Animals* (London: Watts and Company, 1934).

Dickens, David B., 'The German Matrix of Stoker's *Dracula*', Elizabeth Miller ed., *Dracula: The Shade and the Shadow* (Westcliff-on-Sea: Desert Island Books, 1998) pp. 31–41.

Donelly, J.S., 'Landlords and Tenants', W.E. Vaughan, ed., *A New History of Ireland* V (Oxford: Clarendon Press, 1989) pp. 346–9.

Doyle, Arthur Conan, *The Adventures of Sherlock Holmes* (New York: Belmont Tower Books, 1974).

Doyle, Arthur Conan, *The Memoirs of Sherlock Holmes* (Harmondsworth: Penguin, 1952).

Du Maurier, George, *Trilby* (London: Osgood, McIlvaine and Company, 1895).

Easton, M.G., *The Illustrated Bible Dictionary* (London: Nelson, 1893).

Edwards, Robert, 'The Alien and the Familiar in *The Jewel of Seven Stars* and

*Dracula'*, William Hughes and Andrew Smith, eds, *Bram Stoker: History, Psychoanalysis and the Gothic* (Basingstoke: Macmillan, 1998) pp. 96–115.

Ellenberger, H.F., 'Charcot and the Salpêtrière School', L.T. Benjamin ed., *A History of Psychology* (New York: McGraw-Hill, 1988), pp. 136–46.

Ellmann, Richard, *Oscar Wilde* (London: Hamish Hamilton, 1987).

Empson, William, *Milton's God* (London: Chatto and Windus, 1961).

Evans, E.J., ed., *Social Policy 1830–1914* (London: Routledge and Kegan Paul, 1978).

Fancher, R.E., *Pioneers of Psychology* (New York: W.W. Norton, 1979).

Farson, Daniel, 'The Sexual Torment of the Man who Created Dracula', *The Mail on Sunday*, 3 January 1993, pp. 35 and 43.

Farson, Daniel, *The Man Who Wrote Dracula: A Biography of Bram Stoker* (London: Michael Joseph, 1975).

Fleetwood, J.F., *The History of Medicine in Ireland* (Dublin: Skellig, 1983).

Fontana, Ernest, 'Lombroso's Criminal Man and Stoker's Dracula', *Victorian Newsletter* 66 (1984) 25–7.

Foote, Edward Bliss, *Home Cyclopedia of Popular Medical, Social and Sexual Science* (London: L.N. Fowler, 1901).

Foucault, Michel, *The History of Sexuality: An Introduction* (London: Penguin, 1984).

Frayling, Christopher, *Vampyres: Lord Byron to Count Dracula* (London: Faber and Faber, 1991).

Garsault, Alain, 'Pozzuoli (Alain): *Bram Stoker: Prince des Ténèbres'*, *Positif*, 353 (1990) 128.

Gelder, Ken, *Reading the Vampire* (London: Routledge, 1994).

Gilbert, Arthur N., 'Doctor, Patient, and Onanist Diseases in the Nineteenth Century', *Journal of the History of Medicine*, 30 (1975) 217–34.

Gilmour, Robin, *The Idea of the Gentleman in the Victorian Novel* (London: George Allen and Unwin, 1981).

Girouard, Mark, *The Return to Camelot* (New Haven: Yale University Press, 1981).

Glover, David, *Vampires, Mummies, and Liberals* (Durham, NC: Duke University Press, 1996).

Gogarty, Oliver St John, *Intimations* (London: Sphere, 1985).

Gonzáles, Antonio Ballasteros, 'Portraits, Rats and Other Dangerous Things', Bruce Stewart, ed., *That Other World* (Gerrards Cross: Colin Smyth, 1998) 2 vols, Vol. 2, pp. 18–29.

Graham, Colin, 'A Late Politics of Irish Gothic: Bram Stoker's *The Lady of the Shroud'*, Bruce Stewart, ed., *That Other World* (Gerrards Cross: Colin Smyth, 1998) 2 vols, Vol. 2, pp. 30–9.

Grand, Sarah, *The Heavenly Twins* (London: William Heinemann, 1897).

Haining, Peter, and Tremayne, Peter, *The Un-Dead* (London: Constable, 1997).

Haley, Bruce, *The Healthy Body and Victorian Culture* (Cambridge, Mass.: Harvard University Press, 1978).

Hall, Lesley A., 'Forbidden by God, Despised by Men: Masturbation, Medical Warnings, Moral Panic, and Manhood in Great Britain, 1850–1950', John C. Fout, ed., *Forbidden History* (Chicago: University of Chicago Press, 1992) pp. 293–315.

Hartnell, Elaine, 'Thoughts Too Long and Too Intensely Fixed on One Object:

Fictional Representations of Brain Fever', Nickianne Moody and Julia Hallam, eds, *Medical Fictions* (Liverpool: MCCA, 1998) pp. 201–12.

Hatlen, Burton, 'The Return of the Repressed/Oppressed in Bram Stoker's *Dracula*', M.L. Carter ed., *Dracula: The Vampire and the Critics*, (Ann Arbor: U.M.I. Research Press, 1988) pp. 117–35.

Henschen, F., *The History of Diseases* (London: Longmans, 1986).

Hiatt, Charles, *Henry Irving, A Record and Review* (London: George Bell and Sons, 1903).

Hogg, James, *The Private Memoirs and Confessions of a Justified Sinner* (Harmondsworth: Penguin, 1987).

Hoggan, F.E., 'Women in Medicine', T. Stanton, ed., *The Woman Question in Europe* (London: Sampson Low, Marston, Searle and Rivington, 1884) pp. 63–89.

Hogle, Jerrold E., 'Stoker's Counterfeit Gothic: *Dracula* and Theatricality at the Dawn of Simulation', William Hughes and Andrew Smith, eds, *Bram Stoker: History, Psychoanalysis and the Gothic* (Basingstoke: Macmillan, 1998) pp. 205–24.

Hollander, Bernard, *Nervous Disorders of Women* (London: Kegan Paul, Trench, Trubner and Company, 1916).

Horn, Pamela, *High Society: The English Social Élite 1880–1914* (Stroud: Alan Sutton, 1992).

Housman, A.E., *A Shropshire Lad* (New York: Dover, 1990).

Howell, Michael and Ford, Peter, *The Ghost Disease* (Harmondsworth: Penguin, 1986).

Hughes, Thomas, *Tom Brown at Oxford* (London: Macmillan, 1880).

Hughes, William, '"Introducing Patrick to his New Self": Bram Stoker and the 1907 Dublin Exhibition', *Irish Studies Review* no. 19 (Summer 1997) 9–14.

Hughes, William, '"So unlike the normal lunatic": Abnormal Psychology in Bram Stoker's *Dracula*', *University of Mississippi Studies in English*, New Series 11–12 (1993–5) 1–10.

Hughes, William, *Bram Stoker: A Bibliography* (Brisbane: University of Queensland, 1997).

Humphry, L., *A Manual of Nursing: Medical and Surgical* (London: Charles Griffin and Company, 1900).

Hutchinson, John, *The Dynamics of Cultural Nationalism* (London: Allen and Unwin, 1987).

Irving, Laurence, *Henry Irving: The Actor and his World* (London: Faber and Faber, 1951).

Johnson, Joseph, *Noble Women of Our Time* (London: T. Nelson and Sons, 1886).

Katz, Jacob, *From Prejudice to Destruction, Antisemitism 1700–1933* (Cambridge, Mass.: Harvard University Press, 1980).

Leatherdale, C., *Dracula: The Novel and the Legend* (Brighton: Desert Island Books, 1993).

Leatherdale, Clive, *The Origins of Dracula: The Background to Bram Stoker's Gothic Masterpiece* (London: William Kimber, 1987).

Lennon, Seàn, *Irish Gothic Writers: Bram Stoker and the Irish Supernatural Tradition* (Dublin: Dublin Corporation Public Libraries, 1999).

Linton, Elizabeth Lynn, '"In Custody" and "Emancipation"', *The Illustrated London News*, 6 February 1892, pp. 172–3.

Linton, Elizabeth Lynn, 'The Wild Women as Social Insurgents', *The Nineteenth Century* XXX (1891) 596–605.

Linton, Elizabeth Lynn, 'The Wild Women: No. 1 As Politicians', *The Nineteenth Century*, XXX (1891) 79–88.

Linton, Elizabeth Lynn, *The Girl of the Period and Other Social Essays*, 2 vols (London: Bentley, 1883).

Lombroso, Cesare, *The Man of Genius* (London: Walter Scott, 1891).

Loomis, R.S., *The Grail* (Princeton: Princeton University Press, 1991).

'Lorna', 'Mr. Bram Stoker. A Chat with the Author of "Dracula"', *The British Weekly*, 1 July 1897, p. 185.

Ludlam, Harry, *A Biography of Dracula: The Life Story of Bram Stoker* (London: Foulsham, 1962).

M'Gregor-Robertson, J., *The Household Physician* (London: Blackie and Son, n.d.).

Maclear, G.F., and Williams, W.W., *An Introduction to the Articles of the Church of England* (London: Macmillan, 1896).

Mancoff, D.N., *The Return of King Arthur: The Legend through Victorian Eyes* (London: Pavilion, 1995).

Marryat, Amy, *Half-Hours with My Girls* (London: Rivingtons, 1890).

Mason, Diane, 'Un-like a Virgin: Female Masturbation and Virginity in *Fin-de-Siècle* Medical Advice Literature', Nickianne Moody and Julia Hallam, eds, *Medical Fictions* (Liverpool: MCCA, 1998) pp. 213–25.

Mayo, Herbert, *On the Truths Contained in Popular Superstitions – With an Account of Mesmerism* (Edinburgh: William Blackwood and Sons, 1851).

McCormack, W.J., 'Irish Gothic and After, 1820–1945', Seamus Deane, ed., *The Field Day Anthology of Irish Writing* (Londonderry: Field Day Publications, 1991) pp. 842–6.

McWhir, Anne, 'Pollution and Redemption in *Dracula*', *Modern Language Studies*, 17 (1987) 31–40.

'Medical Man, A', *Cassell's Family Doctor* (London: Cassell and Company, 1897).

'Medicus' [Dr Gordon Stables], 'When Bud and Burgeon Come Again', *The Girl's Own Paper*, XVIII (1897) 295.

Melton, J. Gordon, 'Stoker, Abraham "Bram"', *The Vampire Book* (Detroit: Visible Ink Press, 1994) pp. 583–7.

Milburn, Diane, '"For the Dead Travel Fast": *Dracula* in Anglo-German Context', Elizabeth Miller, ed., *Dracula: The Shade and the Shadow* (Westcliff-on-Sea: Desert Island Books, 1998) pp. 41–53.

Newton, R., *The Giants and How to Fight Them* (London: S.W. Partridge, n.d.).

Nicholson, John, 'Scared Shitless: the Sex of Horror', Clive Bloom, ed., *Creepers* (London: Pluto, 1993) pp. 123–46.

Nutt, Alfred, *Studies on the Legend of the Holy Grail* (London: The Folk-Lore Society, 1888) pp. xi–xiv.

Owen, A.R.G., *Hysteria, Hypnosis and Healing: The Work of J.-M. Charcot* (London: Dennis Dobson, 1971).

'Pat', 'Pioneering on the West Coast', *The World's Work*, IX (1907) 630–3.

Pauwels, Louis, and Bergier, Jaques, *Le Matin des Magiciens* (Paris: Gallimard, 1960).

Pearsall, Ronald, *The Table-Rappers* (London: Book Club Associates, 1973).

Pearson, J., *An Exposition of the Creed*, ed. Bradley (London: Valpy, 1870).

Pick, Daniel, '"Terrors of the Night": *Dracula* and "Degeneration" in the Late Nineteenth Century', *Critical Quarterly* 30 (1989) 71–87.

Pinkerton, Mark, 'Why Westenra?', *The Bram Stoker Society Journal*, no. 7 (1995) 12–15.

Pozzuoli, Alain, *Bram Stoker: Prince des Tenénèbres* (Paris: Librairie Séguier, 1989).

Proctor, R.A., 'The Mystery of the Pyramids', *Belgravia*, XXXII (1877) 434–52.

Propp, Vladimir, *Morphology of the Folktale*, second edition, trans. Scott (Austin: University of Texas Press, 1973).

Punter, David, *The Literature of Terror: A History of Gothic Fictions from 1765 to the Present Day*, 2 vols (London: Longman, 1996).

Raible, C.G., 'Dracula: Christian Heretic', *Christian Century*, 96 (1979) 103–4.

Richardson, Maurice, 'The Psychoanalysis of Ghost Stories', *The Twentieth Century*, 166 (1959) 419–31.

Ritchie, John, *Contested Truths of the Word* (Kilmarnock: Ritchie, 1917).

Ross, J.M., *The Illustrated Globe Encyclopædia*, 12 vols (London: Thomas C. Jack, 1882).

Roth, Phyllis, *Bram Stoker* (Boston: Twayne, 1982).

Sage, Victor, *Horror Fiction in the Protestant Tradition* (Basingstoke: Macmillan, 1988).

Said, Edward, *Orientalism* (New York: Pantheon, 1978).

Searle, G.R., *The Quest for National Efficiency* (Oxford: Basil Blackwell, 1971).

Seed, David, 'The Narrative Method of *Dracula*', *Nineteenth-Century Fiction*, 40 (1985) 61–75.

Senf, Carol A., '*Dracula, The Jewel of Seven Stars* and Stoker's "Burden of the Past"', Carol Davison, ed., *Bram Stoker's Dracula* (Toronto: Dundurn Press, 1997) pp. 77–94.

Senf, Carol A., '*Dracula*: Stoker's Response to the New Woman', *Victorian Studies* 26 (1982) 33–49.

Senf, Carol A., '*The Lady of the Shroud*: Stoker's Successor to *Dracula*', *Essays in Arts and Sciences*, 19 (1990) 82–96.

Shaffer, Talia, '"A Wilde Desire Took Me": The Homoerotic History of *Dracula*', *English Literary History*, 61/2 (1994) 381–425.

Shepard, Leslie, 'The Library of Bram Stoker', *The Bram Stoker Society Journal* 4 (1992) 28–34.

Simon, Brian, and Bradley, Ian, eds, *The Victorian Public School: Studies in the Development of an Educational Institution* (Dublin: Gill and Macmillan, 1975).

Skal, David, *Hollywood Gothic* (New York: W.W. Norton, 1991).

Skal, David, *V is for Vampire: The A–Z Guide to Everything Undead* (London: Robson, 1996).

Smiles, Samuel, *Self-Help* (London: John Murray, 1902).

Smith, Andrew, 'Bram Stoker's *The Mystery of the Sea*: Ireland and the Spanish-Cuban-American War', *Irish Studies Review*, 6/2 (1998) 131–8.

Smith, Andrew, *Dracula and the Critics* (Sheffield: Pavic, 1997).

Smith, Roger, *Trial by Medicine: Insanity and Responsibility in Victorian Trials* (Edinburgh: Edinburgh University Press, 1981).

Somerville, Edith and Ross, Martin, *Some Experiences of an Irish R.M.* (London: Longmans, Green and Company, 1903).

Spehner, Norbert, *Dracula: Opus 300, Un Siècle d'Edition (1897–1997)* (St-Hyacinthe: Ashem Fictions, 1996).

St. John, John, *William Heinemann: A Century of Publishing 1890–1990* (London: William Heinemann, 1990).

Stoker, Bram, *Under the Sunset* (London: Sampson Low, Marston, Searle and Rivington, 1882).

Stoker, Bram, *A Glimpse of America* (London: Sampson Low, Marston and Company, 1886).

Stoker, Bram, *The Snake's Pass* (Dingle: Brandon, 1990).

Stoker, Bram, 'The Red Stockade', *Cosmopolitan Magazine*, 17 (1894) 619–30.

Stoker, Bram, *The Watter's Mou'*, Charles Osborne, ed., *The Bram Stoker Bedside Companion* (London: Victor Gollancz, 1973) pp. 166–224.

Stoker, Bram, *The Shoulder of Shasta* (Westminster: Constable, 1895).

Stoker, Bram, *Dracula* (Oxford: Oxford University Press, 1996).

Stoker, Bram, *Miss Betty* (London: New English Library, 1974).

Stoker, Bram, *The Mystery of the Sea* (Stroud: Sutton Publishing, 1997).

Stoker, Bram, *The Jewel of Seven Stars* (Oxford: Oxford University Press, 1996).

Stoker, Bram, *The Man* (London: William Heinemann, 1905).

Stoker, Bram, *Personal Reminiscences of Henry Irving*, 2 vols (London: William Heinemann, 1906).

Stoker, Bram, *Lady Athlyne* (London: William Heinemann, 1908).

Stoker, Bram, *Snowbound: The Record of a Theatrical Touring Party* (London: Collier, 1908).

Stoker, Bram, *The Lady of the Shroud* (Stroud: Sutton Publishing, 1994).

Stoker, Bram, 'The Great White Fair in Dublin', *The World's Work*, IX (1907) 570–6.

Stoker, Bram, 'The 'Eroes of the Thames', *The Royal Magazine*, October 1908, 566–70.

Stoker, Bram, 'The Censorship of Fiction', *The Nineteenth Century and After*, 66 (1909) 974–89.

Stoker, Bram, *Famous Impostors* (London: Sidgwick and Jackson, 1910).

Stoker, Bram, *The Jewel of Seven Stars* (London: William Rider, 1912).

Stoker, Bram, *The Lair of the White Worm*, bound with *Dracula* (London: Foulsham, 1986).

Stoker, Bram, *Dracula's Guest* (Dingle: Brandon, 1990).

Stoker, Bram, 'Greater Love', *The London Magazine*, 33 (1914–15) 161–8.

Tennyson, Alfred, Lord, *The Marriage of Geraint, Geraint and Enid* (London: Macmillan, 1892).

Thompson, Raymond, *The Return from Avalon: A Study of the Arthurian Legend in Modern Fiction* (Westport: Greenwood Press, 1985).

Thomson, Spencer, and Steele, J.C., *A Dictionary of Domestic Medicine and Household Surgery* (London: Charles Griffin and Company, 1899).

Thornton, John, *Elementary Practical Physiology* (London: Longmans, Green and Company, 1919).

Veith, Ilza, 'On Hysterical and Hypochondriacal Afflictions', *Bulletin of the History of Medicine*, 30 (1956) 233–40.

Veith, Ilza, *Hysteria: The History of a Disease* (Chicago: University of Chicago Press, 1965).

Weininger, Otto, *Sex and Character* (New York: A.M.S. Press, 1975).

White, Andrew, 'The Victorian Development of Whitby as a Seaside Resort', *The Local Historian*, 28 (1998) 78–93.

Whyte, L.L., *The Unconscious before Freud* (London: Social Science Paperbacks, 1967).

Wilcox, R.T., *The Dictionary of Costume* (London: Batsford, 1969).

Wilde, Oscar, *A Letter from Oscar Wilde* (Dublin: The Tragara Press, 1954).

Williams, Anne, *Art of Darkness: A Poetics of Gothic* (Chicago: University of Chicago Press, 1995).

Wills, Christopher, *Plagues: Their Origin, History and Future* (London: Harper Collins, 1996).

Wixson, Kellie Donovan, '*Dracula*: An Anglo-Irish Gothic Novel', Elizabeth Miller, ed., *Dracula: The Shade and the Shadow* (Westcliff-on-Sea: Desert Island Books, 1998) pp. 247–56.

Zanger, Jules, 'A Sympathetic Vibration: Dracula and the Jews', *ELT*, 34 (1991) 33–43.

# Index

Allan, J.M.,
'On the Real Differences in the
Minds of Men and Women',
105, 133
Allen, Grant,
*The Woman Who Did*, 135, 193 n.
45
America, United States of, 55–6, 77,
90
Americans, 55–6, 58–9, 69, 91, 95–6,
139
Anglican Church, *see* England,
Church of
*see also Common Prayer, Book of;*
Ireland, Church of;
Protestantism
Anglo-American
identities, 58–9, 69–70, 76, 91, 199
n. 82
relationships, 58–9, 69, 76, 77, 116
Anglo-Irish
identities, 7, 14, 63
relations, 59, 60, 62, 63, 64, 66
*see also* Ireland
Anglo-Saxons, 85, 91, 139
anti-Semitism, 63, 68
*see also* Jews
aquiline physiognomy, 70–5, 84, 114,
178, 192 n. 25
Aristotle, 15
Arrowsmith, J.W., 97–8, 100
Athurianism, 57, 59–60, 83, 96
Asquith, Herbert Henry, 8

Balcombe, Florence, *see* Stoker,
Florence
Balfour, Arthur James, 8
Belford, Barbara,
*Bram Stoker*, 8, 16–17, 24
Bible
allusions to, 16, 18, 19, 20, 29–30,
63, 68, 113–14, 131
language of, 22, 29–30

miscellaneous references, 21, 23,
25, 26, 28, 29, 32, 34, 43, 44,
45, 49, 114, 175
narratives from, 17–20, 26–8, 33–4
biologism, 98, 100, 101, 103, 105, 110,
117, 122–5, 132–3, 136, 193 n. 33
Blackwood, Algernon,
'A Psychical Invasion', 187 n. 63
blasphemy, 43, 44, 45, 52, 175
blood
healthy, 58, 69, 139
and perspiration, 166, 169, 176,
198 n. 59
and physiology, 139, 140, 141,
143, 148, 149, 151, 153, 177
and semen, 12, 112, 140–1, 163,
166, 174, 198 n. 59
as signifier, 12, 59, 69, 78, 102,
103, 135, 139–40, 142, 143,
175, 176, 177
*see also* blush; pallor; spermatic
economy
blush, 58, 69, 104–6, 129, 135, 138,
143, 149, 156, 178
*see also* pallor
Boucicault, Dion, 8
Braddon, M.E., 8
brain fever, 160–1, 197 n. 54
*British Weekly, The*, 15
Budge, E.A. Wallis, 37
*The Mummy*, 37–8
Burton, Sir Richard, 8, 74, 75, 84, 85,
186 n. 46

Caine, Hall, 1, 2
canine teeth, 72–5, 85
Carlyle, Thomas,
*Past and Present*, 80, 83, 96
Carpenter, W.B., 142, 168, 172, 173
'Electrobiology and Mesmerism',
168
'Mesmerism, Odylism, Table-
Turning and Spiritualism', 168

216   *Index*